Industrialization and Growth

A WORLD BANK RESEARCH PUBLICATION

with contributions by

Gershon Feder
Yuji Kubo
Jeffrey Lewis
Jaime de Melo
Mieko Nishimizu

INDUSTRIALIZATION AND GROWTH
A Comparative Study

Hollis Chenery
Sherman Robinson
Moshe Syrquin

PUBLISHED FOR THE WORLD BANK
Oxford University Press

Oxford University Press

NEW YORK OXFORD LONDON GLASGOW
TORONTO MELBOURNE WELLINGTON HONG KONG
TOKYO KUALA LUMPUR SINGAPORE JAKARTA
DELHI BOMBAY CALCUTTA MADRAS KARACHI
NAIROBI DAR ES SALAAM CAPE TOWN

Manufactured in the United States of America
First printing October 1986

Library of Congress Cataloging-in-Publication Data

Chenery, Hollis Burnley.
  Industrialization and growth.

  Bibliography: p.
  Includes index.
  1. Economic development. 2. Industrialization.
I. Robinson, Sherman. II. Syrquin, Moshe.
III. International Bank for Reconstruction and
Development. IV. Title.
HD82.C472 1986   338.9   86–21837
ISBN 0-19-520547-2

Contents

Preface

DEVELOPMENT is now conceived as the successful transformation of the structure of an economy. In his historical studies of modern economic growth, Kuznets (1966) identified the shift of resources from agriculture to industry as the central feature of this transformation. While the postwar experience of developing countries shows industrialization to be highly correlated with rising income, it also reveals substantial differences due to resource endowments and government policies.

The causal factors behind these relations are a matter of dispute. The sources of industrialization range from the need to adapt the composition of supply to shifts in domestic demand to the exploitation of comparative advantage in labor-intensive activities. In the past decade such historical trends have been modified as some countries have accelerated their industrialization to offset worsening terms of trade, while favored primary producers have suffered from "Dutch disease" and a tendency to deindustrialize. Both the long-term tendency of middle-income countries to industrialize and variations from it need to be evaluated in designing development policy.

The present volume is one of a series of studies of the structural transformation that have been supported by the World Bank. Earlier work by Chenery and Syrquin (1975, 1980) extended the Kuznets research program to cover the postwar development patterns of lower-income countries and also developed a methodology for comparing the sources of industrialization in different economies. A broader approach to the analysis of structural change, using a general equilibrium framework, was developed by Dervis, de Melo, and Robinson (1982); this enabled them to compare the effects of different policies. These two lines of analysis have been consolidated in the present volume, which tries to explain the postwar experience of semi-industrial countries.

Research for this study was undertaken in two stages, which were designed to take advantage of the expanding data on the productive structure of developing countries.[1] The centerpiece of the first stage was the development of a comparable set of input-output accounts for nine semi-industrial economies in a framework that facilitates economy com-

1. The first stage corresponds to World Bank research project 671-32, "A Comparative Study of Sources of Industrial Growth and Structural Change"; the second to research project 671-79, "The Sources of Growth and Productivity Change." Selected findings of these studies are listed in chapter 1 of this volume and in the World Bank's annual *Abstracts of Current Studies* for 1978–83.

parisons over time. This stage led to a series of publications on the methodology and findings for individual economies.

The second stage of our research focused on the growth of total factor productivity: the apparent differences between developed and less developed countries, the effects of alternative development strategies, and the variation among sectors. In this context, more detailed studies were carried out for four economies—Japan, the Republic of Korea, Turkey, and Yugoslavia. Computable general equilibrium models, in addition to our standard input-output model, were used to test the relative importance of different factors.

The design of both phases of research was carried out in collaboration with the authors of the principal country studies in order to reconcile the theoretically desirable and the empirically feasible approaches. Our main collaborators in the first stage were Bela Balassa, Merih Celasun, Kwang Suk Kim, Shirley W. Y. Kuo, Yuji Kubo, Jeffrey Lewis, Jaime de Melo, Tsunehiko Watanabe, and Larry Westphal. Gershon Feder, Mieko Nishimizu, and Shujiro Urata joined us in the second stage. All contributed to the specialized studies that provide the background for this volume.

We are also indebted to a number of other colleagues and friends for their comments on successive drafts of the manuscript. We should especially like to thank Jeffrey Williamson, whose many comments were invaluable in producing a more coherent whole. Others include Irma Adelman, Alain de Janvry, Kemal Dervis, Shantayana Devarajan, Frank Lysy, Dwight Perkins, Betty Sadoulet, Lance Taylor, Simon Teitel, and Adrian Wood.

We have also benefited greatly from a series of able research assistants: Tim Condon, Hazel Elkington, Kathy Jordan, Murat Koprulu, Maria Kutcher, and Narayana Poduval. For their help in typing many drafts, we thank Trinidad Angeles, Nenita Bencio, Cheryl Cvetic, Teresita Kamantigue, Isabelle Kim, and Kim Tran. Our editor, Jeanne Rosen, patiently and expertly took us in hand and greatly improved the final product.

Like most comparative studies, this final product is both more and less than might have been hoped for. Initial hypotheses tend to explain less than was expected, yet the first results have led to new and more interesting questions. Although our views have converged in the process, we have found it useful to identify the authors of each chapter rather than seek a common interpretation.

1 Introduction

THE RELATION between industrialization and economic growth is a subject of continuing controversy. Historically, the rise in the share of manufacturing in output and employment as per capita income increases, and the corresponding decline of agriculture, are among the best documented generalizations about development. But how does this transformation of the structure of production affect the rate of growth and the distribution of its benefits? And what has been the effect of policies designed to accelerate this shift or to alter its composition? These and related questions are still in dispute.

This book attempts to clarify the role of industrialization in development by conducting a series of comparative studies of semi-industrial economies. The studies address three main topics: industrialization as a stage in the overall transformation that constitutes modern economic growth; the similarities and differences in the experiences of nine industrializing economies; and the relation between rising productivity and structural change. This chapter traces the background of the principal issues to be considered; summarizes the studies' main findings; and gives the reader a guide to the countries chosen, the topics discussed, and the analytical techniques employed.

The Issues

Many of the issues considered in this volume were debated intensively but inconclusively in the 1950s. Although these debates defined the logic of different positions, they failed to resolve important questions about the role of industrialization or the choice of a development strategy. Only after the experience of the 1960s and the early 1970s was assessed did the empirical questions become more focused and the relevant policy issues emerge. A decade later, we can distinguish more clearly among the principal approaches to development that have been tried and analyze the role played by industrialization in each.

Advantages of Industrialization

Early arguments for accelerated industrialization were based largely on the assumed properties of technology in manufacturing and related sectors. Authors such as Rosenstein-Rodan (1943, 1961) and Mandelbaum (1945) stressed the importance of economies of scale and growth of productivity in manufacturing and the cumulative benefits that these bring about in the form of external economies. With some additional assumptions, these factors argue for balanced investment in heavy as well as light

1

industry and a reduced share of manufactured imports in the gross national product (Mahalanobis 1955).

Industrialization was also advocated by Prebisch (1950) and Singer (1950) to offset the supposed disadvantages of specialization in primary production and the associated secular deterioration in the terms of trade. Nurkse (1961), noting the limited world demand for exports of primary products and the rising domestic demand for manufactured goods, proposed a policy of balanced growth of the industrial and primary sectors. In modified form, this approach has been a fruitful starting point for subsequent empirical work on the ways in which the conditions of demand limit the patterns of development.

These arguments for early industrialization were criticized by Viner (1952) and Fleming (1955) as conflicting with the neoclassical analysis of comparative advantage and the benefits of specialization. More recently, the longer-term comparative advantage of many developing countries has been seen to lie in those branches of manufacturing that use the growing skills of the labor force. The neoclassical position has thus come to be identified with the export of labor-intensive manufactured goods induced by outward-oriented trade policies.

Nurkse's arguments for balanced growth were clarified by Scitovsky (1954, 1959) and Streeten (1959). This discussion weakened the case for limiting trade and stressed the differences in country conditions of demand and supply. Perhaps more important, it showed the limitations of partial equilibrium analysis as a means of resolving such economywide questions.

Changing Perceptions

Kuznets (1957, 1966) and his followers have put the issues of industrial growth into a broader perspective. Instead of focusing narrowly on the allocation of resources, Kuznets describes the increase in industrial output as part of the general transformation that he identifies as "modern economic growth." In this context, industrialization is not only a response to changing demand and supply conditions but also a principal means of acquiring modern technology.

The style of comparative analysis initiated by Clark (1940) and Kuznets led to a number of empirical generalizations—"stylized facts"—that underlie much subsequent work. Although the earlier attempts to identify theoretical grounds for advocating a particular pattern of resource allocation were inconclusive, Kuznets's empirical findings have stimulated a search for the causes and implications of these stylized facts. Much of this book is an attempt to interpret the interaction of the principal factors that cause the structural changes reflected in Kuznets's cross-country and time-series patterns.

The sustained growth of the world economy from the mid-1950s to the mid-1970s led to a more optimistic view of the benefits of trade for developing countries than had prevailed. As manufactured exports from developing countries grew at more than 10 percent a year, the assumption that export markets were limited became much less tenable. At the same time, comparative studies of the effects of import substitution by Macario (1964), Bruton (1970), and Little, Scitovsky, and Scott (1970) demonstrated that these policies become less and less efficient if they are maintained for long periods.

The argument for shifting from an inward-oriented to an outward-oriented strategy was greatly strengthened by the success of a small group of "newly industrializing economies" and particularly of the four East Asian economies in this group: Hong Kong, the Republic of Korea, Singapore, and Taiwan.[1] These four "superexporters" have followed a new pattern of industrialization characterized by very rapid growth of manufacturing based on increasing participation in the international economy. Their experience has raised questions about the extent to which this pattern is suitable for larger economies, whether it depends on the particular social and political features of East Asian societies, and so forth. In our search for answers to such questions, we shall try to identify the common sources of growth and structural change in these and other industrializing countries and to pinpoint the main differences.[2]

Although outward-oriented policies have received great attention in recent years, they have been only one of several ingredients in successful development strategies. Japan, the original model of export-led growth, has been more notable in the postwar[3] period for attaining a great increase in productivity than for having a particularly open economy. Among countries with favorable natural resource endowments, Malaysia and Thailand have pursued strategies of delayed industrialization; after a late start, manufacturing has increased rapidly in response to the growth of domestic demand, without the distortions introduced by premature attempts to accelerate industrialization. Even among countries with very autarkic policies in the early 1960s, one finds examples (Brazil, Spain, and Turkey) of relatively successful development based on a shift to more neutral trade policies and the growth of manufactured exports. These relatively large economies resemble the early Nurkse model of balanced growth, in which industrialization arises primarily from the growth of domestic demand; at the same time, export growth must be fast enough to

---

1. An OECD (Organisation for Economic Co-operation and Development) study, *The Impact of the Newly Industrializing Countries on Production and Trade in Manufactures* (1979), is the most comprehensive analysis of this group as a whole. The ten economies that it covers are Hong Kong, Korea, Singapore, and Taiwan (East Asia); Greece, Portugal, Spain, and Yugoslavia (Mediterranean); and Brazil and Mexico (Latin America).

2. Ranis (1981) compares Latin American and East Asian trade policies and their consequences.

3. Throughout the book, "postwar" and "prewar" refer in general to the times after and before World War II; the exact year varies depending on the economy under discussion.

avoid serious trade bottlenecks. Although all these cases incorporate shifts to more outward-oriented policies, they do not exhibit the extreme specialization characteristic of the four East Asian superexporters.

The adaptability of countries pursuing different strategies has been tested in the past decade by the periodic disruption and slower growth of the world economy. Those economic structures distorted by past efforts to reduce imports have proven vulnerable because of the limited margin for additional import substitution. Furthermore, it has been more difficult and disruptive of growth for inward-oriented countries to shift to export expansion than for more outward-oriented countries to make the smaller structural adjustments needed. The prospect of slower growth of world trade is therefore causing strategies of both export orientation and import substitution to be reassessed.

The experience of the past twenty years has been subject to varying interpretations. Balassa (1981), Ranis (1981), and Little (1982) see the growth of the East Asian superexporters as the predictable result of freeing trade and removing discrimination against exports; their success points the way for others to follow. But skeptics such as Diaz-Alejandro (1975), Datta-Choudhuri (1981), and Streeten (1982) stress that the strong role of government, favorable human resource endowments, and the expansive international environment of the 1960s are special features that limit the transferability of the superexporters' experience.

Despite these differing views, there is considerable common ground among economists debating development strategies. Krueger (1984) points out that the main issue between the proponents of neoclassical trade policy and its critics is not whether to industrialize but what form the industrialization should take. It is also generally agreed that the static gains achieved in shifting to more efficient patterns of trade are not the most important reason for the high growth rates of successful countries. Increased productivity is even more important. Identifying the virtues of outward-oriented trade policies is thus only a starting point for unraveling the causal links between industrialization and economic growth.

Questions Addressed

The first of the three sets of questions that we shall take up in this book concerns the uniform features of development patterns, especially the tendency to shift from primary production to manufacturing. How essential is industrialization for development? What is the importance of changes in demand in comparison with changes in such supply-side factors as capital accumulation and comparative advantage? Before the answers to these questions can be applied to policy analysis, the causal links among them need to be better understood.

The second set of questions concerns the relation between growth and structural change. Although neoclassical theory points to the significance of changes in factor supplies and productivity, studies of developing countries show that changes in demand and trade are equally important to continued growth. Industrialization thus can be viewed as a way to satisfy similar patterns of demand growth with varying combinations of factor supplies. In analyzing these issues, we must recognize the importance of initial conditions and of the differences in resource allocation associated with such structural features as the size of an economy and its natural resource endowment.

The third set of questions concerns the means by which policies are carried out. Is excessive import substitution inefficient mainly because it raises the cost of traded goods or because it is associated with other policies that lead to balance of payments bottlenecks or reduce productivity growth? This type of question is perhaps the most difficult, but it must be addressed if we are to use the results of comparative studies to improve policy choices.

The Research Design

Two main approaches have been used to study the issues outlined above. One stems from trade theory and stresses external policies. The other stems from planning models and stresses the internal aspects of resource allocation. In designing the research for the present volume, a central problem was to combine elements of both techniques in a methodology that also takes into account the data available for the industrializing economies.

One technique for comparative country analysis has evolved over the past fifteen years in a series of studies on trade and development policy, beginning with the pioneering work of Little, Scitovsky, and Scott (1970). Succeeding studies have taken up specific topics that relate trade to development: the levels of effective protection (Balassa 1971), the impact of different trade regimes (Donges 1976; Bhagwati 1978; Krueger 1978; Balassa 1981), and the indirect effects of these regimes on employment (Krueger 1983). These authors have held their studies to manageable proportions by focusing on the implications of trade theory and policy without examining other circumstances affecting growth and resource allocation in any detail.

A second approach is based on multisectoral models designed to study changing patterns of resource allocation. Originally developed to isolate the implications of alternative policies in individual countries, such models have rarely been applied to comparative studies. The early versions were based on open input-output systems, in which exports were usually treated as exogenous. Subsequent studies have used linear programming or computable general equilibrium models, which integrate the internal and external policies affecting resource allocation but are more demanding of data. Although multisectoral models are typically used to analyze the economic structure and policies of a given country, they have occasionally been extended to examine more general questions. Representative exam-

ples are the analysis of comparative advantage in a general equilibrium
context for Israel (Bruno 1966) and for India (Weisskopf 1971), and the
analysis of policies affecting income distribution for Korea (Adelman and
Robinson 1978).

The two techniques are essentially complementary. The various policy
comparisons (Little, Scitovsky, and Scott 1970; Krueger 1978, 1983;
Bhagwati 1978) rely on classifications of trade policy regimes in selected
countries and on statistical descriptions of their effects. Although empirical models are not used explicitly, trade theory provides a unifying analytical framework. Multisectoral analysis, in contrast, is designed to study
phenomena revealed only by models that are explicitly based on a
social accounting framework. It is particularly suited to the study of
industrialization because the indirect effects of structural change often
outweigh the direct effects that are visible in the national accounts aggregates.

This book began as an attempt to generalize from the growing number
of multisectoral analyses of developing countries. Such studies now exist
for twenty countries and cover periods of up to twenty years. From this
group, we have selected eight semi-industrial economies that have had at
least average growth rates throughout the postwar period; they form a
spectrum of trade and development policies from inward-oriented (Mexico and Turkey) to outward-oriented (Korea, prewar Japan, and Taiwan).
(The sample comprises a quarter of the semi-industrial group identified in
chapter 4. Postwar Japan and Norway were added to illustrate the shift to
a mature economy.)

To prepare the book, studies of these selected economies were undertaken to analyze growth and structural change in the postwar period with
the common accounting framework and methodology described in chapters 3 and 5. The authors were encouraged to extend the analyses to
problems of particular interest for each economy. The main publications
on individual economies that have resulted from these efforts range from
full-scale monographs on Korea, Taiwan, and Turkey to articles on Israel,
Japan, Norway, and Yugoslavia. (Only the standard accounts used in
country comparisons were prepared for Colombia and Mexico.) These
publications are:

Colombia
"Sources of Growth Data for Colombia" (de Melo 1983)

Israel
"Sources of Growth Data for Israel" (Frankel 1983)
"Economic Growth and Structural Change in Israel: An International
    Perspective" (Syrquin 1984)

Japan
"Role of Industrialization in Japanese Development" (Chenery and
    Watanabe 1976)

Korea
"Industrialization and Structural Change in Korea" (Kim 1978)
Growth and Structural Transformation (Kim and Roemer 1979)

Mexico
"Sources of Growth Data for Mexico" (Syrquin 1983)

Norway
"Accounting for Economic Growth: The Case of Norway" (Balassa 1979a)

Taiwan
"Economic Growth and Structural Change in the Republic of China" (Kuo 1979)
The Taiwan Economy in Transition (Kuo 1983)

Turkey
Sources of Industrial Growth and Structural Change: The Case of Turkey (Celasun 1983)
The Foreign Exchange Gap, Growth and Industrial Strategy in Turkey 1973–1983 (Dervis and Robinson 1978)

Yugoslavia
Yugoslavia: Self-Management Socialism and the Challenges of Development (Schrenk, Ardalan, and El Tatawy 1979)

In addition, uniform data on the sources of growth in the form described in chapter 5 were compiled for all countries by Yuji Kubo and Jeffrey Lewis in collaboration with the authors listed above (see Kubo 1983).

A Reader's Guide

This book consists of several types of comparative study that are unified by common themes. Nearly half of it is devoted to what can be learned from the nine economies that were studied in some detail. These results are presented in part II and chapter 10. The rest of the book comprises four comparative studies in which we develop the principal hypotheses and test their applicability to a broad spectrum of semi-industrial countries. These cross-country studies are:

- A comparison of the results of Solow-type estimates of the sources of aggregate growth in thirty-nine economies (chapter 2).
- A multisector simulation of the structural transformation of a representative semi-industrial economy (chapter 3). A dynamic version of this model is developed in chapter 8 to study the effects of resource reallocation on productivity growth.
- An econometric model of the sources of growth under disequilibrium conditions, estimated from data for thirty-four semi-industrial economies (chapter 9).

- A computable general equilibrium (CGE) model of the effects of alternative external policies on transformation and growth, based on data for Korea and other economies in our sample (chapter 11).

Table 1-1 shows how these studies are fitted together in the four parts of the book. The first two are combined in part I to provide an overview of the structural transformation and its relation to aggregate growth. Chapter 2 justifies our focus on semi-industrial countries by showing the characteristic differences between their growth processes and those of more mature economies. The cross-country model is then used to analyze the common features of the transformation in chapter 3 and to establish a basis for a typology of all semi-industrial countries in chapter 4. The three chapters in part I together provide a background for characterizing the nine economies in our sample.

Table 1-1. *The Organization of the Book*

Part of book	Topic	Analysis[a]	Results[a]
I. Structural transformation	Sources of growth: demand versus supply	Mature versus semi-industrial: 39 economies (2)	Varying role of productivity growth (2)
	Uniformity of transformation	Cross-country model (3)	Components of transformation (3)
		Semi-industrial economies (4)	Country typology (4)
II. Experience of industrialization	Causes	Methodology of comparisons (5)	Outward- versus inward-oriented strategies (6)
	Similarities	Multisectoral models: 9 economies (6, 7)	Industrial structure (7)
III. Productivity and structural change	Decomposition of productivity growth	Dynamic cross-section model (8)	Measurement of reallocation effects (8, 9)
	Importance of reallocation effects	Econometric analysis: 34 semi-industrial economies (9) Productivity by sector: 4 economies (10)	Country versus sector effects (8, 10)
IV. Development strategy	Policy instruments	CGE model of representative strategies (11)	Effects of policy changes (11)
	Synthesis	Synthesis of supply and demand factors (12)	Role of price changes (11)

a. Numbers in parentheses refer to chapters.

Part II analyzes the postwar experience of industrialization as it is reflected in comparable multisectoral models of the nine economies. This approach has the advantage of relating changes in the internal structure of demand and production to changes in the external structure of trade and resource inflows. This, in turn, facilitates detailed comparisons between inward- and outward-oriented strategies in which the relative importance of the several sources of growth and structural change can be measured.

Part II also reveals several aspects of industrialization that have not received much attention. Particularly notable is the growing importance of intermediate demand for industrial inputs in all the economies studied. This type of structural change is incorporated into the cross-country model and helps to explain the rapid growth of heavy industry.

Part III is concerned with the relation between industrialization and productivity growth. For this purpose, the multisectoral model is extended in chapter 8 to include the use of labor and capital by sector. The principal issues discussed are the differences in productivity growth among countries and sectors and the effects of reallocating resources.

Industrializing economies differ from mature economies in that the reallocation of resources from sectors of lower productivity to sectors of higher productivity can make an important contribution to overall growth. Chapters 8 and 9 examine the quantitative significance of several such shifts: from agriculture to industry, from light to heavy manufacturing, from domestic markets to foreign ones. In addition to the detailed comparison of four countries (Japan, Korea, Turkey, and Yugoslavia), part III contains an econometric model in which the effects of such shifts are estimated for the semi-industrial economies as a group (chapter 9).

The studies of factor use and productivity have led to some revisions in our original hypotheses. Although sectoral differences in productivity growth are significant, differences among countries are equally so. Total factor productivity growth tends to be higher in all sectors in countries of high growth. In the econometric model, the overall effect of these country differences can be measured as country residuals from the predicted rate of growth and can be associated with general economic policies.

Part IV develops a general equilibrium framework for the analysis of individual policy instruments. This allows the outward-oriented package to be broken down into several components, including the effects of capital inflows as well as increased exports. Efficient and inefficient methods of achieving import substitution are also simulated. In this way, we can compare a spectrum of policy combinations ranging from a stylized version of the superexporters based on the experience of Korea and Taiwan to representative combinations of protection and lower capital inflows based on the experience of Mexico and Turkey (chapter 11). These results, in turn, make possible a synthesis of the demand and supply sides of growth accounting.

PART I

Structural Transformation

THE POTENTIAL of the concept of structural transformation to unify the study of various aspects of development is demonstrated by the use of such terms as agricultural transformation, industrialization, demographic transition, and urbanization, each of which describes one or more dimensions of the overall transformation process. Part I incorporates the transformation of demand, trade, production, and employment into a single framework for analyzing long-term growth phenomena.

Our analysis focuses on the interaction between growth and structural change. What are the main features of the transformation that affect the ways in which economies grow and that distinguish developed from developing countries? Two of the best known of these structural relations are:

- Engel's law of the declining share of food in consumption
- Lewis's hypothesis of the elastic supply of labor in most developing countries.

Our findings suggest several other relations of comparable importance:

- Balassa's "stages of comparative advantage," derived from the Heckscher-Ohlin model
- Kuznets's observation of systematic differences in the level and growth of labor productivity by sector
- The demographic transition, a set of factors that produces first a rise and then a decline in population growth as per capita income rises.

Taken together, these income-related structural changes imply that the growth processes of developing economies may differ substantially from those of advanced economies.

Chapter 2 explores this hypothesis first by extending the techniques of growth accounting. The Solow methodology (Solow 1957) is applied to a large sample of developing and developed countries; this reveals some characteristic differences between the two groups in their sources of growth. These sources are then disaggregated to investigate the interaction between changes in the composition of demand and trade on the one hand and factor supplies and productivity growth on the other.

Chapter 3 attempts to model the factors that produce the typical patterns of the structural transformation. The model incorporates stylized facts of the kind indicated above and is estimated from cross-country data. It allows for differences in factors (such as size and resource base) that affect the structural transformation, as well as for differences between inward- and outward-oriented development policies. Several representative patterns of resource allocation are simulated by increasing the level of income over the range of the transformation.

The main purpose of these cross-country simulations is to provide a standard of comparison for the studies of individual economies in part II. They also suggest several generalizations about the uniformity of the transformation itself. For example, industrialization (measured by a rise in the share of manufacturing in gross national product [GNP]) must occur unless there is a sufficient rise in the value of exports of primary products or services to outweigh both the Engel effects of income growth on demand and the intensified use of industrial inputs. Although the phenomenon of deindustrialization (or the Dutch disease) has been observed in the short run, there are few examples of it persisting in developing countries for more than a decade. The longer-term analysis of chapter 3 indicates that the main issue of transformation is not whether countries need to industrialize but when and in what manner.

Chapter 4 addresses the problem of using these results for policy analysis. It proposes a general typology of industrialization based on the main distinctions that have emerged in simulating patterns of resource allocation. A category of industrializing or semi-industrial economies, intermediate between the less developed and the developed economies, emerges from these simulations. Its characteristics are then used to identify all the semi-industrial economies in the period 1960–80. Finally, distinctions in size, resource endowment, and trade policies are shown to be important in comparing the effects of development policies.

2 Growth and Transformation

HOLLIS CHENERY

THERE ARE TWO contrasting views of the way economic growth occurs. In the neoclassical tradition, GNP rises as the result of the long-term effects of capital formation, labor force expansion, and technological change, which are assumed to take place under conditions of competitive equilibrium. Shifts in demand and the movement of resources from one sector to another are considered relatively unimportant because labor and capital produce equal marginal returns in all uses.

In the second, broader view, economic growth is regarded as one aspect of the transformation of the structure of production that is required to meet changing demands and to make more productive use of technology. Given imperfect foresight and limits to factor mobility, structural changes are most likely to occur under conditions of disequilibrium; this is particularly true in factor markets. Thus a shift of labor and capital from less productive to more productive sectors can accelerate growth. Although this type of structural analysis has not received the same rigorous formulation as general equilibrium theory, it can provide a basis for empirical analysis.

When general equilibrium is not treated as axiomatic, the question of how much the reallocation of resources to sectors of higher productivity contributes to growth becomes an empirical one. It is likely to be more important for developing countries than for developed ones to recognize the potential of reallocation, for developing countries show more pronounced symptoms of disequilibrium in factor markets as well as more rapid change in the structure of production.

This chapter sets forth the background for analyzing the relation between industrialization—or, more broadly, the structural transformation of an economy—and the growth of per capita income. The results of neoclassical studies of equilibrium growth in both developed and developing countries are summarized, after which the effects of changing patterns of demand and trade in promoting or limiting the shift of resources to more productive uses are considered. As the chapter will show, determining the sources of growth calls for a synthesis of demand and supply factors and the use of multisectoral models.

Some fundamental differences between the growth processes of developing or transitional economies and those of mature, industrial economies emerge from this survey. In particular, disequilibrium phenomena are shown to be more significant for the former than for the latter. Thus, although neoclassical theory is a useful starting point for the study of growth, it must be modified substantially if it is to explain the essential features of economies in the process of transformation.

The Sources of Growth

Measurement of the sources of economic growth has progressed greatly since the pioneering work of Abramovitz (1956), Solow (1957), and Denison (1962). The main objective has been to estimate the relative contributions of the growth of capital and labor inputs (corrected for quality changes) on the one hand and of total factor productivity on the other. There are now many studies of the industrial countries, covering much of the postwar period, that use variants of neoclassical theory. This methodology has also been applied to a growing number of semi-industrial countries, and therefore some of the differences in the growth processes of the two groups can be identified.

Because the study of the disequilibrium aspects of growth requires a more detailed model than that of equilibrium growth, the principal econometric efforts have tested the significance of these aspects in explaining differences in growth among countries. This work, which is reviewed below, has established the importance of moving resources from lower-productivity to higher-productivity uses—for example, by expanding exports or by turning from agriculture to industry. These shifts are more important sources of growth in developing than in developed countries.

This empirical work suggests some answers to several questions of concern in this book:

- How useful is the neoclassical methodology as applied to developing countries? Are there significant differences among groups of countries that should be taken into account?
- Which departures from the general equilibrium framework appear to be most significant? To what extent is more explicit analysis of the changing composition of demand and trade needed?
- Are there systematic variations with per capita income in the factors affecting growth that should be allowed for?

In considering these questions, it may be useful to contrast the assumptions underlying neoclassical and structural views of the sources of growth. Since the basic assumptions of neoclassical theory are well known, they can serve as a point of departure in explaining the hypotheses of the structural approach.

The most important distinction between the two views is between their systemic assumptions rather than between any one of their elements. Neoclassical theory assumes the efficient allocation of resources (Pareto optimality) over time from the point of view of both producers and consumers. At any given moment it is impossible to increase aggregate output by shifting labor and capital from one sector to another: reallocation takes place only as the economy expands. In contrast, the structural approach does not assume fully optimal resource allocation; consequently, there may be systematic variations in the returns to labor and capital in different uses.

Some of the assumptions that contribute to this basic distinction are outlined in table 2-1. Maintaining equilibrium in the face of shifts in internal demands and in external trade is helped by high elasticities of substitution among both commodities and factors and by rapid responses to market signals. Neoclassical theory assumes that the economic system has sufficient flexibility to maintain equilibrium prices, whereas the structural approach identifies some conditions that make complete adjustment unlikely. One of the best documented sources of disequilibrium is the duality of the labor market—a duality which has been accentuated in many developing countries by a population growing too rapidly to be absorbed in the high-productivity sectors of the economy. The result is an elastic supply of unskilled labor concentrated in the agricultural and service sectors.

A second widely studied source of disequilibrium is the failure to reallocate resources efficiently to increase exports or replace imports. The factors contributing to a chronic balance of payments deficit include the tendency for import demands to expand more rapidly than total GNP, the lack of incentives for producers to enter new markets, and shortsighted

Table 2-1. *Alternative Views of Growth*

Neoclassical approach	Structural approach
Assumptions	
Factor returns equal marginal productivity in all uses	Income-related changes in internal demand
No economies of scale	Constrained external markets and lags in adjustment
Perfect foresight and continuous equilibrium in all markets	Transformation of productive structure producing disequilibria in factor markets
Empirical implications	
Relatively high elasticities of substitution in demand and trade	Low price elasticities and lags in adjustment
Limited need for sector disaggregation	Segmented factor markets
	Lags in adopting new technology
Sources of growth	
Capital accumulation	Neoclassical sources plus:
Increase in labor quantity and quality	Reallocation of resources to higher-productivity sectors
Increase in intermediate inputs	
Total factor productivity growth within sectors	Economies of scale and learning by doing
	Reduction of internal and external bottlenecks

policies that favor import substitution over export expansion. Whatever the factors limiting balance of payments adjustment in the past, there is little doubt that these factors have been a source of disequilibrium in many developing countries and have impeded growth.

Although the level of income in a hypothetical neoclassical economy is by definition higher than it would be under any set of disequilibrium assumptions, the growth potential of this economy may be less over time. Disequilibrium phenomena such as segmented factor markets and lags in adjustment imply a potential for accelerating growth by reducing bottlenecks and reallocating resources to sectors of higher productivity. This potential is likely to be greater in developing countries—which are subject to greater disequilibrating shocks and have greater market disequilibrium—than in developed countries. In addition, developing countries can take advantage of the more productive technology available from advanced countries. These two factors offer a plausible explanation for the acceleration of growth that has been noted in many industrializing countries.

In summary, the structural approach focuses on differences among sectors of the economy that may inhibit the equilibrating adjustments in resource allocation implied by neoclassical theory. Disequilibrium is more often manifested by the differences in returns to labor and capital in different uses than by the shortages and surpluses that indicate the complete failure of markets to clear. In contrast, neoclassical theory assumes that equilibrium is maintained over time, which limits the sources of growth to factors on the supply side.

Equilibrium Growth

The assumptions of competitive equilibrium that underlie neoclassical theory are a convenient starting point for growth analysis because they permit any group of inputs to be aggregated on the basis of their marginal productivities.[1] For economywide studies, all primary inputs can be categorized as either capital or labor. Each of these can then be consolidated on the basis of its share in the total product. The difference between the growth of total output and the weighted average growth of capital and labor serves as a measure of the increase in total factor productivity for the economy as a whole. This procedure is sufficiently general to permit comparisons among studies using different methodologies, so long as they maintain the assumptions of competitive equilibrium.

Analyses designed to measure the importance of these three sources of growth have now been carried out for thirty-nine economies for several periods. They indicate that the growth of capital, labor, and productivity are of comparable importance for the sample as a whole but vary signifi-

---

1. This section also provides a background for the country studies in chapter 10 and was written in consultation with Mieko Nishimizu.

cantly with the structure of an economy and the effectiveness of its policies.

Methodology

The methodology commonly used to estimate the sources of growth in a neoclassical framework has evolved from Solow's basic formulation (1957). An aggregate production function of the following general form is assumed:[2]

$$(2\text{-}1) \qquad Q = F\,(K,\,L,\,t)$$

where Q is the aggregate output of the economy, K and L are aggregate capital and labor inputs, and t is time. The simplest assumption about the effects of time (and the one made in most of the studies reported in table 2-2 below) is that technical progress is neutral in the (Hicksian) sense that it raises the output achievable from a given combination of capital and labor without affecting their relative marginal products. On this assumption, the production function can be written as

$$(2\text{-}1a) \qquad Q_t = A_t\,F\,(K_t,\,L_t).$$

The three sources of output growth can then be derived by differentiating this equation with respect to time and dividing by Q:

$$\frac{\dot{Q}}{Q} = \frac{\dot{A}}{A} + A\,\frac{\partial F}{\partial K}\,\frac{\dot{K}}{Q} + A\,\frac{\partial F}{\partial L}\,\frac{\dot{L}}{Q},$$

where dots indicate time derivatives. Substituting $\beta_K = (\partial Q/\partial K)(K/Q)$ and $\beta_L = (\partial Q/\partial L)(L/Q)$ gives the basic neoclassical growth equation:2

$$(2\text{-}2) \qquad G_V = G_A + \beta_K G_K + \beta_L\,G_L$$

where G_V, G_K, and G_L are the growth rates of aggregate output (value added), capital, and labor.

The growth of total factor productivity (TFP), G_A, is defined as the difference between G_V and the weighted sum of input growth, $\beta_K G_K + \beta_L G_L$. Each input coefficient, β_i, is defined as the elasticity of output with respect to input i, thus indicating the effect on output growth of a 1 percent increase in the growth of that input. This formulation can be extended to any number of inputs.

Under conditions of competitive equilibrium, each factor receives its marginal product, so that the real wage, w/p, equals $\partial Q/\partial L$. This assumption leads to the important result that in equilibrium the coefficient β_L is also equal to the share of labor in the total product, wL/pQ. Similarly, $\beta_K = rK/pQ$. In the absence of economies of scale, the sum of all the share

---

2. This formulation follows Solow (1957). The conditions underlying it and alternative assumptions are discussed in Branson (1979) and Nadiri (1970). A more general approach using a flexible form of the production function is discussed in chapter 10.

coefficients is equal to unity. Because output elasticities can rarely be estimated directly, these product shares based on equilibrium assumptions are normally used to estimate the growth equation 2-2.

Starting with the work of Denison (1962) and Griliches and Jorgenson (1966), major improvements in empirical analysis of the sources of growth have come from subdividing capital and labor by type and weighting them by their imputed returns. This can be done either for different types of capital assets or for the labor characteristics that affect productivity (education, age, sex, and so on). The formulation adopted by Elias (1978) in studies of many of the developing economies in our sample is representative:

$$(2\text{-}3) \qquad G_V = \beta_L G_L + \beta_L \Sigma \frac{w_i}{w} \left(\frac{\dot{L}_i}{L} \right) + \beta_K G_K$$

$$+ \beta_k \Sigma \frac{r_j}{r} \left(\frac{\dot{K}_j}{K} \right) + G_A$$

where the effects of varying returns on different kinds of capital assets and on different qualities of labor are reflected in the terms w_i/w and r_j/r. Although this method of treating labor quality differences is generally accepted, the extent to which it should be followed in measuring the growth of capital is a matter of dispute.[3]

For the group of developed countries listed in table 2-2 below, the effect of the quality terms in equation 2-3 is to add 25 percent to the growth of the capital stock and to offset the decline in the average hours worked. Compared to studies that do not include quality changes, this method increases the contribution of factor inputs and reduces measured factor productivity growth by a corresponding amount. For the developing countries, Elias (1978) attributes a smaller proportion of input growth to quality improvements; in some studies, this element is omitted entirely. Despite these conceptual differences, it will be shown that the Solow-Denison framework is a valuable basis for comparing the growth processes of developing and developed countries.

Developing versus Developed Countries

Similarities in the growth processes of developed countries have been explored in several recent studies. Earlier results tended to stress the relatively small proportion of growth accounted for by the increase in capital and labor, which leaves a large unexplained residual. Fuller allowance for quality improvements in the estimates of Christensen, Cummings,

---

3. Equation 2-3 is a simplified version of the methodology used by Christensen, Cummings, and Jorgenson (1980), which stems from earlier studies by Griliches and Jorgenson (1966, 1967).

and Jorgenson (1980), which are used here, has reduced the residual for the developed countries to an average of about half of total growth.[4]

Few efforts have been made to compare the performance of any substantial group of developing countries with that of industrial countries. In a pioneer attempt, Bruton (1967) analyzed data for five Latin American countries and concluded that total factor productivity growth (the residual) was much lower in this group than in developed countries. Nadiri (1972) reached a similar conclusion for the period 1950–62. This test will be repeated for the larger sample used here.

My analysis tries to identify the main differences in the sources of growth between developed and developing countries by focusing on the role of factor inputs compared with productivity growth. Since many studies provide only rough estimates of the shares of capital and labor in factor inputs, the analysis will consolidate the two into a single factor input, F. The growth equation 2-2 is then simplified to

$$(2\text{-}2a) \qquad\qquad G_V = G_A + G_F(G_K, G_L)$$

where G_V = growth of value added, $G_F = \beta G_K + (1 - \beta) G_L$ equals the combined contribution of factor inputs to growth, and G_A = growth of TFP. The average values of these variables for a sample of thirty-nine economies are reported in table 2-2 along with the underlying estimates for capital and labor shares.

These thirty-nine economies include virtually all the cases for which roughly comparable studies have been published. The sample contains one or two observations for each economy (depending on the availability of studies for different periods) and is divided into three groups based on conventional distinctions between developed, developing, and centrally planned economies. All twenty developing economies fall into the semi-industrial category (defined in chapter 4).[5]

Some preliminary distinctions among the three groups can be drawn from the average values of the variables given in table 2-2. The *developed economies* are characterized by little growth of labor inputs (1.1 percent), moderate growth of capital (5.2 percent) and output (5.4 percent), and a relatively large contribution of TFP to aggregate growth (50 percent). The *developing economies*, in contrast, have high growth of labor inputs (3.3 percent), a higher total factor growth (4.3 percent), and a relatively small contribution of TFP to aggregate growth (30 percent).

The *centrally planned economies* are in most respects closer to the

4. Using the Denison methodology, Kendrick (1982) estimates that increased total factor productivity accounted for about two-thirds of the growth in GNP of nine industrial countries for the period 1960–73, compared with the 50 percent estimated by Christensen, Cummings, and Jorgenson for this period.

5. With respect to income level, Ireland, Israel, and Spain are at the upper end of the semi-industrial category; Ecuador, Honduras, and India are at the lower end.

Table 2-2. *The Growth of Output, Inputs, and Total Factor Productivity*
(percent)

Economy	Years	Growth of value added (G_V)	TFP Growth rate (G_A)	TFP Share	Total factor input Growth rate (G_F)	Total factor input Share	Growth of capital input (G_K)	Growth of labor input (G_L)	Capital income share (β_K)	Labor income share (β_L)	Source
Developed											
Belgium	1949–59	2.95	2.05	69.5	0.90	30.5	2.55	0.25	30.0	70.0	ECE[b]
Canada	1947–60	5.20	3.50	32.5	1.70	67.6	6.80	1.10	42.0	58.0	CCJ[c]
	1960–73	5.10	1.80	35.3	3.30	64.7	4.90	2.00	44.9	55.1	CCJ
Denmark	1950–62	3.51	1.64	46.7	1.87	53.3	3.84	1.21	25.0	75.0	D[d]
France	1950–60	4.90	2.90	59.5	2.00	40.4	4.70	0.30	38.2	61.8	CCJ
	1960–73	5.90	3.00	50.8	2.90	49.2	6.30	0.40	41.7	58.3	CCJ
Germany, Fed. Rep.	1950–60	8.20	3.60	56.8	4.70	43.0	6.90	1.60	36.7	63.3	CCJ
	1960–73	5.40	3.00	55.6	2.40	44.4	7.00	-0.70	40.1	59.9	CCJ
Italy	1952–60	6.00	3.80	62.7	2.30	37.5	3.30	1.60	40.5	59.5	CCJ
	1960–73	4.80	3.10	64.6	1.60	35.4	5.40	-0.70	38.3	61.7	CCJ
Japan	1960–73	10.90	4.50	41.3	6.40	58.7	11.50	2.70	41.5	58.5	CCJ
Netherlands	1951–60	5.00	2.30	46.5	2.70	53.6	4.00	1.40	47.0	53.0	CCJ
	1960–73	5.60	2.60	46.4	3.00	53.6	6.60	0.30	42.9	57.1	CCJ
Norway	1953–65	5.40	2.88	53.3	2.52	46.7	5.10	0.80	40.0	60.0	BB[e]
Sweden	1949–59	3.40	2.50	73.5	0.90	26.5	2.00	0.50	30.0	70.0	ECE
United Kingdom	1949–59	2.50	1.20	48.0	1.30	52.0	3.10	0.60	30.0	70.0	ECE
	1960–73	3.80	2.10	55.3	1.70	44.7	4.60	0.00	38.7	61.3	CCJ
United States	1947–60	3.70	1.40	37.5	2.30	62.9	4.00	1.40	39.3	60.7	CCJ
	1960–73	4.30	1.30	30.2	3.00	69.8	4.00	2.20	41.4	58.6	CCJ
Average		5.40	2.70	49.0	2.70	51.0	5.20	1.10	38.5	61.5	

Country	Period									Source
Developing										
Argentina	1950–60	3.30	1.05	31.8	2.25	68.2	2.65	1.10	—	—	E[f]
	1960–74	4.10	0.70	17.1	3.30	82.9	3.80	2.20	—	—	E
Brazil	1950–60	6.80	3.65	53.7	3.15	46.3	3.10	2.80	—	—	E
	1960–74	7.30	1.60	21.9	5.70	78.1	7.50	3.30	—	—	E
Chile	1950–60	3.50	0.85	24.3	2.65	75.7	2.60	2.50	—	—	E
	1960–74	4.40	1.20	27.3	3.20	72.7	4.20	1.90	—	—	E
Colombia	1950–60	4.60	0.95	20.7	3.65	79.3	4.25	2.75	—	—	E
	1960–74	5.60	2.10	37.5	3.50	62.5	3.90	2.80	—	—	
Ecuador	1950–62	4.72	2.18	46.2	2.54	53.8	2.82	3.41	38.0	62.0	Co[g]
Greece	1951–65	6.90	2.39	34.5	4.52	65.5	7.10	2.80	40.0	60.0	BB
Honduras	1930–62	4.52	1.40	31.0	3.12	69.0	3.65	2.93	26.0	74.0	Co
Hong Kong	1955–60	8.25	2.40	29.1	5.85	70.9	4.68	6.63	40.0	60.0	Ch[h]
	1960–70	9.10	4.28	47.0	4.82	53.0	7.60	2.97	40.0	60.0	Ch
India[a]	1959/60 –78/79	6.24	−0.18	−2.9	6.42	102.9	4.77	1.65	52.5	47.5	Ah[i]
Ireland	1953–65	4.70	2.00	42.6	2.70	57.4	4.20	1.70	40.0	60.0	BB
Israel	1952–58	9.80	3.90	39.8	5.90	60.2	11.80	3.20	30.0	70.0	Au[j]
	1960–65	11.00	3.40	30.9	7.60	69.1	13.10	5.00	30.0	70.0	G[k]
Korea, Rep.	1955–60	4.22	2.00	47.4	2.22	52.6	2.18	2.25	40.0	60.0	Ch
	1960–73	9.70	4.10	42.3	5.50	57.7	6.60	5.00	36.7	63.3	CCJ
Mexico	1950–60	5.65	1.60	28.3	4.05	71.7	5.20	2.65	—	—	E
	1960–74	5.60	2.10	37.5	3.50	62.5	3.90	2.80	—	—	E
Peru	1950–60	4.50	−0.70	−15.6	5.20	115.6	7.65	2.70	—	—	E
	1960–70	5.30	1.50	28.3	3.90	71.7	4.40	2.70	—	—	
Philippines	1947–65	5.75	2.50	43.5	3.25	56.5	—	—	—	—	L[l]
Singapore	1972–80	8.00	−0.009	−0.1	8.01	100.1	9.48	5.52	61.1	38.9	T[m]
Spain	1959–65	11.20	5.02	44.8	6.18	55.2	8.70	4.50	40.0	60.0	BB
Taiwan	1955–60	5.24	3.12	59.5	2.12	40.5	2.68	1.75	40.0	60.0	Ch

(Table continues on the following page.)

Table 2-2 (continued)

Economy	Years	Growth of value added (G_V)	TFP Growth rate (G_A)	TFP Share	Total factor input Growth rate (G_F)	Total factor input Share	Growth of capital input (G_K)	Growth of labor input (G_L)	Capital income share (β_K)	Labor income share (β_L)	Source
Turkey	1963–75	6.40	2.23	34.8	4.17	65.2	6.82	1.02	55.0	45.0	KT[n]
Venezuela	1950–60	7.85	2.15	27.4	5.70	72.6	7.20	3.70	—	—	E
	1960–74	5.10	0.60	11.8	4.40	88.2	4.50	3.30	—	—	E
Average		6.30	2.00	31.0	4.30	69.0	5.50	3.30	45.30	54.7	
Centrally planned[a]											
Bulgaria	1953–65	12.50	3.30	26.4	9.20	73.6	11.60	7.60	40.0	60.0	BB
Czechoslovakia	1953–65	7.00	2.74	39.1	4.26	60.9	6.60	2.70	40.0	60.0	BB
Hungary	1953–65	6.50	1.78	27.4	4.72	72.6	7.30	3.00	40.0	60.0	BB
Poland	1961–65	6.60	2.20	33.3	4.40	66.7	6.50	3.00	40.0	60.0	BB
Romania	1953–65	11.10	5.32	47.9	5.73	52.1	8.30	4.10	40.0	60.0	BB
U.S.S.R.	1950–62	6.30	1.82	28.9	4.48	71.1	—	—	—	—	B[o]
Yugoslavia	1953–63	11.80	4.78	40.5	7.02	59.5	7.50	6.70	40.0	60.0	BB
Average		8.20	2.50	35.0	5.70	65.0	8.00	4.50	40.0	60.0	

— Not available.

Note: All variables are defined in equations 2-3 and 2-5.

a. Refers to manufacturing only.
b. Economic Commission for Europe (1964).
c. Christensen, Cummings, and Jorgenson (1980).
d. Denison (1967)
e. Balassa and Bertrand (1970).
f. Elias (1978)
g. Correa (1970).

h. Chen (1977).
i. Ahluwalia (1985).
j. Aukrust (1965).
k. Gaathon (1971).
l. Lampman (1967).
m. Tsao (1980).
n. Krueger and Tuncer (1980).
o. Boretsky (1966).

semi-industrial economies than to the developed ones. The studies for these economies apply only to the manufacturing sector, in which both output and input growth have been considerably higher than in the other sectors. Like the developing economies, the centrally planned economies rely more heavily on expanding factor inputs than on increasing productivity.[6]

The availability of these fifty-seven country studies makes possible a regression analysis of the differences in the growth processes of the three groups. For this purpose, an average growth equation will be estimated for each group to study the relation of productivity growth to other elements in equation 2-2. I allow for the possibility that productivity growth may be affected by the rate of growth of factor inputs, by output growth, or by unspecified differences among the country groups.

It is widely held that productivity advances are at least partly embodied in additions to the stock of physical or human capital. The following equation expresses this possibility:

$$G_A = \gamma_0 + \gamma_F G_F.$$

Substituting this expression for TFP, G_A, in equation 2-2a gives the more general growth equation

(2-4) $$G_V = \gamma_0 + (1 + \gamma_F) G_F.$$

The corresponding regression equation takes the form

(2-5) $$G_V = \alpha_0 + \alpha_F G_F$$

where $\alpha_F = 1 + \gamma_F$ and $\alpha_0 = \gamma_0$. (Estimates of equation 2-5 for the total sample as well as for the three country groups are given in table 2-3 below.)

Although the growth equation for the whole sample shows some evidence of embodiment, the corresponding value of the embodiment coefficient γ_F (0.12) is not significantly different from zero. The average behavior of all countries is therefore adequately characterized by equation 2-2a, with a constant value of TFP growth (γ_0) of about 2 percent.

This picture changes markedly when the sample is divided into three groups. The embodiment coefficient for the developed countries (0.35) is quite significant, but the developing-country regression is little changed from that for the whole sample.

The interpretation of these results is made easier if both the scatter diagrams and the regression estimates for each country group are examined. Figure 2-1 shows the production function data along with the

---

6. In the absence of estimates of the elasticity of output with respect to labor and capital, the authors of the estimates for the centrally planned economies (Balassa and Bertrand 1970) used a range from 35 to 55 percent for the capital share. A shift in the capital share from 40 to 50 percent, for example, would raise the contribution of factor inputs on average from 65 to 70 percent of manufacturing growth.

Figure 2-1. *Relationships between Value Added Growth and Factor Input Growth*

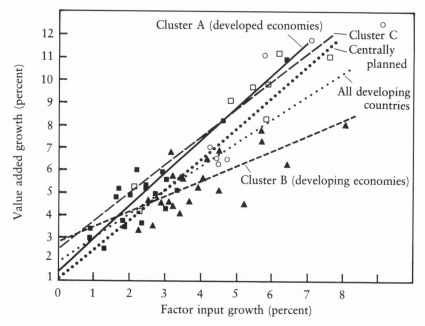

Key: ■ Developed economies
      ○ Centrally planned economies
      ▲ Developing economies
      □ Hong Kong, Israel, Korea, Spain, and Taiwan

regression lines of equation 2-5. Figure 2-2, which shows the relation between factor inputs and productivity growth in each economy in a form corresponding to equation 2-2a, plots lines of constant aggregate growth as the sum of G_A and G_F. The second graph compares factor inputs and TFP as sources of growth in the three country groups, whereas figure 2-1 focuses on the relation between input and output.[7]

Figure 2-2 shows that most of the developed countries fit within a small cluster, A, defined by relatively low factor growth, with TFP accounting for between 50 and 70 percent of overall growth. Japan is the chief exception; it has not only double the average growth rate for a developed country but also a higher proportion resulting from factor inputs.[8] (The United States

---

7. Figure 2-2 omits the centrally planned economies and India because their data are limited to manufacturing. All the observations from table 2-2 appear in figure 2-1, but only the most recent observation for each country appears in figure 2-2. In all but a few cases (Brazil and Korea), the most recent observation gives a good indication of the country's sources of growth for the whole period.

8. Japan fits the production function estimated for this group, but it is so far out of the range of the other observations that this has little significance.

Figure 2-2. *Relationship between Total Factor Productivity Growth and Total Factor Input Growth*

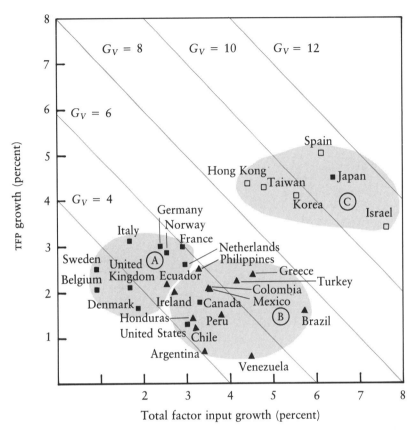

and Canada have a somewhat higher share of labor and a somewhat lower share of TFP than the European countries.)

The developing countries in figure 2-2 divide into two clusters. The larger one, B, is characterized by TFP growth between 0.5 and 2.0 percent. The smaller one, C, is composed of five developing economies plus Japan, with aggregate growth, G_V, averaging more than 10 percent. This performance was achieved by both higher factor inputs and higher factor productivity than the typical developing countries. The origins of the differences between clusters B and C are explored in the next section of this chapter, which tests the effects of resource reallocation as a source of growth.

To pursue this analysis a step further, the nine observations for the five developing economies in cluster C—Hong Kong, Israel, Korea, Spain, and Taiwan—were treated as a separate group in the regression analysis (indicated by a dummy variable for each economy); the results are given in

Table 2-3. *Cross-Country Estimates of Growth and Productivity*
(percent)

| Economy group | Production function | | | | Productivity and growth | | |
| | $(G_V = \alpha_o + \alpha_F G_F;$ equation 2-5) | | | | $(G_A = \beta_o + \beta_V G_V;$ equation 2-6) | | |
	α_o	α_F	R^2	N	β_o	β_V	R^2
Developed (cluster A)	1.71	1.35	0.83	19	0.63	0.39	0.66
	$(0.41)^b$	(0.15)			(0.36)	(0.07)	
All developing	1.76	1.07	0.59	31	-0.78	0.45	0.48
	(0.76)	(0.17)			(0.57)	(0.09)	
Developing (cluster B)	2.74	0.68		22	0.28	0.21	0.61
	(0.61)	(0.14)			(0.87)	(0.15)	
Developing (cluster C)^a	2.49	1.23		9	1.07	0.30	
	(1.13)	(0.23)			(1.48)	(0.20)	
Centrally planned (manufacturing only)	0.98	1.38	0.77	7	-0.53	0.42	0.68
	(1.79)	(0.30)			(1.18)	(0.13)	
All economies	1.89	1.12	0.73	57	0.16	0.36	0.45
	(0.40)	(0.09)			(0.36)	(0.05)	

a. Values computed by using a dummy variable for cluster C economies.
b. Standard errors in parentheses.
Source: Table 2-2.

table 2-3. The estimates for C resemble those for the developed economies, as shown in figure 2-1, whereas the estimates for B imply that an increase in factor inputs has a less than proportional effect on growth.

These estimates also give some support to the Kaldor (1967)-Verdoorn (1949) hypothesis that TFP is a function of overall growth, however achieved.[9] The corresponding regression equation is

$$(2\text{-}6) \qquad\qquad G_A = \beta_0 + \beta_V G_V.$$

The results of estimating this equation for the present sample are also given in table 2-3. Although they show a significant association between productivity increase and overall growth in each group, this does not tell much about the causal factors involved. (The validity of this hypothesis is examined on a sectoral basis in chapter 10.)

Both sets of regressions point to the relative inefficiency of the growth processes of the typical developing economies in cluster B. In terms of the production functions of figure 2-1, a representative developing economy with relatively high factor input growth of 5 percent can expect aggregate growth of about 6 percent, whereas the regressions for either developed economies (cluster A) or efficient developing economies (cluster C) predict

9. The Kaldor-Verdoorn hypothesis was actually formulated in terms of *labor* productivity growth.

growth of about 9 percent. Later chapters will compare in detail four members of cluster C—Israel, Japan, Korea, and Taiwan—and three members of B—Colombia, Mexico, and Turkey—to identify some of the sources of this difference.

Disequilibrium Growth

Disequilibrium growth is characteristic of an economic system that exhibits significant departures from the neoclassical assumptions described above. It falls into the category of the "theory of second best," where for various reasons the optimal (equilibrium) solution is unattainable. In empirical terms, the main questions are whether one can identify the effects of disequilibrium in factor or product markets and incorporate them into an analysis of growth and development.

The growth characteristics of an inflexible economy are in general the opposite of those of neoclassical theory, which implicitly assumes a high degree of substitution among both commodities and factors of production. For example, a fixed coefficient model will almost automatically generate capital shortages and labor surpluses in a developing economy that has a relatively high growth of the labor force; yet this problem is virtually ruled out by neoclassical assumptions. Similarly, the growth of income produces a more than proportional rise in the demand for manufactured goods and a resulting tendency for manufactured imports to outrun exports. The structural adjustments through export expansion, import substitution, and capital inflows needed to maintain a balance of payments equilibrium will reduce growth unless they are carried out efficiently. (This problem, which has been studied in the literature on two-gap models, is taken up in detail in part II.)

In each area of potential disequilibrium, the actual performance of developing countries lies somewhere between the extremes of flexibility and inflexibility assumed by the neoclassical and the input-output systems respectively. The next section tests the importance of disequilibrium factors by comparing the results of statistical studies that incorporate them with those that do not.

The Effects of Disequilibrium

To incorporate the effects of disequilibrium into the study of growth, I shall attempt to establish which of the several factors suggested are of general significance for developing countries. Those shown to be important can then be studied in more detail for individual countries.

Several economists have done regression analyses of large samples of countries with the common objective of testing the significance of structural variables in explaining growth rates. (This approach was first applied in Hagen and Havrylyshyn 1969; Robinson 1969, 1971; and Chenery, Elkington, and Sims 1970. Data were for different periods between 1950 and 1965.) The main factors tested were:

Neoclassical variables
Growth of capital stock
Growth of the labor force (or population)
Improvements in the quality of labor (or a rise in the level of education)

Structural variables
Reallocation of labor and capital
Growth of exports
Capital inflow (two-gap hypothesis)
Level of development

Each study started from a version of the neoclassical growth formula given in equation (2-2) and added other explanatory variables. Because analysts were forced to use proxies for the underlying factors, the regression coefficients in these equations cannot necessarily be identified with parameters in a specific model. The cross-country regression equations are of the general form

$$(2\text{-}7) \qquad G_Y = a_0 + a_1 \left(\frac{I}{Y}\right) + a_2 G_L + a_3 X_3 + a_4 X_A$$
$$+ a_5 X_E + a_6 X_F + a_7 X_D$$

where
    I/Y = the ratio of investment to GNP (a proxy for the growth of capital
        stock)
    G_L = growth of the labor force
    X_3 = a measure of increase in labor quality (or education)[10]
    X_A = a measure of the shift of labor or capital out of agriculture
    X_E = a measure of the growth of exports
    X_F = a measure of the balance of payments deficit
    X_D = a measure of the level of development.

The use of only the first two explanatory variables yields results that can be compared with the time-series estimates of neoclassical growth for individual countries. In making this comparison, it should be noted that the coefficient for the investment term, a_1, can be identified with the marginal productivity of capital only to the extent that capital-output ratios are the same in all countries.[11] Because this form of estimation does not rely on the assumption that factors are paid their marginal products, it gives some indication of the effects of this assumption.

The results of four studies covering periods before 1965 are given in table 2-4. Each study illustrates the effects of adding one or more structural variables to a model that includes only the growth of capital and

10. This variable was omitted from the summary of results in table 2-3 because it was not found to be significant in the studies surveyed.
11. To estimate the aggregate production function, the variable should be I/K—which is not observable—instead of I/Y, as discussed by Hagen and Havrylyshyn (1969).

Table 2-4. *Growth Regressions, 1950–73*

Regression equation	Sample size	Explanatory variables							R^2
		I/Y	L	A	E	F	$\ln y$	$(\ln y)^2$	
		DEVELOPING ECONOMIES; EARLY PERIODS							
		1958–66 (Robinson 1971)							
1	39	0.17**	0.55						0.22
2	39	0.15**	0.37	1.70**					0.35
3	39	0.09	0.35	2.01**		0.17**			0.52
		1955–60 (Hagen and Havrylyshyn 1969)							
4	33	0.21**	0.40	0.07					0.29
5	33	0.16	0.34	0.25*	0.03	0.11			0.54
		1950–59 (Chenery, Elkington, and Sims 1970)							
6	31	0.15*				0.16*			0.22
7	31						0.18**	−0.02**	0.36
8a	31	0.14**	0.59**		0.75**	0.21**	0.09*	−0.01**	0.77
8b	19[a]	0.08	1.09**		0.37				0.84
		1955–63 (Feder; chapter 9)							
9	31[b]	0.14**	0.74**						0.26
10	27[b]	0.05	0.88**	0.82**					0.19
11	31[b]	0.09	0.57*		0.37				0.30
		SEMI-INDUSTRIAL ECONOMIES, 1964–73 (Feder; chapter 9)							
12	30	0.25**	0.78*						0.46
13	30	0.14**	0.43*	0.80**					0.67
14	34	0.10**	0.59**			0.30**			0.79
15	32	0.11*	0.74**	0.90**	0.23**				0.81

Empty cells: Not applicable.
*Significant at 10 percent with two-tailed test.
**Significant at 5 percent with two-tailed test.
Note: Dependent variable: annual growth of GNP.
a. Developed economies.
b. Semi-industrial economies.
Sources: Equation 2-7; tables 9-1, 9-4, and 9-6.

labor. The studies cover samples of thirty to forty developing countries for periods of five to ten years.[12]

In almost all cases the addition of structural variables (as in regression equations 3, 5, and 8a in table 2-4) substantially improved the explanation of differences in growth rates among developing countries. The proportion of the variance explained by each equation typically increases from about 0.25 to more than 0.50. Feder's results for the period 1964–73 (table 2-4; also see chapter 9) show even greater improvement when the sample is limited to the semi-industrial economies. Because each explanatory variable is correlated to some extent with per capita income, the

12. Hagen and Havrylyshyn (1969) and Chenery, Elkington, and Sims (1970) made separate estimates for the 1950s and for 1960–65. In almost all cases the fits for 1960–65 were worse, so I rely mainly on the studies for longer periods. Chenery, Elkington, and Sims also present comparable results for developed countries that will be discussed below.

Table 2-5. *Sources of Growth in Developing Economies,*
Two Studies, 1958–73

	1958–66 (Robinson 1971)				1964–73 (Feder; chapter 9)				
Source	Sample mean	1	2	3	Sample mean	12	13	14	15
Investment (I/Y)	0.168	2.90	2.56	1.56	0.201	4.97	2.80	2.14	2.20
		(59)[a]	(51)	(31)		(78)	(44)	(33)	(34)
Labor ($\dot{L}/L$)	2.74	1.49	1.00	0.95	2.07	1.62	0.89	1.39	1.72
		(30)	(20)	(19)		(25)	(14)	(22)	(27)
Reallocation			0.77	0.90			2.00		0.50
			(16)	(18)			(31)		(8)
Exports				0.70				1.85	1.96
				(14)				(29)	(31)
Residual		0.56	0.62	0.84		−0.18	0.72	1.04	0.01
		(11)	(13)	(17)		(−3)	(11)	(16)	(0)
Total growth		4.95	4.95	4.95		6.41	6.41	6.43	6.39

Empty cells: Not applicable.
a. Figures in parentheses are percentages of total growth.
Sources: Table 2-4; Robinson (1971, table 6); and tables 9-2 and 9-7.

values of most regression coefficients tend to decline as additional variables are included. This is illustrated by the coefficients for labor and capital in each of the studies cited.

Although almost all the structural variables that were tested make a statistically significant contribution to this explanation, little can be said about the underlying causal relations. When the mean values of each explanatory variable are inserted into the regression equations, the equations give a breakdown of the implied sources of growth for the given period. To show the relative importance of each factor, the main findings of Robinson and Feder are compared in this way in table 2-5.[13]

Five conclusions emerge:

- The growth of capital is still the most important single factor, but its relative contribution is reduced from well over 50 percent of average growth in the neoclassical model to 30–40 percent in the structural formulations.
- The growth of the labor force is similarly reduced in importance; in some developing-country samples, it is no longer statistically significant. These findings are consistent with the evidence that many developing countries are characterized by surplus labor.
- The reallocation of capital and labor from agriculture to more productive sectors accounts for about 20 percent of average growth.
- The growth of exports makes a significant contribution to growth for

13. The sample means are shown for labor and capital, the only variables specified in the same form in both studies.

all developing countries in the period 1964–73; however, it does not appear to have been significant before 1960. If both factor reallocation and export expansion are included in the same regression, the latter appears to be more important. (This interaction is discussed in chapter 9.)

• The capital inflow (excess of imports over exports) shows a significant effect on growth in two of the studies cited in table 2-4, in addition to its effects on investment and exports. This finding gives some support to the two-gap hypothesis that imports may constitute a limit to growth. (Chapter 9 gives an alternative interpretation of the results for 1964–73 according to this hypothesis.)

Developing versus Developed Countries

Virtually all the structural factors in table 2-4 that affect the rate of growth are correlated with the level of development. That other factors are also significant is shown by adding per capita income as an explanatory variable in table 2-4 (equations 7 and 8a), which improves the regression results for developing countries although it has little effect on the developed group. The extent of multicolinearity makes it necessary to estimate specific models—as is done in chapter 9—before attributing causal significance to any particular statistical finding.

Despite these qualifications, the cross-country studies of growth yield two general results. First, they identify several aspects of structural change that affect the rate of growth and that have a varying importance at different levels of development. Taken together, these lead to a pattern of an accelerating and then a declining rate of growth as per capita income rises. Second, the structural factors in the cross-country regressions are all more significant for the developing countries than for the developed ones, whereas the growth of the labor force has more effect in developed countries. Investment is the only source of growth shown to be important for both groups, although one may speculate about the relative importance of technological improvements.

These comparisons suggest not only that there are somewhat dissimilar sets of growth factors for developing and developed countries but also that there is a need for different research strategies to more clearly identify each set. Although cross-country regressions and time-series analyses yield fairly consistent results for the developed countries, they give two quite different pictures for developing countries. To reconcile the two, it is necessary to take explicit account of the changing structure of demand and production, something omitted from the conventional description of the sources of growth.

Structural Transformation

The structural transformation of a developing economy may be defined as the set of changes in the composition of demand, trade, production, and factor use that takes place as per capita income increases. A main thesis of this book is that to understand country differences in sources and rates of growth, the transformation as a whole must be analyzed. More specifically, changes in demand and trade may affect the sources of growth as much as the changes in factor supply that have been stressed so far.

The central role of international trade in the structural transformation can be revealed only if the sectors that produce tradable commodities are isolated so that the relations between demand, trade, and productivity growth can be examined. Differences in resource endowments among countries are also manifested in variations in the patterns of trade over time. This section outlines the relations between changes in demand and trade on the one hand and the sources of growth on the other and suggests ways of integrating this demand-side analysis with the supply-side approach.

Accounting for Sectoral Differences

The sources-of-growth methodology referred to in the first section of this chapter relies on a combination of accounting identities and a few economic assumptions in order to compare the growth processes of different countries. I shall first disaggregate this supply-side analysis by sector and then combine it with a corresponding breakdown of demand and trade. The result is a demand-side view of the factors leading to structural change and growth that is consistent with supply-side analysis. The construction of comparable statistical accounts for the economies in the sample will in turn make possible comparative analysis and the development of more complete models.

The disaggregation of the sources of growth on the supply side is quite straightforward. In the equilibrium version, a growth equation of the form of equation (2-2) can be specified for each sector of the economy:

$$(2\text{-}8) \qquad\qquad G_i = \beta_{K_i} G_{K_i} + \beta_{L_i} G_{L_i} + \lambda_i$$

where each term has a meaning similar to the aggregate model, equation 2-3. The growth of the economy is given by a weighted average of the sectoral growth rates:

$$(2\text{-}9) \qquad\qquad G_V = \Sigma \bar{\rho}_i \, G_i$$

where the weights are the average shares of each sector, $\bar{\rho}_i$, derived from the analysis of demand given below. When the analysis of supply is separated from the analysis of demand, these sectoral weights must be exogenously given. This disaggregated analysis can be used with different forms of production functions and can include sector-specific inputs (such as natural resources) that may set a limit to the growth of particular sectors.

The corresponding system of growth accounting from the demand side is developed in chapters 3 and 5. It is based on the following accounting identity for each sector of production (see equation 3-3):

$$X_i = D_i + (E_i - M_i) + \sum_j X_{ij}$$

where

X_i = gross output of sector i

D_i = domestic final demand (consumption plus investment)

$(E_i - M_i)$ = net trade (exports minus imports)

$X_{ij} = a_{ij}X_j$ = intermediate use of commodity i by sector j (a_{ij} is assumed to vary with the level of per capita income).

The properties of the input-output system make it possible to eliminate intermediate demand as a separate source of growth by attributing it to the elements of final demand (see equation 5-11). In this way, the increase in production of sector i is equated to the sum of four factors:

- *The expansion of domestic demand* (DD), which includes the direct demand for commodity i plus the indirect effects on sector i of the expansion of domestic demand in other sectors
- *Export expansion* (EE), or the total effect on output from sector i of increasing exports
- *Import substitution* (IS), or the total effect on output from sector i of increasing the proportion of demand in each sector that is supplied from domestic production
- *Technological change* (IO), or the total effect on sector i of changing input-output coefficients throughout the economy as wages and income levels rise.

Of these four factors, the only one with a strong basis in theory is domestic demand, for which generalized systems of Engel functions have been estimated in many countries.[14]

There are three formal similarities between the two approaches to accounting for growth. First, the supply-side analysis states the requirement for a combination of inputs to produce a given commodity; the demand-side approach specifies the need for that commodity throughout the economy to "produce" a given level of GNP. Second, the supply decomposition allocates productivity growth by sector as a residual; the demand decomposition measures a similar factor—technological change—by changes in input-output coefficients throughout the economy. Third, each approach can be applied as a first approximation by ignoring price effects (or assuming constant prices). Once prices are explicitly introduced, the separation between supply-side and demand-side analysis breaks down because both are necessary to determine relative prices.

14. See Lluch, Powell, and Williams (1977).

The importance of disaggregation depends on the sectoral differences in either production functions or demand conditions. On the supply side, large differences in production functions exist among agriculture, mining, manufacturing, utilities, and services. On the demand side, large differences stem from income elasticities, tradability, and the extent of intermediate use. These are illustrated in the prototype model of the transformation developed in the next chapter.

Interactions between Supply and Demand

The two accounting systems presented above describe the results of the interaction of the several factors affecting economic growth and structural change. Although an accounting system cannot disentangle causal relations, it can indicate the relative importance of various factors. This chapter therefore concludes by juxtaposing the results of applying demand and supply decompositions to a single set of data taken from the prototype model (set forth in chapter 3).

Table 2-6 shows a supply-side decomposition of the sources of growth

Table 2-6. *Sectoral Sources of Growth, Supply-Side Decomposition, Income Range $560–$1,120*

Sector	Capital β_{K_i}	Capital $\beta_{K_i} \cdot G_{K_i}$	Labor β_{L_i}	Labor $\beta_{L_i} \cdot G_{L_i}$	TFP growth (λ_i)	Sector growth (G_i)	Average sector share $(\bar{p}_i)$	Contribution to growth $(\bar{p}_i G_i)$
Primary		2.69		0.41	1.00	4.09	17.4	0.71
Agriculture	0.46	2.41	0.54	0.26	0.86	3.53	14.8	0.52
Mining	0.50	4.26	0.50	1.19	1.81	7.26	2.6	0.19
Manufacturing		3.62		1.86	2.14	7.57	27.4	2.07
Light industry	0.42	2.87	0.58	1.94	2.11	6.91	16.7	1.15
Heavy industry	0.54	4.79	0.46	1.74	2.19	8.60	10.7	0.92
Nontradables		2.46		2.14	1.77	6.37	55.2	3.51
Social overhead	0.55	3.29	0.45	1.34	1.96	6.59	15.4	1.01
Services	0.35	2.16	0.65	2.46	1.66	6.28	39.8	2.50
Total economy								
Aggregate	0.43	2.71	0.57	1.31	2.28	6.30	100	6.30
		(43)[a]		(21)	(36)			
Average of sectors		2.82		1.77	1.72			
		(45)		(28)	(27)			
Reallocation effect					0.56			
					(9)			

Note: Empty cells mean not applicable. Each row gives the breakdown of sector growth using equation 2-8. The last column gives the breakdown of total growth (6.30 percent) using equation 2-9.

a. Figures in parentheses are shares of total growth.

Source: Chapter 8.

for six sectors of a representative economy. For each sector, the rate of growth is determined (as in equation 2-8) as the weighted sum of the growth of factor inputs plus total factor productivity growth. These elements are aggregated (as in equation 2-9) to give a total growth of 6.30 percent over the specified income range.

Table 2-7 gives a corresponding breakdown of the sources of growth from the demand side (using equation 5-16). In this case, the growth of each sector is expressed as a share of the total increment in GNP so that it can be compared with the initial composition of output. If a given rate of aggregate growth is assumed, the table shows the typical breakdown of the sources of demand growth starting from a middle-income level of $560.

The most notable differences in the sectoral results are between primary production and manufacturing and between tradables and nontradables (social overhead and services). Exports and import substitution together account for 30 percent of the growth of tradables but have a relatively small effect on the growth of nontradables. Both exports and changes in input coefficients reinforce the growth of demand for manufactures.

Tables 2-6 and 2-7 also reconcile the two ways of accounting for the aggregate growth rate of 6.30 percent. On the supply side, the column totals in table 2-6 attribute 45 percent to the growth of capital, 28 percent to the growth of labor, and 27 percent to the growth of total factor productivity. The row totals in table 2-7 (incremental share of value added) attribute 33 percent to the growth of manufacturing, 11 percent to the growth of primary production, 40 percent to the growth of services, and 16 percent to the growth of social overhead capital.

These statements cannot be taken as separate explanations except under an extreme assumption either that demand adjusts fully to the increase in

Table 2-7. *Sectoral Sources of Growth, Demand-Side Decomposition, Income Range $560–$1,120*

Sector	Share of value added (percent)		Contribution to Growth (annual percent)			
			Sources			Total,
	Initial	Incremental	Demand	Trade	IO	$\bar{p}_i G_i$
Primary	20.6	10.9	0.51	0.31	−0.11	0.71
Manufacturing	24.4	33.2	1.50	0.53	0.04	2.07
Light industry	15.8	18.4	0.88	0.25	0.02	1.15
Heavy industry	8.6	14.8	0.62	0.28	0.02	0.92
Nontradables	54.9	55.9	3.14	0.39	−0.01	3.52
Social overhead	15.0	16.2	0.91	0.11	0.00	1.02
Services	39.9	39.7	2.23	0.28	−0.01	2.50
Total	100.0	100.0	5.15	1.23	−0.08	6.30

Source: Cross-country model in chapters 3 and 6.

supply by sector or, conversely, that supply adjusts to the pattern of the increase in demand. In all other cases, together they describe the outcome of equilibrating adjustments.

Chapter 3 extends the analysis of the sectoral sources of growth to the whole structural transformation (see figure 3-7 below) to show the interaction between the level of income and the sources of growth by sector. The rise of industry—defined below as manufacturing plus social overhead facilities—becomes the dominant source of growth over the later stages of the transformation. An explanation of the factors determining these changes, and of the ways in which they are influenced by both the initial structure and government policy, constitutes the principal agenda for this book.

3 Typical Patterns of Transformation

HOLLIS CHENERY

MOSHE SYRQUIN

CHAPTER 2 ARGUED that the growth processes of a developing country can best be understood as part of the overall transformation of its economic structure. This interdependence works in both directions: income growth causes changes in the composition of domestic demand and production, and, conversely, rising investment rates and the reallocation of labor tend to increase aggregate growth. The transformation is by no means uniform across countries, however, for it is affected by resource endowments and the initial structure of the economy as well as by the choice of development policies. In extreme cases, large structural changes may be associated with little or no growth.

To pursue this argument further, it is necessary to move beyond the traditional growth accounting approaches of chapter 2 toward a more explicit model of the structural transformation that incorporates some of the most basic underlying relations. In doing so, our main objective is to design a form of analysis that takes advantage of both the aggregate data available for large numbers of countries and the detailed time series available for individual countries.

This chapter constitutes a first step in this direction. It presents a simple multisectoral model designed to simulate the effects of changing demand and trade on the structure of production. Since these are aspects of the transformation for which data are relatively plentiful, the underlying structural relations can be estimated from cross-country data as well as from data for individual countries over time. This enables us to identify some common features of the transformation to be used as benchmarks in comparing the experience of various countries.

Having allowed for these common elements, we can better analyze the sources of variations in the transformation. We shall concentrate on the interplay between two sets of factors: the pattern of specialization and the level of income already achieved. Differences in specialization are largely the result of a country's size, resource endowments, and trade policies. Different trade patterns, in turn, are associated with variants of the production pattern in which industrialization is either accelerated or retarded. We shall simulate three representative patterns that embody the main differences in country experience and that set the stage for the comparative studies of later chapters.

Modeling the Structural Transformation

The structure of an economy can be defined by its supplies of productive factors—labor, capital, and natural resources—and their employment in different uses or sectors. The term structural transformation encompasses the changes in the economic structure that lead to, and are caused by, a rise in the national product, together with the proximate causes of these changes. A narrow definition of proximate causes would include the accumulation of capital and skills, the effects of rising income on the composition of demand, and changes in comparative advantage. A broader definition would incorporate some aspects of productivity growth and the effects of government policies on resource allocation.

The Conceptual Framework

To simplify the problem of modeling the structural transformation, we divide the task into two parts: an explanation of the rate of growth, and an explanation of the changes in economic structure. Although the two parts are interrelated, they can be separated initially by treating one or the other as exogenously given. This procedure was followed in chapter 2, which analyzed the effects of specified structural changes on growth. Here the procedure is reversed; we shall begin by trying to explain changes in the economic structure with GNP growing at a given rate.

Our basic measure of the economic structure is the share of GNP originating in each sector of the economy ($\rho_i = V_i/V$). The main purpose of a model of structural transformation is to explain the variations in ρ_i and V_i as per capita GNP rises. By estimating the model from cross-country data, we attempt to simulate the full range of the transformation, which typically involves at least a tenfold increase in per capita GNP. In this way, cross-country analysis supplements studies of individual developing countries, which typically cover only 20 to 30 percent of this range.

The study of patterns of economic development, initiated by Clark and Kuznets, has led to the identification and measurement of a number of structural changes associated with rising income. In an earlier study (Chenery and Syrquin 1975), we estimated many of these relations for the postwar period in a uniform econometric framework that takes into account a country's size and resources as well as its per capita income. The degree of similarity found between time-series studies and cross-country estimates of the principal relations provides support for the use of cross-country estimates in modeling these features, although care must be taken in interpreting the results.

The most notable feature of the structural transformation, confirmed in both cross-country and time-series studies, is the rise in the share of manufacturing, ρ_m, in GNP and the corresponding decline in the share of agriculture, ρ_a. The reallocation of capital and labor from rural to urban areas, along with many related aspects of industrialization, stems from this basic change in the productive structure. The various hypotheses advanced to explain this process can be grouped as *demand explanations*, based on generalizations of Engel's law; *trade explanations*, based on shifts in comparative advantage as capital and skills are accumulated; and *technological explanations*, which include the substitution of processed for natural materials and the effects of differential rates of productivity growth.

Our first objective is to capture the interactions among these three sets of factors as they affect the structure of production. This results in what can be described as a model of industrialization. We shall take the rates of growth of GNP and population as given, thus deferring consideration of the effects of structural change on growth to the final section of this chapter. In simplified terms, the static model of industrialization explains structural change for a given period, whereas the more complete dynamic model incorporates the interaction between demand and supply in explaining changes of growth rates for several periods.

The static model of industrialization is intended for use in the historical analysis of individual countries as well as for cross-country simulations. This dual purpose requires that definitions of economic sectors and of the structural relations among variables be compatible across countries. Each approach has its strengths and weaknesses. On the one hand, because individual country models incorporate some behavioral relations omitted from the cross-country model, they can be used to analyze the effects of government policy. On the other hand, since the cross-country model covers a much wider range of income levels, it can be used to analyze the structural transformation as a whole. In this sense the two types of application are complementary; each helps to generalize the results of the other.

Elements of the Model

Two traditions of multisectoral analysis can be drawn on in modeling structural transformation: the input-output approach of Leontief (1951) and the applied general equilibrium approach pioneered by Johansen (1960). The main difference between them is the explicit incorporation of price effects by Johansen, which makes his model much more demanding of data but potentially more useful for policy analysis. This book draws on extensive experimentation with both types of analysis.

The input-output system was first applied to the analysis of structural change in the American economy by Leontief and others (1953). The main problem studied was the effect of changes in input coefficients between 1919 and 1939 on the structure of production and labor use, with external trade and domestic demands held constant. A similar procedure was followed by Chenery, Shishido, and Watanabe (1962) in tracing the transformation of the structure of production in Japan between 1914 and 1954 to changes in demand, trade, and technology. Attempts to generalize the results of this study led to the development of the cross-country model of transformation presented here, to which the experience of Japan and other countries will be compared.

Johansen's 1960 study of the Norwegian economy addressed the causes and effects of nonproportional growth among sectors in more general terms. While retaining Leontief's input-output system to describe interindustry relations, he included demand and production functions that depend on relative prices. This general equilibrium approach has been developed further in a number of recent studies of developing countries designed to simulate the effects of alternative policies (see chapters 5 and 11).

Although a general equilibrium approach is clearly preferable on theoretical grounds, the choice must also be tailored to both the analytical objectives and the available data. Significant differences between the two methods arise only in cases where relative prices change substantially. In the long term, the most important of these is the rising cost of labor, which leads to the substitution of capital for labor and to shifts in comparative advantage. Whereas applied general equilibrium models can, in principle, distinguish between capital-labor substitution and technological change, input-output models lump them together.

For historical analysis, the potential advantages of a general equilibrium approach are likely to be offset by the limited data on prices and capital stocks. In analyzing alternative policies, however, general equilibrium models yield important insights, even when the relevant functions must be approximated from scattered observations. In the present volume, the input-output approach is used in this chapter and in the country studies of part II, whereas a general equilibrium model is used for the policy comparisons of chapter 11.

THE ACCOUNTING FRAMEWORK.   The accounting framework underlying the model must specify a breakdown of the national income and product accounts and their relation to international trade and factor use. A simple input-output system that satisfies these requirements is shown in table 3-1. The accounting unit is the productive sector, which can be defined either in aggregate terms (primary, industry, services) or with sufficient disaggregation to distinguish industries and products at the two-digit or even three-digit level of the standard international classifications of production and trade.

Table 3-1 represents a consolidation of elements of the national and international accounts in a standard input-output format. The breakdown of the gross national product by use is shown under (I), interindustry transactions under (II), and the sectoral origins of the GNP under (III). (The sectoral value added is broken down into returns to capital and to labor when data are available.)

Table 3-1. *The Accounting Framework*

				Use					
Source (producing sector)	Intermediate use			Final use					Total
	$1 \cdots j \cdots n$			C	I	G	E	M	X
	(II)			(I)					
1	X_{11}	X_{1j}	X_{1n}	C_1	I_1	G_1	E_1	M_1	X_1
i	X_{i1}	X_{ij}	X_{in}	C_i	I_i	G_i	E_i	M_i	X_i
n	X_{n1}	X_{nj}	X_{nn}	C_n	I_n	G_n	E_n	M_n	X_n
	(III)								
Value added	V_1	V_j	V_n						V
Capital stock	K_1	K_j	K_n						K
Labor	L_1	L_j	L_n						L
Total	X_1	X_j	X_n	C	I	G	E	M	

Symbols

C_i	Private consumption	W_i	$\Sigma_j X_{ij}$
I_i	Investment	X_j	Output
G_i	Government consumption	V_j	Value added
E_i	Exports	K_j	Capital stock
M_i	Imports	L_j	Labor
X_{ij}	Commodity i used by sector j	i	Producing sector
U_j	$\Sigma_i X_{ij}$	j	Using sector

Five identities can be derived from the elements in table 3-1:

First, for gross domestic product by use:

$$(3\text{-}1) \qquad Y = (C + I + G) + (E - M) = D - F$$

where Y is gross domestic product, D is domestic final demand, and F is capital inflow.

Second, for gross domestic product by source:

$$(3\text{-}2) \qquad V = \Sigma_j V_j.$$

Third, for commodity supply and use:

$$(3\text{-}3) \qquad X_i = \Sigma_j X_{ij} + D_i + E_i - M_i = W_i + D_i + T_i$$

where T_i is net trade by sector.

Fourth, for the use of intermediate and primary inputs by sector:

$$(3\text{-}4) \qquad X_j = \Sigma_i X_{ij} + V_j = U_j + V_j.$$

Fifth, for aggregate sources and uses:

$$(3\text{-}5) \qquad \Sigma_j X_j = \Sigma_j U_j + \Sigma_j V_j = \Sigma_i W_i + \Sigma_i D_i + \Sigma_i T_i$$

where $-\Sigma_i T_i = F$, the net capital inflow.

These identities are illustrated in tables 3-4, 3-5, and 3-6 below, which give estimates for three benchmark levels of income ($140, $560, and $2,100 in 1970 dollars) corresponding to the beginning, middle, and end of the transformation process.

In these and other tables, the accounts are shown in a condensed eight-sector format. Two principles have been followed in designing these sectoral disaggregations: to focus on those sectors that are important to the analysis of industrialization and structural change; and to allow for the use of data from the maximum number of countries, including those for which only sectoral totals are available. These criteria lead to a substantial disaggregation of the manufacturing sectors, which are the main focus of the analysis, but much more aggregate treatment of the rest of the economy. In the basic sectoral classification adopted as our standard form (see table 3-2), manufacturing constitutes fourteen out of the twenty-three sectors. The aggregation of the results into eight sectors for presentational purposes maintains the distinction between heavy and light industry used in the U.N. international standard industrial classification (ISIC).[1]

STRUCTURAL RELATIONS. The model of industrialization is designed to show how factors directly related to the level of income generate changes in the structure of production and factor use. Starting from the accounting framework of table 3-1, we do this in two steps. First, the five aggregate components of the gross domestic product in equation 3-1 are expressed as functions of per capita income and other exogenous variables. Second, each aggregate is broken down by sector, so that each component of demand and trade is expressed as a function of the corresponding aggregate. This two-stage formulation takes advantage of the much larger body of data available for cross-country estimates of the aggregate relations. Since the application of the model to individual countries is described in chapter 5, the present discussion is limited to the cross-country version, whose purpose is to explain the stylized facts of industrialization.

The exogenous variables in the cross-country model are of two kinds: universal factors, which vary fairly uniformly with the level of income, and particular factors, which produce the chief differences in development patterns among countries. The universal factors include: Y/N, gross domestic product (GDP) per capita; K/N, capital stock per capita; and S/N, skills per capita. The particular factors, which serve to distinguish different allocation patterns, include: N, population size; R/N, natural resources per capita; and Φ, allocation policies.

---

1. The characteristics of industrial sectors are examined further in chapter 7. In principle, a corresponding disaggregation of agriculture would be desirable to allow for differences in demand, production functions, and trade. Although this can be done for individual countries, it has not proved feasible for cross-country comparisons.

Table 3-2. *Sector Classification and Aggregation*

Four sectors	Eight sectors	Twenty-three sectors	ISIC[a]
Tradables			
I. Primary	1. Agriculture	1. Agriculture	01–04
	2. Mining	2. Coal and oil	12, 13
		3. Other mining	14, 19
II. Manufacturing			
Light industry	3. Food processing and tobacco	4. Food, drinks, and tobacco	20–22
	4. Consumer goods	5. Textiles	23
		6. Clothing	24
		7. Lumber and wood products	25, 26
		8. Paper and printing	27, 28
		9. Leather products	29
		10. Miscellaneous manufacturing	39
Heavy industry	5. Producer goods	11. Rubber products	30
		12. Chemicals	31
		13. Coal and petroleum products	32
		14. Nonmetallic minerals	33
		15. Metal products	34, 35
	6. Machinery	16. Machinery	36, 37
		17. Transport equipment	38
Nontradables			
III. Social overhead	7. Social overhead	18. Construction	40
		19. Electricity, gas, and water	51, 52
		20. Transport and communication	71–73
IV. Services	8. Services	21. Trade	61
		22. Real estate	64
		23. Other services	62, 63 81–84, 90

a. From United Nations (1958).

DOMESTIC DEMAND. To analyze the variation in domestic demand with level of income, we rewrite equation 3-1 as

$$(3\text{-}6) \qquad Y + F = C(y,\Phi) + I(y,\Phi) + G(y,\Phi)$$

where F is the trade balance $(M - E)$. It is assumed that each component of demand is a function of the level of income, y, and of a set of allocation policies, Φ. The theoretical basis for this relation is strongest for the aggregate consumption function, $C(y)$, but the accounting identity implies that any variable that affects one component of demand must affect the others as well. Similarly, although raising the level of investment is a typical purpose of Φ, the total effect is to shift resources from public and private consumption to investment at a given level of income.

Next, it is assumed that each sectoral component of domestic demand is a function of the corresponding total:

$$
\begin{aligned}
\text{(3-7)} \qquad\qquad C_i &= C_i(C) \\
I_i &= I_i(I) \\
G_i &= G_i(G).
\end{aligned}
$$

The form of these equations is illustrated by the several variants of the linear expenditure system, which has been estimated from both cross-country and time-series data.[2] These and other equations in the cross-country model are expressed on a per capita basis.

Two phenomena dominate the shift in the overall pattern of demand as income rises. The most important is the decline of the share of food in private consumption, which permits all other components to rise. The second is the increase in the share of investment in GDP. Overall, the income-related changes in domestic demand summarized in equations 3-6 and 3-7 will be shown to account for, at most, half the observed rise in the share of manufacturing in GDP, which is the principal phenomenon to be explained.

EXTERNAL TRADE.   The analysis of shifts in external trade parallels that of domestic demand. It starts from the identity $E + F = M$. Each of these aggregates is then expressed as a function of variables that have been shown to affect the level of trade. For intercountry analysis, these include natural resource endowments, R, and population size, N, each of which has a more important effect on the share of exports in GDP than does per capita income. The third component, F, is largely determined by national and international policies. These relations can be stated symbolically as

$$
\text{(3-8)} \qquad\qquad E(R, y, N, \Phi) + F(\Phi) = M(y, N, \Phi).
$$

Rich natural resources tend to raise the level of exports and imports, whereas a large domestic market tends to decrease the share of trade.

The Heckscher-Ohlin factor-proportions theory of trade provides a starting point for breaking down E and M by sector. The assumption that the composition of exports depends on the relative availability of natural resources, R, physical capital, K, and human capital, S, yields the following expression for exports of commodity i:

$$
\text{(3-9)} \qquad\qquad E_i = E_i(E, R, K, S, \Phi).
$$

2. The extended linear expenditure system of Lluch, Powell, and Williams (1977) demonstrates this approach and provides a basis for evaluating the results.

A similar set of factors affects the composition of imports:

(3-10) $M_i = M_i(M, K, S, \Phi)$.

Although statistical studies by Balassa (1979b) and others provide empirical support for this type of explanation of trade patterns, the lack of acceptable measures of factor intensities—particularly of resource availability—makes it difficult to estimate these equations directly. Instead, as explained below, we have made separate estimates for each of three groups of countries, which differ significantly in size and factor endowments.

On balance, the change in trading patterns with rising income is as important to the explanation of industrialization as is the shift in domestic demand. Differences in trading patterns associated with factor endowments and policy approaches also constitute the largest source of variation in the patterns of structural change, which are analyzed in the last section of this chapter.

TECHNOLOGY AND SUBSTITUTION. The rising cost of labor and the availability of new technology affect industrialization in two ways: through direct substitution of capital for labor in each sector and through changes in input-output coefficients. Technological change in sectors such as agriculture and services leads to an increase in the intermediate use of commodities because of the mechanization of hand operations. In addition, technological change tends to increase the use of processed inputs, such as electric power or steel, in all sectors. We have incorporated the common tendencies observed in many countries into the estimates of the cross-country model.[3] The net effect is to make the input coefficients, and hence intermediate demand, a function of per capita income: $X_{ij} = a_{ij}(y)X_j$.

COMPOSITION OF OUTPUT. The three sets of relations for sectoral demand, trade, and technological change can be substituted in the accounting identity 3-3 to give the following equation for the output of each sector:

(3-11) $X_i = C_i(y,\Phi) + G_i(y,\Phi) + I_i(y,\Phi) + E_i(y,N,\Phi)$
            $- M_i(y,N,\Phi) + \Sigma_j a_{ij}(y)X_j$.

The level of output in each sector is then determined by solving the input-output system of equations:

(3-12) $X_i = \Sigma_j r_{ij}(y)(D_j + T_j)$

where $D_i = C_i + G_i + I_i$; $T_i = E_i - M_i$, and $r_{ij}(y)$ is an element of the Leontief inverse matrix for income level y (see chapter 5).

---

3. The rationale for this procedure is given in Syrquin (1976) and Chenery and Syrquin (1980).

Finally, the value added in each sector is proportional to sectoral output:

$$(3\text{-}13) \qquad\qquad V_j = v_j(y)\,X_j$$

where the value added ratio, v_j, may vary with per capita income. The specification of the production function underlying this input-output relationship is discussed below.

Cross-Country Simulation

The purpose of simulating the effects of rising income levels in the cross-country model is to establish an average or standard pattern with which individual country experience can be compared. In this way, comparative analysis can be extended beyond individual structural features to the processes by which structural change comes about. For this purpose, it is more important to have a consistent set of estimates of the economic structure at successive points in the transformation than to have more accurate estimates of isolated features.

The set of general relations outlined above indicates the underlying logic of the model that we have estimated from cross-country data. It traces changes in the economic structure to the evolution of two main factors: the level of total demand (or per capita income) and the composition of factor supply (capital, skills, and natural resources per person). Rises in income lead to fairly uniform changes in the composition of demand, whereas changes in factor supply lead to shifts in trade patterns and technology.

Since changes in supply conditions are less uniform across countries, they are the major sources of differences in development patterns as well as the main focus of development policies. The variation in factor endowments has provided the basis for several typologies of development strategies, an approach we shall also adopt in an attempt to identify more homogeneous subgroups of developing countries.

ESTIMATION. The procedure for estimating the model from cross-country data has been described in Syrquin and Elkington (1978) and Chenery and Syrquin (1980).[4] It is designed to establish a standard of comparison for country studies; to decompose the standard pattern into components that can be derived from the equations of the general model; and to use data from several country samples—which has led to the specification of the model at two levels of aggregation.

Consistency among estimates of the aggregate variables in equations 3-6 and 3-8 is achieved by specifying the same regression equation for each component of GDP, denoted by x, and by using the same sample of countries. The equation is of the following form:

$$(3\text{-}14) \quad x = \alpha + \beta_1 \ln y + \beta_2 (\ln y)^2 + \gamma_1 \ln N + \gamma_2 (\ln N)^2 + \varepsilon F.$$

4. A summary of the more important parameters in the model is given in Chenery and Syrquin (1980).

Estimates of this equation for the period 1950–70 are given in Chenery and Syrquin (1975) and give rise to the standard pattern derived for that period.

To identify the main sources of deviation from the standard pattern, we have tested two alternatives. The first is to introduce additional exogenous variables into the specification of the structural relations, as illustrated by population size, N, and capital inflow, F, in equation 3-14. The other alternative is to use the variables representing differences in factor proportions and trade policies to identify different types of economies. After experimenting with both approaches,[5] we have chosen the more general typological method in specifying representative patterns for the present study.

The breakdown of each aggregate by sector as specified in equations 3-7 and 3-9 is derived primarily from a sample of fifteen countries having input-output accounts. For the major components—food and nonfood in consumption, and primary products and manufactures in exports and imports—these have been supplemented by data from other countries, so that greater attention is given to the chief sources of variation.

For our purposes, the main test of this set of estimates lies in the overall performance of the model in simulating long-term structural change. Its ability to replicate cross-country patterns of production has been shown in Chenery (1979, pp. 85–90). At the four-sector level, the agreement between observed and simulated structural changes appears to be quite satisfactory. The discrepancies are larger with less aggregation because the country samples are smaller and less representative of low-income economies. The overall performance of the model is examined in the next section.

INDUSTRIALIZATION. The cross-country model will be used for two purposes: to give an overview of the interaction among the factors leading to industrialization and to provide a basis for comparing the nine economies that will be studied in detail in subsequent chapters. We shall first simulate the standard pattern of industrialization, which is defined by a set of solutions to equation 3-12 that correspond to average demand and trade patterns at each level of income, with population size and capital inflow held constant. Country comparisons will then be made for each of the common features.

The income levels used in these simulations covered the complete transition from less developed to mature industrial economies. This range is broken down into six periods, each of which is defined by the interval between successive benchmark levels of per capita income (see table 3-3). Most of the simulations cover only the first four periods, which encompass the transition from a less developed to a mature economy. All the semi-industrial countries identified in chapter 4 now fall into the income range

5. See Chenery and Syrquin (1975, chap. 4).

Table 3-3. *Breakdown of Transition for Simulations*

	Income range (dollars per capita)[b]	
Period[a]	1964 dollars	1970 dollars
1	⎰ 100	⎰ 140
2	⎱ 200	⎱ 280
3	400	560
4	800	1,120
5	1,500	2,100
6	2,400	3,360
	3,600	5,040

Note: Another period, 0, is introduced in chapter 8; see footnote 3 in that chapter for explanation.

a. Semi-industrial countries typically fall into periods 2, 3, and 4.

b. The benchmark income ranges were originally defined in 1964 dollars in Chenery and Syrquin (1975). They are expressed here in the 1970 dollars used throughout this book, with a conversion factor of 1.4. A comparison factor of about 2.6 can be used to convert these 1970 dollars to 1982 prices. Also see the appendix to this chapter.

of periods 2 to 4. Periods 5 and 6 have been added to analyze the changes related to the cessation of growth in the share of manufacturing in output and employment, which now characterizes virtually all mature industrial economies.

Tables 3-4, 3-5, and 3-6 summarize three solutions to the cross-country model, corresponding to the beginning, middle, and end of the structural transformation. The results are presented in the form of equation 3-11, which includes three components for each sector: domestic final demand, exports and imports, and intermediate demand. Changes in the composition of output and value added can be traced to changes in the composition of each of these elements.

Before proceeding to a more detailed analysis, we shall give an overview of transformation as a whole. Table 3-7 compares the economic structure at level 5 (table 3-6) with that at level 1 (table 3-4) using a four-sector aggregation. To focus on structural change, each element is expressed as a percentage of GDP. In this form, the increment in total output of each sector from level 1 to level 5 remains equal to the sum of the three components in equation 3-3:

$$(3\text{-}15) \quad \left(\frac{X_i^5}{V^5} - \frac{X_i^1}{V^1}\right) = \left(\frac{D_i^5}{V^5} - \frac{D_i^1}{V^1}\right) + \left(\frac{T_i^5}{V^5} - \frac{T_i^1}{V^1}\right) + \left(\frac{W_i^5}{V^5} - \frac{W_i^1}{V^1}\right)$$

Although aggregate value added remains constant at 100 percent, total

Table 3-4. *Standard Solution to the Cross-Country Model, Income Level 1 ($140 per capita)*
(dollars per capita)

	Domestic final demand					Trade			Inter-mediate demand (W)	Gross output (X)	Value added (V)	Per-centage of V
Sector	Consumption	Invest-ment	Govern-ment	Total demand	Per-centage of total demand	Ex-ports	Im-ports	Net trade				
Primary												
1. Agriculture	25.5	0	0.5	26	18	21	3	18	17	61	51	37
2. Mining	0	0	0.5	1	0	1	1	0	2	3	2	1
Subtotal[a]	26	0	1.0	270	18	22	4	18	19	64	53	38
Manufacturing												
3. Food	15	0	1	16	11	0	3	-3	10	23	7	5
4. Consumer goods	11	0	0	11	8	1	4	-3	9	17	8	6
5. Producer goods	3	0	0	3	2	1	7	-6	11	8	4	3
6. Machinery	0	7	1	8	6	0	8	-8	1	1	1	1
Subtotal[a]	29	7	2	38	27	2	22	-20	31	49	20	15
Nontradables												
7. Social overhead	7	12	1	20	14	1	1	0	7	27	15	11
8. Services	41	1	16	58	40	3	4	-1	13	70	51	36
Total[a]	102	21	20	143	100	28	31	-3	70	210	140	100
Percentage of total final demand	71	15	14	100								

a. Totals may not add because of rounding.
Source: World Bank data.

Table 3-5. *Standard Solution to the Cross-Country Model, Income Level 3 ($560 per capita)*
(dollars per capita)

| | Domestic final demand | | | | | Trade | | | Inter-mediate demand (W) | Gross output (X) | Value added (V) | Per-centage of V |
Sector	Consump-tion	Invest-ment	Govern-ment	Total demand	Per-centage of total demand	Exports	Imports	Net trade				
Primary												
1. Agriculture	45	0	1	46	8	62	21	41	62	149	101	18
2. Mining	1	0	1	2	0	3	6	−3	19	18	15	3
Subtotal[a]	46	0	2	48	8	65	27	38	81	167	116	21
Manufacturing												
3. Food	61	0	4	65	11	6	11	−5	48	108	33	5
4. Consumer goods	51	0	3	54	10	14	13	1	65	120	56	10
5. Producer goods	18	0	1	19	3	15	31	−16	78	81	38	7
6. Machinery	2	39	1	42	8	1	36	−35	13	20	10	2
Subtotal[a]	132	39	9	180	32	36	91	−55	204	329	137	24
Nontradables												
7. Social overhead	32	65	7	104	18	10	7	3	42	149	84	15
8. Services	161	6	68	235	42	24	17	7	65	307	223	40
Total[a]	371	110	86	567	100	135	142	−7	392	952	560	100
Percentage of total final demand	65	20	15									

a. Totals may not add because of rounding.
Source: World Bank data.

50

Table 3-6. *Standard Solution to the Cross-Country Model, Income Level 5 ($2,100 per capita)*
(dollars per capita)

| Sector | Domestic final demand | | | | | Trade | | | Inter-mediate demand (W) | Gross output (X) | Value added (V) | Per-centage of V |
	Consump-tion	Invest-ment	Govern-ment	Total demand	Per-centage of total demand	Ex-ports	Im-ports	Net trade				
Primary												
1. Agriculture	64	0	4	68	3	117	101	16	89	253	137	6
2. Mining	19	0	4	23	1	12	78	−66	125	82	62	3
Subtotal[a]	83	0	8	91	4	129	179	−50	294	335	199	9
Manufacturing												
3. Food	186	0	19	205	10	59	32	27	180	412	126	6
4. Consumer goods	202	0	15	217	10	91	45	46	332	595	270	13
5. Producer goods	104	0	6	110	5	95	104	−9	480	581	263	12
6. Machinery	15	172	4	191	9	60	132	−72	73	192	99	5
Subtotal[a]	507	172	44	723	34	305	313	−8	1,065	1,780	758	36
Nontradables												
7. Social overhead	115	283	26	424	20	41	28	13	150	587	330	16
8. Services	549	25	300	874	42	105	72	33	219	1,126	813	39
Total[a]	1,254	480	378	2,112	100	580	592	−12	1,728	3,828	2,100	100
Percentage of total final demand	59	23	18	100								

a. Totals may not add because of rounding.
Source: World Bank data.

51

Table 3-7. *Structural Change during the Transformation, Income Level 5 Compared with Level 1* (percentage of GDP)

Sector	Domestic demand (D)			Net trade (T)			Intermediate demand (W)			Gross output (X)ᵃ			Value added (V)		
	Initial	Final	Increment	Initial	Final	Increment	Initial	Final	Increment	Initial	Final	Increment	Initial	Final	Increment
Tradables															
Primary	18	4	−14	13	−2	−15	14	14	0	46	16	−30	38	9	−29
Manufacturing	28	34	+6	−14	0	+14	22	51	+29	36	85	+49	15	36	+21
Nontradables															
Social overhead	14	20	+6	0	1	+1	5	7	+2	20	28	+8	11	16	+5
Services	42	42	0	−1	2	+1	9	10	+1	50	53	+4	36	39	+3
Totalᵇ	102	100	−2	−2	−1	+1	50	82	+32	151	182	+31	100	100	0

Note: Period 1 is defined by a GDP level of $140 per capita (table 3-4); period 5 is defined by a level of $2,100 (table 3-6).
a. $X = D + T + W$.
b. Totals may not add because of rounding.
Source: Tables 3-4, 3-6.

gross output increases from 151 to 182 percent of GDP, an increase reflecting the growth in intermediate use of industrial products.

Industrialization is commonly measured by the rise in the share of manufacturing in GDP, shown in table 3-7 as an increase from 15 to 36 percent. In a general-equilibrium context, however, industrialization is a property of the system as a whole, in which the fall in the share of primary production from 38 to 9 percent is offset by a rise in social overhead as well as in manufacturing. The share of services, in constant prices, changes little.[6]

The causes of the rise in manufacturing differ considerably from those of the decline in primary output. An initial account of these differences is given by equation 3-15, in which intermediate demand is treated as a separate factor (which is later decomposed into separate sources). Table 3-7 shows that the decline of the primary share can be attributed equally to the fall in domestic demand and to the shift in net trade.[7] Intermediate demand for primary products remains constant in relation to GDP.

The proximate causes of the rise in manufacturing are quite different. The increase in intermediate demand accounts for more than half the total, whereas the rise in the share of domestic demand is only 12 percent of the rise in gross output. Even after the growth of intermediate demand is distributed between domestic demand and trade (see chapter 5), the former will be shown to account for less than half the rise of the industrial share. This finding requires a substantial revision in the common view that industrialization is largely explained by Engel effects.

COUNTRY COMPARISONS. The changing economic structure that is simulated by the cross-country model can be thought of as the path that a hypothetical country, whose behavior is based on postwar relations, would follow as its income rises. Because the earlier transformations of the now-developed countries have taken place over a century or more, we could not hope to validate these relations from historical experience even if the relevant data were available. Instead, the validity of this approach can best be judged by the extent to which it captures important aspects of the experience of the countries in the postwar era for which it has been estimated.

The cross-country model is used in this book as one of the ways of generalizing about the experience of a large sample of developing coun-

6. At this level of aggregation, the changes in value added simulated by the model are quite close to those derived from cross-country regressions (Chenery 1979, pp. 85–90). Because the regressions are based on current prices in each country, they reflect the rise in the relative price of services. Kravis (1984, p. 30) shows that the share of services in domestic final demand remains quite constant across rising income levels when valued in constant international prices.

7. In this aggregation, food processing is treated as part of manufacturing. Since tables 3-4, 3-5, and 3-6 show that the share of processed food remains almost constant, shifting it to agriculture would have little effect on this result.

tries. Its results are considered in conjunction with detailed country studies in which we can come closer to inferring causal relationships between policies and performance. In this context, we are as much interested in the differences between individual country experience and the standard pattern as we are in the similarities.

The nine economies in our sample were chosen to cover the full range of transformation that has been simulated above. On the basis of their per capita incomes, Colombia, Korea, Taiwan, and Turkey fell in period 1 in the 1950s and Mexico and Yugoslavia in period 2. At the upper end of the scale, Israel, Japan, and Norway reached income levels exceeding $2,000 by the early 1970s.[8] Because identical accounts have been constructed (in constant 1970 prices) for benchmark years in each of these economies, a comparison can be made with the cross-country simulations for each element of the economic structure. The common features of industrialization that can be identified in this way are discussed in the following section.

Although the cross-country model is generally consistent with the stylized facts of postwar industrialization, the limitations of this approach should be kept in mind when comparing country experience with the model simulations. Cross-country estimates of value added by sector have been compared with historical changes in developed countries by Temin (1967) and Kuznets (1971) and with postwar time series for developing countries by Chenery and Syrquin (1975). Both types of comparison point to a significant time-related shift from primary production to services that is separate from the effects of rising income. This may be largely the result of rising relative prices of services. For industry, however, the cross-section and time-series estimates are quite similar and the time trends are relatively small.[9]

Common Features of Industrialization

The model of industrialization traces the rise of industry to shifts in domestic demand, the growing intermediate use of industrial products, and the transformation of comparative advantage as factor proportions change. Although these phenomena can be observed in virtually all developing countries, their relative importance varies according to each

8. As discussed in the appendix to this chapter, the methodology of comparative analysis can be improved by the use of international conversion factors for national income based on purchasing power rather than on exchange rates when the former become more widely available. Within our sample, the purchasing power of Israel is somewhat overstated and that of Japan understated by the use of 1970 exchange rates. However, the comparisons in this chapter are limited to changes over time, which are not significantly affected by differences in conversion factors of the magnitude that have been observed.

9. See Chenery and Syrquin (1975, p. 124) for a comparison of predictions with and without time trends. Extension of our previous work (Syrquin 1985c) up to 1982 indicates that the recent, more turbulent period has not significantly affected the nature of the transformation. A negative time shift is still in evidence for agricultural production, but it is now offset by a time-related increase in mining rather than in services.

country's initial structure, natural resource endowment, and development policies.

This section discusses these three phenomena as they are simulated by our model under typical assumptions and as they are reflected in the experience of the nine economies in our sample. In addition to explaining the model results, this procedure brings out the differences among these economies. The causes of variation in patterns of industrialization and sources of growth are explored further in the final section.

Shifts in Domestic Demand

Figures 3-1 and 3-2 show the estimated changes in the principal components of domestic demand—food and nonfood consumption, investment,

Figure 3-1. *Changes in Main Components of Demand in Sample Economies*

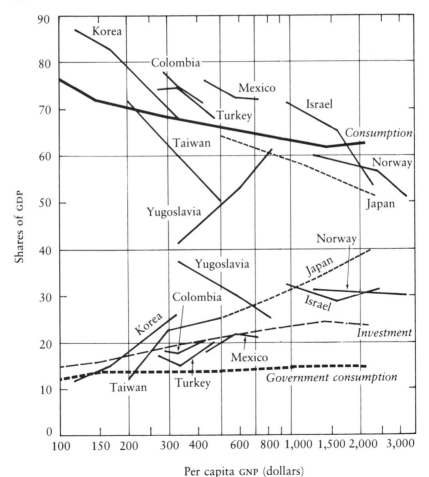

Figure 3-2. *Changes in Shares of Food and Nonfood Consumption in Final Demand*

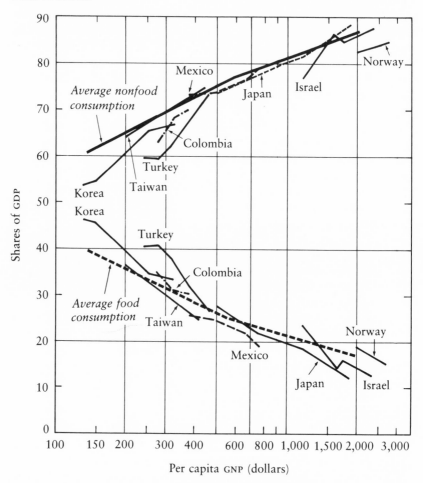

Per capita GNP (dollars)

and government consumption—for the standard pattern and for each economy. In almost all cases, the largest single change in demand is the fall in the share of food consumption, which is therefore treated as a separate component in figure 3-2. In the average patterns shown in figure 3-2 and table 3-8, this share falls from 29 percent of national income at level 1 ($140) to 19 percent at level 3 ($560) and to 13 percent at level 5 ($2,100). (*Note:* Unless otherwise indicated, all dollars are 1970 dollars.) The reduction is even steeper for Israel, Japan, Korea, and Turkey in relation to their levels of income.

The total fall in the share of food in domestic demand (by 16 percentage points) is offset in the standard pattern by a rise in the share of investment (by 8 points) plus a rise in nonfood and government consumption (by 9 points). However, differences in initial conditions and development policies produce substantial variation in this pattern. In Japan, Korea, and Taiwan, which had the highest rates of GNP growth, virtually the entire fall in food consumption was offset by a rise in investment of more than 10 percentage points. At the other extreme, Israel, Norway, and Yugoslavia, which had already reached investment levels of over 30 percent in the mid-1950s, chose to offset the fall in food consumption primarily by an increase in public consumption. The remaining economies—Colombia, Mexico, and Turkey—followed the standard pattern.

Not only does the proportion of nonfood demand change substantially with rising income, so does its composition. In contrast, there is relatively little variation in the commodity breakdown of either investment or government expenditure.[10]

The combined effects of rising income on the composition of total domestic demand are shown in table 3-8, which compares the cross-country estimates for the six main sectors to the changes in each economy. Two major shifts occur in virtually all cases: first, a substantial fall in the share of food demand with the rise in per capita income; and second, increases in producer goods, machinery, and social overhead, produced by rises in both investment and consumer demand.

The same trends are shown in the cross-country model, although there is somewhat less departure from proportional growth. This is due in part to the fact that this sample of semi-industrial economies is growing faster than the average; consequently, the share of investment-related sectors has increased more rapidly.

Rise in Intermediate Use

As countries industrialize, their productive structures become more "roundabout" in the sense that a higher proportion of output is sold to other producers rather than to final users. As with final demand, this phenomenon can be broken down into two parts: first, a shift in output mix toward manufacturing and other sectors that use more intermediate inputs; and second, technological changes within a sector that lead to a greater use of intermediate inputs. The second aspect is illustrated by the increased use of manufactured inputs in agriculture and transportation that accompanies increasing mechanization.

The tendency for the share of intermediate use of commodities to increase with rising income is found throughout our sample and has also been observed in cross-country studies (Chenery 1963). As seen in figure 3-3 and table 3-7, the industrialization model simulates a rise in the

10. The principal inputs into investment are construction (59 percent) and machinery (36 percent), which are assumed in the model to be fixed. Within the sample, the share of machinery varies between 35 and 40 percent of investment costs.

Table 3-8. Shares of Final Domestic Demand in Sample Economies

Economy[a]	Benchmark years and change	Per capita income (dollars)	Change (percent)	Shares of demand (percent)					
				Agriculture and food	Consumer goods	Producer goods	Machinery	Social overhead	Services
Colombia	1953	274		34.9	8.1	3.5	6.4	12.7	32.0
	1970	369	35	30.2	9.5	6.2	6.0	14.8	33.3
				-4.7	1.4	2.7	-0.4	2.1	1.3
Mexico	1950	380		25.1	10.8	4.0	5.6	10.7	42.0
	1975	736	94	19.5	8.4	6.1	12.2	14.8	37.0
				-5.6	-2.4	2.1	6.6	4.1	-5.0
Turkey	1953	239		40.1	6.2	4.5	6.0	18.3	24.7
	1973	461	93	26.1	7.6	9.3	8.8	20.3	27.6
				-14.0	1.4	4.8	2.8	2.0	2.9
Yugoslavia	1962	469		33.9	8.3	2.0	10.2	28.6	16.3
	1972	781	67	22.8	11.0	4.2	16.0	25.2	19.6
				-11.1	2.7	2.2	5.8	-3.4	3.3
Japan	1955	500		27.0	7.9	0.9	5.8	15.3	43.5
	1970	1,897	279	11.6	7.4	3.9	18.2	23.5	35.4
				-15.4	-0.5	3.0	12.4	8.2	-8.1

Korea	1955	131		46.1	9.4	1.9	3.7	10.6	28.0
	1973	323		33.1	9.9	4.7	10.9	18.2	23.1
			147	−13.0	0.5	2.8	7.2	7.6	−4.9
Taiwan	1956	203		36.1	2.8	5.2	4.1	9.6	41.6
	1971	426		24.5	8.5	5.4	14.7	14.1	32.6
			110	−11.6	5.7	0.2	10.6	4.5	−9.0
Israel	1958	1,067		23.0	10.0	4.6	10.6	24.6	27.2
	1972	2,372		12.6	8.7	16.1	18.5	26.1	18.1
			122	−10.4	−1.3	11.5	7.9	1.5	−9.1
Norway	1953	1,171		20.9	12.3	16.7	1.9	20.0	28.0
	1969	2,769		14.9	12.4	20.0	2.5	28.5	31.6
			136	−6.0	0.1	3.3	0.6	−1.5	3.6
Cross-economy model	Level 1	140		29	8	2	6	14	40
	Level 3	560		19	10	3	8	18	42
	Level 1 to level 3		300	−10	+2	+1	+2	+4	+2
	Level 5	2,100		13	10	5	9	20	42
	Level 1 to level 5		1,400	−16	+2	+3	+3	+6	+2

Note: Mining is omitted because of negligible final use.

a. Listed according to broad development strategy, in descending order from inward- to outward-oriented, as discussed in chapter 4 (see especially table 4-3). This order of listing for the semi-industrial economies will be used throughout the tables in the book.

Source: World Bank data.

Figure 3-3. *Share of Intermediate Use in Gross Output, Sample
Economies*

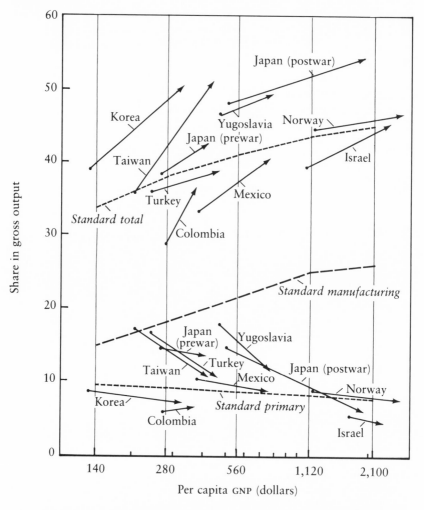

average share of intermediate use in total domestic demand from 33 to 45
percent over the period of transformation. The four higher-income economies follow this pattern fairly closely, whereas the five poorer ones show
more rapid increases.[11]

In addition to this overall rise in intermediate use, the substitution of
manufactured goods for primary inputs is uniformly observed in our
sample. This phenomenon is also captured in the general model, as shown
in figure 3-3. The model produces a gradual decline in the intermediate use

11. Although there are not enough observations to analyze this aspect of technological
change in greater detail, this comparison suggests that we may have underestimated its effects
in the lower income levels. This phenomenon is discussed further in chapter 7.

of primary products. A more rapid decline has occurred in economies that started from relatively high levels of primary inputs: Japan, Taiwan, Turkey, and Yugoslavia. The increase in the intermediate use of manufactures tends to be more rapid than is simulated in the standard pattern. The largest deviations are associated with the very rapid transformation that has taken place in Korea and Taiwan.

To separate the effects of changing input coefficients from the effects of changing output composition, table 3-9 gives two calculations of intermediate demand for each economy. The first shows the actual change in

Table 3-9. *Actual versus Predicted Intermediate Use in Sample Economies*
(constant output shares)

Economy	Initial and terminal year	Primary		Manufacturing		Total	
		Actual	Pre-dicted	Actual	Pre-dicted	Actual	Pre-dicted
Colombia	1953	5.9	6.7	12.3	13.3	28.7	30.9
	1970	6.3	6.3	18.5	18.7	36.3	36.2
	Change	0.4	−0.4	6.2	5.4	7.6	5.3
Mexico	1950	10.1	10.0	12.7	13.4	33.2	33.5
	1975	8.5	9.0	20.9	18.9	40.3	38.4
	Change	−1.6	−1.0	8.2	5.5	7.1	4.9
Turkey	1963	16.5	14.8	12.6	12.3	35.9	34.5
	1973	10.3	11.1	18.5	15.7	38.8	36.4
	Change	−6.2	−3.7	5.9	3.4	2.9	1.9
Yugoslavia	1962	17.7	17.5	17.8	14.9	46.2	41.4
	1972	11.3	14.8	27.3	19.2	49.3	43.3
	Change	−6.4	−2.7	9.5	4.3	3.1	1.9
Japan	1955	14.6	10.0	24.4	20.5	48.0	43.2
	1970	6.0	9.0	36.6	27.6	54.3	47.8
	Change	−8.6	−1.0	12.2	7.1	6.3	4.6
Korea	1963	11.8	11.7	24.5	29.6	43.6	49.9
	1973	7.0	7.0	35.0	33.5	50.4	48.7
	Change	−4.8	−4.7	10.5	3.9	6.8	−1.2
Taiwan	1956	17.0	16.3	10.2	22.5	35.9	49.4
	1971	10.4	10.6	32.1	30.9	50.8	50.0
	Change	−6.6	−5.7	21.9	8.4	14.9	0.6
Israel	1958	5.3	8.2	18.0	25.2	39.5	48.0
	1972	4.3	6.0	27.9	32.2	45.4	49.5
	Change	−1.0	−2.2	9.9	7.0	5.9	1.5
Norway	1953	8.7	9.4	20.3	22.0	44.7	47.0
	1969	7.3	9.7	23.7	26.6	46.9	52.4
	Change	−1.4	0.3	3.4	4.6	2.2	5.4

Note: Intermediate use is defined as $\Sigma\ a_{ij}\ (X_j/X)\ (k)$, where k indicates the actual or constant shares of the using sectors. For Colombia, Japan, Mexico, Turkey, and Yugoslavia, the standard of comparison was the average output mix of Mexico (1960) and Turkey (1963). For Korea, Israel, Norway, and Taiwan, the standard was the average of Korea (1970) and Taiwan (1971).
Source: World Bank data.

intermediate use between the extreme benchmark years, and the second shows the predicted effect of holding the composition of output constant. Thus the second column isolates the effects of changing coefficients, which account for well over half the total change in most cases.

In agriculture, evidence is available for a large number of countries on the rising share of intermediate inputs (or decline in value added) in the total value of output. Figure 3-4 gives data on the value added ratio in

Figure 3-4. *Value Added Ratio in Agriculture*

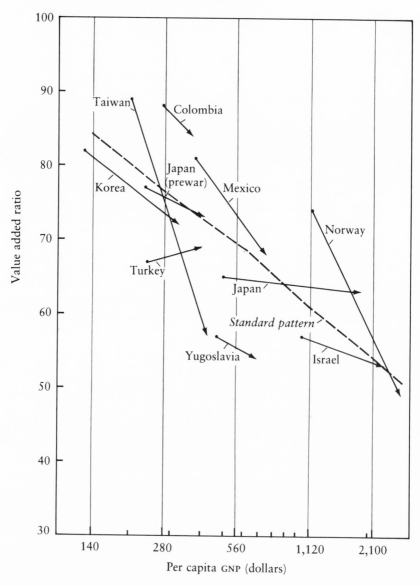

agriculture, as well as the estimated relation to the level of per capita income.[12] There is a decline in the value added ratio—and a corresponding rise in intermediate use in agriculture—in the entire sample except for Turkey. The regression equation implies that during the course of the transformation intermediate inputs into agriculture typically increase from less than 20 percent to more than 45 percent of the value of output. This relation is incorporated into the general model.

In summary, the combination of rising purchases by other sectors, together with substitution of manufactured for primary commodities, produces rapid growth in the intermediate demand for manufactured goods. This aspect of industrialization can only be analyzed by an interindustry model, which makes it possible to trace growing intermediate use to the changes in final demand and trade that are responsible for it. Although our estimates of changes in input coefficients are fairly arbitrary, they provide a much better representation of the stylized facts than do models that ignore this aspect of structural change.

Changes in Comparative Advantage

The third major source of industrialization is the transformation of international trade. Through import substitution and the expansion of manufactured exports, developing countries shift away from the specialization in primary products that is characteristic of early stages of development. Underlying this shift are changes in supply conditions—accumulation of skills and physical capital plus the greater availability of intermediate inputs—as well as economies of scale based on a growing domestic market for manufactured goods. As table 3-7 shows, these changes typically contribute more to increasing the share of manufacturing in total output than do the changes in domestic final demand.

Although shifts in comparative advantage ultimately affect all developing countries, their magnitude and timing vary greatly. Countries with small populations have relatively specialized economies and a high share of trade in GNP, but the trade share declines markedly with increasing population size. A country's natural resources, and how they are exploited, have a substantial impact on its comparative advantage; this is most pronounced in small countries and at low income levels. The effects of historical and geographical factors tend to be accentuated by differences in national policies: large countries have been prone to adopt inward-oriented policies, which appear more feasible to them than to small countries.

The effects of size and resource endowments on trading patterns, being complex, can be brought out more readily by subdividing the sample and estimating separate patterns for each group. In an earlier study (Chenery

---

12. See Syrquin and Elkington (1978). The regression equation used in the cross-country model is $v_{ag} = 1.388 - .111 \ln y$, where v_{ag} is the value added ratio in agriculture.

and Syrquin 1975), we tested a two-way classification of countries based on their population size and their relative specialization in primary or manufactured exports. Because large countries (those with populations of more than 20 million in 1970) are—with few exceptions—considerably less specialized than small ones, they were treated as a single group in estimating typical trade patterns.

Figure 3-5 shows the average export patterns of the three main country groups: large (L); small and oriented toward manufactured exports (SM); small and oriented toward primary exports (SP). The figure compares the estimated export pattern in each group with the standard pattern derived from the pooled regression for all countries; representative population sizes are used in each case.[13]

The large-country pattern has less than half the share of exports of the pooled regression, and the shift from primary to manufactured exports takes place at a lower income level. This group of large developing countries is more homogeneous than the full sample, as shown by the smaller standard deviations from the average trade and production patterns (see chapter 4). Only in a few cases (such as Korea) do differences in resources and trade policies lead to substantial departures.

The small countries are subdivided according to the natural resource content of their exports into primary-oriented and manufacturing-oriented trade patterns.[14] Although the indexes used to make this division are rather arbitrary, the typical patterns that result are not much affected by the choice of criteria. Figure 3-5 shows that the differences between the trade patterns for the two groups are very substantial. In the SM group, manufactured exports overtake primary exports at an income level of $250, which parallels the transformation of domestic demand. The typical SP economy, on the other hand, maintains a strong comparative advantage in primary exports throughout the transformation, while manufactured exports make little or no contribution to the rise of industry. In this case industrialization is largely the result of the demand effects of rising income.

The identification of three typical trade patterns not only improves the explanatory power of the regressions but also brings out important variations in the role of trade in industrialization. These are explored further in the final section of this chapter, in which the effects of policy differences are also considered.

Reallocation of Capital and Labor

The shift in the composition of output with rising income is reflected in varying degree in the reallocation of labor and capital from primary

13. The population sizes are specified as 5 million for small countries, 40 million for large, and 10 million for the pooled sample, which are close to the median values for each.

14. The basis for this division is described in Chenery and Syrquin (1975, pp. 68–69) and in chapter 4.

Figure 3-5. *Trade Patterns for Three Groups of Countries*

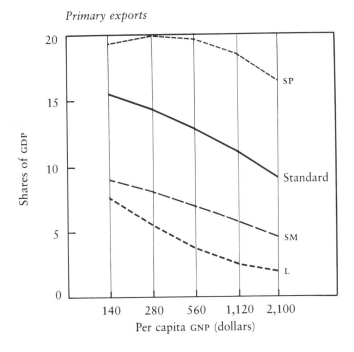

Primary exports

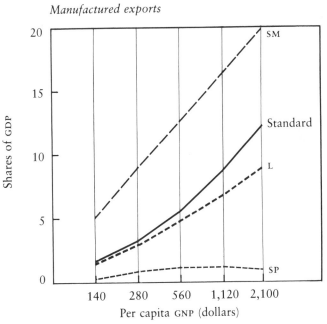

Manufactured exports

Key: L: large country pattern
SM: small, manufacturing-oriented country pattern
SP: small, primary-oriented country pattern

production to manufacturing and services. We shall extend the cross-country model to analyze these shifts by means of the following input functions:

(3-16) $K_j = k_j(y)X_j$

and

(3-17) $L_j = l_j(y)X_j$

where the input coefficients k_j and l_j are functions of the level of income and reflect the growing capital intensity of the economy as a whole.[15]

Changes in the composition of value added, labor, and capital that are generated by the cross-country model are shown in figure 3-6. Although the same basic pattern can be detected in each, it is exaggerated in the case of employment and minimized in the case of capital. These differences are due to variations in rates of productivity growth and in factor proportions among sectors.

The typical employment pattern reflects the lag in the movement of workers out of agriculture and the correspondingly lower growth in labor productivity in this sector throughout most of the transformation. This trend is only reversed toward the end of the transformation as surplus labor is absorbed. As will be shown in chapter 4, most semi-industrial economies demonstrate a similar pattern.

The rise of employment in industry is much smaller than the decline in agriculture, and consequently most of the shift takes place from agriculture to services.[16] Within our sample, Colombia, Japan, Mexico, Taiwan, and Yugoslavia are quite typical of the general pattern of employment seen in the next chapter in figure 4-5. Turkey and Yugoslavia lag in shifting labor out of agriculture and thus have correspondingly larger differences in labor productivity between agriculture and manufacturing. Israel deviates in the opposite direction and thus has relatively equal labor productivity among sectors.

The pattern of capital use shows a much higher proportion in social overhead, which is larger than primary production and manufacturing combined. Because this difference in capital intensity persists at all income levels, the shift from primary production to manufacturing appears less pronounced. A more detailed breakdown would show a corresponding shift from infrastructure supporting primary production to infrastructure supporting industry.

The first six figures in this chapter provide a multidimensional view of

---

15. The use of this simple form of input function is necessitated by the lack of sufficient data to estimate representative production functions. The properties of these functions are discussed in the next section.

16. These results are quite consistent with the early speculations of Clark (1940), who defined transformation as a shift in employment from primary to secondary to tertiary sectors.

Figure 3-6. *Simulation of Value Added, Employment, and Capital for Cross-Country Model*

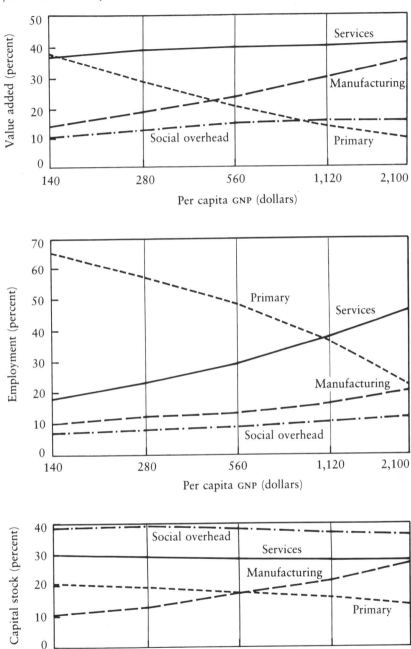

the most persistent features of the transformation as measured by cross-country data. The extent to which individual countries vary from this pattern has been indicated for the nine economies in our sample. We shall now consider the main types of departure from the typical pattern and the ways in which they reflect the dynamics of the transformation.

Dynamics of the Transformation

Up to now we have analyzed the transformation in static terms, focusing on long-term phenomena not much affected by the rate of growth. This chapter has explained the typical relations between increasing levels of income and structural change, whereas chapter 2 analyzed some of the relations between structural change and the rate of growth. We shall now consolidate the two lines of analysis in a dynamic version of the cross-country model.

The dynamic model is designed to explore the interaction between changes in the structure of production, trade, and employment on the one hand and the rate of growth on the other. Two main topics will be addressed: first, the long-term tendency of growth to accelerate in the middle periods of the transformation; second, the relation between the typical patterns of specialization identified above and the rate of growth.

In discussing these questions, the overall transformation will be divided into three stages that correspond to the shift in the relative contributions of primary production and manufacturing to growth. The cross-country model will be extended to simulate both typical changes in the sources of growth from one stage to the next and the effects of alternative patterns of specialization. Although these and other interpretations of the sources of productivity change and growth are quite speculative, they provide an introduction to the principal questions studied in later chapters.

Shifts in the Sources of Growth

Chapter 2 derived aggregate growth from equations of the following form for each sector:

$$(2\text{-}8) \qquad\qquad G_i = \beta_{Ki} G_{Ki} + \beta_{Li} G_{Li} + \lambda_i$$

$$(2\text{-}10) \qquad\qquad G_V = \Sigma_i \bar{\rho}_i G_i.$$

These equations can be added to the cross-country model to derive a dynamic version of the transformation. For each level of income, the solution to the static model determines the composition of value added and hence the weight to be given to each sector, ρ_i.

The rate of aggregate growth results from the interaction of demand and supply forces. In an accounting sense, it is common to express the growth of output as determined by the growth of inputs and their efficiency, as in the growth accounting equation 2-9 or in the Harrod-Domar growth relation:

$$(3-18) \qquad G_V = \frac{I/V - \delta}{h^*},$$

where I/V is the share of gross investment in GDP, δ is the ratio of depreciation to output, and h^* is the realized incremental capital-output ratio.

This relation provides a convenient summary of the pattern of growth in the simulation model.[17] For each income interval, the implied aggregate rate of growth is derived from the income-related investment rate (equation 3-14)[18] and the incremental capital-output ratio. The latter is aggregated from the income-related sectoral capital-output ratios (equation 3-16) with output weights, ρ_i.[19] Combining the values of sectoral outputs at various income levels with the sector growth rate, we can express this aggregate growth rate as a weighted average of the sectoral growth rates, as was illustrated in tables 2-6 and 2-7.

There are several advantages in focusing on the contributions of different sectors to growth. The relative importance of supply and demand constraints varies among sectors and can be reflected in the simulations of the model. Moreover, even though these growth equations can be estimated only for individual countries, their general characteristics can be incorporated into the stylized approximations used in the cross-country model. Although the comparative data from which they are estimated are more limited than for other elements of the model, we have used them in the context of the accounting framework to produce a set of estimates that incorporates certain empirical features. These features are:

- Agricultural growth is assumed to be limited by technology and natural resources to 4 percent or less. Total factor productivity growth is low in the early stages because of the availability of underemployed labor, but it increases as industrialization proceeds.
- Manufacturing output is determined by demand and trade patterns. The latter reflect changes in comparative advantage as capital intensity rises. In keeping with country estimates, productivity growth is somewhat higher in manufacturing than in other major sectors (see chapters 8 and 10).
- The capital-output ratio for social overhead is two to three times the average, but it declines somewhat with rising income.

17. A more complete statement of the dynamic model is given in chapter 8.
18. The rate of depreciation is also assumed to vary with income; see chapter 8.
19. The use of the Harrod-Domar growth relation (equation 3-18) does not imply the adoption of a specific growth theory or the assumption of a technologically fixed capital coefficient. The growth equation is an ex post identity implicit in the set of income-related, reduced-form relations presented above.

Figure 3-7. *Sectoral Sources of Growth*

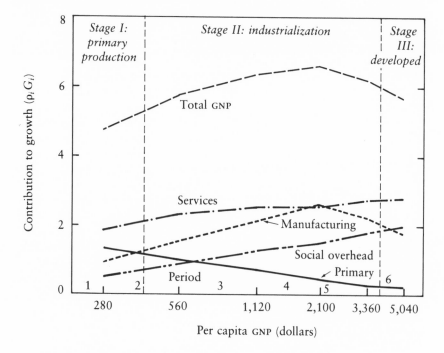

• The income elasticity of demand for services is close to one. Services are traded only to a limited extent.

A solution to the dynamic model for period 3 of the transformation has been given in tables 2-6 and 2-7. The results for the whole range of the transformation are summarized in figures 3-7 and 3-8.[20] The first shows the contribution of each of the major sectors to aggregate growth, $\rho_i G_i$, and the second derives the contribution of labor, capital, and total factor productivity growth from the sectoral results.

The acceleration of growth from 4.9 percent in period 1 to 6.7 percent in period 4 is attributable to the rise in the rate of investment from 13 to 16 percent of GNP (the Harrod-Domar effect) and the shift of resources to sectors with higher productivity growth (the reallocation effect). These results are consistent with the cross-country regressions of chapter 2 and are analyzed further in chapter 8.

Figure 3-7 can also be regarded as a dynamic version of figure 3-6. The contribution of each sector to growth is measured by its average share of total GNP, $\overline{\rho}_i$, weighted by its growth rate, G_i. If all growth rates were identical in a given period, the relative contribution of each sector to

20. These figures plot data for each period at the income level of the terminal years. Thus data for period 3 from table 2-7 are shown at income level $1,120 in figure 3-7.

Figure 3-8. *Factor Contributions to Growth*

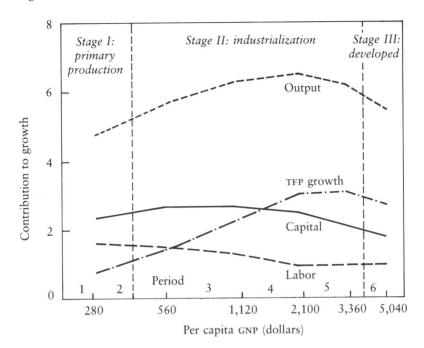

aggregate growth would merely equal its share of GNP. The contribution of a rapidly growing sector, such as manufacturing in the early periods, is greater than its static share, whereas that of primary production is less. For example, in period 3 the growth contribution of primary production is reduced by a third from the static share (from 21 to 14 percent) whereas that of heavy industry is raised by a third (from 9 to 12 percent).

In using these results for country comparisons, a further distinction should be made between outputs that are tradable—primary products and manufactures—and those that are essentially nontradable (social overhead and most services). Since imports and exports increase the range of choice of resource allocation, differences among countries are concentrated in the tradable sectors and in the nontradables related to them.

The further aggregation by factor contributions to growth in figure 3-8 is more speculative. The decline in the contribution of labor reflects the slowdown in population growth at high income levels, which outweighs rising labor productivity. The rise in total factor productivity growth in the early periods stems from the existence of underutilized labor and the subsequent shift of resources out of agriculture. The relative constancy of the capital contribution results from the decline in its marginal product, which offsets the rise in the investment rate. As indicated in chapters 2 and

8, however, each of these tendencies is subject to considerable variation among the countries that have been studied.

For convenience in making intercountry comparisons, we utilize these typical shifts in the sources of growth to define three stages of transformation: I, primary production; II, industrialization; and III, the developed economy. Because there are no significant discontinuities in the processes that lead from one to the next, the dividing lines between them are somewhat arbitrary.[21] We shall consider the extent to which different trade patterns cause this sequence to vary after summarizing the principal features of each stage.

STAGE I. PRIMARY PRODUCTION. The first stage of the transformation is identified by the predominance of primary activities—principally agriculture—as the main source of the increasing output of tradable goods. Even though primary production typically grows more slowly than manufacturing, this difference is more than offset at low income levels by the limited demand for manufactured goods. The large weight of agriculture in value added is also one of the main reasons for slower overall growth during this stage.

On the supply side, stage I is characterized by low to moderate rates of capital accumulation, accelerating growth of the labor force, and very low growth in total factor productivity. As figure 3-8 shows, it is the absence of productivity growth more than low investment rates that causes the lower aggregate rates of growth in stage I. Although comprehensive studies of productivity growth in poor countries are few, this conclusion is consistent with the evidence cited in chapter 2.

STAGE II. INDUSTRIALIZATION. The second stage of the transformation is characterized by the shift of the center of gravity of the economy away from primary production and toward manufacturing. The main indicator of this shift is the relative importance of the contribution of manufacturing to growth, as shown in figure 3-7. In the standard pattern generated by the dynamic model, manufacturing makes a larger contribution to growth than primary production above an income level of about $400. This shift occurs at lower or higher levels of income depending on the resource endowments and trade policies of different countries, as shown in figure 3-9.

(In stage III of the transformation, the relation between growth and structure is reversed. The elasticity of demand for manufactures declines at higher income levels and the contribution of manufacturing to growth falls from period 4 onward.)

On the supply side, the contribution of capital accumulation remains

21. The criteria used to distinguish the semi-industrial economies (stage II) are discussed in chapter 4.

Figure 3-9. *Sectoral Contributions to Growth: Alternative Trade Patterns*

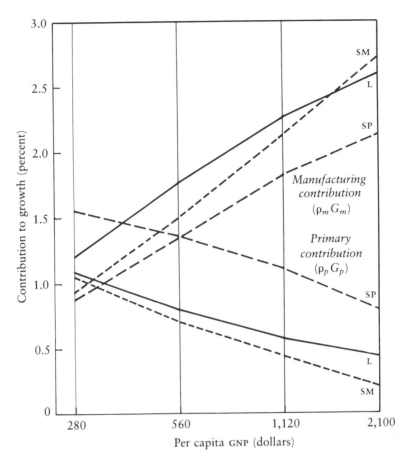

high for most of stage II because the rise in the rate of investment tends to offset the decline in the weight of capital in the sectoral production functions. The dominant feature of the average pattern of figure 3-8 is the rise in the contribution of productivity growth associated with the shift from agriculture to industry, which fully accounts for the acceleration of growth in stage II. This phenomenon will be the subject of detailed analysis in part III.

STAGE III. THE DEVELOPED ECONOMY. The transition from stage II to stage III can be identified in several ways. On the demand side, income elasticities for manufactured goods decline, and at some point their share in domestic demand starts to fall. Although this tendency is offset for a while by the continued growth of exports, it is ultimately reflected in a decline in the share of manufacturing in GNP and in the labor force. This turning point has occurred in virtually all the industrial market economies within the past twenty years.[22]

On the supply side, the main difference between stage II and stage III is the decline in the combined contribution of factor inputs as conventionally measured. The contribution of capital falls because of both its slower growth and its declining weight. In addition, because of a slow-down in population growth, only a few developed countries still have a significant increase in their labor force.

Although the level of total factor productivity growth has remained relatively high in the advanced countries—at least until the mid-1970s—it is less associated with industrialization and more widely diffused throughout the economy than in stage II. The most notable change is in agriculture, which has shifted from being a sector of low productivity growth to being the sector of highest growth of labor productivity in most of the developed countries. The underlying cause is the continued movement of labor out of agriculture and the closing of the wage gap between agriculture and other sectors, which has stimulated the substitution of capital for labor as well as technological improvements.[23]

The Effects of Specialization

Differences in international specialization have been identified above as the primary source of variation from the standard growth pattern just described. They include not only the effects of factor proportions on comparative advantage but also policy decisions about the levels of trade and external capital inflows.

How much do different patterns of specialization affect the sources of growth? This question will be explored by simulating the sources of growth in the cross-country model with alternative levels and composition of trade and then comparing the results with the experiences of individual countries.

The alternative export patterns in figure 3-5 illustrate the central tendencies of three subgroups within a total sample of approximately ninety countries. The differences among the three export patterns are large and statistically quite significant. To determine their effects on the sectoral sources of growth, we substitute alternative vectors estimated for each of the three groups (L, SM, and SP) for the average export and import vectors of the standard pattern. At a given level of per capita income ($560) and with demand and technology held constant, the total effect of a change in the trade vectors can be measured by the shifts in value added by sector

---

22. Of the seventeen countries that are generally recognized as industrial market economies, all except Finland have shown declines in the share of manufacturing in GNP since 1960 as well as in the share of the labor force in manufacturing. See World Bank (1984).

23. A recent comparison of the sources of growth in the OECD countries is given in Kendrick (1982).

Table 3-10. *Effects of Alternative Trade Patterns on Sources of Growth, Income Level 3 ($560 per capita)*
(percent)

Sector	Standard pattern ρ_i	Standard pattern $\rho_i G_i/G$	L pattern ρ_i	L pattern $\rho_i G_i/G$	SM pattern ρ_i	SM pattern $\rho_i G_i/G$	SP pattern ρ_i	SP pattern $\rho_i G_i/G$
Primary	21	14	16	11	15	9	26	20
			(−5)	(−3)	(−6)	(−5)	(+5)	(+6)
Light industry	16	18	17	18	19	21	15	16
			(+1)	(0)	(+3)	(+3)	(−1)	(−2)
Heavy industry	9	12	13	16	6	10	8	11
			(+4)	(+4)	(−3)	(−2)	(−1)	(−1)
Nontradables	55	56	54	55	60	60	51	53
			(−1)	(−1)	(+5)	(+4)	(−3)	(−3)

Note: Changes from the standard pattern are shown in parentheses.
Source: World Bank data.

from the standard pattern. Repeating the calculation for rising levels of income gives the sectoral shares and growth rates that determine the differences in the sources of growth.[24]

The shifts from the standard composition of value added, ρ_i, are shown in table 3-10 for each of the specialized trade patterns. Because exports are only one element in demand, the effects of a given change in exports on value added are substantially reduced. For example, the SP export pattern is characterized by primary exports about 50 percent higher than the standard level (figure 3-5). This shift results in a 23 percent increase in primary output, equivalent to a shift of 5 percent of GNP from other sectors to primary production (table 3-10).

The characteristic features of each of the three trade patterns can thus be identified by a set of intersectoral shifts of resources at each level of income. For the small primary exporter, table 3-10 shows that the increase in the share of primary production of 5 percent is offset by proportional reductions in the other sectors. Similarly, the SM pattern can be identified at this income level with a 3 percent shift of GNP to light industry through export expansion plus a 5 percent shift from tradables to nontradables. The L pattern involves a 4 percent shift to heavy industry, mainly through import substitution.

The second column in table 3-10 gives the sources of growth by sector, $\rho_i G_i/G$, for each pattern, as measured from equation 2-8. The table also compares the three specialized patterns with the standard pattern. The main difference from the static comparisons in the first column is the lower

24. To isolate the effects of different trade patterns, we have assumed constant aggregate growth rates.

weight given to the slowly growing primary sector, which offsets the higher share of the manufacturing sectors. The deviations from the standard pattern, however, are similar in both columns.

The different trade patterns have a large impact on the timing of industrialization. These effects are brought out in figure 3-9, which shows the growth contributions of primary production and manufacturing under each trade pattern. (Nontradables are omitted since they show relatively little variation from the standard pattern of figure 3-7.) We shall measure the timing of industrialization by the beginning of stage II, the income level at which the growth contribution of manufacturing begins to exceed that of primary production.

With this measure, large countries typically reach the semi-industrial stage at an income level of about $250, the standard pattern at about $400, and small primary exporters at $600. In the L pattern, early industrialization results from the widespread policy of import substitution in manufacturing. In the SP pattern, manufactured imports are replaced much more slowly. The SM pattern is more complex because it starts with a relatively high inflow of external capital, which is later replaced as a source of foreign exchange by the rapid growth of exports of light manufactures.

Our nine-economy sample contains several examples of each of these typical patterns as well as several deviants from them. Table 3-11 gives a decomposition, for selected periods, of the increment in GNP by sector; this can be compared with table 3-10.[25] Allowing for the income levels in each economy, we can identify the two periods in Colombia as primary oriented. Israel and Taiwan have the typical features of an SM economy, the former showing the effect of a high capital inflow in raising nontradables and lowering the production of tradables. The late periods in Japan, Korea, Mexico, Turkey, and Yugoslavia are characteristic of large economies: all show a rapid fall in the growth contribution of primary production and a rise in that of heavy industry. These comparisons will be pursued further in chapters 6 and 7.

Issues for Country Analysis

Simulations of the cross-country model have provided considerable insight into the relation between economic structure and growth. In addition to the topics on which we have suggested some general conclusions, there are three others for which the comparative evidence suggests hypotheses that require further exploration for individual countries:

- *Structural determinants of productivity growth.* Cross-country studies have associated productivity growth with shifts from agriculture to industry, with the growth of exports, and with macroeconomic

---

25. These incremental shares in value added ($\Delta V_i/\Delta V$) are equivalent to the decomposition of aggregate growth used in table 3-10 ($\rho_i G_i/G$).

Table 3-11. *Sectoral Sources of Growth*

Economy	Years	Initial income (dollars)	Sectoral percentage of total growth			
			Primary	Light industry	Heavy industry	Nontrad-ables
Colombia	1953–66	274	23.7	12.2	12.1	52.0
	1966–70	330	42.2	19.4	9.3	29.1
	1953–70		29.8	14.5	11.2	44.4
Mexico	1950–60	380	17.7	12.1	7.8	62.4
	1960–70	479	14.9	14.8	11.6	58.7
	1970–75	670	5.4	14.5	17.3	62.8
	1950–75		12.6	14.2	12.5	60.7
Turkey	1963–68	319	10.7	11.3	18.4	59.6
	1968–73	377	6.4	10.3	25.9	57.4
	1963–73		8.2	10.7	22.8	58.3
Yugoslavia	1962–66	469	21.5	13.9	20.7	43.9
	1966–72	581	−4.1	18.0	24.1	62.0
	1962–72		7.2	16.2	22.6	54.0
Japan (prewar)	1914–35	265	16.0	16.8	10.7	56.5
Japan (postwar)	1955–60	500	4.5	9.0	27.2	59.3
	1960–65	753	2.4	12.4	26.9	58.3
	1965–70	1,159	1.2	13.7	34.6	50.5
	1955–70		2.0	12.7	31.5	53.8
Korea	1955–63	131	37.1	19.5	17.1	26.3
	1963–70	149	18.1	18.2	12.0	51.7
	1970–73	250	8.9	26.2	23.9	41.0
	1955–73		16.3	21.4	16.9	45.4
Taiwan	1956–61	203	28.2	16.3	7.1	48.4
	1961–66	231	17.4	12.4	18.9	51.3
	1966–71	305	1.5	24.1	24.7	49.7
	1956–71		10.5	19.3	20.2	50.0
Israel	1958–65	1,067	6.7	11.1	14.6	67.6
	1965–72	1,587	5.0	13.5	17.2	64.3
	1958–72		5.7	12.5	16.2	65.6
Norway	1953–61	1,171	0.7	10.2	18.0	71.1
	1961–69	2,028	1.0	10.1	17.5	71.4

Source: World Bank data.

policies. This issue will be analyzed in the detailed country studies of chapter 10.

- *The rate of structural change.* For each trade pattern, the cross-country model implies an association between the rate of growth and the rapidity of structural change. Further evidence of this relation is given in chapter 7. It is not possible to conclude, however, that growth can be accelerated by measures to speed up structural change, unless they are derived from a country model that incorporates market behavior. Such a model is proposed in chapter 11.

- *The necessity of industrialization.* The three typical patterns of transformation derived here all include a stage at which a substantial increase in manufacturing output occurs, with associated changes in trade, employment, and urbanization. Is this result merely a phenomenon of the postwar period, or is it a more general requirement? We provide a partial answer to this question in the next chapter by analyzing the experience of the full sample of middle-income economies.

Appendix. Comparisons of Real Income across Countries and over Time

In various parts of this book, particularly in chapters 3, 4, and 8, we analyze the relation between economic structure and the level of development. The latter is measured by income per capita in U.S. dollars at official exchange rates.[26] The income benchmarks in the simulation model in chapters 3 and 8 have the same interpretation, namely, income levels in U.S. dollars.

It is well known that exchange rates are an imperfect measure of the purchasing power of the various national currencies. Price structures vary across countries, and exchange rates at best reflect only the prices of internationally traded goods in the absence of impediments to trade. The alternative to using exchange rates as conversion factors for international comparisons is to reprice the local components of income in every country at a uniform set of prices. This is equivalent to the use of purchasing-power parities (PPPs) as conversion factors, where PPPs, following Kravis (1984), refer to the number of currency units required to buy one U.S. dollar worth of output. PPPs are a weighted average of the ratios of domestic price (P_i) to the price of the same good i in the country chosen as numeraire (P_i^*) or to its price in some international units.

There have been various attempts to estimate real incomes for small samples of countries; these attempts designated a high-income country as numeraire. Until recently, similar estimates for a large number of developing countries were not available. This deficiency has begun to be remedied by the International Comparisons Project (ICP). In a series of studies, the ICP has estimated real incomes for an ever increasing number of countries. Phase III of the project, which includes thirty-four countries, became available in 1982. Phase IV, yet to be published, covers more than sixty countries. The sample of real income estimates that was available when the present study was in progress was too small to make it a suitable alternative to exchange rate conversions.

The purpose of this appendix is to clarify some of the issues related to real income comparisons and to assess the effect of using exchange rates

---

26. Following the methodology described in the *World Bank Atlas* (World Bank 1977), which uses an average of 1965–71 annual exchange rates.

for conversion on the nature of the results about the transformation of economic structure in chapters 3 and 8 (see also the technical appendix to Chenery and Syrquin 1975).

Exchange Rates and PPPs *as Conversion Factors*

The principal result of the ICP and similar studies is that differences across countries in incomes converted at exchange rates tend to exaggerate the real differences in income.

Let *YE* stand for GDP converted at exchange rates and *YR* for real income. If GDP is expressed in a country's own currency, the two income figures are obtained as:

$$YE = \text{GDP}/e$$
$$YR = \text{GDP}/\text{PPP}$$

where *e* is the exchange rate and PPP the purchasing power parity rate.

The systematic divergence between *YE* and *YR* per capita has been analyzed in two equivalent ways:

- The ratio *YR/YE*, labeled by Kravis and associates the "exchange rate deviation index" (ERD), declines steadily with the level of income per capita from levels close to 3 for very low-income countries to a value of 1 for the United States.
- The reciprocal of the ERD is the national price level (PPP/*e*), which increases systematically with per capita income.[27]

Several explanations have been proposed to account for the systematic pattern of the ERD or of its inverse, the price level. The main one, which is most relevant for our purposes, is the "differential productivity model," of which there are various versions going back at least to Ricardo (see Kravis and Lipsey 1983). Its modern version (see Balassa 1964 and Samuelson 1964), accepts the law of one price as approximately valid for traded goods but introduces a sector producing nontraded goods. Assuming that productivity differences among countries are larger for traded than for nontraded goods, that the production of the latter is relatively more labor-intensive, and that labor is relatively more abundant (relatively less expensive) in low-income countries, the relative price of nontraded goods can be expected to be positively associated with per capita income. Since the prices of traded goods are similar across countries, the model also predicts that the national price level will be higher in high-income countries.

The differential productivity model relies on real factors related to the structure of the economy. In addition to the level of per capita income, other such influences that have been suggested for examination include the

27. The variation across countries in the national price level is analyzed in Kravis and Lipsey (1983) and Clague (1985).

industrial structure of output and employment and the degree of openness of the economy. These long-run factors determine the underlying price level, while short-run, mainly monetary, variables are the cause of deviations from the basic level (Kravis and Lipsey 1983, p. 10).

The rise in the relative price of nontraded goods with the level of income across countries can also be derived from a model where differences in total factor productivity among sectors do not vary in a systematic way with income. Bhagwati (1984) has recently shown that the price effect is compatible with the traditional factor-proportion model in trade theory.

Effects of Using Exchange Rates

There are two types of international comparisons in chapters 3 and 8 that could be affected by using exchange rates as conversion factors rather than purchasing power parities. The first one relates measures of economic structure to per capita income across countries and is essentially a static comparison. The second one refers to the dynamic simulation of an economy over time.

Static Cross-Country Comparisons

Static comparisons include studies of the structure of demand and production across countries as well as comparative static simulations of changes in structure with incomes (for example, the static model of chapter 3).

The patterns using exchange rates show the average transformation in relation to income changes which incorporate a systematic variation in prices. If the price variation is not correlated with per capita income among countries, then the use of YE instead of YR may affect the precision of the estimates but will not necessarily bias the results. When the deviation of YE from YR is systematic, the results will be biased. However, a close relation between YE and YR per capita implies that there is a simple transformation between the results using YE and the ones that would obtain if YR were to be used.

When the bias in using exchange rates affects all components of GDP equally, the transformation in economic structure studied in chapter 3 will take place over a narrower real income range than the one shown there. The pace of the transformation is therefore underestimated in our analysis.

As mentioned above, a major component of the deviation between YE and YR is caused by differences in price structures. To correct for these differences, separate correction factors are needed for different components of GDP. The ICP reports give detailed information on the price structures of the countries studied. The principal results are that the relative price of government consumption generally rises with income while the relative price of investment declines. Since the ICP examined expenditure categories, it does not provide information on the relative prices of goods by sector of origin.[28] For this a production approach to real income is necessary (see Maddison 1983).

The conclusion of this discussion is that the main effect of using exchange rates is on the rate of the transformation but not on its nature. Moreover, the expected biases usually strengthen the changes reported (as with the increase in investment shares); where they do not (the case of services), they are mentioned as important qualifications in the text.

The position of individual countries is of course unknown and cannot be determined from an average relation between YE and YR, such as the ones estimated from observations for the countries in the ICP sample and used to predict YR for countries not in the sample. The best known of these "short-cut" derivations of real incomes used an estimated relation between YR and YE based on sixteen observations to predict "Real GDP Per Capita for More than One Hundred Countries" (Kravis, Heston, and Summers 1978). The short-cut relations are useful, but they do not reduce the uncertainty about the position of individual countries.

An additional potential problem when converting local currencies by exchange rates relates to the choice of the base year. The simulation model in chapter 3 was partly based on econometric estimates from pooled cross-section and time-series data. Incomes in U.S. dollars were obtained by applying the exchange rate for a base year and domestic growth rates for other years. The choice of the base year can affect the estimated patterns if variations in real exchange rates over time are correlated with per capita income. The problem was not serious before the 1970s. In Chenery and Syrquin (1975) all figures were in 1964 U.S. dollars. These figures are converted in chapter 3 to 1970 values by a uniform factor of 1.4 based on the U.S. price deflator.[29]

Since the collapse of the Bretton Woods system in the early 1970s, exchange rates became more volatile and have increasingly departed from predictions based on simple purchasing-power-parities comparisons. Some simple comparisons reported in Syrquin (1985c) suggested that currencies have, on the average, appreciated relative to the U.S. dollar and that the extent of the appreciation increases with income per capita. At low income levels, various countries show a real depreciation in their currencies. This association between changes in real exchange rates and income has the effect of stretching the income range for a group of countries when using exchange rates for recent years instead of 1964 exchange rates. The gap among countries for a given year appears wider in 1980 U.S. dollars than in 1964 U.S. dollars.

The choice of the base year affects the estimates of transformation from

---

28. See, nevertheless, the attempt by Kravis, Heston, and Summers (1983) to use expenditure data to examine the share of services in GDP.

29. The conversion factor also includes a switch from factor cost to market prices (see Syrquin 1985c).

cross-country regressions as well as the results from short-cut regressions for predicting real incomes.

In chapter 3 (note to table 3-3), it was mentioned that a factor of 2.6 is needed to convert the 1970 dollars there to 1982 prices. This factor, based on the U.S. price deflator, is an average of the differential factors for different income levels actually observed during this period. For the lowest-income countries, the factor is closer to 2.3, and for the industrial countries it is about 3 (Syrquin 1985c).

Dynamic Simulations

Once the time element comes in, the deviation of YE from YR becomes more significant. Growth rate calculations and comparisons, such as those in figures 3-7 and 3-8, are intended to be in real terms, whereas the changes across benchmark levels of YE incorporate a price effect. The growth rates between benchmark levels of YE in figures 3-7 and 3-8 (and in chapter 8, which derives them) give the time required to traverse the distance between the various levels of YE. The results are overestimates since they do not take into account the variation in the price level during the same interval. The quantitative results are sensitive to the use of exchange rates, but the important question is the extent to which the qualitative results about the transformation are also affected. As mentioned above, the use of exchange rates as conversion factors stretches the income range studied. A uniform stretching would be the least damaging to the nature of the results and the easiest to incorporate into the analysis. A uniform stretching implies a logarithmic relation between YR and YE, and most of the short-cut studies have postulated such a logarithmic relation and estimated it with quite good results. (See, for example, Kravis, Heston, and Summers 1978 and Marris 1981.) Based on the results of Phase III of the ICP, we estimated the following relation for twenty-seven economies:[30]

$$\ln YR = 2.81 + 0.68 \ln YE, \qquad \bar{R}^2 = 0.97$$
$$(16.7) \quad (28.9)$$

The implication of the results is that real growth amounts to 68 percent of growth in income converted at exchange rates *at all income levels*. The remaining 32 percent represent the systematic price effect.

The effect of switching to income converted at PPPs instead of exchange rates on the income intervals in tables 3-3 and 8-2 would be to reduce all of them *uniformly* by 32 percent, but, most important, all the acceleration and declaration effects on growth would still remain.

The main conclusion is that the results from the simulation model are not unduly sensitive to the use of exchange rates.

---

30. The sample includes data for Israel, Norway, and Turkey from Marris (1981). They were not in the ICP study but are in the sample studied in detail in part II of this book. The regression excludes six European countries with an ERD in 1975 below one. Including them lowers the elasticity to 0.66.

Real Investment and Growth

A final simple exercise relates to the statistical analysis of growth across countries in chapters 2 and 9. In those chapters the growth rate of real GDP during 1964–73 is analyzed in terms of a simple neoclassical and more complex models. In the former model two variables enter as explanatory: the growth rate of the labor force (or population as a proxy) and the investment share in current prices. Summers, Kravis, and Heston (1980) used the results of Phase II of the ICP (sixteen countries) to derive expenditure shares in domestic and international prices for a large number of countries for 1950–77. We used their results to estimate the simple neoclassical model for twenty-nine semi-industrial countries during 1964–73 in two alternative versions: the investment share in domestic prices (I/Y) *dom.* and in international prices (I/Y) *int.* Using the notation of chapter 2, the results are:

$$G_Y = 0.002 + 0.40G_L + 0.24\ (I/Y)\ dom. \quad \bar{R}^2 = 0.34$$
$$(1.2) (3.9)$$

$$G_Y = 0.008 + 0.53G_L + 0.23\ (I/Y)\ int.\ \bar{R}^2 = 0.25$$
$$(1.4) (3.2)$$

The similarity of results from the versions in this rather simple exercise is quite reassuring for chapters 2 and 9.

4 The Semi-Industrial Countries

HOLLIS CHENERY

MOSHE SYRQUIN

IN CHAPTER 3, we identified an industrializing stage of economic development in which manufacturing growth becomes the dominant source of the increasing supply of tradable commodities. Semi-industrial countries were portrayed as those economies which have diversified their production and trading structure and have exceeded some threshold level of per capita income. In this chapter, we shift our attention from these general features of the structural transformation to a survey of those economies that were semi-industrial—that is, that were in the industrializing stage—during some portion of the period 1950–80. This gives us a group of thirty-nine economies, including all those in our sample except Norway.[1] Our primary objective is to characterize the group as a whole in terms of the analytical concepts introduced in chapters 2 and 3, as a background for the comparative studies in part II. Because most of these economies have been widely studied, we will draw on several comparative analyses in classifying their development strategies.

This chapter discusses the main sources of variation in postwar industrialization using a simple typology of development strategies that incorporates the principal features thought to produce differences in patterns of growth and structural change. This typology includes the structural differences associated with size and resource endowments that have already been discussed, as well as a breakdown of external policies along a spectrum from outward-oriented (export promotion) to inward-oriented (import substitution). The external dimension of a development strategy is stressed because it represents one of the most important choices facing policymakers and explains some of the main differences in recent economic performance.

Our two basic hypotheses are, first, that the long-run transformation of the economic structure is similar for all types of countries and, second, that differences in initial structure and development strategy have affected the timing of the industrialization process and the sequencing of specific activities more than they have affected the overall pattern. The typology described in this chapter is designed to identify the main variations in the

1. Including Japan, which by 1970 could no longer be considered semi-industrial.

postwar experience of semi-industrial economies and to explore the association of policy, structure, and performance during this period.

Types of Industrialization

In the early 1950s it was possible to make a fairly sharp distinction between developed (industrial) and developing (nonindustrial) countries, with less than a dozen intermediate cases that would now be classed as semi-industrial.[2] The following two decades were characterized by accelerating growth and rapid industrialization throughout the world. This was also a period when countries experimented with a variety of development strategies, particularly in the fields of international trade and finance. Together these trends produced a great increase in the number of semi-industrial countries as well as considerable diversity in the sequence of structural changes that they have followed.

Identifying the Semi-Industrial Countries

If there were only a single feasible route to development, such as the "standard pattern" of chapter 3, it would be a simple matter to identify the actual countries corresponding to each stage. Furthermore, if all measures of structure—such as industrial output or share of manufactured goods in total exports—bore a fixed relation to each other, as in the standard pattern, then any one of them could serve equally well to characterize a semi-industrial country. As illustrated in chapter 3, however, different initial conditions and patterns of specialization have a considerable effect on the timing and sequence of structural changes.

The cross-country model provides several measures that might be selected as benchmarks in dividing the transformation into an earlier (primary) and later (semi-industrial) stage. The most essential are indexes of the shifts in internal demand, exports, and production from the primary sector to manufacturing. The principal benchmark used in this chapter is the point at which the contribution of manufacturing to growth exceeds that of primary production. Supplementary benchmarks are a minimal per capita GNP (as a proxy for domestic demand for manufactures) and a minimal share of manufactures in exports and production.

---

2. The structural comparisons of Kuznets (1966) and Chenery and Syrquin (1975) identify fifteen developed (or industrial) countries in 1950 (in order of highest to lowest per capita income): the United States, Canada, Switzerland, Sweden, Australia, New Zealand, the United Kingdom, Denmark, Norway, Belgium, France, the Federal Republic of Germany, Finland, the Netherlands, and Austria. By 1960 Japan, Italy, Czechoslovakia, the U.S.S.R., and the German Democratic Republic had also reached this stage. The centrally planned economies are omitted from this discussion for lack of comparable data on their structures.

By the criteria used here, the semi-industrial group of 1950 included several Mediterranean countries (Spain, Portugal, Israel, and Yugoslavia) and several Latin American ones (Argentina, Mexico, Brazil, and Uruguay). In Asia, only Japan and Hong Kong had reached this stage, and elsewhere only the Union of South Africa.

Table 4-1. *Benchmarks for Semi-Industrial Countries*

Index	Standard pattern	Large	Primary-oriented
Per capita income (dollars)	350	300	500
Manufacturing output			
Share of GDP (percent)	18	19	14
Value added per capita (dollars)	60	55	70
Incremental share of growth in tradables (percent)[a]	50	50	50
Manufactured exports			
Share of merchandise exports (percent)	20	25	10
Per capita (dollars)	15	8	10

a. Computed in tables 4-2 and 4-4 as the industry index: $\rho_m G_m / (\rho_p G_p + \rho_m G_m)$.

In selecting benchmark levels for these indexes, we have taken account of the actual values for representative economies as well as the values simulated by the cross-country model. To allow for differences in timing resulting from variations in size, resource endowments, and development strategies, we shall adopt a specific set of criteria for the standard case and a somewhat different set for each of the extreme patterns of specialization described earlier: the large country and the primary-oriented country.

The benchmarks for large countries are adjusted for the lower levels of trade and the earlier import substitution that characterize this group. The resource-rich primary product exporters deviate in the opposite direction: they have relatively high levels of trade, but their comparative advantage in primary production delays the development of manufactured exports. Because these countries industrialize mainly for the domestic market, the export test is replaced by a higher level of domestic output. A summary of the benchmarks suggested for the three country groups is given in table 4-1.

This flexible classification scheme gives us a consistent way to identify the semi-industrial countries. Because we wish to arrive at an all-inclusive classification, countries that meet only two of the three criteria are considered marginal but are included in the statistical analyses.

Table 4-2 lists the thirty-eight economies that we have classified as having been semi-industrial in 1976, with large and primary-oriented countries shown separately so that appropriate benchmarks can be applied to each group. It includes twenty-one economies that meet all three criteria, fifteen that meet two, and two poor countries (India and Kenya) that satisfy only one. Most small economies having a total GNP of less than $2 billion in 1970 are omitted because their structures tend to be unrepresentative.[3]

3. See Chenery and Syrquin (1975, pp. 102–03) and Chenery (1979, pp. 28–32). Japan was no longer in the semi-industrial category in 1970.

A Typology of Industrialization

Several attempts have been made to analyze the postwar experience of developing countries by identifying selected characteristics of economic structure and policy that have a systematic effect on resource allocation. The structural characteristics used have included the resource base for primary exports, the size of the domestic market, and dualistic labor markets. The most widely analyzed policy difference has been the inward or outward orientation of trade policy, defined by the extent of discrimination against exports.

Some of the studies have classified the countries and periods analyzed according to structural and policy variables and thus have given rise to a partial typology of development performance. Examples of such typologies are the family of dual economy models stemming from W. A. Lewis's original analysis (1954); the import substituting strategy of industrialization studied by Little, Scitovsky, and Scott (1970) and Balassa (1971); and the trade regimes of Krueger (1978) and Bhagwati (1978).[4]

The procedure of this chapter is somewhat different, although our ultimate objectives are similar. We start from a statistical analysis of the structural transformation that focuses on changes in demand, trade, and production. As in other approaches, we select a critical phase of the transformation—the rise of industry—for more detailed study. Unlike them, however, we then try to identify all the semi-industrial economies in the postwar period and to develop a typology by subdividing this universe instead of by starting from a few prototypes. The two approaches are essentially complementary in that each provides a check on the other.[5]

Depending on the problem being analyzed and the objectives of the study, alternative typologies can be designed by combining policy dimensions with structural features. We have a choice between emphasizing internal policy (resource mobilization) or external policy (trade strategy). Although the earlier development literature stressed the former, there are several reasons for preferring to focus on the latter in analyzing differences in industrialization. First, except in the centrally planned economies, trade policy has become the main instrument used by governments to influence resource allocation. Second, differences in trade policy have led to the substantial variation in economic structures and in the indirect effects on performance that have been documented in several countries. Differences in resource mobilization, in contrast, show only a weak association with variations in structure or performance across countries.

The typology used for this study extends our earlier classification of allocation patterns (Chenery and Syrquin 1975, table 16), which was based on a statistical analysis of the level and orientation of exports in a

---

4. A partial typology is also implicit in studies of "mineral exporters," "superexporters in East Asia," "newly industrialized countries," and so on.
5. Ranis (1984) discusses the convergence that has taken place so far.

Table 4-2. *Structural Characteristics of Semi-Industrial Economies, 1976*
(1970 dollars)

Economy	Population midyear (million)	Per capita GNP	Shares in GDP (percent)		Industry index, 1953–73[a]	Value added in manufacturing per capita	Manufactured exports	
			Agriculture	Manufacturing			Percentage merchandise exports	Per capita
Primary-oriented								
Venezuela	12	1,754	6	17	0.41	300	2	10
South Africa	26	914	8	24	0.66	203	42	54
Malaysia	13	587	30	16	0.38	99	16	49
*Iran	34	1,317	10	11	0.23	141	1	5
*Iraq	12	949	3	7	0.23	67	0	0
*Algeria	16	676	8	11	0.51	76	1	2
*Ecuador	7	437	21	15	0.45	69	2	2
*Côte d'Ivoire	7	416	26	12	0.56	54	8	13
Other large								
Spain	36	1,993	10	28	0.82	532	69	115
Yugoslavia	22	1,146	15	32	0.75	326	70	108
Argentina	26	1,058	13	37	0.76	360	25	26
Brazil	110	778	11	30	0.71	193	25	16
Mexico	62	744	10	27	0.78	203	31	11
Turkey	41	676	30	17	0.56	103	24	8
Korea	26	457	25	25	0.60	102	88	129
Colombia	24	430	30	21	0.53	86	22	10
*Philippines	43	280	28	24	0.39	67	24	9
*Thailand	43	259	31	19	0.34	49	19	9
*Egypt	38	191	30	23	0.50	38	27	7
*China[b]	836	115	32	43	0.84	—	49	—
*India	620	102	40	17	0.23	15	53	3

Other small

Israel	3	2,675	7	28	0.87	518	78	361
Singapore	2	1,843	2	25	0.95	468	46	899
Greece	9	1,767	19	20	0.66	296	49	93
Ireland	3	1,747	15	20	0.78	—	53	399
Hong Kong	5	1,440	2	25	0.95	332	97	1,254
Portugal	10	1,153	15	34	0.77	335	68	87
Uruguay	3	949	11	29	0.43	237	34	44
Taiwan	16	730	12	37	0.84	269	85	290
Chile	11	717	8	22	0.72	160	5	5
Costa Rica	2	710	20	20	0.55	144	29	58
*Tunisia	6	573	21	11	0.38	53	26	25
*Peru	16	546	17	21	0.61	98	8	5
*Dominican Republic	5	532	20	21	0.57	116	18	18
*Syria	8	532	20	9	0.75	111	10	9
*Guatemala	7	430	27	16	0.42	—	17	14
*Morocco	17	369	20	16	0.44	42	16	8
*Kenya	14	164	34	13	0.47	20	12	4

— Not available.

*Marginal economies: those economies that do not satisfy all three criteria in table 4-1.

Note: Economies in each group are in order from highest to lowest per capita income. All figures are for 1976 or closest available year. Economies included in sample in part II are in italics.

a. Industry index computed as $\rho_m G_m / (\rho_p G_p + \rho_m G_m)$.

b. All data on China are preliminary.

Sources: Population, per capita GNP, and manufactured exports from World Bank 1978, 1979, 1980b, 1981b, 1982, 1983, 1984. Shares in GDP from World Bank 1980c. Value added from table 4-4.

large sample of developing and industrial economies.[6] This study led to the three-way classification of patterns of specialization (large; small, primary-oriented; and small, industry-oriented) used in chapter 3 and also in chapters 6 and 7.

The typology of semi-industrial economies in table 4-3 recognizes the effects of structural features such as size and resources as well as trade policy. However, because abundant primary resources are conducive to outward-oriented policies whereas large domestic markets favor import substitution, it is not possible to make sharp distinctions between the influences of structure and of policy.

Three types of trade strategy are defined—inward-oriented, outward-oriented, and neutral—and the countries representative of them in about 1970 are identified. The association between trade policy and the two structural indicators reduces the number of relevant combinations in the typology; by further concentrating only on the main variants in development patterns during the period, we end up with the eight groups in table 4-3.[7] Because our only use of the typology is to provide a comparative framework for detailed studies, the summaries in table 4-3 and in table 4-5 below are limited to the predominant features of policy during the period 1960–75, with structural measures given for 1965 and 1975.

Virtually all developing countries practiced inward-oriented policies—that is, policies having the effect of discriminating against exports—before 1960. The most sensitive indicator of a movement away from these policies that is widely available is the development of manufactured exports. This is the main factor in the trade orientation index, the principal structural measure used to distinguish among the four groups.

Although it is useful to start from such a classification of all semi-industrial countries, those with some continuity in policy and with adequate data are more valuable for our purpose. The following comments on the principal strategies are based on a comparison of five or six such examples in each category.[8]

---

6. The classification was based largely on a trade-orientation index that compares actual trade bias to the one predicted from cross-country regressions. The trade bias was defined as $TB = (E_p - E_m)/E$, and the trade orientation index as $TO = TB - T\hat{B}$, where E_p, E_m, and E stand for primary, manufactured, and total exports. The index considers the pattern of specialization as well as the level of total exports and is further discussed in the appendix to this chapter.

7. Our earlier classification of allocation patterns in 1965 compressed these eight groups into four by neglecting the effects of size, as shown in the first column of table 4-3. The distinctions among the four strategies are similar.

8. Countries having some continuity and coherence in their economic policies can be said to be following a development strategy, regardless of the policymaking process and of the institutional structure that accompanies it. These characteristics apply to more than half the economies in table 4-3, including the eight in our sample. Chapter 6 takes explicit account of changes in strategy in the latter group.

Representative Postwar Strategies

To illustrate the effects of development policies on structure and performance, we have tried to identify several typical examples of the four
strategies and to compare some of the features of each strategy. Almost all
countries followed a policy of import substitution fostered by some degree
of protection in the 1950s, including those that have since had the greatest
success with outward-oriented policies. Our comparisons are based on
structural changes since 1960, together with descriptions of the policies of
the countries cited as examples.

OUTWARD-, PRIMARY-ORIENTED ECONOMIES. Because our sample is
limited to the semi-industrial stage, the eight economies in this category
are those with a particularly strong comparative advantage in primary
production. They differ among themselves in their industrial policies,
however. Although most of them protect manufacturing to try to accelerate its growth, Malaysia has maintained an outward orientation with
relatively neutral incentives among sectors; the result has been substantial
growth of manufactured exports while primary exports have stayed at a
high level. Ecuador, Iran, and Venezuela illustrate the effects of the more
typical policy of industrial protection, which makes export earnings entirely dependent on primary products, as indicated by large positive values
of the trade orientation index. The negative impact on the industrial share
in output associated with the enormous rise in the price of energy in the
1970s (the Dutch disease) is also apparent in several countries in this
group (Algeria, Ecuador, Iraq, and Venezuela).

INWARD-ORIENTED ECONOMIES. Because most developing economies
are characterized by substantial protection in some form, only those that
have followed this policy to the extent of holding exports below the
statistical norm are put in this category. The eleven countries listed for this
policy in table 4-3 (including seven in Latin America) have a long history
of deliberately following policies that favor production for the domestic
market. In time, these policies produce the "second stage" import substitution syndrome of pushing domestic production into sectors of manufacturing in which comparative disadvantages are increasingly pronounced.[9]

In most countries, protective policies had been modified somewhat by
1970. This is reflected in the rise in the share of manufactured exports
toward the norm by 1975 (shown in table 4-5 below). Where this change

---

9. Ranis (1981) gives a detailed comparison of the later stages of import substitution in
Latin America as contrasted to the neutral or outward-oriented industrial policies of East
Asia.

Table 4-3. A Typology of Industrialization

Size, type, and name of economy	Chenery and Syrquin typology[b] (1965)	Relative export level		Trade orientation index[c]		Capital inflow		Relative efficiency[d] (8)
		1965	1975	1965	1975	1965	1975	
Large, LP								
*Iran	P	1.77	2.71	0.36	1.03	−0.064	−0.091	3.19
South Africa	B	1.46	—	0.06	—	0.000	—	−2.71
			Outward-, primary-oriented[a]					
Small, SP								
Venezuela	P	1.52	1.12	0.61	0.59	−0.105	−0.080	3.73
Malaysia	P	2.80	1.95	0.09	0.03	−0.044	−0.005	0.35
*Iraq	P	1.70	2.02	0.61	0.63	−0.150	−0.134	−1.37
*Algeria	P	1.06	1.14	0.34	0.41	0.030	0.118	−1.57
*Ecuador	IS	0.66	0.99	0.46	0.60	0.030	0.065	0.40
*Côte d'Ivoire	P	1.59	1.46	0.33	0.29	−0.014	−0.002	0.03
			Inward-oriented[a]					
Large, LI								
Argentina	IS	0.54	0.49	0.65	0.47	−0.014	0.002	−1.04
Mexico	IS	0.49	0.29	0.28	0.35	0.010	0.027	−0.51
Brazil	IS	1.01	0.78	0.57	0.67	−0.021	0.038	2.06
Turkey	IS	0.53	0.34	0.25	0.19	0.014	0.084	0.44
*China	—	0.49	0.70	—	—	−0.003	0.002	−0.77
*India	IS	0.54	0.70	—	—	0.021	0.011	−2.14
Small, SI								
Uruguay	IS	0.71	0.36	0.53	0.09	−0.070	0.036	−2.37
Chile	IS	0.53	0.89	0.53	0.40	−0.011	0.020	−1.47
*Peru	B	0.77	0.35	0.36	0.34	0.012	0.087	−1.44
*Dominican Republic	P	0.62	0.94	0.43	0.35	0.023	0.000	1.22
*Syria	B	0.70	0.70	0.32	0.48	0.000	0.125	0.72

Neutral[a]

Large, LN							
Spain	B	0.35	0.49	0.14	-0.20	0.034	0.039	-0.33
Colombia	IS	0.77	0.81	0.09	0.12	-0.010	-0.010	-0.51
*Philippines	B	1.08	1.07	0.08	0.13	0.000	0.068	-1.75
*Thailand	B	1.21	1.12	0.10	0.12	0.013	0.047	0.09
*Egypt	M	1.01	0.77	-0.27	-0.31	0.038	0.211	-0.66
Small, SN							
Greece	B	0.30	0.44	0.35	-0.18	0.114	0.106	0.71
Ireland	B	—	1.06	—	-0.19	—	0.052	-1.28
Costa Rica	B	0.57	0.73	0.06	0.01	0.100	0.085	0.63
*Tunisia	M	0.79	0.97	0.05	0.23	0.131	0.048	-0.07
*Guatemala	B	0.80	0.79	0.21	0.13	0.028	0.018	1.26
*Morocco	B	1.05	0.81	-0.16	-0.07	-0.013	0.109	0.14

Outward-, industry-oriented[a]

Large, LM							
Japan	M	1.03	0.85	-0.18	-0.07	-0.014	0.000	-0.40
Yugoslavia	M	0.77	0.94	-0.78	-0.74	-0.003	0.078	-2.39
Korea	M	0.50	1.81	-0.95	-0.97	0.073	0.085	2.91
Small, SM							
Israel	M	0.45	0.49	-0.64	-0.77	0.135	0.261	0.28
Singapore	M	3.09	2.46	-0.16	-0.20	0.121	0.106	4.55
Hong Kong	M	1.70	2.01	-1.21	-1.19	0.070	-0.023	1.87
Portugal	M	0.94	0.58	-0.76	-0.79	0.047	0.116	1.77
Taiwan	M	0.91	1.33	-0.52	-1.18	0.029	0.033	3.18
*Kenya	M	1.57	0.98	-0.69	-0.31	-0.015	0.047	-0.21

— Not available.
*Marginal economies.
Note: Economies in each group are in order of highest to lowest per capita income. See table 4-2 for definition. Economies included in sample in part II are in italics.
a. See appendix to this chapter for criteria for this classification.
b. Chenery and Syrquin (1975, chapter 4).
c. See appendix to this chapter for derivation of this index.
d. Residual between predicted growth from the neoclassical growth equation in table 9-1 and actual growth for the period 1964–73.
Source: World Bank data.

was pronounced, as in Spain and Brazil, it led to a fairly rapid rise from the very low level of manufactured exports in 1965.[10]

Two countries in our sample—Mexico and Turkey—are typical of the distortions produced by an inward orientation, as indicated by low manufactured exports and a positive trade orientation index. Their overall performance, however, has been somewhat better than the average for this group.

NEUTRAL ECONOMIES. Although the neutral category in table 4-3 contains countries that do not fit in one of the other groups, for some of them—such as Costa Rica, Thailand, and Tunisia—this is an accurate description. These countries are identified by average levels and patterns of trade and by only moderate levels of protection. Within our sample, Colombia comes closest to this type, particularly since 1970.

OUTWARD-, INDUSTRY-ORIENTED ECONOMIES. This strategy combines outward-oriented policies and a lack of comparative advantage in primary exports. Except for the two city-states of Hong Kong and Singapore, Korea and Taiwan come closest to this ideal type. Korea has pursued this pattern of specialization further than any other large economy (including the industrialized countries) and hence resembles the smaller manufacturing-oriented economies. Korea and Taiwan are used as the prototypes of the industry-oriented strategy in chapters 7 and 11.

The effects of an outward-oriented policy become pronounced only after the onset of the semi-industrial stage (after 1970 in the case of Korea). The only large countries in this category in the postwar period are Italy, Japan, and Yugoslavia, all of which began with a period of reconstruction. Because of their large domestic markets, industrial output in these countries is less specialized than in smaller countries, as the subsequent analysis of Japan and Yugoslavia will indicate.[11]

The strategy of outward-oriented industrialization has often been accompanied by a large inflow of capital, which implies a shift from production of tradable commodities to nontradables. This pattern is reflected in Israel and Korea and is analyzed in detail in chapter 11.

Strategy and Performance

The typology of semi-industrial countries is used in subsequent chapters as a guide to systematic comparisons among countries. These include comparisons by types of strategy (inward-oriented with outward-

---

10. Spain is classed as neutral on these grounds, despite the lag in trade behind normal levels, even in 1975. The Philippines exemplifies a shift from neutral to more inward-oriented policies between 1965 and 1975, although without any fall in the export ratio.

11. Because Yugoslavia is the only centrally planned economy in our sample, we shall not attempt to generalize from its experience.

oriented) and by structural characteristics (large with small), as well as more detailed comparisons between two economies of the same type (such as Mexico with Turkey, or Korea with Taiwan), for which the typology helps in selecting appropriate pairs. The study of industrialization requires both approaches, since detailed country analyses must be supplemented by comparisons derived from larger samples.

This section examines the relation between trade strategies and sources of growth by extending the analysis of chapters 2 and 3 to the strategies identified in table 4-3. We shall explore the similarities within each strategy as well as the evidence of the importance of other variables not yet included in the analysis.

Efficiency and Factor Use

Development strategies try to accelerate growth either through increasing the supply of labor and capital or through more efficient use of resources. In comparing developed and developing countries in chapter 2, we found large differences in the relative importance of increased factor inputs and increased efficiency as a source of growth. We now wish to extend this analysis to the four strategies of our typology, which generally implies that more open economies are more efficient.

The statistical studies of chapter 9 are designed to address this question by applying alternative growth equations to our sample of semi-industrial economies. In that chapter, the principal comparison is between the neoclassical growth equation, which explicitly considers only the growth of inputs (labor and capital), and an extended model incorporating the efficiency-enhancing effect of shifting resources to the more highly productive external sector. In this chapter, the residuals from regressions based on the neoclassical growth equation are used as indicators of the relative efficiency of different economies.[12]

In both time-series and cross-country estimates of sources of growth, the efficiency of an economy is measured by the difference between its observed growth rate and that predicted from the growth of its factor inputs. In a time-series study of a single country, this difference defines the growth of total factor productivity, as given by equation 2-3. In a cross-country analysis, this difference is a measure of the efficiency of an economy relative to that predicted by the estimated productivity of capital and labor, as given in the neoclassical model of table 9-1.[13]

12. This shift from time-series to cross-country analysis also enables us to increase the coverage from nineteen of the twenty (all except Honduras) semi-industrial economies considered in table 2-2 to nearly the full list of table 4-3.

13. The identification of the residuals as measures of relative efficiency implicitly assumes that there is no correlation between the omitted efficiency variables and the variables included in the regression. In figure 4-1 and in the text, only substantial differences are emphasized.

To make them symmetrical with the time-series analysis, we can express the cross-country results as

$$(4\text{-}1) \qquad\qquad G_V = \hat{G}_V + \delta,$$

where $\hat{G}_V$ is the growth predicted from the increase in factors and δ is the residual between predicted and actual growth for each country.[14] The values of the residuals are given in the last column of table 4-3; they are used to plot the three elements of equation 4-1 in figure 4-1. This figure can be compared with the presentation of time-series results in figure 2-2, with allowances made for the conceptual differences between the two equations.[15]

To what extent are the trade strategies associated with differences in efficiency? And what is the relative importance of growth in factor inputs and of efficiency in explaining differences in the growth rate among countries? These two questions can be examined by referring to figure 4-1. Five of the nine examples of the outward-, industry-oriented strategy are clustered in one group, labeled M, with a median efficiency of $+2.9$ percentage points, while seven of the eleven inward-oriented economies are clustered in another group, labeled I, with a median efficiency of -1.4 percentage points. The median values of the other two groups are close to zero.[16]

Between the inward- and outward-oriented strategies, the difference in efficiency is much more important than the difference in growth of factor inputs; it accounts for over 80 percent of the spread in the median growth rates of about 5 percentage points.[17] This finding provides a starting point for chapter 11, which simulates the effects of different trade and borrowing strategies in an effort to identify the quantitative significance of individual policies.

Several of the observations in figure 4-1 are suggestive of other factors that need to be taken into account in interpreting the comparative results. Although Yugoslavia is classed as industry-oriented because of its relatively high level of manufactured exports, it exhibits the low efficiency thought to characterize centrally planned economies (see chapter 2). On the positive side, Brazil and Turkey both grew over 2 percentage points faster than is typical of countries with an inward-oriented strategy.

Within our sample, Korea and Taiwan are typical of outward-, indus-

---

14. The intercept of the neoclassical model in table 9-1 is close to zero.

15. The time-series analysis of chapter 2, in which factor shares in income are taken to represent factor elasticities, assumes that the return to each input represents its marginal product; the cross-section regression estimates the average contribution of each factor without making this assumption but ignoring intercountry differences. The latter results are discussed in chapter 9.

16. The median deviation for all nine economies in the M group is $+1.8$; for the eleven in the I group it is -0.8.

17. Including the points outside their corresponding clusters, the difference in median efficiency accounts for most of the spread of nearly 3 percentage points in median growth.

Figure 4-1. *Factor Inputs and Relative Efficiency of Semi-Industrial Economies*

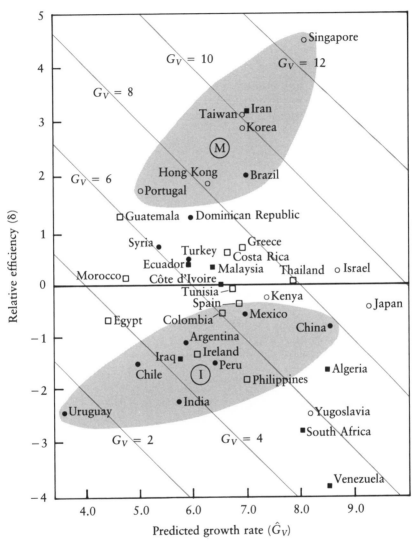

Key: ■ Primary-oriented
       ● Inward-oriented
       □ Neutral
       ○ Industry-oriented
      G_V Growth rate in percent
      M, I Medians

Source: chapter 9.

try-oriented economies with their high efficiency, whereas Mexico and Turkey are representative of large, inward-oriented economies. In addition to Yugoslavia, Israel is an outlier in achieving high growth through high factor inputs rather than through high efficiency. In general, the eight economies that we shall study in considerable detail appear as somewhat above average performers of the three strategies they represent.[18]

Sectoral Sources of Growth

Although industrialization plays an important part in the development of all semi-industrial countries, its timing and contribution to growth vary greatly with the country's initial structure and development strategy. Having illustrated the typical effects of specialization in the previous chapter, we now examine some aspects of intercountry variation in the context of the semi-industrial typology of table 4-3.

In chapter 3, the causes of industrialization were traced to three factors: shifts in final demand, increased intermediate use of industrial products, and shifts in comparative advantage away from primary production. In the early stage of development, the need to industrialize can be offset for long periods by increasing primary exports; in the late stage, the rise of manufactures ceases because final demand for manufacturing no longer grows more rapidly than GNP. In between is a period of industrialization during which a substantial shift from primary production to manufacturing takes place.

How uniform are these tendencies? Has industrialization always been the path followed in practice? We shall examine these questions first for the two decades ending in 1973, a period when the world economy was expanding rapidly and international policies were generally supportive of growth. As elsewhere in this chapter, our primary concern is to characterize the group of all semi-industrial economies as a background for our subsequent study of the smaller sample.

A complete set of data on sectoral sources of growth for the semi-industrial economies is given in table 4-4. It includes the average shares and growth rates for the three main sectors: primary, manufacturing, and services (including social overhead). The industry index in the last column shows the relative contribution of manufacturing to the production of tradable commodities. The contribution of manufacturing to total growth at various income levels is shown in figure 4-2 for the sample (including Norway) and for some developed countries.[19]

Against this background, we can summarize some of the principal relations of these factors to the semi-industrial typology.

18. The exception is Yugoslavia, which is the only centrally planned economy included.
19. For the economies in our sample, the periods shown in figure 4-2 are those in table 3-11, except for the initial period in Japan, which is here 1914–55. The last period in Japan refers to 1970–79 (World Bank 1982). For the industrial countries, the information generally refers to 1950–60, 1960–70, and 1970–77 and is taken from World Bank (1980c).

In the eight industry-oriented economies in table 4-4, manufacturing makes a larger contribution to growth than in other countries at the same income level. The effect of the rising share of manufacturing on aggregate growth is shown in figure 4-2 for Japan (over a longer period) as well as for other members of our sample. Korea and Taiwan stand out as examples of rapid industrialization.

In the eight primary-oriented economies, manufacturing uniformly contributes less to growth than is typical of other countries at the same income level. But the inhibiting effects of the growth of primary exports on manufacturing (the Dutch disease) are outweighed by the accelerated growth of domestic income: there is no case among the semi-industrial economies in which the share of manufacturing declined from 1953 to 1973.[20]

The relative contribution to growth of the sectors with limited trade, namely social overhead and services, is more or less constant across strategies because it is determined mainly by domestic demand.[21] The predicted effect of high capital inflows in raising the share of services is noticeable in some small countries, including Costa Rica, Greece, Israel, and Syria.

The Timing of Structural Change

Each development strategy implies a different sequence of changes in the composition of production, trade, employment, and other structural features. The policies adopted to carry out a given strategy are designed to stimulate certain aspects of this sequence—such as the shift from imports to production of manufactured goods—and inhibit others. But the success of a given set of policies also depends on its indirect effects on trade, employment, and income distribution throughout the economy—effects which are often more important than those for which the strategy was designed.

Issues of timing affect virtually all aspects of development strategy. The exploitation of natural resources for export tends to slow the development of other tradable goods and hence the transformation of the labor force. Direct attempts to accelerate the development of manufacturing, in contrast, tend to distort prices and inhibit the evolution of trade in accordance with comparative advantage. Before these phenomena are studied in detail, therefore, it is helpful to have an overview of the typical relations among different aspects of structural change in industrializing countries.

How similar are the sequences of structural change among countries? This question will be addressed by looking first at the differences between large and small economies and then at the effects of different trade

20. Symptoms of the Dutch disease are evident for Ecuador and Iraq in table 4-6, which extends the analysis of structural change through 1980.
21. Service exports are substantial, however, in Hong Kong, Singapore, and Tunisia.

Table 4-4. Sectoral Sources of Growth in Semi-Industrial Economies, 1953–73

Size, type, and name of economy	Years	Annual growth rates						Value added shares (percent of GDP)[b]		Contribution to growth of GDP			Industry index[c]
		Population[a]	Per capita GDP	GDP	Primary (G_p)	Manufacturing (G_m)	Services (G_s)	Primary (ρ_p)	Manufacturing (ρ_m)	$\rho_p G_p$	$\rho_m G_m$	$\rho_s G_s$	
Large, LP													
*Iran	1955–73	2.9	6.9	9.8	13.4	12.8	5.4	43	13	5.75	1.73	2.35	0.23
South Africa	1953–73	3.1	2.2	5.3	3.5	6.6	5.5	24	25	0.84	1.64	2.81	0.66
						Outward, primary-oriented							
Small, SP													
Venezuela	1953–73	3.3	2.9	6.2	7.6	7.5	5.2	26	18	1.97	1.38	2.90	0.41
Malaysia	1955–73	2.8	2.9	5.7	5.0	8.4	5.6	42	15	2.09	1.27	2.41	0.38
*Iraq	1953–73	3.3	5.4	8.7	7.0	10.1	11.1	53	11	3.74	1.11	3.95	0.23
*Algeria	1953–73	3.2	2.5	5.7	4.9	6.6	5.8	29	22	1.42	1.46	2.83	0.51
*Ecuador	1955–73	3.3	2.1	5.4	4.8	7.1	5.0	36	20	1.72	1.42	2.21	0.45
*Ivory Coast	1960–73	3.7	3.9	7.6	4.2	11.9	8.9	36	16	1.53	1.91	4.24	0.56
						Inward-oriented							
Large, LI													
Argentina	1953–73	1.4	2.2	3.6	2.6	4.4	3.4	18	34	0.48	1.49	1.62	0.76
Mexico	1953–73	3.5	2.9	6.4	3.6	7.2	6.9	17	29	0.60	2.08	3.76	0.78
Brazil	1953–73	2.9	3.9	6.8	4.2	8.4	7.1	21	27	0.89	2.22	3.72	0.71
Turkey	1953–73	2.6	3.3	5.9	3.4	9.6	6.9	41	18	1.39	1.76	2.81	0.56
*India	1953–73	2.3	1.5	3.8	3.9	3.1	4.1	52	19	2.03	0.60	1.18	0.23
Small, SI													
Uruguay	1955–73	0.5	-0.2	0.3	1.4	0.7	-0.3	17	26	0.24	0.18	-0.17	0.43
Chile	1955–73	2.0	2.0	4.0	4.2	6.8	2.4	18	29	0.76	1.98	1.27	0.72
*Peru	1953–73	2.9	2.8	5.7	3.2	7.7	6.5	32	20	1.02	1.56	3.12	0.61
*Dominican Republic	1955–73	2.9	2.9	5.8	4.4	6.4	6.2	24	22	1.05	1.41	3.36	0.57
*Syria	1956–73	3.4	3.3	6.7	2.3	8.0	8.2	25	21	0.57	1.67	4.46	0.75

Neutral

Large, LN												
Spain	1954–73	1.1	5.4	6.5	3.1	7.0	7.4	18	35	0.54	2.43	3.53	0.82
Colombia	1953–73	2.8	2.1	4.9	3.5	6.6	5.2	36	21	1.25	1.41	2.23	0.53
*Philippines	1953–73	3.0	2.6	5.6	5.8	6.2	5.1	38	23	2.19	1.42	2.01	0.39
*Thailand	1953–73	3.1	3.7	6.8	5.5	7.0	8.5	45	18	2.47	1.29	3.12	0.34
*Egypt	1954–73	2.5	1.8	4.3	4.1	7.9	3.2	34	17	1.38	1.38	1.57	0.50
Small, SN												
Greece	1953–73	0.6	6.4	7.0	4.5	9.7	7.3	28	25	1.25	2.38	3.47	0.66
Ireland	1953–73	0.7	3.1	3.8	1.6	4.7	4.6	25	30	0.40	1.43	2.05	0.78
Costa Rica	1953–73	3.1	3.0	6.1	3.7	6.5	7.3	30	20	1.09	1.32	3.66	0.55
*Tunisia	1961–73	2.2	3.6	5.8	6.8	7.0	5.0	27	16	1.86	1.12	2.83	0.38
*Guatemala	1953–73	3.2	1.9	5.1	4.4	6.1	5.2	30	16	1.34	0.98	2.78	0.42
*Morocco	1953–73	2.4	0.3	2.7	2.0	2.8	3.2	33	18	0.65	0.51	1.58	0.44
Outward-, industry-oriented												
Large, LM												
Yugoslavia	1953–73	1.0	4.9	5.9	3.5	5.8	7.7	24	42	0.83	2.43	2.66	0.75
Korea	1953–73	2.3	5.2	7.5	4.5	13.4	7.7	40	20	1.78	2.64	3.13	0.60
Small, SM												
Israel	1953–73	3.3	5.5	8.8	5.7	9.5	8.9	9	34	0.49	3.27	5.07	0.87
Singapore	1960–73	2.0	7.3	9.3	5.4	15.4	7.6	3	23	0.17	3.53	5.63	0.95
Hong Kong	1953–73	2.2	5.8	8.0	5.1	9.2	7.6	3	31	0.14	2.89	5.00	0.95
Portugal	1953–73	0.2	7.4	7.6	4.0	9.8	8.0	25	35	1.00	3.43	3.19	0.77
Taiwan	1953–73	2.8	5.4	8.2	2.7	12.8	8.4	28	31	0.74	4.00	3.47	0.84
*Kenya	1954–73	3.2	2.1	5.3	3.3	6.3	6.7	39	18	1.28	1.16	2.88	0.47

*Marginal economies. See table 4-2 for definition.

Note: Economies in each group are in order of highest to lowest per capita income. Economies included in sample in part II are in italics.

a. 1960–75.

b. Average of the initial and terminal years.

c. $\rho_m G_m / (\rho_p G_p + \rho_m G_m)$.

Sources: Population, World Bank (1977); output, Poduval (1978).

Figure 4-2. *Contribution of Manufacturing to Growth in Selected Developed and Sample Developing Economies*

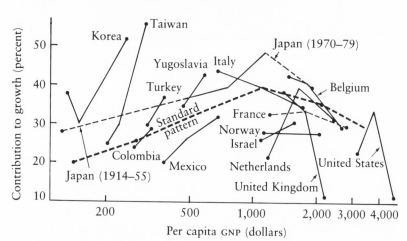

Per capita GNP (dollars)

strategies. Because large countries typically have much lower levels of trade than small countries at any given level of income, we expect them to have a more uniform pattern of production and less scope to alter it by changing the composition of exports. A uniform pattern of production does not necessarily carry over to employment because of variations in productivity.

Large and Small Countries

Our discussion is based on figures 4-3, 4-4, and 4-5, which portray the transformation of production and exports during the period 1953–73, and employment during the period 1960–80. Large and small semi-industrial economies are shown separately to highlight the differences between the two groups. Because industrialization is characterized by a rising share of manufacturing in the production, exports, and employment of the tradable sectors, the three figures concentrate on these dimensions.

In figure 4-3, per capita value added in primary production is plotted on the vertical axis and in manufacturing on the horizontal axis. The change in these magnitudes over the period of observation (fifteen to twenty years depending on available data) is shown by a vector, the length of which is proportional to the rate of growth. A more rapid transformation is indicated by a more nearly horizontal vector as well as by its length (for example, Japan and Korea among the large economies). A similar interpretation applies to the transformation of exports in figure 4-4. The transformation of employment is shown in figure 4-5 in terms of the shares of total employment represented by employment in agriculture and in industry.[22]

The average patterns of transformation are given by the plots for large and for small countries based on cross-country regressions, all of which show a shift toward higher manufacturing shares of production, exports, and employment. A country that lags behind the average transformation of production or exports will appear above the regression line; from such a position, "catching up" is shown by a vector that converges toward the average pattern, as for Colombia or Turkey. For reasons discussed earlier, the transformation of production and exports takes place at an earlier stage in large countries than in small ones.

To compare the paths followed by different countries at a similar point in the transformation, we have plotted lines for constant levels of tradable output and exports. Along these lines, production combinations for the large economies range from Iran to Brazil; those for small economies range more widely from Iraq to Hong Kong. Similar comparisons are made for exports and employment.

The timing of structural change is more uniform in all countries for production than for either exports or employment. Moreover, there is less variation in production among large countries, where changing domestic demand is the dominant factor, than among smaller ones. In fact, figure 4-3 gives considerable support to the idea that larger countries have a fairly limited choice in the balance between primary production and manufacturing.

To develop a rough measure of the variability in the timing of the transformation, we shall use the isoquant for $V_p + V_m = \$200$ in figure 4-3 (where V_p and V_m stand for value added per capita in primary production and manufacturing, respectively), which corresponds to the beginning of the semi-industrial stage. From this we can measure the share of tradable goods provided by primary production in each country at a comparable level of income. For large countries, the range is from highs of 77 percent (Iran) and 65 percent (South Africa and Turkey) to lows of 40 to 45 percent (Brazil, Mexico, and Yugoslavia). This is somewhat less than the corresponding range for small economies: from highs of 80 percent (Iraq) and 72 percent (Malaysia) to 35 percent in Israel and Taiwan (not to mention 10 percent or so in Hong Kong and Singapore).

A similar comparison of the transformation of exports in large and small economies is given in figure 4-4. The large countries follow expansion paths that tend to parallel the average, with countries that lag in manufactures—Brazil, Colombia, Thailand, and Turkey—tending to move toward the average path. These are countries that have been identified earlier as moving away from inward-oriented policies. (Argentina

22. Industry is defined broadly to include mining, construction, and utilities.

Figure 4-3. *Composition of Commodity Output in Semi-Industrial Economies*

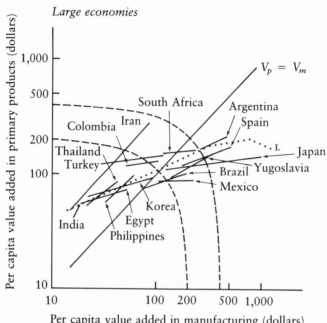

Large economies

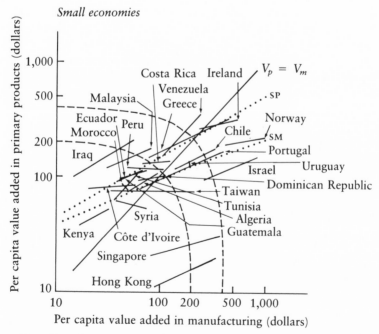

Small economies

Note: Along the ray $V_p = V_m$, value added per capita in primary production equals that in manufacturing. For explanation of L, SM, and SP, see table 4-3.

Figure 4-4. *Composition of Merchandise Exports in Semi-Industrial Economies*

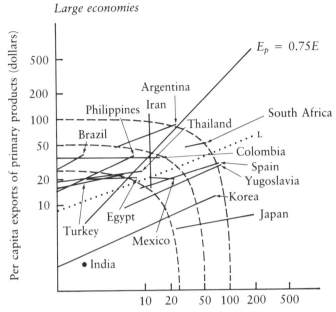

Large economies

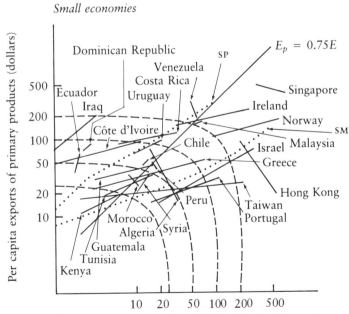

Small economies

Note: Along the ray $E_p = 0.75E$, exports of primary products represent 75 percent of total merchandise exports.

and the Philippines do not exhibit such tendencies.) At a constant export level ($E_p + E_m = \$50$), the variation in the share of primary exports in total merchandise exports is quite wide, ranging from more than 80 percent in Argentina, Brazil, Iran, and the Philippines to less than 20 percent in Japan and Korea. This wide variation has relatively less effect on production in large economies than in small ones because of the lesser share of trade in GDP.

Small economies show an equally wide variation in the composition of exports but considerably more diversity in the direction of change over time. For several mineral exporters—Algeria, Ecuador, Morocco, and Tunisia—improved terms of trade for primary exports have temporarily reversed the tendency to shift toward manufactured exports. For others that have experienced a very rapid transformation—Hong Kong and Taiwan—virtually the total increase in exports has come from manufactures. These tendencies carry over into the production patterns, since exports comprise a high proportion of GDP.

The transformation of the labor force (figure 4-5) falls somewhere between trade and production in its variability, but it bears little relation to country size. The average pattern for both groups shows a reduction in the agricultural labor force that is offset by equal increases in industrial and service employment. There are no exceptions to this decline in the share of agricultural employment in semi-industrial economies over the twenty-year period, but there is considerable variation in the way in which the increase is divided between industry and services. Because the transformation of the labor force involves rural-urban migration as well as upgrading of human capital, this shift is inherently slower than the other transformations, and it often continues well beyond the point at which they are virtually completed.

The typical lag in the shift of resources out of agriculture results in a lower productivity of labor than in the other sectors and, usually, in a corresponding lag in the growth of labor productivity in agriculture. This widening gap in intersectoral labor productivity in the early stages of transformation is documented and analyzed in chapter 8.

Differences among Strategies

The trade strategy of a country is only one of several factors that affect the magnitude and timing of structural transformation. Others are the rate of growth achieved, the initial structure, the population size, and the effectiveness with which the chosen strategy is carried out. Because we cannot hope to disentangle these influences by comparative analysis alone, for now we shall only illustrate some of the typical sequences observable in the period 1960–80.

The previous section has discussed the variability in timing of the transformation of production, trade, and employment and the greater homogeneity of large countries in this respect. To illustrate the effects of the trade strategy and other factors, we have selected twenty-eight econo-

Figure 4-5. *Composition of the Labor Force in Semi-Industrial Economies*

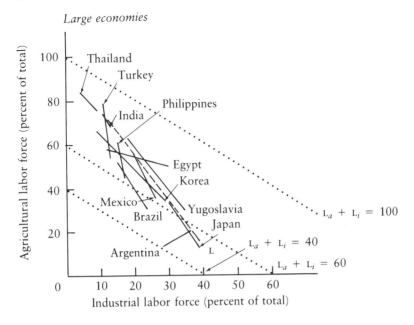

Large economies

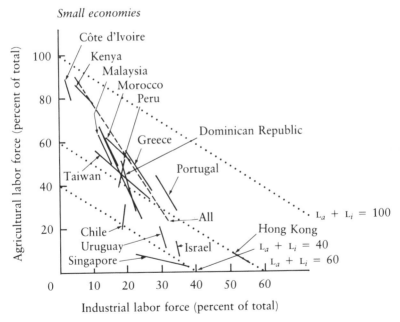

Small economies

Note: The line $L_a + L_i = 40$ represents combinations of employment in agriculture and industry totaling 40 percent of the labor force; the other two lines are similar.

mies from the complete list in table 4-3, omitting eleven that had erratic policy changes or other disruptions to growth. To take into account the variation in initial conditions, we have separated the more advanced economies from those that have only recently reached the semi-industrial stage. This procedure yields table 4-5, in which economies are classified by both trade strategy and level of development. (Further information is given in tables 4-6, 4-7, and 4-8.)

Table 4-5 gives two measures for each dimension—value added, exports, and employment—of the shift of resources over the period 1960–80: the decrease in the share of primary products and the increase in the share of manufactures. Except that they refer to a more recent period, these measures correspond to the slopes of the vectors in figures 4-3, 4-4, and 4-5. Juxtaposing the three dimensions of structural change in this way shows the differences in the timing of the three sets of changes.

The previous discussion leads to three expected relations among trade strategy, initial conditions, and the timing of transformation. First, the primary-oriented strategy and the later phases of the inward-oriented strategy are associated with a low level of manufactured exports and deferred transformation, whereas the outward-, industry-oriented strategy tends to accelerate the growth of manufactured exports and hence the transformation of production and employment. Second, the indirect effects of these strategies on growth—which were discussed above—tend to accentuate these relations. Third, an initial lag in industrial development—which characterized many countries at the end of World War II—is conducive to rapid transformation if other conditions are favorable.

Turning to the measures in table 4-5, we observe a somewhat slower transformation of production in the primary-oriented countries and a rapid transformation in most of the manufacturing-oriented group. As countries approach the industrial structure of the developed countries, the rate of change slows down, as in Argentina, Israel, Japan, and Yugoslavia.

Examples of rapid transformation of production are found for each of the four trade strategies. Malaysia, which has followed a relatively outward-oriented policy with respect to manufactures as well as primary products, is the main exception to the typical slow transformation of primary-oriented countries. In the inward-oriented group, China and Turkey achieved relatively rapid transformations of production despite limited export growth, partly because of their low levels of industrialization before 1960. Brazil has had the greatest success in growing rapidly with a modified inward-oriented strategy, which in turn has led to a moderately rapid transformation.

Turning to the relations among the three aspects of transformation, we note that exports are more immediately responsive to changes in trade policy than is production, whereas changes in employment patterns lag behind. In the inward-oriented category, the earlier effects of import substitution were subsequently modified by more outward-oriented poli-

Table 4-5. *The Timing of the Transformation, 1960–80*

Economy	Size	Annual growth rate of GDP	Changes in share					
			Value added		Exports		Employment	
			V_p	V_m	E_p	E_m	L_a	L_m
Outward-, primary-oriented								
Recent								
Iran	Large	6.9	−5	−3	3	−3	−15	11
Malaysia	Small	7.2	−9	14	−18	18	−13	14
Côte d'Ivoire	Small	7.4	−18	9	−7	7	−10	2
Sri Lanka[a]	Small	4.4	−3	+2	−17	+11	−2	0
Advanced								
South Africa	Large	5.0	4	2	−25	25	−2	−1
Venezuela	Small	5.5	3	0	−1	1	−17	5
Inward-oriented								
Recent								
Turkey	Large	6.0	−18	9	−25	25	−24	2
China	Large	5.5	−8	15	—	—	—	—
India	Large	3.5	−12	4	−16	16	−5	2
Advanced								
Argentina	Large	3.2	−3	1	−20	20	−7	−8
Mexico	Large	6.2	−5	5	−27	27	−19	6
Brazil	Large	6.9	−4	13	−36	36	−22	9
Chile	Small	3.4	−5	−7	−16	16	−11	−1
Neutral								
Recent								
Colombia	Large	5.5	−8	5	−20	20	−25	2
Philippines	Large	5.7	−1	5	−30	30	−15	2
Thailand	Large	7.8	−13	7	−23	23	−8	5
Egypt	Large	5.8	−7	8	−8	8	−8	18
Costa Rica	Small	6.2	−9	5	−21	21	−22	4
Tunisia	Small	6.1	4	6	−24	24	−22	15
Advanced								
Spain	Large	5.6	−16	1	−51	51	−27	9
Greece	Small	5.9	−5	3	−36	36	−19	8
Ireland	Small	3.9	—	—	−29	29	−18	12
Outward-, industry-oriented								
Recent								
Korea	Large	9.1	−22	14	−75	75	−32	20
Taiwan	Small	9.6	−22	20	−39	39	−37	32
Advanced								
Japan	Large	8.0	−10	−4	−17	17	−21	9
Yugoslavia	Large	5.8	−13	−7	−35	35	−34	17
Israel	Small	6.1	−6	3	−19	19	−7	1
Singapore	Small	8.6	−2	17	−25	25	−6	16
Portugal	Small	5.4	12	7	−21	21	−20	7

— Not available.
Note: Economies included in sample in part II are in italics.
a. Sri Lanka has been added since the period has been shifted to 1960–80.
Sources: Tables 4-6, 4-7, 4-8.

Table 4-6. *Changes in Distribution of Gross Domestic Product*

Economy	Primary (agriculture and mining)		Change in share 1960–80	Manu- facturing		Change in share 1960–80
	1960[a]	1980[a]		1960	1980	
Primary-oriented						
Venezuela	27.2	29.8	2.6	16.0	16.2	0.2
South Africa	26.0	29.7	3.7	20.6	22.6	2.0
Malaysia	41.0	31.9	−9.1	8.7	22.5	13.8
*Iran	45.7	41.3	−4.4	11.0	12.0	1.0
*Iraq	54.4	70.4	16.0	9.6	5.6	−4.0
*Algeria	21.2	38.5	17.3	8.3	11.2	2.9
*Ecuador	26.8	32.9	6.1	16.0	8.8	−7.2
*Côte d'Ivoire	44.1	26.6	−17.5	7.1	10.7	3.6
Other large						
Spain	3.3	7.3	−16.0	27.1	28.1	1.0
Yugoslavia	24.0	11.5	−12.5	36.4	29.5	−6.9
Argentina	17.4	14.4	−3.0	31.5	32.6	1.1
Brazil	17.3	13.5	3.8	25.6	38.6	13.0
Mexico	20.8	15.6	−5.2	19.2	24.1	4.9
Turkey	42.7	24.4	−18.3	12.6	21.5	8.9
Korea	38.9	17.1	−21.8	13.8	28.0	14.2
Colombia	38.0	29.8	−8.2	17.3	22.1	4.8
*Philippines	26.9	26.2	−0.7	20.3	25.6	5.3
*Thailand	40.9	27.5	−13.4	12.6	19.6	7.0
*Egypt	29.9	22.5	−7.4	20.1	28.4	8.3
*China[b]	46.8	38.0	−8.8	30.9	46.0	15.1
*India	50.8	38.8	−12.0	14.1	17.8	3.7
Other small						
Israel	11.2	5.0	−6.2	23.1	26.0	2.9
Singapore	3.8	1.8	−2.0	11.6	28.3	16.7
Greece	24.0	19.5	−4.5	16.3	19.4	3.1
Ireland	22.2[c]	18.2	−4.0	26.2	19.5	−6.7
Hong Kong	4.0	1.3	−2.7	26.5	26.5	0.0
Portugal	25.4	13.4	−12.0	29.0	36.3	7.3
Uruguay	19.1	10.1	−9.0	21.4	25.0	3.6
Taiwan	30.6	8.8	−21.8	21.5	41.6	20.1
Chile	20.9	16.2	−4.7	27.9	20.7	−7.2
Costa Rica	26.0	17.4	−8.6	14.2	19.6	5.4
*Tunisia	25.8	29.9	4.1	7.8	13.9	6.1
*Peru	23.5	22.5	1.0	24.2	27.1	2.9
*Dominican Republic	28.6	23.3	−5.3	17.3	15.0	−2.3
*Syria	26.9	20.9	−6.0	20.4	20.9	0.5
*Guatemala	30.5	—	—	12.9	—	—
*Morocco	28.2	22.6	−5.5	15.5	17.0	1.5
*Kenya	38.9	32.8	−6.1	9.4	13.3	3.9

— Not available.
*Marginal economies. See table 4-2 for definition.
Note: Economies included in sample in part II are in italics.
a. Or closest available year.
b. All data on China are preliminary.
c. Mining included in industry.
Sources: World Bank (1980c, 1982).

Table 4-7. *Composition of Merchandise Exports*

Economy	Total merchandise exports (1980) (millions of dollars)	Percentage share of merchandise exports Total primary 1960	1980	Total manufacturing 1960	1980	Growth rate Merchandise exports, 1960–80	Manufacturing exports, 1960–80
Primary-oriented							
Venezuela	10,621	100	99	0	1	−2.6	−4.2
South Africa	13,472	71	46	29	54	6.3	10.2
Malaysia	7,105	94	82	6	18	6.6	12.4
*Iran	6,972	97	97	3	3	0.8	1.5
*Iraq	13,627	100	100	0	0	3.8	0.0
*Algeria	6,398	93	99	7	1	3.3	−7.7
*Ecuador	1,237	99	97	1	3	5.2	11.7
*Côte d'Ivoire	1,392	99	92	1	8	6.7	19.5
Other large							
Spain	10,684	78	27	22	73	11.4	18.4
Yugoslavia	4,314	63	28	37	72	5.8	10.1
Argentina	4,135	96	76	4	24	6.3	17.4
Brazil	10,379	97	61	3	39	6.4	21.3
Mexico	7,893	88	61	12	39	8.0	13.4
Turkey	1,500	97	72	3	28	1.6	14.3
Korea	9,048	86	11	14	89	23.4	43.4
Colombia	2,024	98	78	2	22	2.0	15.3
*Philippines	3,082	96	65	4	34	4.6	16.7
*Thailand	3,354	98	75	2	25	8.4	23.8
*Egypt	1,570	88	80	12	20	0.1	3.4
*China[a]	9,420	—	51	—	49	—	—
*India	3,451	55	39	45	61	3.3	5.5
Other small							
Israel	2,715	39	20	61	80	10.3	12.0
Singapore	9,990	74	49	26	51	8.0	11.3
Greece	2,652	90	54	10	46	11.3	20.8
Ireland	4,377	72	43	28	57	7.8	11.8
Hong Kong	10,164	20	3	80	97	11.0	11.7
Portugal	2,386	45	24	55	76	4.8	6.6
Uruguay	546	71	52	29	48	3.5	6.0
Taiwan	19,196	—	51	—	49	20.1	—
Chile	2,484	96	80	4	20	5.6	14.6
Costa Rica	497	95	75	5	25	6.5	16.6
*Tunisia	1,135	90	66	10	34	4.5	11.5
*Peru	1,734	99	89	1	11	2.9	15.6
*Dominican Republic	496	98	74	2	26	1.2	16.1
*Syria	1,087	81	92	19	8	5.1	0.6
*Guatemala	784	97	77	3	23	6.7	19.0
*Morocco	1,239	92	77	8	23	2.3	7.7
*Kenya	670	88	86	12	14	3.1	4.3

— Not available.

*Marginal economies. See table 4-2 for definition.

Note: Economies included in sample in part II are in italics.

a. All data on China are preliminary.

Source: World Bank (1980c, 1982). Data are for 1960–80 or for closest available year.

Table 4-8. Changes in Employment and Productivity

	Share of labor force						Relative productivity[a]					
	Agriculture		Industry		Services		Agriculture		Industry		Services	
Economy	1960	1980	1960	1980	1960	1980	1960	1980	1960	1980	1960	1980
Primary-oriented												
Venezuela	35	18	22	27	43	55	0.17	0.33	1.00	1.74	1.67	0.86
South Africa	32	30	30	29	38	41	0.38	0.23	1.33	1.83	1.26	0.98
Malaysia	63	50	12	16	25	34	0.59	0.48	1.50	2.31	1.80	1.15
*Iran	54	39	23	34	23	27	0.54	0.22	1.44	1.69	1.65	1.37
*Iraq	53	42	18	26	29	32	0.32	0.17	2.89	2.81	1.07	0.59
*Algeria	67	25	12	25	21	50	0.24	0.24	2.92	2.28	2.33	0.74
*Ecuador	58	52	19	17	23	31	0.50	0.25	1.00	2.24	2.09	1.58
*Côte d'Ivoire	89	79	2	4	9	17	0.48	0.43	7.00	5.50	4.78	2.59
Other large												
Spain	42	15	31	40	39	45	0.50	0.53	1.26	0.93	1.48	1.22
Yugoslavia	63	29	18	35	19	36	0.38	0.41	2.50	1.23	1.63	1.25
Argentina	20	13	36	28	44	59	0.80	1.00	1.06	1.64	1.05	0.70
Brazil	52	30	15	24	33	46	0.31	0.33	2.33	1.54	1.49	1.15
Mexico	55	36	20	26	25	38	0.29	0.28	1.45	1.46	2.20	1.37
Turkey	78	54	11	13	11	33	0.53	0.43	1.91	2.31	3.46	1.42
Korea	66	34	9	29	25	37	0.56	0.47	2.22	1.41	1.72	1.16
Colombia	51	26	19	21	30	53	0.67	0.08	1.37	1.43	1.33	0.79
*Philippines	61	46	15	17	24	37	0.43	0.50	1.87	2.18	1.92	1.08
*Thailand	84	76	4	9	12	15	0.48	0.33	4.75	3.22	3.42	3.07
*Egypt	58	50	12	30	30	20	0.52	0.46	2.00	1.17	1.53	2.10
*China[b]	75	71	15	17	10	12	—	0.44	—	2.77	—	1.83
*India	74	69	11	13	15	18	0.68	0.54	1.82	2.00	2.00	2.06

Other small

Israel	14	7	35	36	51	57	0.79	0.71	0.91	1.00	1.12	1.04
Singapore	8	2	23	39	69	59	0.50	0.50	0.78	0.95	1.13	1.05
Greece	56	37	20	28	24	35	0.41	0.42	1.30	1.19	2.13	1.53
Ireland	36	19	25	37	39	44	0.61	—	1.04	—	1.33	—
Hong Kong	8	3	52	57	40	40	0.50	—	0.75	—	1.43	—
Portugal	44	24	29	36	27	40	0.57	0.54	1.24	1.28	1.44	1.03
Uruguay	21	11	29	32	50	57	0.91	0.91	0.97	1.03	1.06	1.00
Taiwan	56	19	11	43	33	38	0.50	0.42	2.64	1.21	1.30	1.05
Chile	30	19	20	19	50	62	0.33	0.37	2.55	1.95	0.78	0.90
Costa Rica	51	29	19	23	30	48	0.51	0.59	1.05	1.26	1.80	1.13
*Tunisia	56	34	18	33	26	33	0.43	0.50	1.00	1.06	2.23	1.46
*Peru	52	40	20	19	28	41	0.35	0.20	1.65	2.37	1.75	1.15
*Dominican Rep.	67	49	12	18	21	33	0.40	0.37	1.92	1.50	2.38	1.67
*Syria	54	33	19	31	27	36	0.46	0.61	1.11	0.87	2.00	1.47
*Guatemala	67	55	14	21	19	24	—	—	—	—	—	—
*Morocco	62	52	14	21	24	27	0.37	0.35	1.93	1.52	2.08	1.85
*Kenya	86	78	5	10	9	12	0.44	0.44	3.60	2.10	4.89	3.75

— Not available.
*Marginal economies. See table 4-2 for definition.
Note: Economies included in sample in part II are in italics.
a. Relative productivity is measured by the share of value added divided by the share of the labor force.
b. All data on China are preliminary.
Source: World Bank (1982, tables 3, 19). Data are for 1960–80 or for closest available year.

cies, which produced rapid growth of manufactured exports in several of these countries.[23]

These comparisons show that the eight semi-industrial economies in our sample are generally representative of the trends observed in the three strategies they represent. Korea and Taiwan are unique, however, in that they combine all the factors associated with rapid transformation: low initial levels of manufacturing, high capital inflow, outward orientation, and rapid growth. Subsequent attempts to explain their exceptional performance will show that it can be accounted for only by a combination of these factors—along with high productivity growth—and not by the direct effects of the trade strategy alone. The three outward-oriented countries that started from a higher level of industrialization—Israel, Japan, and Yugoslavia—have maintained moderate to high growth rates with less structural change. Finally, the two inward-oriented countries—Mexico and Turkey—are quite typical of the transformation that has taken place in this group.

Appendix. The Index of Trade Orientation

The typology presented in Chenery and Syrquin (1975, table 16) was based primarily on a statistical analysis of the level and composition of exports. An update of this analysis forms the basis for the typology of semi-industrial economies in table 4-3. This appendix describes the principal indicator in the classification—the index of trade orientation. (See also the technical appendix in Chenery and Syrquin 1975.)

The trade orientation (TO) index measures the deviation of the observed trade bias in a country from that predicted for a typical country of similar income and size. The trade bias is defined as $TB = (E_p - E_m)/(E_p + E_m)$. It is a measure of the composition of commodity exports normalized by total merchandise exports. Let E stand for merchandise exports $(E_p + E_m)$. Then

$$(4\text{-}2) \qquad TO = TB - \widehat{TB} = \frac{E_p - E_m}{E} - \frac{\hat{E}_p - \hat{E}_m}{\hat{E}}.$$

The expected trade bias, $\widehat{TB}$, is computed from the predicted values of E_p and E_m, based on cross-country regressions of the form

$$(4\text{-}3) \quad E_i = \alpha + \beta_1 \ln y + \beta_2 (\ln y)^2 + \gamma_1 \ln N + \gamma_2 (\ln N)^2 + \Sigma \delta_j TD_j,$$

where

$i = p, m$
$y =$ per capita income
$N =$ population
$TD =$ time dummy variables.

For table 4-3, separate regressions were run for large countries (those with a population in 1970 exceeding 20 million) and for small countries

23. Notably Brazil, 21 percent; Argentina, 17 percent; Chile, 15 percent; and Colombia, 15 percent (see table 4-7).

Figure 4-6. *The Trade Orientation Index*

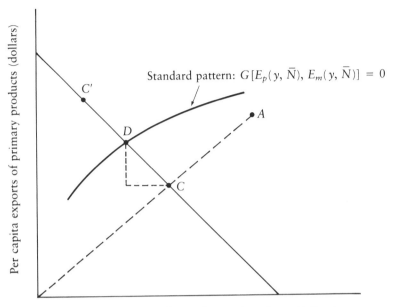

Standard pattern: $G[E_p(y, \bar{N}), E_m(y, \bar{N})] = 0$

for the period 1962–82. The samples consisted of twenty-five large countries with 468 annual observations and fifty-nine small countries with 1,041 observations. Two time dummy variables were included in the regressions—the first to measure a uniform shift after 1973 and the second to measure an incremental shift after 1979. The regression results are summarized in Syrquin (1985c).

The trade orientation index in Chenery and Syrquin (1975) is normalized by total exports including services exports, whereas in equation 4-2 the denominator is merchandise exports alone. This is the only difference between the two. With the definition used here, the TO index has a simple distance interpretation, illustrated in figure 4-6. With size held constant, the "standard pattern" line traces the predicted relation between primary and manufactured exports for various income levels.[24]

For a country with income y, its predicted export bundle is given by point D, whereas its actual position is at A. This country is a high exporter, with both Ep and Em exceeding the predicted levels.

The TO index in equation 4-2 can also be expressed as

$$(4-4) \qquad \text{TO} = -\frac{1}{\hat{E}}\left[\left(\frac{E_p}{EL} - \hat{E}_p\right) + \left(\hat{E}_m - \frac{E_m}{EL}\right)\right]$$

24. In the regressions, the dependent variables appear as shares of GDP. In the graph, it is convenient to express them in per capita value terms in a way parallel to figure 4-4. The TO index in equation 4-1 is invariant to this transformation provided only that the predicted per capita values are derived from the predicted shares.

where $EL = E/\hat{E}$ is the relative export level shown in table 4-3. Dividing the actual point by EL shifts its location from point A to point C on a line of merchandise exports constant at their predicted level. The expression in brackets is the signed "city block" distance between points D and C. The TO index is obtained by dividing this distance by $\hat{E}$. Moreover, because $(E_p + E_m)/EL = \hat{E}_p + \hat{E}_m$, equation 4-3 can be simplified to the following:[25]

$$(4\text{-}5) \qquad \text{TO} = 2\left[\frac{E_p}{E} - \frac{\hat{E}_p}{\hat{E}}\right] = -2\left[\frac{E_m}{E} - \frac{\hat{E}_m}{\hat{E}}\right].$$

An Illustration

Figure 4-7 illustrates the elements involved in computing the trade orientation index for two countries with significantly different trade strategies, Korea and Argentina. The actual trade proportions (as shares of GDP) in 1975 and the predicted values for their income level and size are as follows:

	Actual export shares			Predicted export shares		
	E_p	E_m	E	$\hat{E}_p$	$\hat{E}_m$	$\hat{E}$
Korea	0.044	0.196	0.240	0.089	0.044	0.133
Argentina	0.056	0.018	0.074	0.079	0.073	0.152

The merchandise export ratio in Korea in 1975 (0.240) greatly exceeded the predicted share for a country of its characteristics (0.133), and in addition the actual composition of exports departed significantly from the expected one. This can be seen from figure 4-7 by comparing the rays through the actual point (A) and through the predicted bundle (D). The TO index can be computed thus:

$$(4\text{-}6) \qquad \frac{0.044 - 0.196}{0.240} - \frac{0.089 - 0.044}{0.133} = -0.97$$

or thus:

$$(4\text{-}7) \qquad 2\left|\frac{0.044}{0.240} - \frac{0.089}{0.133}\right| = -0.97$$

In contrast to the case of Korea, the export ratio of Argentina in 1975 fell short of its predicted value, whereas its composition was biased toward primary exports and so had a positive TO index. Its value (0.48) can easily be computed from figure 4-7.

Criteria for the Classification in Table 4-3

In table 4-3, countries were assigned to a category on the basis of their relative export levels ($EL = E/\hat{E}$) and the TO index, measures supplemented by dynamic considerations and an evaluation of their trade strategies. If a country experienced a significant shift in policy or in the two indicators, we tended to classify it by its position in 1975 or by the direction of the shift.

25. The Euclidean distance between points D and C equals $\sqrt{2}\,\hat{E}\mid E_p/E - \hat{E}_p/\hat{E}\mid$, which except for the factor of $\sqrt{2}$ gives the same absolute figures as the "city block" measure but is always positive. It does not distinguish a manufacturing orientation (at C) from an equidistant primary orientation (at C').

Figure 4-7. *The Trade Orientation Index in Korea and Argentina,*
1975

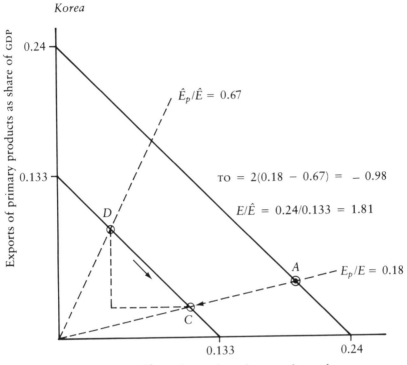

Korea

$\hat{E}_p/\hat{E} = 0.67$

TO $= 2(0.18 - 0.67) = -0.98$

$E/\hat{E} = 0.24/0.133 = 1.81$

$E_p/E = 0.18$

Exports of primary products as share of GDP

0.24

0.133

D

A

C

0.133   0.24

Exports of manufactured products as share of GDP

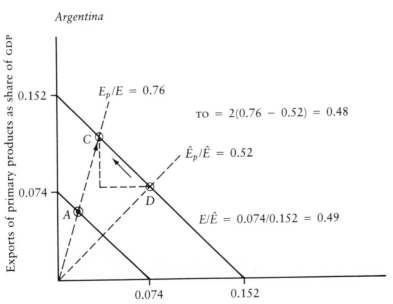

Argentina

$E_p/E = 0.76$

TO $= 2(0.76 - 0.52) = 0.48$

$\hat{E}_p/\hat{E} = 0.52$

$E/\hat{E} = 0.074/0.152 = 0.49$

Exports of primary products as share of GDP

0.152

0.074

C

A

D

0.074   0.152

Exports of manufactured products as share of GDP

Figure 4-8. *Boundaries for the Typology*

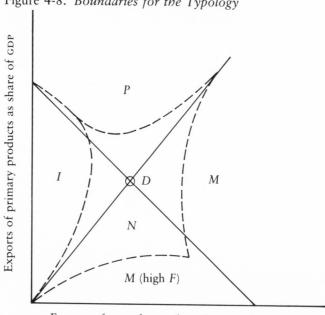

Exports of manufactured products as share of GDP

Apart from dynamic considerations, the critical values of the indicators for inclusion in the various groups are:

- Outward-, primary-oriented: EL > 1.5 and TO > 0. Economies with EL between 1.0 and 1.5 and a large positive TO index were also put in this group.
- Inward-oriented: EL < 0.5 and TO > 0. Economies with EL between 0.5 and 1.0 and a large positive TO index were also put in this group.
- Outward-, industry-oriented, normal capital inflow: Relatively high EL and TO < 0, or normal EL with a large negative TO index.
- Outward-, industry-oriented, high capital inflow: High levels of capital inflow tend to be associated with low export ratios, especially for exports of primary products (Chenery and Syrquin 1975, p. 43). Therefore, a country with a high capital inflow (F) ratio but otherwise balanced will have a low EL value and a negative TO index. To accommodate these effects, we did not include in the industry-oriented group such countries as Greece with high F and a small negative TO index.

Figure 4-8 sketches the boundaries of the classification. Point D represents the predicted export composition and level for the country being classified.

The changes in policies and in the indicators between 1965 and 1975 were significant for Algeria, Brazil, Ecuador, Egypt, Greece, and Spain.

PART II

The Experience of
Industrialization

IN THE NEXT three chapters, we turn our attention to the experience of a small sample of semi-industrial economies during the postwar period. In contrast with the long-run focus of the analysis in chapters 2 to 4, we shall make comparisons over time within a single economy, as well as comparisons across the sample. By concentrating on shorter subperiods, we are able to examine in more detail the impacts of the various development strategies discussed in chapter 4. Our analysis will focus on the characteristics of industrialization and on the effects of different trade strategies on growth as well as on the interactions between aggregate growth and the sectoral structure of demand, production, and trade.

In looking at a small sample and relatively short subperiods, it is always difficult to discern general patterns and to draw lessons for other countries. Our goal is to examine the impact of the choice of a development strategy on growth and structural change. To help us discriminate between effects that reflect the choice of a development strategy and circumstances that are peculiar to individual economies, we use the cross-country model described in chapter 3 as a benchmark with which the experiences of the individual economies in our sample can be compared. Initial conditions such as country size, resource base, and income are controlled for.

To study the characteristics of industrialization, one must consider the interlinked nature of the economy. Especially important during industrialization is the changing pattern of demand for goods as intermediate inputs. The greater use of intermediate goods in production reflects both increasing specialization and increasing complexity of interindustry relations. These trends are part of the defining characteristics of industrialization. The appropriate analytical framework for examining such trends is provided by the input-output accounts and models based on them.

In chapter 5, we discuss a variety of models that start from the basic input-output accounts. In our analysis, such models serve two functions.

First, a model imposes a theoretical structure on historical data. It can be used as a tool for analyzing historical experience by providing a framework for sorting out the relative magnitudes of various important effects. Second, a model can serve as an empirical laboratory for doing controlled experiments. Such counterfactual analysis can provide important insights into the nature of the processes under study.

In chapters 6 and 7, we use the approaches described in chapter 5 to analyze the experiences of our sample of economies: Colombia, Israel, Japan, Korea, Mexico, Norway, Taiwan, Turkey, and Yugoslavia. Inclusion in the sample was determined by availability of comparable input-output data in real terms for more than two benchmark years. As we have discussed in chapter 4, the sample is representative of the semi-industrial countries and spans a variety of development experiences in the postwar period.

In chapter 6, we analyze the relation between different trade strategies and the aggregate structure of growth. The intent is to relate aggregate performance to policy choices and, more particularly, to explore the links between trade strategies, demand structure, and economywide growth. An input-output model enables us to identify which sectors and sources of demand serve to drive the economy forward as "engines of growth." In chapter 7, we turn to the sectoral structure of production and to the determinants of structural change. In examining changes in the composition of output induced by changes in demand, trade, and production technology, and in searching for systematic relations between these changes and industrialization, we turn to such structural parameters as input-output coefficients, import coefficients, the pattern of trade, and expenditure shares for final demand. We also consider the relation between the speed and character of structural change and an economy's trade strategy.

5 The Methodology of Multisector Comparative Analysis

YUJI KUBO
SHERMAN ROBINSON
MOSHE SYRQUIN

THE FIRST PART of this book presented a general analysis of growth and structural change in semi-industrial countries. The variety of development strategies and of levels of performance indicate that there is no one "best" or "necessary" way to achieve economic development. But patterns are discernible, and some strategies appear to be more successful than others. Comparative analysis reveals important lessons and uniformities that invite a more detailed analysis of the mechanisms at work.

In this chapter, we systematically discuss the methods of multisector comparative analysis. Although this will take us back over some of the ground covered in part I, the discussion here will center on methodology. No actual data will be presented except for a simple numerical example.

Comparisons that focus on the structure of production must capture the interlinked nature of the economy and, in particular, the flow of products for intermediate as well as final use. Greater use of intermediate goods in production reflects increasing specialization (that is, more division of labor) and increasing complexity, features that are among the defining characteristics of the process of industrialization. The national product accounts, which measure value added, purposely net out flows of intermediate goods and so cannot provide a suitable framework for analyzing intersectoral linkages. We must turn, therefore, to the input-output accounts and to models based on them.

The input-output accounts present, in tabular form, a picture of all the flows of products in the economy in a given year and thus provide a static view or "snapshot" of the economy. Although such a view is useful for making structural comparisons, it does not suffice for analyzing dynamic processes. In this chapter, we start from the static input-output model and go on to discuss two ways to make comparisons over time. The first is to compare changes between two points in time—the method of comparative statics. The second is to build models that explicitly capture dynamic processes and to use them to provide simulation laboratories for making dynamic comparisons.

The numerical example used in the following sections consists of a four-sector hypothetical economy that expands by 50 percent: per capita income goes up from \$400 in the initial year, t_1, to \$600 in the terminal year, t_2. The four sectors are primary, light industry, heavy industry, and services. The numbers in the example are arbitrary, although the relative magnitudes roughly reflect the main features of typical semi-industrial countries as presented in chapters 3 and 4. (The data are presented in table 5-1 below.)

The Static Input-Output Model

In this section, we first present the accounting elements for a comparative analysis of economic structure. This will be followed by a discussion of some of the problems that arise in such an analysis.

Material Balance Equations

The starting point for making structural comparisons is the material balance equation of the input-output accounts (which was given in slightly different form as equation 3-3):

$$(5\text{-}1) \qquad X_i = W_i + D_i + E_i - M_i$$

where

X_i = gross output of sector i
W_i = intermediate demand for the output of sector i
D_i = final demand for the output of sector i
E_i = export demand for the output of sector i
M_i = total imports of products classified in sector i

Assuming that each sector produces only one output and that intermediate inputs are required in a fixed proportion to output in each sector, we can write the demand for intermediate inputs by a sector as a function of its output:

$$(5\text{-}2) \qquad W_i = \Sigma_j X_{ij} = \Sigma_j a_{ij} X_j$$

where X_{ij} is the intermediate use of commodity i by sector j and a_{ij} is the corresponding input-output coefficient.

Typically, input-output data are presented with imports classified as either competitive—that is, perfect substitutes—or as noncompetitive. If they are noncompetitive, then they are not grouped with domestic products but are viewed as a nonproduced input into a sector, analogous to labor and capital. In the data in part II, we have consistently regarded all imports as competitive so that they share the same sector classification as domestic production.[1]

---

1. For some countries, such as Korea, this adjustment required the reclassification of data for noncompetitive sectors in various years. See Kim (1977) for the details of how this was done.

Imports of commodity i, M_i, are demanded for intermediate use, M^w, and for final use, M^f. In equation 5-1 they appear in the total import supply and as part of both intermediate and final demand. Let u_i^w and u_i^f stand for the domestic supply ratios (the proportion of intermediate and of final demand produced domestically). Substituting these ratios and equation 5-2 in equation 5-1, we obtain the material balance equation for domestic production:

(5-3) $$X_i = u_i^w \Sigma_j a_{ij} X_j + u_i^f D_i + E_i$$

and similarly for imports:

(5-4) $$M_i = m_i^w W_i + m_i^f D_i$$

where the import coefficients are defined as $m_i = (1 - u_i)$ for both intermediate and final goods.

Three points should be noted about equations 5-3 and 5-4. First, exports are netted out of production in defining the domestic supply ratios. This is appropriate when there is no direct re-export of imports. Second, the formulation implicitly assumes that imports and domestic goods with the same sector classification are alternative sources of supply and are perfect substitutes in all uses. But for many intermediate and capital goods such an assumption might be incorrect. Another approach that allows for less than perfect substitution between imports and domestic goods is explored in chapter 11. Third, the domestic supply ratio for intermediate use, u_i^w, is assumed to be the same for all sectors using commodity i as an input but to be different from the domestic supply ratio for final use, u_i^f. In the application in chapters 6 and 7, information about this distinction between intermediate and final imports was not available for the entire sample; therefore, a unique coefficient was defined for each sector irrespective of the source of demand. (For some economies, full import matrices detailing the sectoral use of intermediate imports of commodity i were available, and these were used in the calculations for table 7-7.) The presentation in this chapter will continue to distinguish between intermediate and final imports as in equations 5-3 and 5-4, with occasional references to the more complete formulation.[2]

Equations 5-3 and 5-4 can be conveniently restated in matrix notation:

(5-5) $$X = \hat{u}^w AX + \hat{u}^f D + E$$

and

(5-6) $$M = \hat{m}^w AX + \hat{m}^f D$$

where ^ over a variable denotes a diagonal matrix and A is the matrix of input-output coefficients.

---

2. The general approach is developed in Syrquin (1976, 1985b); the extended equations are given in detail in Kubo (1980).

The A matrix represents the technology of interindustry relations. It has a domestic component and an imported one:

$$(5\text{-}7) \qquad\qquad\qquad A = A^d + A^m$$

where

$A^d = \hat{u}^w A$ = domestic input-output matrix
$A^m = \hat{m}^w A$ = import matrix of intermediate use.[3]

For the domestic material balances, A^d is the relevant matrix. The system in equation 5-5 can be solved to yield the domestic production needed to satisfy a specific level of domestic and export demand with a given technology, A, and import structure, $\hat{u}^w$ and $\hat{u}^f$. The solution is:

$$(5\text{-}8) \qquad X = (I - A^d)^{-1}(\hat{u}^f D + E) = R(\hat{u}^f D + E)$$

where R is the inverse of the identity matrix minus the matrix of *domestic* coefficients.

Table 5-1 presents the material balance accounts of our hypothetical economy at an initial year, t_1, and a terminal year, t_2. The structure of this hypothetical economy and its change over time are designed to reflect the main features of an average semi-industrial country. Table 5-2 summarizes the structural parameters, that is, the input-output matrices and the domestic supply shares. Also shown is the domestic inverse matrix of the terminal year, which is used in the computations below.

In the initial period, value added in manufacturing is already larger than value added in primary production; together, these tradables account for more than half of total GDP. During the period, manufacturing grows at a faster than average rate and primary production at a slower than average rate. Services grow at the same rate as total GDP.

Chapters 6 and 7 demonstrate the importance of further disaggregation within manufacturing. In this chapter, two branches are distinguished— light industry and heavy industry. This distinction serves primarily to illustrate the reduced scope for import substitution in light industry, which is reflected in the large share of domestic supply in that sector at t_1, when almost half the demands for heavy industry products are supplied by imports. These figures are representative of the initial conditions in the sample in chapters 6 and 7.

The technology matrix, A, becomes denser over time. This shows up in the reduction in the value added coefficient for the economy and for all sectors except services, for which it remains constant. Other representative features of the hypothetical economy are mentioned below in the discussion of the results.

Equation 5-8 and the associated import balance equation 5-6 can provide a framework for consistency planning. The simple input-output

---

3. These approximations are needed when a full import matrix is not available.

Table 5-1. *Material Balances for a Hypothetical Economy*
(dollars per capita)

Sector	D	+ E	− M^f	− M^w =	Y	+ W =	X	V
			Initial year					
Primary	51	40	2	12	77	77	154	100
Light industry	113	14	8	11	108	92	200	80
Heavy industry	69	10	33	32	14	73	87	40
Services	181	20	0	0	201	64	265	180
Total	414	84	43	55	400	306	706	400
			Terminal year					
Primary	85	51	4	23	109	115	224	123
Light industry	197	28	10	19	196	192	388	132
Heavy industry	110	22	44	62	26	162	188	75
Services	237	32	0	0	269	128	397	270
Total	629	133	58	104	600	597	1,197	600

Note: Variables refer to equation 5-1. Y is final demand for products of a sector; V is value added.

model can be used to derive the domestic production and imports required to support any projected level of final demand and exports. The analysis, of course, is static, and projections of investment demand must be provided exogenously along with projections of other components of final demand. This framework can then be extended to include dynamic processes either through comparative statics or through the design of explicit dynamic models. Before considering such extensions, however, we discuss some of the problems of using the basic framework for making intertemporal or intercountry comparisons.

Problems of Structural Comparisons

In virtually all countries, input-output data are gathered and tabulated as nominal flows; that is, the entries in the table indicate nominal payments by a column account to a row account. Corresponding to each payment is a flow of real goods and services from a row account to a column account. The problem is to start from the nominal flows and derive the corresponding real flows so that they are comparable over time and across countries.

To see the nature of the problem, define the nominal balance equation explicitly, including prices (but ignoring exports and imports):

$$(5\text{-}9) \qquad P_i X_i = P_i X_{ij} + P_i D_i$$

where P_i is the price of a good i and X_{ij} is the flow of intermediate goods from sector i to sector j. The input-output coefficients are given by

$$a_{ij} = \frac{X_{ij}}{X_j}$$

Table 5-2. *Structural Parameters for a Hypothetical Economy, Initial and Terminal Years*
(all entries multiplied by 100)

Sector	A_1, by sector				A_2, by sector				Domestic supply shares				Inverse matrix for terminal year $(R_2 = (I - \hat{u}_2^w A_2)^{-1})$, by sector			
									Final		Intermediate					
	1	2	3	4	1	2	3	4	u_1^f	u_2^f	u_1^w	u_2^w	1	2	3	4
1. Primary	17	13	10	6	17	11	8	5	96	95	85	80	119	17	13	8
2. Light industry	5	22	16	10	7	25	19	11	93	95	88	90	14	138	31	17
3. Heavy industry	7	16	20	5	12	18	24	5	52	60	56	62	13	20	123	7
4. Services	6	9	8	11	9	12	9	11	100	100	100	100	15	22	18	116
$\Sigma_i a_{ij}$	35	60	54	32	45	66	60	32								
Value added ratio, v_j	65	40	46	68	55	34	40	68								

and the ratio of nominal intermediate flows to nominal output is given by

$$(5\text{-}10) \qquad \frac{P_i a_{ij}}{P_j} = \frac{P_i X_{ij}}{P_j X_j}.$$

For a set of nominal input-output accounts, it is convenient and traditional to define the units of the real flows so that all prices equal one. The coefficient a_{ij} is defined as a dollar's worth of input from sector i required to produce a dollar's worth of output in sector j. When relative prices differ across countries or over time, the units of the various real magnitudes are no longer the same and cannot be compared.

Ideally, the data for all economies and periods should be deflated to a comparable set of base prices—presumably a set of world prices for some representative year. Unfortunately, such comprehensive data are not available, and the comparative analysis relies instead on deflating the input-output tables over time within each economy so that the flows are expressed in constant domestic prices.[4] Thus, although direct comparisons of economies' production levels are not possible, comparisons of production structures and of growth and structural change can be made.

The most straightforward way to deflate to constant prices is to divide the material balance equation for each sector (equation 5-9) by an index of that sector's output prices. Intrasectoral disaggregation, both by source and by destination, has permitted the use of more refined procedures in several of the economies in our sample.[5] Nonetheless, the limitations of the available data have resulted in some estimates that are rather crude. All such comparative work entails a tradeoff between the quality of the data and the scope of the comparison. Although acknowledging the inclusion of data of inferior quality for some countries, we feel that the gains from wider country coverage outweigh the drawbacks.

A problem of consistency arises from the deflation of the material flows. If value added at constant prices is taken to be the residual when the constant price value of intermediate inputs is subtracted from the constant price value of output, then it is possible for the real value added in some sectors to be negative. The problem is that the concept of real value added is theoretically ambiguous, with no obvious single way to measure it.[6] For our comparative work, we define real sectoral value added by deflating current price value added by an index of the sector's own output prices. The resulting set of input-output flows in real terms does not satisfy the accounting identities: real GDP calculated as the sum of real sectoral value added will not, in general, equal real GDP calculated as the sum of sectoral

4. World price data, however, are available for Korea and Taiwan. See Kim (1977) and Kuo (1979).

5. Starting from equation 5-10, separate deflators can be defined for each entry in the input-output matrix. This approach has been used for Israel, Japan, Korea, Taiwan and—on an ad hoc basis—for Turkey.

6. See David (1962) and Bruno (1978).

net final demand. Such consistency is not required for any of our comparative analyses. With our focus on comparing production structures, it seems
best to use a deflation procedure that is theoretically appropriate on the
output side.

Exports and imports raise additional problems. Ideally, exports and
imports should be valued in domestic market prices. In producers' prices,
exports are typically entered at their f.o.b. (free on board) value whereas
imports are expressed at their c.i.f. (cost, insurance, and freight) value plus
tariffs. For identical products, f.o.b. export prices do not equal the corresponding domestic producers' prices when, as often occurs, there is differential pricing. In turn, tariff rates do not equal the corresponding
realized rates of nominal protection under various circumstances known
to have prevailed for many products in all the economies in our sample.
Corrections have been attempted for most of these economies, with
varying degrees of sophistication.[7]

The problems of deflation and data adjustment are sensitive to the level
of aggregation at which the comparative analysis is pursued. In general,
the goal has been to define an aggregation scheme that is comparable
across countries and periods and has as many sectors as possible. For each
economy, we started with the most disaggregated data available; the range
is from 118 sectors in Korea to 20 sectors in Colombia. The finest disaggregation that is perfectly comparable across the entire sample is 14
sectors. We have also used 8-sector and 4-sector aggregations for comparisons when finer detail is not needed. The various sectors and aggregations
are defined in table 3-2 above. Table 5-3 indicates the nature of the
underlying data. From tables 3-2 and 5-3, it can be seen that the comparisons are roughly at the two-digit ISIC level, with some at the three-digit
level. At these levels, the comparisons are probably relatively insensitive to
random measurement errors owing to distortions, although systematic
variations across economies or periods would still cause problems. In the
following chapters, only distinct and robust results are emphasized. The
data base is described in Kubo (1983).

Sources of Growth and Structural Change

The static input-output model described above has been used as an
analytical framework for making structural comparisons. The extensive
data set described above, however, will be used to go beyond static
comparisons to the analysis of growth and structural change over time
during the process of economic development. In this section, we first
discuss some issues in the measurement of sources of growth and structural change and then describe a comparative statics framework that
facilitates intertemporal comparisons.

7. See the studies listed in chapter 1 for a detailed discussion.

Table 5-3. *Data Characteristics of the Sample Economies*

Economy	Number of sectors[a]	Price de-flator[b]	Import matrix avail-able?	World prices avail-able?	Benchmark years[c]
Colombia	20	1958	No	No	1953, 1966, 1970
Mexico	45	1960	No	No	1950, 1960, 1970, 1975
Turkey	25	1968	No	No	1953, 1958, 1963, 1968, 1973
Yugoslavia	29	1972	No	No	1962, 1966, 1972
Japan	41	1965	Yes	No	1914, 1935, 1955, 1960, 1965, 1970
Korea	118	1968	Yes	Yes	1955, 1963, 1970, 1973
Taiwan	58	1971	Yes	Yes	1956, 1961, 1966, 1971
Israel	84	1965	Yes	No	1958, 1965, 1972
Norway	25	1955/1961	Yes	No	1953, 1961, 1969

a. Refers to the lowest level of aggregation at which at least part of the data were available. For further details, see Kubo (1983).

b. Base year for price deflator. For Norway the base year is 1955 for the 1953 and 1961 tables and 1961 for the 1961 and 1969 tables.

c. Years for which data are available.

Source: World Bank data; described in Kubo (1983).

Growth Accounting

The process of development entails both the growth of aggregate output and changes in the structure of the economy. Variations in the structures of production and factor use can only be analyzed in a multisectoral framework. Such a framework is also required for studying the interrelations between structural change and growth. That is, looking at growth only at the aggregate level or simply adding up the sectoral results leaves out an important dimension of the process.

Studies of growth, whether at the sectoral or aggregate level, try to identify its determinants by one of two approaches. The first approach is to build a model (ideally a general equilibrium one) incorporating behavioral, technological, and institutional relations as well as assumptions about the function of markets (see chapter 11). The second approach, more limited but simpler to implement, derives the proximate sources of growth from identity-based decompositions and a few economic assumptions. The following examples all refer to segments of the same accounting framework (see table 3-1). The first two were presented in chapter 2 as applications of the growth accounting approach.

Basic equation or identity		*Growth accounting equation*
$Y_i = f(K_i, L_i, t)$	(2-10)	$G_i = \beta_{Ki} G_{Ki} + \beta_{Li} G_{Li} + \lambda_i$
$Y = \Sigma Y_i$	(2-11)	$G_V = \Sigma \rho_i G_i$
(5-1) $\quad X_i = W_i + D_i + E_i - M_i$	(5-1a)	$\Delta X = \Delta W + \Delta D + \Delta E - \Delta M$

The first growth accounting equation, 2-10, is the standard Abramo-vitz-Solow-Denison decomposition of the sources of growth. It starts from a production function, not from an accounting identity, and relies more on economic theory than the other equations do.[8] The problem with this approach is that a substantial source of growth (λ or TFP growth) has been obtained as a residual, which implies that important factors affecting growth were not incorporated into the original production function.

The second equation 2-11, is illustrated graphically in figure 3-7. It allocates growth to its sectoral origins. In combination with equation 2-10, it gives the aggregate growth accounting from the supply side (see table 2-7 and chapter 8).

The calculation of the sources of growth from the demand side starts from the material balance equation 5-1. Its corresponding growth accounting equation, shown in terms of increments,[9] matches the change in output with changes in its various uses and in imports. This very simple and only mildly illuminating decomposition is the starting point of the more elaborate approach in the following section. As presented below in equation 5-11, the equation is derived from an accounting identity without any further assumptions. Its relation to economic theory is limited to the economic basis underlying the selection of categories in national income accounting. Adding to this accounting identity the assumption of a linear technology for interindustry relations—represented by the matrix A—and an import structure that reflects the imperfect substitutability of similar commodities with different sources of supply (domestic or imported)—represented by the sets of coefficients $\hat{u}^f$ and $\hat{u}^w$—we obtain the more elaborate accounting identity in equation 5-8. The derivation of the growth accounting relation corresponding to 5-8 is the subject of the next section. Before turning to that analysis, we offer some observations on the growth accounting approach.

- The identification of the "sources" of growth does not imply that causal relations have been established or that these proximate sources are exogenous; they may, in turn, be the result of more fundamental underlying causes. They are, however, first approximations and give orders of magnitude of the various effects. Often they provide essential starting points for more structured models and a guide for further research.
- When growth accounting starts from an identity, one must consider whether the categories are analytically relevant and whether the weights associated with them are economically meaningful.

8. See, however, Taylor (1979, chapter 6), which has a useful discussion of identity-based decompositions.
9. This is to facilitate the comparisons in the following sections. The expression in growth rates can be easily derived from the one in absolute changes.

Figure 5-1. *Measures of Growth and Structural Change*

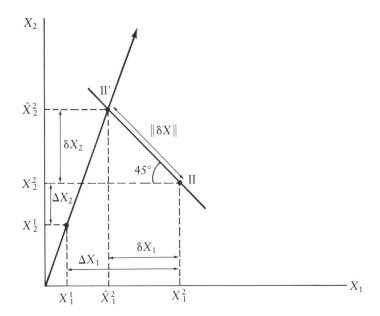

- In interpreting the results, it is important to determine how independent the various sources—such as TFP growth and capital accumulation—are from each other and how responsive they are to policy instruments.
- The supply-side and the demand-side decompositions are partial and complementary representations of the process of growth. Only in extreme cases can we rely on just one of them. Chapter 2 and part III include some attempts at integrating the two. Chapters 6 and 7 focus on the demand decomposition of the sources of growth and structural change.[10] To clarify the measures of growth and structural change used in these chapters, we give a graphic representation and then develop the algebra of a more extensive decomposition methodology.

A Graphic Representation

Figure 5-1 is a graph of growth and structural change in a two-sector model. Initially, the economy is at point I and is producing X_1^1 and X_2^1 (the subscript refers to the sector and the superscript to the period). Later, the economy is at point II and is producing X_1^2 and X_2^2. Aggregate output has

10. For further discussion of these issues, see chapters 2 and 11 and the final section of this chapter.

grown from $X^1 = X_1^1 + X_2^1$ to $X^2 = X_1^2 + X_2^2$, where real output is defined simply as the sum of sectoral outputs in constant prices.

The change in aggregate output is given by the sum of the changes in sectoral output: $\Delta X = \Delta X_1 + \Delta X_2$ (where $\Delta X_i = X_i^2 - X_i^1$). The change in aggregate output, however, conceals significant changes in the structure of production. To measure this structural change, the movement from point I to point II is decomposed into two steps. First, the economy is assumed to grow so that all sectors expand proportionately. This balanced growth takes the economy from point I to point II′, with outputs $\hat{X}_1^2$ and $\hat{X}_2^2$, and the same aggregate output as at point II. Then, holding aggregate output fixed, the structure of production is changed; the changes in sectoral production generated by moving from point II′ to point II are given by δX_1 and δX_2. Henceforth, we shall use the notational convention that small delta, δ, represents a change in structure and large delta, Δ, a change in output between the initial and terminal points. Note that since aggregate output is fixed along the line connecting II and II′, the sum of changes in δ over all sectors must equal zero. With only two sectors, δX_1 must be equal in magnitude and opposite in sign to δX_2.

It is possible to devise a number of summary measures of structural change based on the sectoral measures of δ. One summary measure from figure 5-1 is the "distance" between points II and II′ (denoted by $\|\delta X\|$). The measure $\|\delta X\|$ is the Euclidean distance between points II and II′ and is given by the square root of the sum of squares of the sectoral δ measures.[11] The measure of distance generalizes naturally to the multisector case and will be expressed as a ratio to a measure of aggregate output.

In chapter 7, we use such summary measures of structural change not only for gross output but also for separate components of supply and demand. In all cases, the baseline against which structural change is defined is that of balanced growth, such that sector shares remain fixed. Thus "structural change" is defined as deviations from proportional growth while "growth" alone refers to the change in output.

Decomposing Growth and Structural Change

We next present the equations for separating the sources of growth and structural change. The calculations are illustrated with our numerical example.

OUTPUT GROWTH. Equation 5-8 solves for domestic production given final demand—both domestic, D, and exports, E—domestic supply ratios, u_i^f and u_i^w, and the input-output coefficients, a_{ij}. Between two periods, a change in output, ΔX, depends on changes in the sets of structural param-

---

11. Another measure, used by Chenery, Shishido, and Watanabe (1962), is the average of the absolute values of the sectoral measures.

eters, $\hat{u}^f$, $\hat{u}^w$, and A. After some algebraic manipulations, the change in sectoral outputs can be written as:[12]

$$\Delta X = R_2 \hat{u}_2^f \Delta D + R_2 \Delta E + R_2 \Delta \hat{u}^f D_1 + R_2 \Delta \hat{u}^w W_1 + R_2 \hat{u}_2^w \Delta A X_1$$

or, for sector i:

(5-11) $\Delta X_i = \sum_j r_{ij2} u_{j2}^f \Delta D_j =$ domestic demand expansion (DD)

$\qquad + \sum_j r_{ij2} \Delta E_j =$ export expansion (EE)

$\qquad + \sum_j r_{ij2} \Delta u_j^f D_{ji} =$ import substitution of final goods (IS^f),

$\qquad + \sum_j r_{ij2} \Delta u_j^w W_{ji} =$ import substitution of intermediate goods (IS^w)

$\qquad + \sum_j r_{ij2} u_{j2}^w \sum_k \Delta a_{jk} X_{ki} =$ changes in input-output (IO) coefficients

where R is the inverse of the identity matrix minus the matrix of domestic input-output coefficients $[R = (I - A^d)^{-1}]$, r_{ij} is an element of R, and the number subscripts refer to the periods.[13]

The first two terms on the right-hand side of equation 5-11 are changes in the output of sector i induced by the expansion of domestic demand and exports in all sectors, given a constant import structure. The third and fourth terms measure the direct and indirect effects of changes in the import structure of final and of intermediate goods. The last term gives the direct and indirect effects of changes in the total (domestic and imported) matrix of input-output coefficients, which represent the widening and deepening of interindustry relations brought about by the changing mix of intermediate input requirements. The changes in input-output coefficients are caused, in turn, by changes in production technology as well as by

12. With continuous time and denoting for any variable z, dz/dt by Δz, the time derivative of equation (5-8) is

$$\Delta X = R(\hat{u}^f \Delta D + \Delta \hat{u}^f D + \Delta E) + \Delta R(\hat{u}^f D + E).$$

The derivative of an inverse matrix is given by

$$\Delta R = -R \Delta(I - A)R = R(\hat{u}^w \Delta A + \Delta \hat{u}^w A)R.$$

Since $AR(\hat{u}^f D + E) = AX = W$, substituting in the first equation in this note gives the result in the text.

In discrete fixed weights decompositions, interaction terms arise, but not when the weights of both periods are mixed as in equation 5-11. This index number problem is further discussed in the text. In this and later equations, we present one version of the weights. In all applications, an average of the Paasche and Laspeyres versions is used.

13. This derivation is taken from Syrquin (1976). It elaborates the direct type decomposition first developed in Chenery (1960), which was incorporated into an explicit interindustry framework in Chenery, Shishido, and Watanabe (1962) and in Chenery (1969).

substitution among various inputs (perhaps in response to changes in relative prices), although we cannot separate these two effects without more information.

All the terms in equation 5-11 give the total effects of changes, including the indirect linkages through intermediate input flows in the input-output matrix. It is also possible to define a direct decomposition in which the changes in the demand for intermediate inputs appear as an independent source of total sectoral demand, as in the growth accounting equation 5-1 above. Such an approach disregards the linked nature of the economy and is useful when concentrating on the behavior of particular sectors.[14] In this book, we generally use the total decomposition measures. In chapters 3 and 10, the direct measure is used for analysis that does not focus on linkages.

Four points are worth noting about the decomposition equation 5-12. First, import substitution is defined as arising from changes in the ratio of imports to total demand for each sector. This treatment is natural given the view, discussed earlier, that imports are imperfect substitutes for domestic goods, so that the source of supply is an integral part of the economic structure.[15] With this definition, imports and domestically pro- duced goods in each sector can then be treated separately, while the aggregate contribution of import substitution to growth is sensitive to the level of sectoral disaggregation. For example, it is possible for import substitution to be positive in every sector but for the ratio of total imports to total demand still to increase because of changes in the sectoral com- position of demand.

Second, since the domestic supply ratios for intermediate use are assumed to be the same for all users, the import substitution term for intermediates, IS^w, is an average of the changes in the import matrix. Data permitting, it is possible to incorporate these separate changes into a more elaborate import substitution effect. Since such data are available for only a few economies (see table 5-3), we have not used this refinement in our comparative work.[16]

Third, the effect of changes in input-output coefficients includes changes in the total coefficients without distinguishing between imported and

14. Frank, Kim, and Westphal (1975) argue that the direct measures are more relevant to assess how producers in specific sectors react to various incentive policies. Direct and total measures are compared in Syrquin (1976) and in Chenery (1979).

15. This treatment differs conceptually from the treatment in Chenery, Shishido, and Watanabe (1962), where imports are considered as perfect substitutes for domestic goods. There is an extensive literature on the appropriate definition of import substitution in multisector models; see Arrow (1954), Desai (1969), Morley and Smith (1970), Fane (1971, 1973), Syrquin (1976), and Balassa (1979a).

16. The algebra of the decomposition equation, including this refinement, has been developed by Syrquin (1976, 1985b). The available import matrices are used in chapter 7 (see tables 7-7 and 7-8). Kubo (1980) also summarizes the algebra of the measures used in chapters 6 and 7.

domestically produced goods. Thus, the input-output coefficients may remain constant ($\Delta A = O$), in which case the last term in the decomposition will be zero, even though changes in domestic supply ratios result in changes in $\hat{u}^w A$ (and hence in R). Changes in input-output technology are defined as changes in the aggregate coefficients, including imports, while any changes in the intermediate domestic supply ratios are included in the import substitution term. For example, a change in the total amount of steel required to produce a car is classified as a change in the input-output coefficient, while a change in the mix of domestically produced and imported steel is classified as import substitution.

Fourth, an index number problem is implicit in the decomposition equation because the decomposition can be defined either by the terminal-year structural coefficients and the initial-year volume weights (as in equation 5-11) or by the initial-year structural coefficients and the terminal-year volume weights. The two versions are analogous to Paasche and Laspeyres price indexes. In the analysis below, both indexes have been computed separately for the decomposition in each period, and averages of the two are presented.[17]

The total change in sectoral output is decomposed into its sources by category of demand. The total change in output equals the sum of the changes in each sector and can also be decomposed either by sector or by category of demand. The relations (with the two IS terms combined) can be shown schematically:

$$
\begin{array}{ccccccccc}
\text{DD}_1 & + & \text{EE}_1 & + & \text{IS}_1 & + & \text{IO}_1 & = & \Delta X_1 \\
\text{DD}_2 & + & \text{EE}_2 & + & \text{IS}_2 & + & \text{IO}_2 & = & \Delta X_2 \\
\vdots & & \vdots & & \vdots & & \vdots & & \vdots \\
\text{DD}_n & + & \text{EE}_n & + & \text{IS}_n & + & \text{IO}_n & = & \Delta X_n \\
\hline
\Sigma \text{DD}_i & + & \Sigma \text{EE}_i & + & \Sigma \text{IS}_i & + & \Sigma \text{IO}_i & = & \Sigma \Delta X_i & = \Delta X
\end{array}
$$

Reading down columns gives the sectoral composition of each demand category; reading across rows gives the decomposition of changes in sectoral demand by different demand categories. When making comparisons across countries and time periods, it is convenient to divide the entire table by $\Sigma \Delta X_i$ so that all components across sectors and demand categories sum to 100. Alternatively, it is sometimes convenient to divide the rows by ΔX_i and then look at the percentage shares of the contribution of each demand category to the change in sectoral output. Both presentations are used in this book (see chapters 2, 6, and 7).

---

17. It is possible to define an appropriate Divisia index by specifying the time path of the different variables. See, for example, Fane (1971, 1973). Syrquin and Urata (1985), in a similar context, use mean weights to compute a discrete approximation to the Divisia index.

Computing equation 5-11 for the hypothetical economy yields three forms of the sources of growth (see table 5-4): absolute growth in dollars, the percentage of each sector's growth in output, and the percentage of the total change in output (as in the schematic above and in table 2-7).

Tables 5-1 and 5-2 provide all the data needed to perform the computations in table 5-4. For example, in panel A of table 5-4, heavy industry output expanded by \$101, of which \$7 originated in increased demands from import substitution of final goods throughout the system:

$$
\begin{aligned}
\text{IS}^f(3) &= \Sigma_j r_{3j} \Delta u_j^f D_{j1} \\
&= 0.13\,(-0.01 \times 51) \\
&\quad + 0.20\,(0.02 \times 113) \\
&\quad + 1.23\,(0.08 \times 69) \\
&\quad + 0.07\,(0.00 \times 181) = 7.2
\end{aligned}
$$

In light industry, the domestic supply ratio increased by 0.02. Had final demand remained at \$113, this would have called for an increased production of \$2.26 ($= 0.02 \times 113$), which in turn would have placed indirect demands on heavy industry through the inverse matrix ($r_{3,2} = 0.20$) of \$0.45. Adding up all the direct and indirect effects, we obtain a total effect

Table 5-4. *The Sources of Growth*

		Source of growth				
Sector		DD	EE	IS^f	IS^w	IO
		A. As absolute growth in dollars				ΔX
Primary		59	18	1	−4	−4	70
Light industry		131	27	5	3	22	188
Heavy industry		55	20	7	5	14	101
Services		92	21	1	1	17	132
Total		337	86	14	5	49	491
	Rate^a	B. As percentage of sectoral output growth				Total
Primary	4.7	85	26	1	−6	−6	100
Light industry	8.3	70	14	3	1	12	100
Heavy industry	9.6	54	20	7	5	14	100
Services	5.1	70	16	1	1	12	100
Total	6.6	69	18	3	1	9	100
						Incremental shares
		C. As percentage of total output growth				
Primary		12	4	0	−1	−1	14
Light industry		27	5	1	1	4	38
Heavy industry		11	4	2	1	3	21
Services		19	5	0	0	3	27
Total		69	18	3	1	9	100

a. Average annual growth rate for an eight-year period computed as $\frac{1}{8}(\ln X_2 / X_1)$.
Source: Data from tables 5-1 and 5-2.

of $7. This includes the *decrease* in demand from agriculture because of its *negative* import substitution (or import liberalization). The other numbers in table 5-4 can be similarly computed. Note that the last term in equation 5-11—the effect of changes in input-output coefficients—involves at each step the change in *all* the coefficients in the matrix.

Panel B of table 5-4 shows the relative contribution of the various sources of growth to sectoral output growth. In the numerical example, domestic demand expansion accounts for 85 percent of the growth of output in agriculture, trade effects for 21 percent, and changes in input-output coefficients for -6 percent. This decline in the demand for agricultural output for intermediate use is due primarily to the uniform decline in the coefficients of the agricultural row in the table (compare A_1 and A_2 in table 5-2). A similar result is commonly found in country studies (see chapter 6), and it reflects the substitution of fabricated for natural materials and the effect of changes in relative prices. Input coefficients *into* agriculture (the first column in the A matrix) generally rise as production becomes more roundabout. This is conveniently summarized by the change in the value added ratio shown in table 5-2 (see also figure 3-4 and chapter 6).

Panel C of table 5-4 presents all entries as a proportion of the expansion of aggregate output. The last column shows the incremental sectoral shares.

MEASURES OF TRADE EFFECTS. There is an important asymmetry in the way we measure the effects of exports and of import substitution, which we have to keep in mind when comparing the results in chapters 6, 7, and 10. Exports enter as a flow and their potential contribution is, in principle, unbounded; this is not the case for imports, which appear as ratios to final or intermediate demand. The importance of this distinction varies by sector and period within a country. The values for domestic supply shares in table 5-2 are representative of the experience in the economies in our sample. Domestic shares for final and intermediate manufactured goods in the initial year are about 90 percent for light industry and 50 percent for heavy industry, or import shares of 10 and 50 percent. The scope for import substitution is ample in heavy industry but not in light industry. This can be compared with the import coefficients for several countries in our sample, which are shown in table 5-5.

By the early 1950s, the potential for further import substitution in light industry was severely restricted except in Korea, where rapid import substitution came after 1955. Significant import substitution in heavy industry took place during the period covered by our study except in postwar Japan, where it occurred earlier.

Another element of asymmetry in measuring exports and import substitution is caused by aggregation. The flow of exports is independent of the level of aggregation, but sectoral import coefficients may hide signifi-

Table 5-5. *Import Coefficients for the Sample*

| | | Import coefficient (percent) ||
Country	Year	Light industry	Heavy industry
Mexico	1929	22	75
	1950	6	46
Turkey	1953	2	34
	1963	2	22
Japan	1914	3	27
	1955	2	4
Korea	1955	22	69
	1963	7	42

Sources: For Mexico 1929, Villarreal (1976). All other figures are World Bank data; described in Kubo (1983).

cant intrasectoral variation. Episodes of trade liberalization usually register a rapid increase in exports and in imported inputs. Sectoral import coefficients change little or even rise; this implies negative import substitution. Any increase in intraindustry specialization and import substitution of specific products within sectors would fail to appear in the data, except at high levels of disaggregation.

STRUCTURAL CHANGE. Equation 5-11 decomposes the change in sectoral output. In the terminology used earlier, it represents a tool for analyzing the sources of growth from the demand side. The analysis of structural change calls for a different decomposition that measures the deviations from proportional growth. This sectoral δ measure for a variable X is defined as $\delta X = X_2 - \lambda X_1$, where λ is the proportional change in national income between two years. It is defined as the ratio of total national income in the second year to that in the first. In making comparisons, data are available for periods of varying lengths. Thus, λ need not be an annual rate of growth but depends on the number of years in the period.

Because of the linearity of the input-output system, if all the elements of domestic demand, exports, and imports were to expand at the same rate, λ, then with a given input-output matrix, output would expand at the exact same rate in each sector, and the structure of production would be unchanged. Changes in this structure can therefore be traced back to deviations from proportional growth in domestic demand and exports and to changes in domestic supply ratios and in input-output coefficients.

From equation 5-8, a δ decomposition can be derived analogous to the Δ decomposition in equation 5-11. After some algebraic manipulations, the decomposition (in matrix notation) is given by:

$$(5\text{-}12) \quad \delta X = R_2 \hat{u}_2^f \delta D + R_2 \delta E + R_2 \Delta \hat{u}^f \delta D_1 + R_2 \Delta \hat{u}^w \delta W_1 + R_2 u_2^w \Delta A \lambda X_1.$$

$$\quad\quad\quad (a) \quad\quad\quad (b) \quad\quad\quad (c_1) \quad\quad\quad\quad (c_2) \quad\quad\quad\quad\quad (d)$$

The deviation from proportional growth in output in sector i is seen to be the sum of five sets of structural changes:

   a. Effects of deviations in domestic demand in all sectors, with a constant import structure in all sectors

   b. Effects of deviations in exports in all sectors, with a constant import structure in all sectors

   c_1. Direct and indirect effects of changes in the import structure of final goods

   c_2. Direct and indirect effects of changes in the import structure of intermediate goods

   d. Effects of changes in the total (domestic and imported) matrix of input-output coefficients (ΔA).

In equation 5-12, the material balance equation in the terminal year is compared not with its counterpart in the initial year but with the hypothetical material balance equation in the terminal year under the assumption of balanced growth. The decomposition differs from the Δ version not only in measuring output growth as deviations from proportional growth but also in measuring growth of domestic final demand and exports as deviations.

In the decomposition of the deviation measure, import substitution and technical change are still defined in terms of changes in domestic supply ratios and input-output coefficients, respectively. Thus, the last three terms in equation 5-12 are almost identical with the corresponding terms in the Δ decomposition. Given that the nonproportional components of domestic demand and export growth are generally smaller than their increments, the relative importance of import substitution and of changes in input-output coefficients will be greater in accounting for compositional changes in output than in accounting for total growth.

In the diagrammatic presentation of the δ measure in figure 5-1, it was noted that the sum of the deviations from proportional growth across all sectors must be zero. This result will also hold for the decomposition equation if λ (the change in national income between two years) is defined in terms of total sectoral production. If the input-output coefficients do not change ($\Delta A = 0$), then—under the assumption of balanced growth— the ratio of the aggregate value of intermediate goods to value added remains constant over time, and both value added and gross output will grow at the same rate. If the input-output coefficients do change, however, then even under the assumption of balanced growth, total value added and gross output will grow at different rates. In this case, since we define λ as the change in total value added, the sum of the δ measures across sectors will not equal zero. The difference from zero will reflect the change in the ratio of aggregate value added to total output.

Table 5-6 presents the sources of deviations from balanced growth in the same format in which table 5-4 presents the sources of growth. To

Table 5-6. *Deviation from Balanced Growth*
($\lambda = Y_2/Y_1 = 1.5$)

Sector	DD	EE	IS^f	IS^w	IO	δX
			Source of deviation			
	A. Absolute deviation in dollars					
Primary	12	−8	1	−6	−6	−7
Light industry	33	11	7	5	32	88
Heavy industry	8.5	9	11	8	21	57.5
Services[a]	−33	4	2	1	25.5	−0.5
	B. As percent of sectoral output deviation from balanced growth					Total
Primary	172	−114	14	−86	−86	−100
Light industry	37	13	8	6	36	100
Heavy industry	15	16	19	14	36	100
Services[a]	−	+	+	+	+	−100
						$\dfrac{\delta x_i}{\Delta X}$
	C. As percent of total output growth					
Primary	2.4	−1.6	0.2	−1.2	−1.2	−1.4
Light industry	6.7	2.2	1.4	1.0	6.5	17.8
Heavy industry	1.7	1.8	2.2	1.6	4.3	11.6
Services[a]	−6.7	0.8	0.4	0.2	5.2	−0.1

a. Because of the small size of the sectoral deviation, only the signs of the sources of deviation from proportional growth are shown and not the relative magnitudes.

Source: Data from tables 5-1 and 5-2.

clarify the computations, we explicitly derive the effect of nonproportional export expansion on light industry:

$$\text{EE}(2) = \Sigma_j r_{2j} \delta E_j = \Sigma_j r_{2j}(E_{2j} - \lambda E_{1j})$$
$$= 0.14 \, [51 - (1.5 \times 40)]$$
$$+ 1.38 \, [28 - (1.5 \times 14)]$$
$$+ 0.31 \, [22 - (1.5 \times 10)]$$
$$+ 0.17 \, [32 - (1.5 \times 20)] = 10.9$$

In explaining structural change, import substitution emerges as much more important than in the decompositions of total expansion. Domestic demand, as expected, is no longer the dominant effect.

Trade and Input Use

The various output decompositions start from the material balance equation for domestic production (5-3). Analogous decompositions for imports can be derived from the balance equation for imports (5-4).[18] This equation analyzes imports by sector of origin. Intermediate imports can also be studied by sector of use by being considered as inputs into the

18. The equations can be found in Syrquin (1976).

sector's production process. This approach recognizes explicitly that to sustain an increase in output, imports—which are imperfect substitutes for domestic products—are going to be needed as intermediate inputs. Ideally, an import matrix should be used in this analysis. When one is not available, it can be approximated by $\hat{m}A$—as in some entries in table 7-7—or by $\hat{m}^w A$—as in the example in this chapter. Considering intermediate imports by sector of use will help us to examine the relation between export expansion and its import requirements.

IMPORT CONTENT OF EXPORTS. The production needed for a given level of exports requires imports as intermediate inputs. We now develop a measure of the total import content of exports (ICE).

Let $Q = A^m R$, where A^m is an import matrix. A typical element of Q—q_{ij}—gives the total imports of commodity i needed to generate one unit of *final* product of sector j. The column sums of Q then give the total import content in one unit of final product in each sector. The Q matrix for the terminal year in our example is given in table 5-7. One dollar of final product from the light industry sector (sector 2) calls for 3.6 cents of imported primary goods, 5.2 cents of imported light industry products, and so on. Adding up all the requirements, we find a total import bill of 20 cents or an import content of 20 percent.

The equation for the import content of exports (ICE) is $\text{ICE} = e' Q S^e$, where e' is the unit row vector $(1, \ldots, 1)$ and S^e is the column vector of export shares. Since $e'Q$ equals the row of column sums, we find in our case that

$$\text{ICE}_2 = 0.161(0.38) + 0.20(0.21) + 0.238(0.17) + 0.072(0.24) = 0.16$$

where the figures in parentheses are the export shares from table 5-1. Each dollar of exports generates imports of 16 cents. The actual computations in our sample appear in table 7-7.

Table 5-7. *Trade and Input Use: Import Content of Final Demand*
(percent)

	Sector			
Sector	1	2	3	4
1. Primary	4.4	3.6	3.9	1.6
2. Light industry	3.4	5.2	5.8	2.1
3. Heavy industry	6.7	9.2	11.7	2.8
4. Services	1.6	2.0	2.4	0.7
Total	16.1	20.0	23.8	7.2

Note: $Q = A^m R$.
Source: Data from tables 5-1 and 5-2.

MANUFACTURING AND THE BALANCE OF TRADE. Our final decomposition computes the effect of manufacturing on the balance of trade. Each sector within manufacturing makes a positive contribution to the trade balance—that is, earns foreign exchange—by exporting, and it generates demands for foreign exchange for two uses: to purchase intermediate imports to sustain production whether for export or not, and to purchase final competitive imports of goods similar to those produced and exported by the sector (intraindustry trade). The various components can be summarized for any period as:

$$BPC_i = \Delta E_i - \Delta M_i^{*w} - \Delta M_i^f$$

where

BPC_i = balance of trade contribution by sector i
ΔE_i = change in exports of sector i
ΔM_i^{*w} = change in intermediate imports *used* by sector i
ΔM_i^f = change in final imports of commodities of sector i

To allow comparisons of the various components across countries and over time, the figures are divided by the change in exports of total manufacturing. The results of such calculations appear in table 5-8 (and in table 7-8). The first column of table 5-8 gives the change in exports for two sectors as a percentage of the change in total manufacturing exports. The second column gives the increase in imports of final goods from the same sector. The minus sign means that foreign exchange flows out. The third column gives the change in intermediate imports from all sectors generated by the expansion of total output (not just exports) in each sector. The net effect on the balance of trade is reported in the last column. In our example, the manufacturing sector in all its manifestations in the economy made a negative contribution to the trade balance.

PRIMARY INPUTS. In the discussion so far, the emphasis has been on the material balance equations and, therefore, on the structure of demand for domestic production and imports. We have ignored the cost structure of production on the supply side, except for intermediate input requirements. Primary inputs—labor and capital—and payments for these services—value added—have not been considered at all.

The ratios of value added, employment, and capital stock to gross output have often been considered as structural parameters reflecting income generation, labor productivity, and capital requirements associated with production processes. Trends in these parameters mirror changes in the factor intensity of production as well as shifts in resource allocation that are the result of changes in production technology, relative prices, demand conditions, and so forth. Such trends crucially affect the sectoral pattern of factor use and value added. In turn, growth and

Table 5-8. *Trade and Input Use: Manufacturing and the Balance of Trade*
(percentage of total manufacturing exports)

Sector	Exports (E_i)	Final imports $(-M_i^f)$	Intermediate imports used $(-M_i^{*\,\omega})$	Contribution to balance of trade $(=BPC)$
Light industry	54	-8	-85	-39
Heavy industry	46	-42	-50	-46
Total manufacturing	100	-50	-135	-85

Source: Data from tables 5-1 and 5-2.

structural change generate increased demands for primary and intermediate inputs and bring about changes in the volume and sectoral structure of value added.

To sort out the various effects of output growth and changes in structural parameters on factor use, the same decomposition framework used above can be applied. For example, the level of employment, L_i, can be expressed by the product of the labor-output ratio (the inverse of labor productivity), l_i, and output, X_i:

$$(5-13) \qquad\qquad L_i = l_i X_i.$$

The change in employment over time can be separated into two effects, one related to a change in the labor coefficient and the other to growth in production:

$$(5-14) \qquad\qquad \Delta L_i = l_i \Delta X_i + \Delta l_i X_i.$$

The change in output can be further decomposed, as in equation 5-11.

The last term in equation 5-14 shows the effect on employment of a change in labor productivity. Labor coefficients usually decline during industrialization, so the last term will generally be negative. The change in labor coefficients reflects an aspect of technological change quite different from that captured by changes in input-output coefficients, although the effects may be related. The decomposition treats the changes in l over time as exogenous. No explanation of the source of such changes in labor productivity is offered. An adequate treatment of factor inputs and their contribution to growth requires an analytical framework different from that used so far. Such a framework will be sketched in part III.

A Dynamic Computable General Equilibrium Model

In the comparative statics analysis, there are no explicit links between the two points being compared. The input-output model for each year is essentially timeless and does not consider the dynamic forces that move the economy from the earlier to the later state. To extend the framework requires an explicit model of the dynamic linkages.[19] In this section, we consider a dynamic computable general equilibrium model, which explicitly includes market interactions that work through price mechanisms.[20] Such a model is used in chapter 11 to analyze the medium- to long-term effect on an economy's performance and structure of different choices of development strategy.

A CGE model differs from the input-output model in two essential respects. First, many of the linear relationships in the input-output model are replaced by nonlinear functions that incorporate possibilities for substitution in both production and demand. Second, and perhaps more important, the model simulates the workings of the markets for labor, goods, and foreign exchange and so embodies prices and market mechanisms as main elements of the economic system. Given the behavioral and technological assumptions, the model endogenously determines wages, profits, product prices, and the exchange rate; sectoral production, employment, consumption, investment, exports, and imports; and the nominal flow of funds, including the accounts of the government, the private sector, and foreign trade. The price system in the CGE model is thus much more elaborate than in the input-output model and requires that the model be fully "closed" in the sense that all elements determining supply and demand are included.

Conceptually, the dynamic CGE model used in chapter 11 consists of two distinct submodels: a static, within-period model and a between-period model that provides the needed intertemporal links. The between-period model takes as exogenous all the variables solved in previous periods and generates all the variables that the within-period model takes as exogenous in the next period. The overall model is thus recursive in time; to solve for the current period requires only solutions from previous periods.

The dynamic model uses two kinds of intertemporal equations: behavioral equations, which depend on the history generated by the model, and time-trend equations, which impose exogenous trends on some variables. The specification of the intertemporal equations depends largely on the focus of the analysis. A model with a five-year time horizon that studies year-to-year adjustments will be very different from a model that focuses

19. An extension of the static input-output model that explicitly incorporates capital accumulation but not incentives and markets is the dynamic input-output model. Chapter 2 of Dervis, de Melo, and Robinson (1982) has a useful presentation of the model. Kubo, Robinson, and Urata (1986) apply such a model to two of the countries in this study.

There have also been attempts—often using linear programming formulations—to extend the basic input-output model to include more possibilities for choice and consideration of costs and prices. For a survey, see Blitzer, Clark, and Taylor (1975).

20. Early CGE models for planning started from the work of Johansen (1960). For a survey of issues and models applied to developing countries, see Dervis, de Melo, and Robinson (1982) and Robinson (1986).

on cumulative processes affecting structural change in the long run, such as the model used in chapter 11.

The recursive structure inherent in using separate within-period and between-period models implies that the dynamic model does not achieve full intertemporal equilibrium; that is, all expectations are not realized. Instead, the intertemporal model provides imperfect dynamic adjustments to intertemporal disequilibria that emerge from the within-period solutions of the static CGE model. During a long period, however, the dynamic model does converge to a growth path with equilibrium characteristics. The details of the dynamic specification are discussed in chapter 11.

The Methodology of Model-Based Comparisons

The models that have been presented in this chapter offer a variety of tools for conducting comparative analysis. Any useful comparative framework should allow one to ask "what if" questions that reveal interesting features of the economic structure being analyzed. For example, the simple input-output model makes it possible to capture the interdependence in an economy arising from the flow of intermediate inputs among sectors; one can describe the indirect as well as the direct demands for gross production arising from a given structure of final demand under the assumption of fixed input-output coefficients. The "what if" question in this case is simple: what are the total sectoral demands if the input-output coefficients are fixed? Nonetheless, even such a simple model is useful in comparing production across countries since it relates variations in production structures to differences in the structure of final demand and in the input-output coefficients.

The comparative statics analysis, which decomposes changes in gross production over time and allocates them among various sources of demand, provides a somewhat more sophisticated comparative framework. Although apparently very simple, the underlying model embodies a host of behavioral as well as technological assumptions. Any comparative analysis based on this structure is contingent on these assumptions, which need to be clearly understood.

As we shall see in chapters 6 and 7, the comparative statics framework permits a much richer analysis than is possible with the simple input-output model. The assumptions relating to technology and foreign trade, while strong, are theoretically justifiable, and they facilitate comparative analysis that focuses on the relative importance of internal and external influences on growth and structural change. Such an approach is crucial to understanding the process of development as it has occurred in the semi-industrial countries in the postwar period.

CGE models differ from input-output models not only in degree but also in kind. The simpler models are valuable because they permit the separate analysis of particular effects, comparable in a sense to partial derivatives in mathematics: holding all other variables constant, what is the effect of changes in one variable? But such a model cannot be used to ask a complex counterfactual question such as: what would have happened in a particular country if it had followed a different development strategy from the one it actually pursued? Such a "what if" question is different in kind from the sort of decomposition analysis that can be pursued with simpler models.

Counterfactual comparative analysis requires a model structure that can capture all the important effects that impinge on the question under consideration. The model serves as a simulation laboratory, providing a framework in which one can do controlled empirical experiments. It is used to make projections conditional on the specification of a set of exogenous variables and parameters that constitute an "interesting" experiment—for example, the specification of an alternative development strategy. The results are then compared with a base run or with actual history to see what would have happened differently. The realism of the comparison depends, first, on how well the model specification captures all the essential features of the economy and, second, on how accurately the set of variables and parameters that define the experiment is specified.

A model suitable for counterfactual analysis can also be used for doing sensitivity analysis and simple decomposition analysis. Indeed, such experiments play an important part in validating a model, that is, in determining whether a model's behavioral structure accurately reflects the important factors under consideration. Although a complex model can be used for simple analysis, one should always remember Occam's razor: when two competing hypotheses both explain the facts, pick the simpler. For comparative modeling, the principle might be restated as: use the simplest and clearest model sufficient to do the job. For example, if relative prices do not change, than a CGE model will not add much to the simpler input-output system.

As social scientists, economists are generally hindered in their enquiries by being unable to do controlled experiments. They must make do with an analysis of the experiments that history has seen fit to provide. In this situation, an empirical model can serve two important functions.

First, the model can be a tool for analyzing historical experience to sort out the relative magnitudes of various important effects. The model imposes a theoretical structure on the historical data. It is a separate problem to test the validity of the theoretical structure—that is a task for statistical analysis. In the work described in the rest of part II, the opportunities for such statistical analysis are limited because of the relatively few observations available over time.

Second, the model can provide an empirical laboratory for doing controlled experiments. Since history's experiments are limited, the model can be designed to capture the important structural features of an economy and then be used for experimental work. Such counterfactual experiments can provide important insights into the nature of the processes under study—insights otherwise not obtainable. Although any structural model must of necessity simplify reality, the complexity that can be captured in such an empirical model often defies analysis by means of theoretical models. The potentially important interactions in even a simple multisector, general equilibrium model usually cannot be sorted out with partial equilibrium tools, although such theoretical analysis is useful in pointing to the principal effects that need to be evaluated empirically.

Inevitably, models that focus on one set of issues must neglect others; it is neither feasible nor desirable to try to capture all the complexity of a developing economy in one model. The models described in this chapter are not intended to provide an all-purpose framework suitable for analyzing any problem, but rather a framework suitable for analyzing the long-term features of industrialization, growth, and structural change. Quite different models would be required to analyze problems of short-term adjustment or income distribution.

Given the need for simplification, a model must be constructed from basic building blocks that capture the important forces at work. A step-by-step approach, using a variety of models, seems best for analyzing complex, dynamic processes. Part I laid the groundwork for such an approach by reviewing the experience of a large number of countries in an effort to identify certain universal features or stylized facts that characterize the process of industrialization. The multisector models described in this chapter provide the framework for a more detailed analysis of the experience of a few economies. These models focus on intersectoral linkages and can provide a more complete picture of industrialization and growth than is possible in a more aggregate analysis.

6 Trade Strategies and Growth Episodes

YUJI KUBO

JAIME DE MELO

SHERMAN ROBINSON

IN CHAPTER 4, systematic variations in the development patterns of semi-industrial countries were found to be associated with differences in income, country size, resource base, and trade orientation. Though suggestive, these findings do not enable us to identify the impact of particular policy choices on patterns of development. The purpose of this chapter is to link country policy choices with the structural changes that occur during industrialization while taking into account initial conditions that delineate the boundaries of what is feasible.

The underlying analytical framework is the input-output methodology discussed in chapter 5. Focusing on the sources of growth from the demand side, we turn in this chapter to the connection between different development strategies—particularly trade strategies—and the aggregate structure of demand. Chapter 7 probes the relation between growth and various measures of intersectoral linkages and structural change at a more disaggregated level.

Development strategies have been categorized in various ways. They can be described in terms of factor accumulation; for example, natural-resource-based intensive, physical capital intensive, or human capital intensive. Or they can be described in terms of income distribution; for example, "grow first, redistribute later" or "redistribute first, grow later." Strategies have also been defined by their sectoral emphasis; for example, agriculture-led or industry-led development. Finally, strategies have been defined in terms of trade policies, as, for example, export-led growth or import substituting industrialization.

In this chapter, we concentrate on development strategies defined in terms of trade policies. When we speak of a change in development strategy, we shall be referring primarily to a change in foreign trade regime involving instruments such as the exchange rate and quantitative and price controls on imports and exports. We shall also be looking at policies other than trade policies and shall use the term policy regime to refer to the application of the panoply of government instruments to the economy. Recall that in chapter 3, "typical" countries were defined by trade orientation as well as size: primary versus manufacturing exporters and small versus large countries. In chapter 4 (table 4-3), this categorization was further refined for the semi-industrial countries by distinguishing four trade strategies: primary-oriented, inward-oriented, manufacturing-oriented, and neutral (the last being the residual group which included Colombia). In that discussion (with the exception of Colombia), the economies in our sample were classified as either inward-oriented or industry-oriented on the basis of long-term trends rather than specific policy choices. We examine the effect of changes in trade strategies with the input-output methodology introduced in chapter 5. Because input-output data are available for only a few benchmark years in each economy, our analysis of the impact of different policy regimes has to take place for "episodes" defined by the years for which these input-output data are available.

We begin with a brief discussion of the aggregate performance of our sample of nine economies during the postwar period. This is followed by a comparison of the performance of the sample with that of other semi-industrial countries. Next, we show that in most cases the data-determined benchmark years defining the episodes are characterized by coherent policy regimes and so can be seen as reflecting particular trade strategies. This allows us, later on in the chapter, to use an episode as the unit of analysis for identifying typologies of trade strategies and to examine the growth patterns of the nine economies under different trade strategies. Finally, we examine the sequence of trade strategies through time.

Initial Conditions and Aggregate Performance

Table 6-1 presents some basic indicators for the benchmark years for each economy in the sample. These were years of rapid expansion in world trade, especially in manufactures, and of generally good performance by developing countries. For example, from 1960 to 1970 the middle-income oil-importing countries achieved an average annual growth rate of GDP of 5.9 percent, compared with an average rate of 5.1 percent for the industrial market economies (World Bank 1981, table 2, pp. 136–37). For the same period, total merchandise exports for the middle-income oil-importing countries grew at 6.3 percent a year and imports by 7.7 percent a year (World Bank 1981, p. 148).

The data in table 6-1 indicate that our sample performed well, even by the standards of middle-income countries. The growth rates of per capita GNP are generally respectable and rising during the period. A number of factors contributed to their growth performance. Structural change was important and will be a major theme of the analysis below. Also, average investment rates generally rose, sometimes dramatically. The two exceptions, Norway and Yugoslavia, started with very high rates, which then fell to about 25 percent. Korea and Taiwan benefited from substantial foreign assistance in the early periods, which was later replaced by direct

Table 6-1. *Comparative Economic Indicators for Sample Economies*

Economy	Year[a]	Population		Per capita GNP[c]		Percentage of GDP				
		Number of people (million)	Average annual growth rate[b] (percent)	Level (dollars)	Average annual growth rate[b] (percent)	Imports	Exports	Investment	Primary value added	Industry value added
Colombia	1953	12.5		274		—	—	15.3	40.4	18.0
	1966	18.4	3.0	330	1.4	15.1	12.1	20.4	32.4	22.4
	1970	20.6	2.9	369	2.8	15.8	14.2	21.5	30.7	23.0
Mexico	1950	26.3		380		13.9	14.1	13.5	23.1	24.6
	1960	36.0	3.2	479	2.9	12.8	11.3	20.1	17.5	26.7
	1970	50.4	3.4	670	3.4	10.1	8.1	19.6	12.7	30.9
	1975	60.0	3.5	751	2.3	10.9	7.7	24.4	1.2	32.6
Turkey	1953	22.8		239		—	—	12.4	51.1	12.1
	1963	29.7	2.7	319	2.9	10.3	5.5	15.4	40.7	19.0
	1968	33.5	2.4	377	3.3	7.5	5.3	18.0	32.3	24.4
	1973	38.3	2.7	461	4.1	10.0	7.6	19.0	31.0	24.5
Yugoslavia	1962	18.8		469		17.1	16.0	30.9	24.4	40.1
	1966	19.6	1.0	581	5.5	20.5	19.5	25.5	24.6	40.1
	1972	20.8	1.0	781	5.1	24.1	22.0	26.3	16.8	42.2

Country	Year									
Japan	1914	52.4	—	265	—	17.3	17.7	16.6	28.3	28.8
	1935	69.2	1.3	416	2.2	21.5	21.5	18.1	16.6	34.4
	1955	89.0	—	500	—	10.1	10.7	24.7	25.0	26.5
	1960	94.1	1.1	753	8.5	10.6	11.1	33.7	15.1	38.2
	1965	98.9	1.0	1,159	9.0	9.3	10.8	32.9	10.7	37.9
	1970	104.3	1.1	1,897	10.4	9.8	11.2	39.4	7.2	43.2
Korea	1955	21.6	—	131	—	10.1	1.7	12.0	48.1	13.1
	1963	27.0	2.8	149	1.6	16.4	4.8	18.6	46.8	16.9
	1970	31.4	2.2	250	7.7	24.9	14.8	27.3	32.4	25.5
	1973	32.9	1.6	323	8.9	35.0	31.7	26.0	28.8	29.7
Taiwan	1956	9.2	—	203	—	—	—	15.9	29.8	24.3
	1961	11.0	3.6	231	2.6	19.9	12.8	19.8	29.3	25.4
	1966	12.8	3.1	305	5.7	21.5	20.6	23.1	24.2	29.8
	1971	14.8	2.9	426	6.9	34.2	36.8	26.1	14.8	39.3
Israel	1958	2.0	—	1,067	—	—	—	26.8	13.0	31.7
	1965	2.6	3.6	1,587	5.8	31.9	18.9	27.1	8.2	36.3
	1972	3.1	2.3	2,317	6.5	40.1	27.3	28.8	6.3	38.8
Norway	1953	3.4	—	1,171	—	—	—	29.5	15.5	35.0
	1961	3.6	0.9	2,028	7.1	42.6	39.7	31.1	9.9	32.6
	1969	3.9	0.8	2,769	4.0	38.5	41.2	25.0	6.2	34.0

— Not available.

a. Except for prewar Japan, the economy experiences fall into the period from the 1950–53 Korean war to the 1973 oil crisis. The special characteristics of this period have been discussed in earlier chapters, especially chapter 4.

b. Growth rates refer to the period that starts from the previous benchmark year.

c. In real 1970 dollars.

Sources: World Bank (1976) and World Bank data. See Kubo and Robinson (1984, table 1).

foreign investment (in response to policy incentives and good performance). Except for Mexico, population growth rates were constant or declining. And the stable economic and political environment that prevailed between the 1950–53 Korean war and the oil crisis of 1973 provided a favorable environment for international trade and economic growth.[1]

In addition to the initial diversity of these economies in population, per capita income, and production structure, there was great diversity in the role of foreign trade. The neutral and inward-oriented countries (Colombia, Mexico, and Turkey) and the largest country (postwar Japan) started with relatively low shares of imports and exports in GDP and experienced little change during the period.[2] The outward-oriented economies (Israel, Korea, and Taiwan) had widely differing shares of trade in GDP initially; all three dramatically increased these shares during the period. Pre-1945 Japan and Yugoslavia occupy an intermediate position. They started with similar shares, which then rose moderately but significantly.

Table 6-2 presents the sectoral composition of imports and exports. The similarity of the economies in the structure of their imports is significant. Except for Japan, they depended greatly on imports of heavy industrial products (including intermediates and machinery) throughout the period. None was a large importer of consumer goods. (Only Israel and Korea had initial import shares of more than 20 percent in this category.) Thus, by the initial year, the economies in the sample had largely completed the "easy" or "primary" stage of import substitution, in which imported consumer goods are replaced by domestic substitutes.

The diversity on the export side is greater. Three countries (Colombia, Mexico, and Turkey) are primary exporters; Turkey moved toward a significant share of manufacturing exports only at the end of the period. Korea and Taiwan are the now classic cases of rapid growth led by manufacturing exports. The other countries show a variety of intermediate patterns.

The long-run cross-country model in chapter 3 attributes the rising share of manufacturing in value added to three causes: shifts in the composition of demand, changes in input-output technology that lead to increased demand for intermediate inputs, and changes in comparative advantage. We shall explore the second and third cause in more detail in chapter 7. Here, we analyze the first cause by examining the role of shifts in the structure of demand, using the cross-country model as a benchmark with which to compare the economies in our sample.

---

1. W. A. Lewis (1980) notes the unusually high growth in trade between industrial and developing countries during the period and speculates on the implications of, and remedies for, a slowdown in what he calls "the engine of growth."
2. Norway is both the most developed and the most open of the sample economies and had little change in trade shares during the period.

Sources of Change in Demand and Output

The input-output model is used to trace the indirect linkages by which final demand for the output of one sector generates demand for the output of other sectors. Differentiating among categories of demand, we decompose the change in a sector's output during a period into changes arising from different sources of demand, taking into account indirect effects as well. The decomposition formula was discussed in detail in chapter 5. The decomposition used in this and the next chapter differs slightly from the presentation in chapter 5 in that the same average domestic supply ratios are assumed for all types of demand. The decomposition allocates the change in total output to four different factors: domestic demand expansion (DD), export expansion (EE), import substitution (IS), and changes in input-output coefficients (IO).

The first two terms (DD and EE) arise from direct changes in demand, whereas the third and fourth terms (IS and IO) arise from changes in coefficients. The treatment of exports and imports is not symmetrical. Import substitution is defined in terms of changes in import coefficients. These can be seen as technical coefficients, which seems especially appropriate for semi-industrial economies in which most imports are capital goods and intermediates that are difficult to replace with domestic products. Other treatments of exports and imports have been used in the literature and are discussed in chapter 5.

The total change in aggregate output equals the sum of the changes in the individual sectors and can thus be decomposed either by sector or by category of demand. In chapter 5, we presented a schematic with one row for each sector and five columns giving the change in sectoral output and its decomposition into the four separate terms. Again,

$$DD_1 + EE_1 + IS_1 + IO_1 = \Delta X_1$$
$$DD_2 + EE_2 + IS_2 + IO_2 = \Delta X_2$$
$$\cdot \qquad \cdot \qquad \cdot \qquad \cdot \qquad \cdot$$
$$\cdot \qquad \cdot \qquad \cdot \qquad \cdot \qquad \cdot$$
$$\cdot \qquad \cdot \qquad \cdot \qquad \cdot \qquad \cdot$$
$$\underline{DD_n + EE_n + IS_n + IO_n = \Delta X_n}$$
$$\Sigma DD_i + \Sigma EE_i + \Sigma IS_i + \Sigma IO_i = \Sigma \Delta X_i$$

Reading down the columns gives the sectoral composition of each demand category; reading across the rows gives the decomposition of changes in sectoral demand by demand category. To make comparisons across countries and time periods, it is convenient to divide the entire table by the sum of sectoral output changes ($\Sigma \Delta X_i$) so that all components across sectors and demand categories sum to 100. Alternatively, it is sometimes convenient to divide the rows by the change in each sectoral output (ΔX_i) and then look at the shares of the contribution of each demand category to the change in sectoral output.

Table 6-2. Composition of Imports and Exports of Sample Economies for Selected Years
(percent)

Economy	Year	Import shares				Export shares			
		Pri-mary	Light industry	Heavy industry	Ser-vices	Pri-mary	Light industry	Heavy industry	Ser-vices
Colombia	1953	0.2	17.0	77.6	5.2	86.0	0.8	1.2	12.0
	1966	14.8	11.1	61.8	12.3	71.1	6.3	6.0	16.6
	1970	4.6	13.1	69.1	13.2	78.3	6.7	1.9	13.1
Mexico[a]	1950	11.7	16.6	71.7	0.0	54.3	27.2	1.5	17.0
	1960	10.2	12.5	77.4	0.0	52.7	31.1	4.8	11.5
	1970	8.6	15.1	76.3	0.0	45.4	19.2	21.6	13.9
	1975	11.9	10.4	77.6	0.0	34.4	18.0	30.9	16.7
Turkey	1953	6.6	6.3	85.3	1.8	78.1	3.0	4.5	14.4
	1963	17.3	7.3	65.9	9.6	58.2	8.2	3.8	29.8
	1968	7.9	5.1	75.3	11.8	45.7	19.6	3.1	31.6
	1973	12.0	3.0	78.8	6.2	26.9	27.4	6.8	39.0
Yugoslavia	1962	17.1	10.4	68.3	4.1	11.9	21.9	30.2	35.9
	1966	20.3	11.3	64.9	3.5	14.9	20.7	33.0	31.4
	1972	15.8	14.4	66.8	3.0	11.2	25.3	40.2	23.2

Japan	1914	45.0	10.9	40.0	4.0	10.7	43.8	7.0	38.5
	1935	53.7	10.9	28.0	7.3	2.8	42.2	12.2	42.8
	1955	62.5	18.0	21.1	−1.7	3.0	45.6	28.5	22.8
	1960	53.5	14.2	33.4	−1.1	3.7	44.3	40.0	12.0
	1965	56.8	17.5	26.7	−1.0	2.2	26.7	58.4	12.7
	1970	49.7	16.1	26.5	7.7	1.1	18.4	58.6	22.0
Korea	1955	1.7	38.5	59.6	0.1	23.8	17.2	2.4	56.6
	1963	28.8	13.3	55.7	2.2	20.2	34.2	14.3	31.3
	1970	24.1	19.6	55.7	0.7	8.7	55.0	14.5	21.8
	1973	17.0	19.0	62.5	1.5	3.8	48.5	31.0	16.8
Taiwan	1956	23.4	11.4	59.8	5.4	6.6	78.8	9.4	5.2
	1961	22.1	16.4	56.0	5.5	7.1	66.0	10.0	16.9
	1966	18.6	16.0	60.5	4.9	9.1	49.4	20.0	21.6
	1971	20.3	17.6	58.6	3.5	4.9	48.6	34.0	12.6
Israel	1958	9.7	21.8	45.8	22.7	21.3	33.4	10.5	34.8
	1965	7.0	17.8	47.0	28.2	12.7	30.9	9.6	46.8
	1972	3.2	16.6	67.3	13.0	10.2	35.2	14.4	40.2
Norway	1953	13.7	15.0	46.4	25.0	6.9	20.3	20.4	52.4
	1961	11.3	16.3	51.0	21.6	5.0	16.9	25.2	53.0
	1969	10.1	20.2	50.7	19.0	3.2	15.9	34.3	46.6

a. Data for services in Mexico refers to net exports and are given under the export column. Services imports are defined as zero.
Source: World Bank data; described in Kubo (1983).

Table 6-3. *Sources of Growth for Archetypal Economies*
(percent)

Per capita income and sector	Large (L)					Small manufacturing (SM)					Small primary (SP)				
	DD	EE	IS	IO	Total	DD	EE	IS	IO	Total	DD	EE	IS	IO	Total
$140–$280															
Primary	11.0	2.4	.0	-.8	12.6	9.4	5.7	-1.9	-.5	12.7	10.0	12.9	.0	-.5	22.4
Light industry	19.8	2.7	1.1	1.7	25.3	18.2	8.5	1.1	1.5	29.3	18.4	1.8	1.8	1.7	23.7
Heavy industry	9.5	1.5	3.0	1.3	15.3	2.5	1.2	-.6	.2	3.3	4.0	.8	2.6	.8	8.2
Services	42.9	2.6	.5	.8	46.8	44.0	10.1	-.7	1.3	54.7	40.9	3.2	.5	1.1	45.7
Total	83.2	9.2	4.6	3.0	100.0	74.1	25.5	-2.1	2.5	100.0	73.3	18.7	4.9	3.1	100.0
$280–$560															
Primary	8.8	1.5	-.6	-.7	9.0	6.3	4.5	-2.0	-.9	7.9	7.7	11.4	-.4	-.5	18.2
Light industry	20.3	3.3	.6	1.4	25.6	18.2	9.8	1.2	1.1	30.3	18.9	2.5	1.3	1.4	24.1
Heavy industry	12.7	2.8	2.0	1.6	19.1	3.6	2.9	2.8	.5	9.8	6.9	1.3	3.1	1.1	12.4
Services	42.8	2.9	.2	.4	46.3	41.9	10.3	-.3	.1	52.0	40.7	3.3	.4	.9	45.3
Total	84.6	10.5	2.2	2.7	100.0	70.0	27.5	1.7	.8	100.0	74.2	18.5	4.4	2.9	100.0
$560–$1,120															
Primary	7.3	1.0	-1.1	-.8	6.4	4.3	3.1	-2.1	-.7	4.6	6.3	9.0	-.7	-.7	13.9
Light industry	20.5	4.0	.2	.9	25.6	17.5	10.6	1.3	.9	30.3	18.8	3.4	.9	1.1	24.2
Heavy industry	15.3	4.3	1.4	1.8	22.8	6.5	5.5	4.3	.9	17.2	10.9	1.6	3.3	1.6	17.4
Services	42.0	3.3	-.1	.0	45.2	39.4	9.2	-.1	-.6	47.9	40.8	3.0	.3	.4	44.5
Total	85.1	12.6	.4	1.9	100.0	67.7	28.4	3.4	.5	100.0	76.8	17.0	3.8	2.4	100.0
$1,120–$2,100															
Primary	6.2	.8	-1.2	-.6	5.2	3.2	1.8	-1.7	-.5	2.8	5.5	5.9	-.6	-.7	10.1
Light industry	20.2	5.1	-.1	.6	25.8	16.4	10.6	1.4	.9	29.3	18.1	4.5	.7	1.0	24.3
Heavy industry	17.4	5.6	1.0	2.1	26.1	10.2	8.7	5.4	1.4	25.7	15.7	1.5	3.3	2.4	22.9
Services	40.2	3.6	-.3	-.6	42.9	36.1	7.0	.2	-1.1	42.2	40.4	2.4	.2	-.3	42.7
Total	84.0	15.1	-.6	1.5	100.0	65.9	28.1	5.3	.7	100.0	79.7	14.3	3.6	2.4	100.0

Source: World Bank data; computations from cross-country model. See chapter 3 for description.

Long-Run Comparisons

Tables 6-3 and 6-4 present the decomposition results in the same format as the schematic at the four-sector level. Table 6-3 does this for the cross-country model as applied to three different country patterns or archetypes—large (L), small manufacturing exporter (SM), and small primary exporter (SP)—and four per capita income intervals. The results are described in more detail in chapter 3; see especially table 3-10 and figure 3-9. Table 6-4 presents the results for the sample. Figures 6-1 and 6-2 summarize the sources of growth for the whole economy, as well as the changes in sectoral incremental output shares ($\Delta X_i / \Sigma \Delta X_i$) as income rises for the three archetypes. The variations in decomposition for each archetype are very smooth, which reflects the cumulative effect of the industrialization processes described in chapter 3. The relative contribution to total growth of the primary sector declines in each archetype as income rises, while that of heavy industry (intermediates and machinery) rises as a result of the combined influence of the falling share of food in consumption, the increased share of investment in GDP, and the increased use of fabricated goods as intermediate inputs throughout the economy. The effects of these changes in the composition of final demand are supplemented on the supply side by the accumulation of physical capital and skills, which shifts comparative advantage from goods using primary resources to manufactured products.

The three archetypes generated with the cross-country model are useful in delineating the role of initial conditions in determining the pattern and timing of industrialization. The breakdown between large and small countries takes into account the influence of size on the openness of an economy, while the breakdown between primary and manufacturing exporters takes into account the effect of natural resources on a country's comparative advantage. As figure 6-2 illustrates, all three converge toward a common industrial structure as they grow; the sectoral contributions to growth at the income range $1,120–$2,100 are very similar.[3]

Figure 6-3 (derived from table 6-4) presents the sectoral contributions to total change in output for the sample economies. These results can be compared with those for the archetypes shown in figure 6-2. The economies fall into distinct groups. Korea and Taiwan have strikingly similar patterns, distinguished by the large contribution of light industry. The other open economies, Israel and Norway, also have very similar patterns but are more characteristic of advanced countries in that they have a large contribution by services.[4] Postwar Japan and Yugoslavia show a large

---

3. See figure 6-2 and table 6-3. For a further discussion of this convergence, also see Chenery and Taylor (1968) and chapter 3.

4. The large contribution by services in the case of Israel is partly a reflection of large capital inflows; in the case of Norway, it reflects a long-standing comparative advantage in shipping.

Table 6-4. *Sources of Growth for Sample Economies*
(percent)

Economy and sector	Growth rate	DD	EE	IS	IO	Total
Colombia (1953–70)						
Primary	4.5	12.7	9.1	0.5	0.1	22.4
Light industry	6.8	15.3	1.5	1.5	3.0	21.3
Heavy industry	11.1	9.0	0.8	4.5	1.7	16.0
Services	5.5	36.7	2.6	0.3	0.7	40.3
Total	5.9	73.7	14.0	6.8	5.5	100.0
Mexico (1950–75)						
Primary	4.8	12.8	0.7	−0.3	−0.5	12.7
Light industry	6.0	17.7	0.4	0.5	0.7	19.3
Heavy industry	10.8	16.7	1.8	2.9	1.3	22.7
Services	6.4	43.7	0.7	0.4	0.5	45.3
Total	6.5	90.9	3.6	3.5	2.0	100.0
Turkey (1953–73)						
Primary	2.5	14.9	1.2	0.2	−4.5	11.8
Light industry	6.7	15.3	2.1	0.4	1.7	19.5
Heavy industry	9.6	18.8	0.9	1.6	3.4	24.7
Services	6.7	38.3	2.8	0.2	2.7	44.0
Total	5.9	87.3	7.0	2.4	3.3	100.0
Yugoslavia (1962–72)						
Primary	2.6	10.1	3.9	−3.2	−4.6	6.2
Light industry	11.0	17.7	6.2	−2.6	1.3	22.6
Heavy industry	13.6	23.6	12.2	−6.1	4.4	34.1
Services	8.8	33.0	5.2	−1.3	0.2	37.1
Total	8.7	84.4	27.5	−13.2	1.3	100.0
Japan (1914–35)						
Primary	1.9	7.6	2.8	−2.3	2.3	10.4
Light industry	4.6	15.8	10.5	0.2	−0.4	26.1
Heavy industry	8.1	15.2	4.4	1.9	−3.3	18.2
Services	4.2	35.2	9.0	−0.2	1.3	45.3
Total	4.1	73.8	26.7	−0.4	−0.1	100.0

contribution by heavy industry but probably for different reasons. As is typical for a socialist country, Yugoslavia pursued policies strongly favoring heavy industry. Japan is a large country which was completing its transformation into a mature industrial economy during this period. Prewar Japan, Mexico, and Turkey had more balanced sectoral contributions to growth—a pattern one would expect of large economies. Colombia is the only country in the sample that followed a pattern characteristic of a primary-oriented economy.

Role of Exports

Figure 6-1 shows that one of the main differences in the sources of growth among the three archetypes is the relative importance of exports. As expected, small countries rely more heavily on exports to make up for

Economy and sector	Growth rate	DD	EE	IS	IO	Total
Japan (1955–72)						
Primary	2.2	4.4	0.5	−1.5	−1.9	1.5
Light industry	8.6	14.4	2.0	−0.7	1.1	16.8
Heavy industry	18.0	30.9	8.4	−0.1	3.3	42.5
Services	11.4	35.7	3.0	−0.8	1.3	39.2
Total	11.5	85.4	13.9	−3.1	3.8	100.0
Korea (1955–73)						
Primary	5.7	12.0	3.0	−1.7	−2.5	10.8
Light industry	13.6	19.7	15.1	0.0	−1.9	32.9
Heavy industry	22.1	11.1	10.7	1.4	1.9	25.1
Services	10.3	25.6	6.2	0.2	−0.8	31.2
Total	11.2	68.4	35.0	−0.1	−3.3	100.0
Taiwan (1956–71)						
Primary	7.1	8.8	5.3	−2.0	−1.8	10.3
Light industry	13.6	12.7	17.5	0.6	2.0	32.8
Heavy industry	22.5	10.2	13.5	2.4	1.0	27.1
Services	9.7	23.6	7.1	0.1	−1.0	29.8
Total	12.0	55.3	43.4	1.1	0.2	100.0
Israel (1958–72)						
Primary	6.4	2.6	3.6	−0.3	−0.4	5.5
Light industry	11.2	11.3	12.0	−2.0	1.2	22.5
Heavy industry	14.3	18.7	6.3	−6.6	2.6	21.0
Services	8.9	39.3	13.9	−1.6	−0.6	51.0
Total	9.9	71.9	35.8	−10.5	2.8	100.0
Norway (1953–69)						
Primary	2.5	3.8	2.4	−1.7	0.3	4.8
Light industry	3.7	14.0	6.2	−5.7	3.0	17.5
Heavy industry	7.2	10.7	15.6	−2.2	2.2	26.3
Services	4.8	31.9	21.5	−2.7	0.7	51.4
Total	4.7	60.4	45.7	−12.3	6.2	100.0

Source: World Bank data; described in Kubo (1983).

the limited size of the domestic market, especially at an early stage of industrialization. Moreover, small manufacturing economies exhibit an increasing reliance on exports for growth throughout the transition. The experiences of our sample are compared with those of the three archetypes in figure 6-4. The length of the bars shows the contribution of export expansion to growth as a percentage of the total change in gross output. The bars also indicate the contributions of the four aggregate sectors: primary, light industry, heavy industry, and services. The archetypal economies behave as expected: in the L pattern, contributions by all sectors are balanced; in the SP pattern, a heavy bias toward primary exports is evident; and in the SM pattern, manufactured exports—especially light manufactures—play a large role.

Figure 6-1. *Sources of Growth for Archetypal Economies*

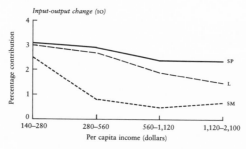

Import substitution (IS)

Per capita income (dollars)

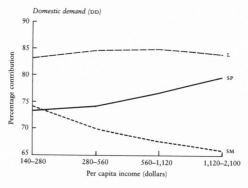

Input-output change (IO)

Per capita income (dollars)

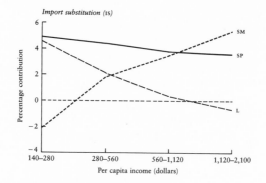

Domestic demand (DD)

Per capita income (dollars)

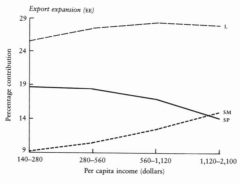

Export expansion (EE)

Per capita income (dollars)

Figure 6-2. *Sectoral Contributions to Growth for Archetypal Economies*

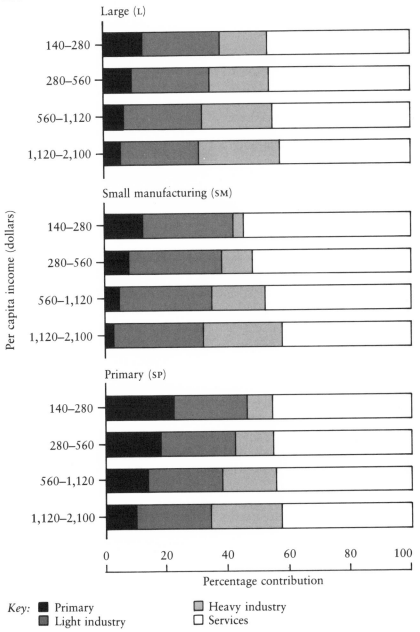

Figure 6-3. *Sectoral Contributions to Growth for Sample Economies*

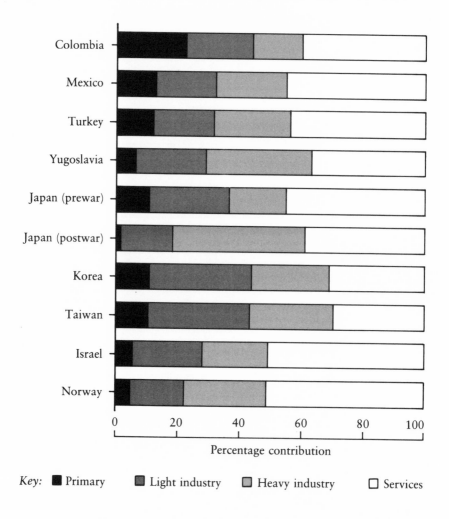

As with the sectoral contributions to total output growth, Korea and Taiwan are again very similar and could be classified as extreme SM economies with relatively larger contributions from heavy industry than in the average SM pattern. Israel and Norway are comparable but show larger contributions by service exports. Mexico and Turkey are the most closed economies, followed by Colombia, which had significant primary exports and is the closest to the SP archetype. Yugoslavia and prewar Japan had a similar aggregate role for exports, but Yugoslavia had a stronger emphasis on heavy industry. Prewar Japan is the closest to the SM archetype. Postwar Japan again looks like a large industrial economy with a significant role for trade, especially in heavy industry. Israel, Korea,

Figure 6-4. *Contribution of Export Expansion to Total Output Change of Sample Economies*

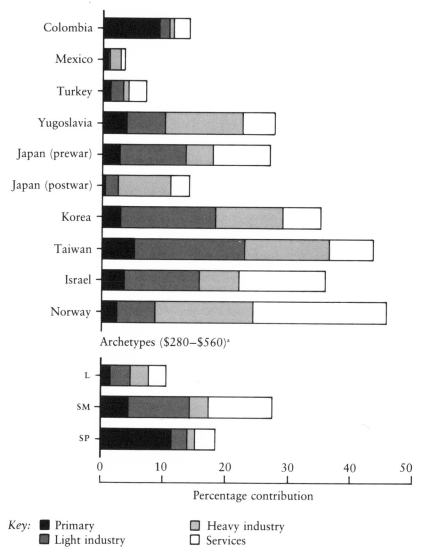

Archetypes ($280–$560)[a]

Percentage contribution

Key: ■ Primary   ▨ Heavy industry
      ▨ Light industry   ☐ Services

a. Only one income range is plotted for the archetypes. This is reasonably close to the income range for most of the sample economies (see table 6-1).

prewar Japan, and Taiwan show a dominant contribution by manufactured exports, led by light industrial exports which are largely labor-intensive. Postwar Japan, Norway, and Yugoslavia favored heavy industrial exports.

Comparing these groups of economies with the cross-country model, we see that the model underestimates the contribution of heavy industry at the income range in question, particularly for Korea, Taiwan, Yugoslavia, and postwar Japan. For the latter two, this can be partly explained by their particular circumstances: Yugoslavia followed a socialist development strategy emphasizing the production of capital goods, while Japan was restoring its industrial base after the war. But for Korea and Taiwan, the contribution of both light and heavy industry far exceeded that predicted for the typical trade patterns of the model.[5] Policies and the choice of development strategy must have accounted for the early industrialization of these two economies. Finally, prewar Japan, Mexico, and Turkey displayed sectoral contributions close to those predicted from the L pattern in the cross-country model. Colombia is the only country that closely resembles the primary-oriented archetype.

For both overall sectoral contributions to growth (figures 6-2 and 6-3) and the role of exports (figure 6-4), a comparison of the experience of the sample economies with the cross-country model confirms some of our earlier conclusions. Colombia follows the SP industrialization pattern, while postwar Japan, Mexico, and Turkey follow the L pattern. In Mexico and Turkey, however, the contribution of export expansion is only about half that predicted by the cross-country model. These countries were much more autarkic than typical countries of their size and per capita income. For Japan, the period 1955–70 was one of import liberalization rather than of import substitution as assumed by the cross-country model. In contrast, prewar Japan fits quite closely the SM pattern, which raises the question of whether this was also true for Mexico and Turkey during the prewar period. Although these countries, like Japan, pursued development strategies based on the substitution of light manufactures for imports, their development strategies were generally more autarkic. They did not have close colonial ties, as did Japan, that permitted an especially advantageous exchange of raw materials for manufactured products.

The remaining economies in the group are outliers on the high side in comparison with the cross-country pattern. Although the choice of benchmark years may be partly responsible, the discrepancy is caused both by the effects of the development strategy for these economies in relation to the "average" development strategy embodied in the cross-section regressions and by special exogenous circumstances, some of which were mentioned earlier. Since the cross-country model was designed to explore the

---

5. Korea and Taiwan started the period with per capita incomes of $131 and $203, respectively (see table 6-1).

process of industrialization that takes place mostly in the transition from a per capita income level of $280–$1,120, it is not surprising that Israel and Norway—with per capita incomes exceeding $1,000 in the initial year—deviate from the predicted pattern. But for Korea, Taiwan, and Yugoslavia, an explanation must lie in a further scrutiny of their choices of development strategy.

Trade Policy Regimes

The analysis so far has been concerned with long-run changes. To consider the effect of different development strategies on the nature and structure of growth, we need to look at episodes that can be characterized by a distinct development strategy. The choice of episodes in the sample economies was determined by the availability of input-output data for benchmark years. We are lucky in that, for our sample, most of the episodes do correspond to periods that reflect a specific development strategy. The benchmark years often fall at or close to a time when an economy underwent a significant shift in its policy regime. This makes it fruitful to use the episodes to explore the relation between different development strategies and the nature of growth in the economy.

A country's development strategy is determined by its choice of policies and its institutional environment. It is also affected by exogenous events such as wars, droughts, and the state of the world economy. To characterize a period as reflecting a particular choice of development strategy implies that the policies chosen reflect a coherent policy regime. A policy may produce different results given different initial conditions, institutional settings, and conditions in the world economy. But within each economy at a given time, one can sensibly characterize policies as being consistent or inconsistent with a development strategy.

In chapter 4, the semi-industrial countries were categorized by three long-term development strategies: inward-oriented, outward-oriented, and neutral. In examining episodes within our smaller sample, it is useful to refine these categories somewhat. We distinguish three trade strategies, one that is inward-oriented and two that are outward-oriented. The first is an import substitution strategy and is characterized by policies that bias production incentives against exports and toward the home market. One of the two outward-oriented strategies, export promotion, is characterized by policies that give roughly equal and positive incentives to production both for export and for the substitution of imports. In contrast with the import substitution strategy, export promotion entails no bias against sales to foreign markets compared with sales in the domestic market.[6] The second outward-oriented strategy, trade liberalization, is characterized by

---

6. In the Bhagwati-Krueger terminology, effective exchange rates for exporting and for import substituting activities are close to one another. See Krueger (1978) and Bhagwati (1978).

policies that give negligible incentives to both import substituting and exporting activities. This case corresponds to a relatively free trade regime, with few quantitative controls or price-related measures.

This classification of development strategies omits important policy and institutional influences that are reflected in the contributions to growth discussed later in the chapter. Particularly important is the role of policies affecting the functioning of factor markets. For example, a change in development strategy, whereby incentives are shifted toward exporting, will not result in increased exports if labor mobility is low and the required investment in new activities is not forthcoming. Moreover, any one of the strategies defined above can be accomplished by a wide variety of policy regimes. Thus, an export-oriented strategy can be achieved by direct quantitative intervention in the market (for example, by applying export targets at the firm level) or by providing price incentives to export sales. Establishing the "equivalence," however defined, of different policy regimes for a development strategy is difficult, even for the simple cases constructed in the theoretical literature.[7]

Episodes and Policy Phases

For each economy in the sample, figure 6-5 relates several episodes framed by two benchmark years for the important policy phases. When no major shifts in policy occurred, no break is indicated. This summary figure seeks to establish whether the benchmark years imposed by the availability of input-output information are unusual in some important way; for example, did they fall in a time of war, acute political instability, poor harvest, or major shifts in policy?

For Colombia, the two episodes (1953–66 and 1966–70) correspond to a period when great changes were taking place in the economy. First, the declining trend in coffee prices, which had been under way since the mid-1950s, was reversed about 1966. Second, that benchmark year was also unusual because it corresponded to a brief but intense liberalization effort, which was followed by a major reform in March 1967 that resulted in a less inward-oriented development strategy. The introduction of a crawling peg and of long-lasting incentives for nontraditional exports inaugurated a reorientation in Colombia's development strategy.[8] This mix of regimes led us in chapter 4 to classify Colombia as having pursued a neutral strategy.

The three episodes in Mexico (1950–60, 1960–70, and 1970–75) constitute the longest time span covered in this study for any country. Throughout the period, Mexico continuously pursued an inward-oriented

7. For example, see Bhagwati (1978) for a good discussion of the equivalence of tariffs and quotas.

8. The incentives took the form of freely negotiable and tax exempt certificates equal to 15 percent of the export value.

Figure 6-5. *Benchmark Years, Major Events, Policy Regimes, and Trade Strategies of Sample Economies*

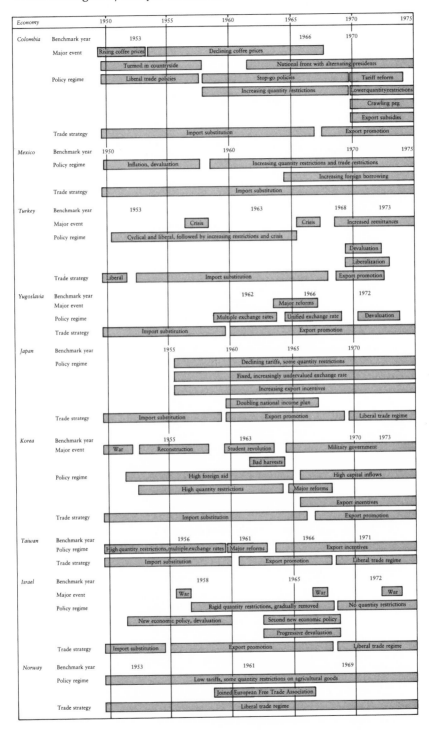

development strategy based on import substitution. Having benefited, as did Colombia, from natural protection during World War II, Mexico had already achieved considerable import substitution in consumer goods by 1950, the initial benchmark year. Significant breaks occurred in 1956 and 1970—the latter corresponding to the third benchmark year. The period in between was one of growth with stability, low inflation, and a fixed exchange rate that was maintained until 1975. Throughout, quantitative restrictions on imports were increasingly relied on to control the current account when foreign exchange imbalances arose. No real attempt at rationalizing or removing foreign exchange controls took place until 1975 so that, from the point of view of policy, Mexico's strategy up until 1970 can be characterized as continuously inward-oriented. During the 1970–75 episode, Mexico experienced increasing inflation and foreign exchange pressures, which ended the previous period of growth with stability. Throughout, few incentives were provided to exporters.

The three episodes in Turkey (1953–63, 1963–68, and 1968–73) cover two major cycles in Turkish postwar economic history, the first culminating in the devaluation of 1958 and the second in the devaluation of 1970. The earlier crisis followed a period of very high inflation, while the later crisis followed a period of remarkable price stability. Like Colombia, Turkey experienced a rapid succession of stop-go policies during the 1953–63 period. During this period, multiple exchange rates, quantitative restrictions, and import surcharges were the main instruments used to control the demand for foreign exchange, though some export incentives were added. Occasionally, these controls were partially removed. On the whole, however, the trend was toward more and more control as the exchange rate became increasingly overvalued. During the 1963–68 period, the exchange rate was unified and a consistent import substitution strategy was pursued. An important shift occurred after the 1970 devaluation when, for the first time in its postwar history, Turkey enjoyed a relative abundance of foreign exchange because of a strong export response to the shift in incentives and unusually high levels of foreign remittances. Notwithstanding this brief liberalization, the basic strategy in the postwar period was to pursue successive phases of import substitution, first in consumer goods and later in capital goods. Export incentives were not sustained over any length of time because of a chronically overvalued exchange rate.

Yugoslavia's two episodes (1962–66 and 1966–72) came well after the intensive period of import substitution during the 1950s, when basic industry was established. Until 1965, Yugoslavia had a system of multiple exchange rates with export subsidies and quantitative restrictions. Rising inflation led to the devaluation of 1965; that year also saw a shift in policy as the foreign exchange regime was rationalized at the same time that a successful stabilization policy was pursued. The result was a unified exchange rate and a reduction in quantitative restrictions on imports. This liberalization of foreign trade was also accompanied by a liberalization of the internal domestic market as the dismantling of the government investment fund led to less central control of the allocation of investment. Thus, Yugoslavia, which had already achieved a substantial substitution of imports by the initial benchmark year, progressively liberalized its foreign and domestic economic policies throughout the period (see Tyson 1980).

After 1945, Japan pursued a stable and successful growth-oriented strategy that combined export incentives with substantial protection for import-competing industries that shifted increasingly away from tariffs and toward quantitative controls of imports. In common with Norway and in contrast with the other economies in the sample, Japan made no important change in its development strategy during the period, although one could argue that the emphasis on growth-oriented policies was heightened around 1960 with the adoption of the so-called doubling national income plan.

The three Korean episodes (1956–63, 1963–70, and 1970–73) straddle one important shift in policy regime in 1965–67 and an earlier, less important shift about 1958, the year that marked the end of post–Korean war reconstruction. The early 1960s were marked by political instability, successive bad harvests, and short-lived efforts to liberalize the foreign trade regime. About 1965, significant reforms in domestic economic policies and foreign trade policies were introduced. On the domestic front, tax and interest rate reforms raised the savings rate, while strong incentives to exporters helped Korea achieve phenomenal rates of export growth up to the end of the period.[9] Korea's economic policy was not one of continuous liberalization throughout the period. The strategy included strong price and nonprice incentives for exporting accompanied by selective measures to promote import substitution.

Taiwan's economic policies were among the most consistent in the group. Beginning with a period of hyperinflation in the early 1950s, Taiwan continuously and progressively liberalized and rationalized its domestic and foreign economic policies. Thus there was continuity throughout the three episodes (1956–62, 1962–66, and 1966–71) with one important change in policy regime following the "nineteen reforms" of 1960–61. These reforms marked a move toward an outward-oriented development strategy since effective export incentives were provided and sustained. By the end of the 1960s, as a result of rapid growth, Taiwan ended its period of labor surplus.

Much like Taiwan, and in contrast with the other countries, Israel pursued sustained economic policies that guided the economy away from direct controls. Israel's two episodes (1958–65 and 1965–72) straddle the

9. On the relationship between financial reforms and savings, see Cole and Lyman (1971) and Brown (1973). For a revisionist interpretation of the interest rate reform, see Giovanni (1983).

reforms of 1962, which marked the replacement of quantitative restrictions with price controls and represented a move toward trade liberalization. In addition to its small size, Israel is also distinctive in the group because of its wars and its political situation, which have necessitated heavy spending on defense. Thus, one can characterize Israel's economic policies as a progressive and sustained liberalization following an acute rationing of resources in the early years of its existence as a state.

Norway consistently followed an outward-oriented strategy after the war. Moreover, Norway is the only one of the nine economies that achieved a truly liberalized trade regime. Indeed, as early as 1954, nominal and effective rates of protection on manufactured imports were less than 10 percent, while quantitative restrictions on imports were also being eliminated. Furthermore, realistic exchange rates were maintained throughout the period, which resulted in a continuously outward-oriented development strategy with a free-trade regime.

The final line for each economy in figure 6-5 notes the trade strategies pursued during the period.[10] To support a trade strategy, a policy regime must be viewed by the economic actors in the system as persisting long enough to justify undertaking large investment projects and a significant reallocation of labor. Short-term stabilization policies whose goal is to control inflation and to establish short-run macroeconomic balance should be excluded from consideration. Unfortunately, adverse medium-term effects result from the stop-go policies often seen in countries suffering from foreign exchange shortages exacerbated by quantitative restrictions, insufficient exchange rate flexibility, and high inflation. In our sample, Colombia, Turkey, and Yugoslavia clearly suffered from such a regime at times, with adverse consequences for economic growth. Even in such cases, however, it is possible to discern long-term trends in policy by looking at trends in incentive measures such as effective rates of protection and effective exchange rates.

Incentive Policies

Most of the economies in our sample have been examined in detail in case studies. Five of them (Colombia, Israel, Korea, Taiwan, and Turkey) were included in the sample studied in the Bhagwati-Krueger project sponsored by the National Bureau of Economic Research (NBER).[11] For these studies, comparable measures of effective exchange rates were calculated for imports and exports. When properly measured, effective exchange rates reflect the actual domestic currency costs for importers and

10. The classification is judgmental and is based on a number of comparative studies. See Little, Scitovsky, and Scott (1970), Bergsman (1979), World Bank (1981), Balassa and others (1982), and Balassa and associates (1971), as well as the NBER series edited by Bhagwati and Krueger.

11. For summaries of the project results, see Bhagwati (1978) and Krueger (1978). The data for Taiwan are drawn from a more recent study by Kuo (1983).

Table 6-5. *Ratio of Effective Exchange Rates for Imports to Exports of Selected Sample Economies*

Year	Colombia[a]	Turkey[a]	Korea	Taiwan[b]	Israel
1954	—	1.48	—	—	1.04
1958	1.28	1.66	0.56	—	0.99
1960	1.02	—	0.68	0.95	1.00
1962	0.88	2.11	0.97	0.98	1.15
1965	1.02	2.39	0.96	0.98	1.15
1968	0.94	2.14	0.85	1.07	1.02
1971	1.00	—	0.82	1.14	1.01

— Not available.

a. The rate for exports refers to "nontraditional" (manufacturing) exports.

b. The ratio is for real effective exchange rates. See Kuo (1983, table 14-4).

Sources: Colombia, Diaz-Alejandro (1976); Turkey, Krueger (1974); Korea, Frank, Kim, and Westphal (1975); Taiwan, Kuo (1983); Israel, Michaely (1975).

the actual domestic currency receipts from export sales for producers in a sector. These rates should, therefore, take into account tariffs, import surcharges, the value of any import premiums, the tariff equivalent of quantitative restrictions, and all types of export subsidies including those of preferential access by exporters to loans and intermediate inputs. The ratio of the effective exchange rates for exports and for imports measures the bias in incentives resulting from the trade regime.[12]

The data on effective exchange rates for the five sample economies in the NBER study are summarized in table 6-5.[13] From these data, certain patterns emerge. In Korea after 1964, the ratio of the effective exchange rate for imports to that for exports was relatively stable, with a slight downward trend indicating an increasing bias in favor of exports. In Taiwan, the ratio was near one (no bias), but with a slight upward trend. In Colombia, there was a distinct cycle, first falling to below one and then rising to about one. Israel also shows a cycle, but with less variation than Colombia. In both countries, there was a move in the latter part of the period to remove incentive biases against exports. In Turkey, the variance in effective exchange rates was quite high; there was a strong bias against exports throughout the period (but data are missing for 1970–73, when incentives evidently favored exports).

An import substitution strategy reflects policies that give rise to incentives with a consistent and marked bias against exports. Export promotion implies either no bias or a bias in favor of exports. A liberalization strategy

12. See Bhagwati (1978) and McKinnon (1980) for discussions of trade bias.

13. Other incentive indicators have been calculated for some of the economies in the sample. Calculations of sectoral effective rates of protection (ERP) are available for some of the sample but only for scattered years. See Balassa and others (1982), and Balassa and Associates (1971).

implies—in addition to no bias toward either exporting or importing—low levels of protection and the maintenance of an equilibrium real exchange rate so that there is no bias toward producing tradables or nontradables. In figure 6-5, the points demarcating a shift in trade strategy are arbitrary in that such policy shifts usually unfold over a period of at least a few years. In some cases (Israel, Korea, and Yugoslavia, for example), the shift in strategy was accompanied by widespread economic changes and reforms that took several years to implement. If each demarcation point is regarded as a zone, in almost every case a benchmark year lies in the zone. Thus, by good fortune, the episodes generally delineate periods characterized by consistent trade strategies.

Economies that pursued gradual shifts in policy regimes include Israel, Japan, Korea, Taiwan, and Yugoslavia. In contrast, Colombia's shift in policy took place rapidly after the March 1967 reforms. Before that date, there had been a succession of stop-go policy cycles, reflecting brief episodes of stabilization and liberalization in the foreign trade regime. In Turkey, a major change in orientation took place about 1970, with a liberalization that was sustained for a few years (until the oil crisis) because of improved foreign exchange availability caused by rising workers' remittances. Exports were helped indirectly through the lower cost of imported intermediate inputs as import rationing became less severe and remittances permitted the exchange rate to be somewhat undervalued. In Mexico, one cannot discern any significant change in trade strategy. Inflation was very low in 1956–70, but without any shift in incentives. Throughout the period, domestic industries were protected, and the incentives to export were few. Norway maintained a liberal trade strategy during the entire period.

Trade and Industry

The preceding discussion presumed a causal link between incentives and the relative effect of import substitution and export expansion policies. But such a link is likely only for marginal activities, that is, for activities having either positive demand elasticities (in the case of imports) or positive supply elasticities (in the case of exports). This means excluding both what are referred to as noncompetitive imports and most exports derived from the exploitation of natural resources whose supply is fixed, such as mining and other extractive activities. Exports of primary commodities such as coffee, which require special growing conditions and have no close substitutes, would also fall into the category of intramarginal export activities. Thus a considerable proportion of primary exports should by and large be fairly insensitive to changes in incentives of the kind discussed earlier since they would be exported under a variety of circumstances and incentives. It is mostly in the manufacturing sector that we expect an association between incentives and contributions to growth.

Figures 6-6 and 6-7 indicate the contributions of export expansion and

Figure 6-6. *Contribution of Export Expansion by Episodes, Selected Sample Economies*

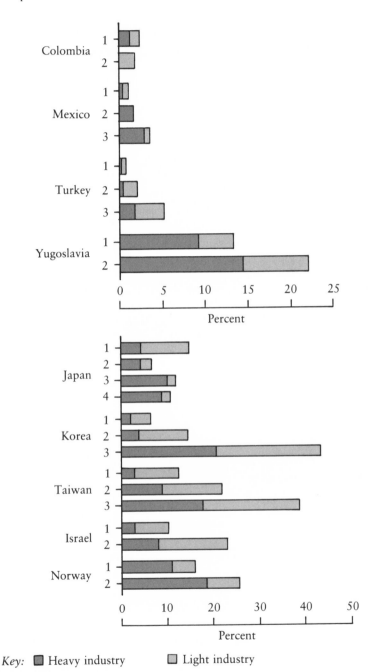

Key: ■ Heavy industry   □ Light industry

Note: Numbers beside economy names refer to episodes delineated by benchmark years (see table 6-6).

Figure 6-7. *Contribution of Import Substitution by Episode, Selected Sample Economies*

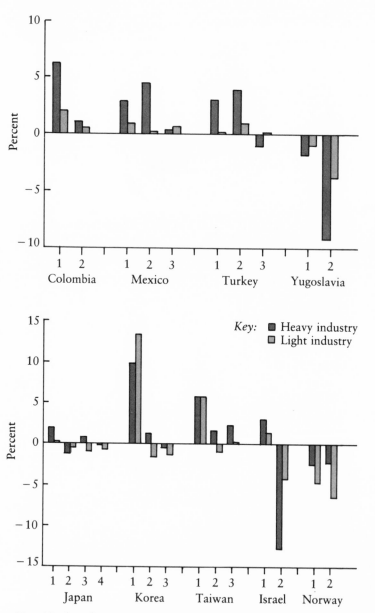

Note: Numbers above economy names refer to episodes delineated by benchmark years (see table 6-6).

import substitution for light and heavy industry (expressed as a percentage of the change in economywide total gross output). The data cover each episode for the sample economies and can be compared with figures 6-3 and 6-4, which cover the entire period. Table 6-6 gives the sources of change in total manufacturing output for each episode, expressed as a percentage of the change in manufacturing output (so that the various contributions add up to 100 for the sector).

Typology of Trade Strategies

Table 6-6 indicates that most of the sample economies went through an episode marked by a sizable effect of import substitution on manufacturing output growth. In Korea and Taiwan, this period corresponded to an

Table 6-6. *Sources of Growth in Manufacturing Output for Sample Economies*

Economy	Years (episode)	Growth rate[a]	Source[b] DD	EE	IS	IO
Colombia	1953–66 (1)	8.3	60.2	6.8	22.2	10.8
	1966–70 (2)	7.4	75.7	4.7	4.2	15.3
Mexico	1950–60 (1)	7.0	71.6	3.1	10.9	14.5
	1960–70 (2)	8.6	86.1	4.0	10.9	−0.9
	1970–75 (3)	7.2	81.4	7.9	2.4	8.3
Turkey	1953–63 (1)	6.4	80.9	2.4	9.1	7.6
	1963–68 (2)	9.9	75.1	4.5	10.5	9.9
	1968–73 (3)	9.6	76.2	10.4	−1.6	15.0
Yugoslavia[a]	1962–66 (1)	16.6	73.7	24.8	−5.0	6.5
	1966–72 (2)	9.1	72.1	37.6	−22.1	12.4
Japan	1914–35 (1)	5.5	70.0	33.6	4.7	−8.4
	1955–60 (2)	12.6	76.2	11.9	−3.3	15.2
	1960–65 (3)	10.8	82.4	21.8	−0.4	−3.8
	1965–70 (4)	16.5	74.4	17.5	−1.5	9.6
Korea	1955–63 (1)	10.4	57.4	11.5	42.2	−11.2
	1963–70 (2)	18.9	70.0	30.2	−0.6	0.4
	1970–73 (3)	23.8	39.0	61.7	−2.6	1.9
Taiwan	1956–61 (1)	11.2	34.7	27.5	25.5	12.3
	1961–66 (2)	16.6	49.1	44.6	1.6	4.7
	1966–71 (3)	21.1	34.8	57.1	3.8	4.3
Israel	1958–65 (1)	13.6	57.0	26.5	11.7	4.8
	1965–72 (2)	11.3	75.8	50.0	−36.6	10.8
Norway	1953–61 (1)	5.0	65.1	36.5	−16.1	14.4
	1961–69 (2)	5.3	51.0	58.3	−19.4	10.0

a. Average annual growth rates of total manufacturing gross output.

b. Expressed as percentages of change in total gross manufacturing output; add up to 100 percent. DD is domestic demand expansion, EE is export expansion, IS is import substitution, and IO is change in input-output coefficients.

Source: World Bank data, described in Kubo (1983).

early phase of industrialization from the mid-1950s to the early 1960s. In the relatively closed economies—Colombia, Mexico, and Turkey—the import substitution phase continued for many years. From figure 6-7, it appears that in the closed economies, and also in Israel, import substitution was concentrated in heavy industry, whereas in Korea and Taiwan it was important in both heavy and light industry.

In many other episodes, changes in input-output coefficients (IO) made a significant contribution to growth, with magnitudes comparable to those for import substitution. As discussed in chapter 5, such a positive contribution reflects an increase in input-output coefficients, that is, a deepening in interindustry linkages. This phenomenon appears to be a universal characteristic of industrialization and will be discussed in more detail in the next chapter.

In the closed economies, export expansion was not an important source of output change in any episode. Both Mexico and Turkey had episodes in which exports increased in importance, but the numbers are significant only in relation to their past values and not in comparison with the rest of the sample. In all the other economies, the role of exports was large in all episodes, but with significant variations across economies, episodes, and sectors. Korea and Taiwan stand out as the star performers. They started with dramatic increases in exports of light industrial products and then shifted toward exports of heavy industrial products. Although less dramatic, this shift in exports from light to heavy manufacturing is also evident in Israel, Japan, and Norway. Only in Yoguslavia was the contribution of heavy industrial exports greater in the early period, which probably reflects a pattern typical of socialist economies with their emphasis on the development of heavy industry.

The observed shifts in the contribution to growth from export expansion and import substitution across episodes parallel the shifts in development strategy discussed above (see figure 6-5). The episodes—twenty-four in all for the nine economies—can generally be categorized as belonging to one of three distinct trade strategies: import substitution, export promotion, or trade liberalization. In table 6-7, the episodes are arrayed according to the contribution of export expansion and of import substitution to the total change in manufacturing output. Within each group, the episodes are listed in ascending order of the contribution of export expansion.

In the initial episodes for Colombia, Korea, and Taiwan, import substitution made a large contribution, which is consistent with their policy regimes. In Mexico and Turkey, significant but smaller contributions of import substitution characterized the first two episodes. Both countries had also pursued an import substitution strategy in the preceding decades. In Turkey's 1968–73 episode, when exports were promoted, the export contribution rose to 10.4 percent. This episode, although short, did reflect a shift in incentives and perhaps provided an indication of what Turkey

Table 6-7. *Typology of Trade Strategies by Contributions to Growth*
(percent)

Export expansion	Import substitution				Row total
	−37 to −16	−5 to +5	9 to 12	22 to 43	
2 to 9		Colombia (2)	Turkey (1)	Colombia (1)	
		Mexico (3)	Mexico (1)		
			Mexico (2)		
			Turkey (2)		7
10 to 28		Turkey (3)	Israel (1)	Korea (1)	
		Japan (2)		Taiwan (1)	
		Japan (4)			
		Japan (3)			
		Yugoslavia (1)			8
30 to 62	Norway (1)	Korea (2)			
	Yugoslavia (2)	Japan (1)			
	Israel (2)	Taiwan (2)			
	Norway (2)	Taiwan (3)			
		Korea (3)			9
Column total	4	12	5	3	24

Note: Economies are arrayed according to contributions of export expansion and import substitution to total manufacturing growth. Within groups, episodes are listed in increasing order of the contribution of export expansion. Numbers in parentheses refer to episodes as defined in table 6-6.

Source: Table 6-6.

could accomplish, as confirmed by the effect of its shift toward an open development strategy in the 1980s. Colombia is an exception: its shift toward export promotion policies in the last episode is not reflected in the results because the effects had only begun to be felt and because of the importance of coffee. An additional explanation is provided by Morawetz (1981), who did a case study of the clothing sector. He argues that Colombian clothing exporters were not able to meet the quality and delivery schedule requirements of the U.S. market even though price incentives existed for part of the period.

In seventeen out of twenty-four episodes, export expansion contributed more than 10 percent to total output growth. In the early episodes in Israel, Korea, and Taiwan, moderate export expansion was coupled with substantial import substitution. More commonly, however, export expansion contributed heavily to growth when incentives favoring import substitution were removed, so that import substitution made little contribution.

In four episodes for Israel, Norway, and Yugoslavia, export expansion was coupled with large negative import substitution. These episodes can be characterized as reflecting trade liberalization policies and as resulting in increased exports and imports.[14] The sizable effect of changes in input-output coefficients for the liberalization episodes in both Israel and Norway may well reflect technological changes in response to international competition, a theme that will be explored in chapter 7.

Sequencing of Trade Strategies

In addition to a clustering of economies according to the contribution of import substitution and export expansion to growth, it also appears from table 6-7 that trade contributions in these economies follow a distinct sequence. Figure 6-8 plots the export expansion and import substitution contributions for all the episodes and shows clearly that periods of significant export expansion are almost always preceded by periods of strong import substitution. Japan is the only exception. It is by far the largest economy in the sample, so the small contribution of import substitution, either positive or negative, is not surprising.

From figure 6-8, it is possible to distinguish three groups of economies. The first group comprises Israel, Korea, and Taiwan—economies in which a period of strong import substitution was followed by a period of export-led growth. The second group comprises Japan, Norway, and Yugoslavia—economies in which the growing role of export expansion in later periods combined with either continued import liberalization (Norway and Yugoslavia) or no significant import substitution (Japan). Colombia, Mexico, and Turkey constitute a third group—economies in which, although the role of import substitution fell over time, export expansion was never very important and growth rates were relatively low. Mexico and Turkey did have episodes with increased export expansion, and Turkey perhaps shares some of the features of the second group.

For the first group, the pattern of observed sequencing of import substitution and export expansion can be attributed to the continuation of a shift in policy toward an export-led development strategy and to the availability of foreign capital at the time when the change in policy was taking place.[15] Indeed, the timely availability of relatively large amounts of foreign exchange is a distinguishing characteristic of Israel, Korea, and Taiwan. For the second group, the situation was somewhat different since these countries were already semi-industrialized in the initial period and are therefore not strictly comparable to the other economies in the sample. It is not surprising to find that countries which are members of the General Agreement on Tariffs and Trade (GATT)—and which participated in the multilateral tariff reductions in the 1960s and 1970s—experienced import

14. Israel is discussed by Michaely (1975), Yugoslavia by Tyson (1980), and Norway by Balassa (1979a).

15. Some have argued that the threat of U.S. aid withdrawal was important in shaping the change in policies. See Krueger (1980b) on Korea.

Figure 6-8. *Trade Sequences in Manufacturing of Selected Sample Economies, by Episode*

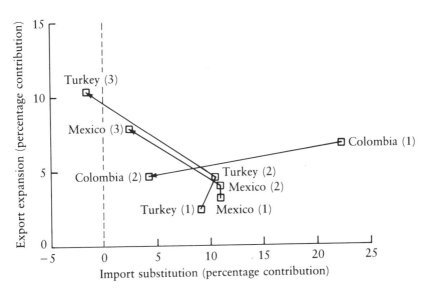

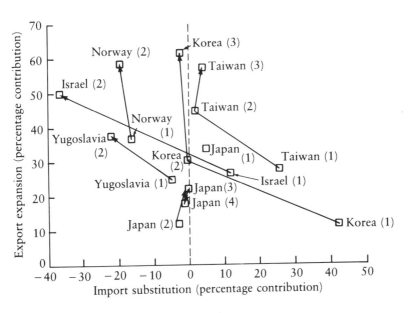

Note: Numbers in parentheses refer to episodes.

liberalization with increased export expansion. For the third group, the minor role of export expansion combined with decreasing import substitution can be attributed to less favorable initial conditions and to an evident reluctance to shift toward a more open development strategy with a reduced bias against exports. In contrast with the first group, the supplies of both foreign exchange and human resources were less favorable in the initial periods and at the time when a shift in strategy seemed desirable.

The observed sequencing raises an immediate question: is a period of significant import substitution, with strong protection of domestic manufacturing, necessary to build the industrial base required for a later shift to an open development strategy led by export expansion? The question is related to a version of the infant industry argument for protection: is a period of protection for manufacturing required to allow firms to grow up before they must face the real world of international markets? It is difficult to generalize from so few cases, and a complete analysis requires consideration of productivity growth, which we discuss in part III. Nevertheless, the evidence presented so far is consistent with the infant industry argument, and it is worthwhile looking at some cases in more detail.[16]

From table 6-7, it appears that Korea and Taiwan are the two economies that experienced the most dramatic switch from import substitution to export expansion. Israel and Turkey also followed such a pattern, but less dramatically. Israel is a very small country and something of a special case, so we do not consider it further. For Korea, Taiwan, and Turkey, we turn to a more detailed analysis of the role of export expansion and import substitution in the growth of the manufacturing sectors.

Table 6-8 presents data on the relative contributions of import substitution and export expansion as percentages of total sectoral output growth during each episode for the three economies. The table also shows the total change in sectoral output as a percentage of the change in aggregate (economywide) output in each episode. The manufacturing sectors are listed in descending order of contribution to total output change, with the leading sectors at the top of each table. For Turkey, the table lists all the manufacturing sectors. For Korea and Taiwan, the miscellaneous and unallocated sectors are omitted.[17]

Even though these economies underwent major shifts in development strategy, table 6-8 indicates that the leading sectors changed little. With a few exceptions, the first five or six sectors led in all episodes. In Korea, machinery moved from sixth to eighth place and then shot up to first place

16. For other analyses of the infant industry argument and sequencing from import substitution to export expansion, see Westphal (1982) and Balassa (1979b).
17. See chapter 5 for a detailed reconciliation of the sector definitions across all the economies. There are some differences in sector definitions. Paper and printing are aggregated in Taiwan and Turkey. Textiles and clothing are aggregated in Turkey, but leather products are a separate sector. Leather products are included with clothing in Korea and Taiwan. Kubo and Robinson (1984) also discuss the sources of growth in particular sectors.

in its contribution to aggregate output growth. Taiwan shows a similar pattern, with machinery moving up as an increasingly important leading sector. In Turkey, machinery actually fell in rank from fifth to seventh place. In Taiwan, the role of food processing declined while that of clothing increased dramatically. In Turkey and Korea, there was less change in the relative importance of these "light" sectors.

Although there was relatively little change in the ranks of the leading sectors, there were significant changes in all three economies in the relative roles of import substitution and export expansion.[18] Figures 6-9, 6-10, and 6-11 plot the import substitution and export expansion contributions from table 6-8. In Korea, the sequencing is quite dramatic. In textiles, chemicals, machinery, petroleum products, paper products, and wood products, import substitution was the main source of growth in the first episode, while export expansion became the main source in the two later episodes. In Taiwan, import substitution in the first episode was very large for basic metals, chemicals, machinery, nonmetallic minerals, clothing, paper products, petroleum products, and transport equipment. In later episodes, the contribution of export expansion to all these sectors was large. The changeover in Taiwan was less dramatic than in Korea, however. In many sectors, export expansion was significant in the first episode, so that import substitution and export expansion occurred simultaneously.

In Turkey, there was significant import substitution in one or both of the first two episodes in petroleum products, basic metals, machinery, nonmetallic minerals, rubber products, and transport equipment. Of these six sectors, four had significant contributions of export expansion in the last episode (but not machinery and transport equipment). The numbers are much smaller for both contributions than in Korea and Taiwan, but the sequencing is evident. In addition, two sectors (food processing and leather products) had significant export expansion contributions during the earlier episodes. In contrast with what happened in Korea and Taiwan, the machinery sector in Turkey did not "mature" during this period—that is, the first episode of extensive import substitution was not followed by any significant export expansion.

The export expansion episode in Turkey was not sustained. The country went through yet another cycle of increasing bias toward import substitution and away from exporting, followed by a crisis in 1977–78.[19] Recently, however, Turkey has shifted toward a more open development strategy, and it now appears that exports, especially of manufactures, are responding successfully. The period of inward-oriented development was quite prolonged in comparison with other semi-industrial countries, but the

18. See Chenery (1980), who uses the same data and discusses this issue in more detail.
19. See Dervis and Robinson (1982) and Celasun (1983) for an analysis of this period.

Table 6-8. *Leading Sectors and Trade Sequences for Selected Semi-Industrial Economies*
(percentage contribution)

	1955–63				1963–70				1970–73			
			Contribution				Contribution				Contribution	
Sector	Output change	Rank	IS	EE	Output change	Rank	IS	EE	Output change	Rank	IS	EE
					Korea							
Food processing	12.6	1	17.7	7.1	9.5	1	−2.9	9.7	11.3	2	1.9	17.5
Textiles	6.5	2	80.7	20.2	4.3	4	−14.3	72.0	6.9	6	−13.7	99.1
Clothing	6.1	3	5.7	6.1	6.0	2	−0.8	45.1	8.6	3	−5.2	70.7
Chemicals	5.4	4	72.8	2.7	4.8	3	8.4	21.2	8.0	4	5.9	44.8
Basic metals	4.5	5	4.1	28.0	3.3	5	11.3	20.4	7.3	5	−13.8	76.1
Machinery	4.3	6	52.7	4.3	2.5	8	−28.7	36.6	12.2	1	2.1	69.1
Petroleum products	3.0	7	97.5	3.1	3.0	6	30.4	17.3	2.1	7	−7.2	40.9
Paper and products	2.3	8	95.5	1.9	1.1	11	−24.2	19.3	1.6	9	−1.9	53.2
Nonmetallic minerals	2.3	9	14.0	2.0	1.9	9	7.2	11.2	1.7	8	−1.7	41.0
Printing	2.0	10	7.1	2.1	0.5	12	−7.5	18.3	0.9	11	4.2	42.8
Transport equipment	1.7	11	10.6	7.7	2.5	7	7.0	7.5	0.8	12	0.3	70.1
Wood and products	1.7	12	64.4	24.0	1.7	10	−0.3	62.0	1.5	10	−0.8	112.5

Taiwan

Food processing	10.5	1	-0.7	35.8	12.7	1	-7.5	29.7	5.8	5	2.1	28.0
Textiles	7.5	2	8.2	41.1	6.6	2	-2.3	67.1	12.9	1	4.0	64.6
Basic metals	3.0	3	63.5	25.0	3.8	5	-9.1	63.2	4.5	6	13.2	59.5
Wood and products	2.9	4	6.9	33.1	1.7	11	0.8	108.8	3.6	7	0.4	66.0
Chemicals	2.5	5	98.0	13.3	5.9	4	10.5	31.2	7.3	4	3.8	52.5
Machinery	1.8	6	23.8	18.5	6.0	3	32.9	31.3	12.4	2	3.9	65.3
Nonmetallic minerals	1.7	7	21.0	32.1	2.6	7	-0.5	48.1	1.1	11	8.1	6.2
Clothing	1.6	8	30.1	23.7	2.2	9	0.0	43.1	7.7	3	-2.4	67.3
Paper and products	1.6	9	13.8	26.2	2.7	6	3.9	23.2	2.5	9	-0.6	30.6
Petroleum products	1.4	10	14.4	33.1	2.5	8	-7.9	24.3	2.3	10	3.5	46.6
Transport equipment	1.0	11	3.4	10.7	2.1	10	-10.0	22.6	2.7	8	18.5	28.5

Turkey

Food processing	11.7	1	-3.0	2.8	6.9	3	6.6	24.2	9.6	1	-0.9	19.4
Petroleum products	5.5	2	21.1	3.5	4.5	4	1.7	1.2	6.7	2	1.7	10.6
Textiles and clothing	4.8	3	8.3	1.6	7.2	2	4.5	2.5	6.0	4	-0.2	22.0
Basic metals	3.0	4	13.5	-2.5	8.7	1	17.7	1.8	6.3	3	-21.0	6.7
Machinery	2.1	5	67.6	0.0	3.3	6	18.9	0.4	4.3	7	8.8	1.9
Chemicals	1.4	6	-24.7	-0.2	3.5	5	-2.3	1.8	4.8	6	-5.7	3.8
Nonmetallic minerals	1.3	7	36.7	0.9	1.7	9	-0.3	1.1	2.7	8	4.2	7.5
Wood and products	1.2	8	2.7	0.8	1.5	11	7.3	0.9	1.4	10	-0.4	3.5
Rubber and products	1.0	9	8.7	1.5	1.3	12	31.3	1.1	1.2	11	-0.9	9.3
Leather and products	0.8	10	5.1	19.0	2.5	7	0.5	-6.8	0.5	12	-11.3	20.9
Paper and printing	0.8	11	-0.9	1.4	1.9	8	1.0	1.1	1.8	9	19.2	4.6
Transport equipment	0.5	12	-39.0	5.2	1.6	10	44.2	1.3	5.0	5	0.4	2.0

Source: World Bank data; described in Kubo (1983).

Figure 6-9. *Import and Export Changes in Korea*

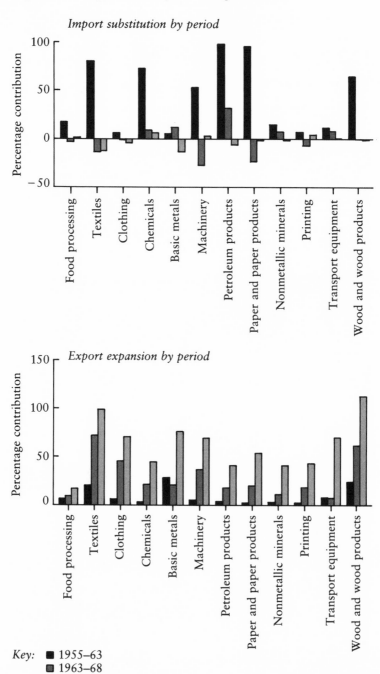

Import substitution by period

Export expansion by period

Key: ■ 1955–63
     ■ 1963–68
     □ 1968–73

Figure 6-10. *Import and Export Changes in Taiwan*

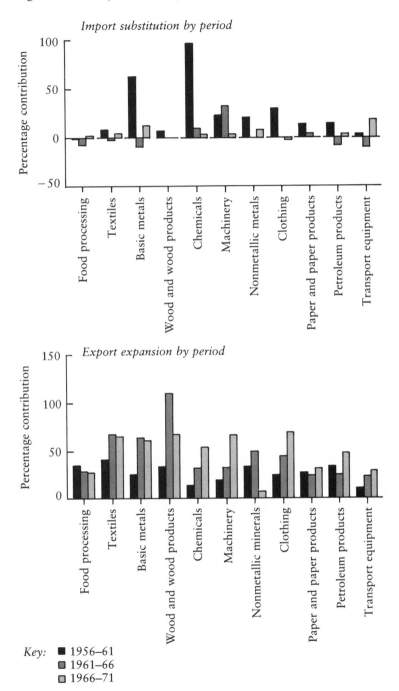

Import substitution by period

Percentage contribution

Food processing
Textiles
Basic metals
Wood and wood products
Chemicals
Machinery
Nonmetallic metals
Clothing
Paper and paper products
Petroleum products
Transport equipment

Export expansion by period

Percentage contribution

Food processing
Textiles
Basic metals
Wood and wood products
Chemicals
Machinery
Nonmetallic minerals
Clothing
Paper and paper products
Petroleum products
Transport equipment

Key: ■ 1956–61
        ▨ 1961–66
        ☐ 1966–71

Figure 6-11. *Import and Export Changes in Turkey*

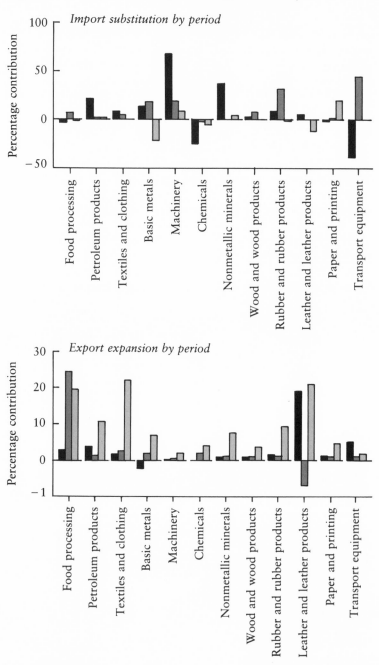

results discussed here indicate that the economy might well have been able to shift strategies successfully in the early 1970s. The advent of the oil crises and the government's misguided response to them delayed the shift for a decade.

Conclusions

This chapter has expanded on the long-run comparisons in chapters 2, 3, and 4. With a smaller sample of economies but with more detailed data, we have analyzed the interrelations between the choice of a development strategy, its supporting policy regimes, and economic performance at both the aggregate and sectoral levels. The results for these economies have been compared with those for the archetypal economies modeled in chapter 3. The analysis has focused both on long-run trends and on shorter-term episodes that can be classified by their trade strategies.

The analysis of the interrelations between the choice of a development strategy, its supporting policy regimes, and economic performance was of necessity heuristic. The input-output model that provides the framework for the analysis does not directly incorporate the links between policy choices, incentives, and performance. Although many of the links we discussed are suggestive, formal modeling of them is beyond the scope of this chapter. Chapter 11 analyzes some of these policy links with a more elaborate model of a single country.

The multisectoral approach used in this chapter has shown how economies pursuing different development strategies exhibit different kinds of structural change. In particular, the analysis has focused on leading sectors and on the roles of different sources of demand as engines of growth. In the next chapter, we focus more on the composition of output and on how the choice of a development strategy affects structural change.

The analysis of trade sequences raises issues about technological change and productivity. In Korea, Taiwan, and Turkey, there were episodes when import substitution was an important source of growth for many manufacturing sectors; these were followed by episodes when export expansion took over as a significant driving force. The results in this chapter for our sample are consistent with the view that a period of import substitution and deepening of input-output relationships is required before an economy can compete successfully in world markets and so shift to either an export-led or open development strategy. This is a theme that will be considered further in later chapters.

7 Interdependence and Industrial Structure

YUJI KUBO
JAIME DE MELO
SHERMAN ROBINSON
MOSHE SYRQUIN

CHAPTER 6 FOCUSED on economywide growth and on the roles of different sectors and sources of demand as the engines of that growth. We identified several typologies of growth and related policy regimes—based largely on aggregate data—which could be used to characterize distinctive subperiods or episodes in the development of the nine economies in our sample. In this chapter, we examine the development experience of these economies from a different angle, stressing sectoral structure and the determinants of structural change.

"Structural change" is a frequently used term in economics, but it is nevertheless hard to pin down.[1] In the absence of a formal model, it is convenient to define structural change as any shifts in the composition of various economic aggregates. In speaking of the causes or sources of structural change, however, one must have in mind some model of the economy that specifies underlying stable relationships—even if only in imprecise terms. Because we have an input-output model, we can be more precise in the measurement of structural change, although the scope of the model limits the aspects of structural change that we can cover.

In the static model, the input-output coefficients are assumed to be given, as are the level and sectoral composition of the components of final demand—consumption, investment, imports, and exports. The model then determines the level and sectoral composition of total production. This treatment implies that changes in the structure of these exogenous elements are the sources or causes of structural change. Thus we shall study changes in the sectoral composition of aggregate output that are induced by changes in demand, trade, and production technology. The emphasis is on the role of such structural parameters as input-output

---

1. See Machlup (1963), and Chenery (1979, pp. 108–09) for a discussion that distinguishes between the structure of an economy and the structure of a formal mathematical model of an economy.

coefficients, import coefficients, and the composition of trade and final demand.[2]

One of the main features of structural transformation is a rapid rise in the relative importance of manufacturing production accompanied by a relative decline in primary production. This chapter is concerned with the various aspects of this transformation. We begin the chapter by looking at some summary measures of structural change over roughly a twenty-year period for the economies in the sample and by setting out the long-term regularities that characterize their growth experience. We then trace these regularities back to changes in three different structural relations: composition of demand, intermediate input technology, and size and composition of trade. We shall also draw on data for the various benchmark episodes discussed in chapter 6 to examine the relation between these structural changes and the choice of a development strategy.

Aggregate Measures of Structural Change

Chapter 3 explored the nature of the long-run transformation of typical developing economies and divided the process into a series of stages or phases. This section examines the industrialization phase and several concomitant structural changes in the sample economies.

Industrialization

According to the model used in chapter 3, the industrialization phase of structural transformation typically entails a shift in the manufacturing share of GDP from about 19 percent to 36 percent, which is associated with an increase in per capita income from $280 to $2,100. In the model, the process was assumed to require about fifty years, with GNP growing at a rate of about 6.2 percent a year (or 3.9 percent per capita). These figures imply that the share of manufacturing increases by an average of 3.2 percentage points each decade throughout the period (which defines the "rate of industrialization").

This performance is about average compared with the record during the nineteenth century of those countries that are now industrialized; however, the variance in historical performance is quite high. Kuznets (1966, table 3-1) estimates rates of industrialization for these countries that range from about 1 to 6 percentage points a decade, with Canada and Italy at the low end and Sweden and the United States at the high end.

Figure 7-1 presents comparable data on the ten-year rates of industrialization (that is, decadal changes in the share of manufacturing in GDP)

---

2. In this chapter, given data limitations, we are not able to analyze separately the roles of investment and consumption demand. Kubo, Robinson, and Urata (1986) consider the role of investment in the framework of a dynamic input-output model applied to two countries in the sample, Korea and Turkey.

Figure 7-1. *Change in Share of Manufacturing in GDP,
Semi-Industrial Economies, 1953–73*

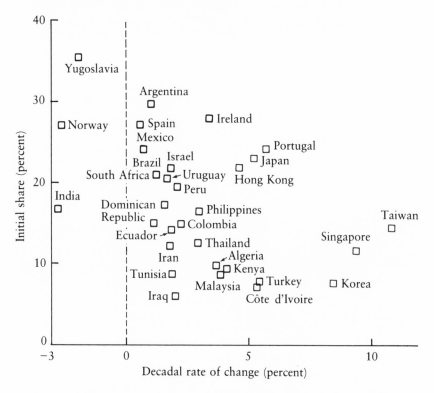

for most of the semi-industrial economies for the period 1953–73.[3]
Although the variation is high, many economies achieved rates of industrialization in excess of 3 percentage points a decade. Korea and Taiwan
are notable outliers; each roughly tripled its share of manufacturing in
GDP during the twenty-year period (from 7.6 to 24.5 percent for Korea
and from 14.4 to 37.2 percent for Taiwan).[4]

The economies in the smaller sample span the range of observations in
figure 7-1, with Norway and Yugoslavia at the lower end and Korea and
Taiwan at the upper end. In general, there is a mild inverse relation
between the initial share of manufacturing in GDP and the rate of industrialization. Norway and Yugoslavia in 1953 were probably approaching
their natural limits for the share of manufacturing in GDP while Korea,

3. See chapter 4, which discusses the semi-industrial countries and their performance in
the postwar period. A number of cross-country studies are discussed in chapter 2.
4. Singapore is also an outlier, but it is a very special case of a city-state economy.

Figure 7-2. *Change in Manufacturing Share in Total Output*

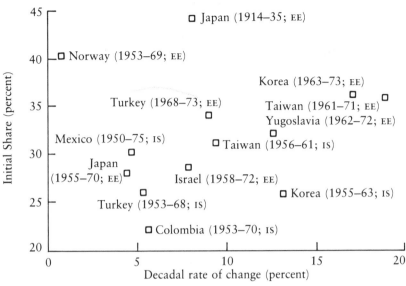

Key: EE Export expansion   IS Import substitution

Source: Episodes are defined in table 6-7. Periods include more than one episode when adjacent episodes had the same classification (EE or IS). Data on shares are described in Kubo (1983).

Taiwan, and Turkey were just starting periods of substantial industrial growth.[5]

The sample reveals interesting variations in the process of structural transformation across episodes. Figure 7-2 presents input-output data on the initial shares and ten-year rate of change in the share of manufacturing in total output (rather than in value added as in figure 7-1). The data are plotted only for periods in which either export expansion or import substitution was an important source of demand growth,[6] which sometimes include more than one episode as defined in chapter 6. Of the thirteen periods plotted, eight are classified as export expansion and five as import substitution.

In general, the episodes of export expansion started from a base of higher manufacturing shares; only Israel and Turkey started such a phase

5. Turkey's low initial share of manufacturing was at least partly caused by its large agricultural resource base. The country has fostered industrial development since before World War II.

6. The classification is based on table 6-7. Episodes characterized by trade liberalization are grouped with those characterized by export expansion.

Table 7-1. *Aggregate Measures of Structural Change of Sample Economies in the Manufacturing Sector*
(average annual percentage change in sectoral shares of each aggregate[a])

Average annual output growth of total gross production	Ratio of manufacturing output to total output[b]	Ratio of intermediate demand to total output[b]	Change in output structure[c]	Change in import structure[c]	Change in export structure[c]
Taiwan 12.0	Taiwan 15.7	Taiwan 10.0	Taiwan 3.8	Japan 4.0	Taiwan 7.3
Japan 11.4	Korea 15.3	Korea 6.1	Yugoslavia 3.7	Israel 4.0	Korea 6.2
Korea 11.2	Yugoslavia 12.5	Colombia 4.4	Japan 3.5	Korea 3.9	Turkey 5.9
Israel 9.9	Japan 8.2	Israel 4.2	Turkey 3.3	Turkey 3.4	Japan 5.7
Yugoslavia 8.7	Israel 8.1	Japan 4.2	Korea 3.2	Taiwan 2.6	Yugoslavia 3.6
Colombia 8.4	Turkey 6.3	Yugoslavia 3.1	Israel 1.6	Yugoslavia 2.3	Israel 3.3
Turkey 6.6	Colombia 5.6	Mexico 2.8	Colombia 1.2	Colombia 2.3	Mexico 2.4
Mexico 6.5	Mexico 3.7	Turkey 2.0	Norway 1.1	Norway 1.4	Norway 1.5
Norway 5.7	Norway 0.8	Norway 1.4	Mexico 1.0	Mexico 0.6	Colombia 1.2

a. Dates for each economy are given in figure 6-5.
b. Decadal rates of change.
c. Computed as $\overline{X} = [\Sigma_i (DX_i(1) - DX_i(0))^2]^{1/2}$; $DX_i = X_i/[\Sigma_i (X_i^2)]^{1/2}$. The unit of measure is a multisectoral generalization of the rate of industrialization defined in chapter 5 for the manufacturing sector. It measures the Euclidean distance between the initial and terminal data in percentage points. All rates are computed at the fourteen-sector level and are in units of percent per decade.

Source: World Bank data; described in Kubo (1983).

with less than a 30 percent share of manufacturing in gross output.[7] It appears that episodes of export expansion also exhibit high rates of industrialization. For the economies in which the sequence from import substitution to export expansion is evident (Korea, Taiwan, and Turkey), the rate of industrialization accelerated substantially in the latter phase—so export expansion appears to have contributed more to industrialization than did import substitution. Yet the fact that the episodes of export expansion started from a relatively high initial share of manufacturing indicates that a country may need to develop a domestic industrial base before it can expand its manufacturing sector through exports (a point discussed in chapter 6 and taken up again in later chapters).

Intermediate Demand and Trade

Industrialization includes certain concomitant structural changes beyond simply an increase in the share of manufacturing in output. Table 7-1 presents some summary measures of aspects of structural change for the sample during the entire period.

There is a significant correlation among the types of structural change measured in table 7-1. As noted above, countries that grow faster tend to have faster rates of structural transformation. They also tend to have more rapid increases in intermediate input demand—"deepenings" of their input-output matrices.[8] These dynamic shifts reflect changes in both technology and the structure of demand.

Colombia is an interesting exception. It had a high rate of increase in intermediate demand even though it ranks relatively low in output growth (sixth) and in rate of industrialization (seventh). During this period, Colombia started from a very low initial manufacturing share in gross output and pursued an import substitution policy that, as these results indicate, achieved significant deepening of its input-output structure.[9] Japan had a very high rate of output growth but ranks lower in rate of industrialization and input-output deepening. Japan's structural transformation was quite far along by 1955; it had the highest initial manufacturing share of any economy in the sample (see figure 7-2). So it is not surprising to observe a slowing in its rate of transformation.

The last three columns of table 7-1 provide a measure of compositional changes in the structure of output, imports, and exports which is comparable across economies. For the postwar period, it appears that international trade did serve the function that theory suggests of permitting a separation

---

7. In the case of Turkey, the export expansion phase was aborted after 1973. See Celasun (1983).

8. This phenomenon was also noted in chapter 3. It will be examined in more detail below. One would also expect to find links between productivity growth and the rate of industrialization, an issue that will be explored in chapter 8.

9. See Diaz-Alejandro (1976) for a good case study of Colombian development during this period.

between the structure of supply and demand.[10] For most of the sample, the change in the composition of imports and exports was greater than the change in the composition of output. (The exceptions are Yugoslavia for exports and Mexico, Taiwan, and Yugoslavia for imports.) It was also generally easier to change the structure of exports than of imports: only Colombia and Israel had higher rates of change in import composition than in export composition.

The analysis so far in this and earlier chapters indicates that the industrialization of the semi-industrial countries since World War II has embraced many different processes. Structural transformation is reflected not only in changes in the manufacturing share but also in changes in input-output technology, demand, and trade. The analysis of these concomitant processes requires a multisectoral perspective.

Sectoral Deviations from Balanced Growth

To examine the causes of changes in the composition of output, it is convenient to measure the deviation of changes in sectoral output from what would have prevailed if there had been balanced growth (that is, if all sectors had grown at the same average rate). To do this, we use the decomposition equation introduced in chapter 5 (equation 5-13), which compares the material balances in the terminal year with the hypothetical values that would have prevailed under balanced growth. Note that in this formulation, as in chapter 6, the same domestic supply ratio is used for all types of demand. To maintain comparability, we have used this formulation in the tables describing the nine economies. We also use the more detailed breakdown described in chapter 5 for some comparisons in a subsample of economies for which the data are available.

In this formulation, deviations (δ) replace increments (Δ), but in fact the two terms that express changes in coefficient ($\Delta \hat{u}$ and ΔA) are nearly the same. Given that deviations are smaller than increments, the relative importance of the import substitution (IS) and input-output (IO) coefficient terms will be greater in the deviation equation. Only nonproportional demand growth has an effect on the composition of output, whereas changes in structural coefficients have a direct effect on structural change.

Table 7-2 presents a decomposition of the sources of sectoral deviation from balanced growth at the three-sector level for the entire period. These deviations from balanced growth reported in table 7-2 again indicate a significant increase in the share of manufacturing. In every case, an increase in manufacturing output above that implied by balanced growth represents the greater part of structural change.[11] Also in every case, the

10. The role of trade in "delinking" demand and supply will be explored in more detail below.
11. These results are consistent with the analysis in chapter 4, in which a larger sample was considered. A few semi-industrial countries suffered from problems of the Dutch disease, but they are exceptions.

output deviation for the primary sector is negative. Along with other forces, Engel's law appears to be at work; the contribution of an expanding domestic demand for the primary sector is negative in every economy. In this sample, there is no offsetting effect of foreign trade. Only in Colombia does export expansion make a significant contribution to the nonproportional growth of the primary sector, and it is not large enough to offset the effect of domestic demand.

For many of the economies—Israel, prewar Japan, Korea, Taiwan, Yugoslavia, and Norway—export expansion accounted for 50 percent or more of the nonproportional growth in manufacturing during the entire period.[12] In the first three (prewar Japan, Korea, and Taiwan), the export effect swamped all other sources of demand and provided clear examples of export-led structural change. In the last three (Israel, Norway, and Yugoslavia), the large positive effect of export expansion was mostly offset by a large negative contribution from import substitution. These countries pursued strategies of trade liberalization with increases in both exports and imports of manufactures and with little net effect of trade on sectoral composition at this level of aggregation.[13]

In Colombia and Mexico, import substitution played the dominant role in structural change. Turkey should also be included in this group because, for most of the period (1958–68), import substitution dominated the other sources of demand (accounting for 30–40 percent of the deviation of manufacturing output from balanced growth). If the brief episode of export expansion (1968–73) is averaged in, the import substitution effect is washed out. We shall examine the episodes separately below.

In all instances except for prewar Japan and Korea, changes in input-output coefficients had a significant effect on structural change in manufacturing.[14] This effect was larger in the import-substituting countries, in which it accounted for a quarter to a third of the nonproportional rise in the share of manufacturing. This fact reflects the introduction of new technologies that make greater use of intermediate inputs and that appear to be necessary for industrialization regardless of the role of trade. However, as we shall discuss below, the choice of a trade strategy can affect the timing of this deepening of intermediate inputs.

Figures 7-3 and 7-4 separate the manufacturing sector into two subsectors, heavy (including intermediates and machinery) and light (including food processing and consumer goods) and provide data for each of the episodes. (See chapter 3 for definitions of the aggregations used.) In most economies, the effect of heavy industry on nonproportional growth in-

---

12. In Japan from 1914 to 1935, the figure was 44 percent.

13. Israel is a special case; it had large capital inflows throughout the period. See Syrquin (1986) for a detailed analysis of Israel that uses this methodology.

14. In both Japan and Korea, there were substantial data problems with the input-output tables. The 1955 Korean table was difficult to estimate and may be affected by recovery from the Korean war. For pre–World War II Japan, the contribution of changes in input-output coefficients was estimated as a residual.

Table 7-2. *Sectoral Deviations from Balanced Growth*
(percentage change in aggregate gross output)

Economy and sectors	Output growth rate	Output deviation[a] (δX)	Domestic demand expansion (DD)	Export expansion (EE)	Import substitution (IS)	Changes in input-output coefficients (IO)
Colombia (1953–70)						
Primary	4.5	-3.7	-7.9	3.8	0.3	0.1
Manufacturing	8.1	16.1	1.4	1.4	7.8	5.6
Services	5.5	1.9	-0.8	1.2	0.4	1.0
Mexico (1950–75)						
Primary	4.3	-5.8	-2.3	-2.6	-0.2	-0.7
Manufacturing	7.7	10.1	3.5	-0.2	4.3	2.5
Services	6.4	1.0	0.5	-0.5	0.6	0.5
Turkey (1953–73)						
Primary	2.5	-18.1	-11.5	-2.1	0.2	-4.7
Manufacturing	8.1	17.2	4.6	4.5	2.4	5.8
Services	6.7	9.0	3.6	2.1	0.2	3.1
Yugoslavia (1962–72)						
Primary	2.6	-17.7	-10.3	1.8	-3.9	-5.4
Manufacturing	12.1	21.1	13.6	10.9	-10.1	6.8
Services	8.8	4.6	4.5	1.4	-1.5	0.3
Japan (1914–35)						
Primary	1.9	-10.8	-9.9	1.1	-3.2	1.2
Manufacturing	5.5	23.6	13.6	10.6	2.5	-3.1
Services	4.2	13.1	6.1	6.4	-0.3	0.9

Japan (1955–70)						
Primary	2.2	−7.6	−3.2	−0.2	−1.9	−2.4
Manufacturing	13.3	12.6	5.0	2.8	−1.2	5.9
Services	11.4	1.0	−1.0	1.2	−1.0	1.7
Korea (1955–73)						
Primary	5.7	−11.3	−7.7	1.8	−2.3	−3.1
Manufacturing	15.8	27.5	4.7	21.1	1.4	0.2
Services	10.3	4.6	0.9	4.3	0.2	−0.7
Taiwan (1956–71)						
Primary	7.1	−7.6	−4.2	1.5	−2.7	−2.2
Manufacturing	16.2	28.2	0.7	20.1	3.5	3.9
Services	9.7	−2.0	−4.5	3.5	0.1	−1.2
Israel (1958–72)						
Primary	6.4	−4.0	−4.8	1.8	−0.4	−0.5
Manufacturing	12.5	15.4	7.0	13.4	−11.8	6.8
Services	9.2	−12.2	−15.2	5.0	−3.5	1.5
Norway (1953–69)						
Primary	2.5	−4.7	−3.1	0.0	−2.0	0.4
Manufacturing	5.2	7.8	−1.6	12.6	−9.2	6.0
Services	4.8	6.2	−0.8	9.3	−3.1	0.8

Note: The first column shows the average annual growth rates of sectoral gross output. Sectoral output deviations and the sources-of-growth contributions are expressed as percentages of the change in aggregate gross output in all sectors during the period specified for each economy. For each sector, the second column is the total of the third through sixth columns. The calculations were done at the 22–24 sector level, and the results were aggregated to 3 sectors. See chapter 5 for a discussion of the methodology.

a. Scaled for comparability across economies and periods by being divided by the total change in aggregate output in the economy.

Source: World Bank data; described in Kubo (1983).

Figure 7-3. *Output Deviations from Balanced Growth in Heavy Industry, Sample Economies*

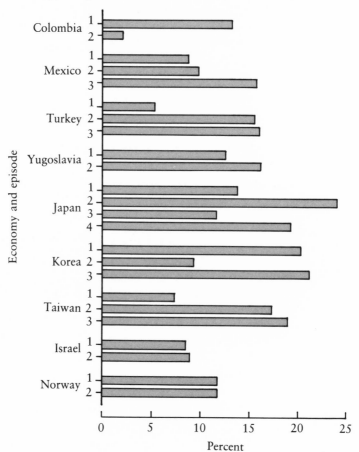

creased with time. In their respective postwar recoveries, each had an episode during which the role of heavy industry was large followed by an episode during which its role declined dramatically. Then, in the final episode in each country, heavy industry again led nonproportional growth. In Colombia, the role of heavy industry declined dramatically during the two episodes for which there are data. In contrast, Israel and Norway, both more developed than the other economies in the sample, showed little change in the role of heavy industry.

The role of light industry varied widely. In the large, more closed economies (Japan, Mexico, and Turkey) light industry was not a significant source of structural change. In the export-led economies (Korea and Taiwan), it was much more significant. In Taiwan, light industry (especially food processing) grew very rapidly in the early episode. Next came a

Figure 7-4. *Output Deviations from Balanced Growth in Light Industry, Sample Economies*

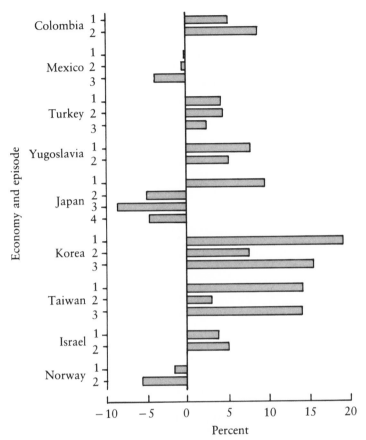

shift toward heavy industry (1961–66) followed by a new spurt (1966–71) in which light and heavy industry were both leading sources of structural change. In Korea, light and heavy industry moved together in their effects on nonproportional growth.

Korea and Taiwan differ markedly from the rest of the sample. The magnitude of their output deviations is larger, and light industry plays a much more important role in the process (accounting for about half their nonproportional growth of manufacturing). The differences are related to the dramatic effects of the export-led development strategies pursued by these two economies, which represent extreme examples of the typical small manufacturing (SM) pattern discussed in chapter 4.

Figure 7-5 presents the decompositions into sources, by category of demand, of the output deviations for heavy and light industry for most of

Figure 7-5. *Output Deviations of Heavy and Light Industry from Balanced Growth, Sample Economies*

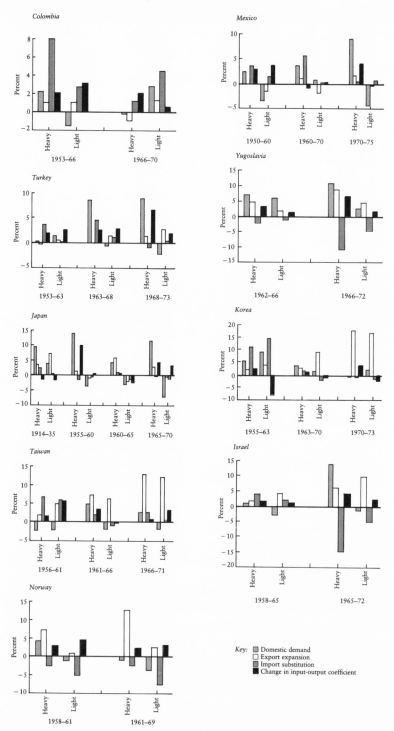

the economies and episodes. The data are shown as percentages of the total deviation for the economy, so the sum of the contributions for each subsector across demand categories equals the contributions given in figures 7-3 and 7-4.

Looking first at Colombia, Mexico, and Turkey, we note that export expansion, when significant, occurred in light industry, whereas import substitution was more important in heavy industry for most of the episodes. In Turkey's brief phase of export-led growth (1968–73), the dramatic increase in the contribution of exports to nonproportional growth of light industry was largely offset by a decrease in the contribution of expanding domestic demand. The export boom represented a diversion of goods from the domestic market with little effect on the overall share of light industry in output.[15]

In contrast, the export expansion episodes in Korea and Taiwan were also led by light industry but with no offsetting decline in the expansion of domestic demand. The result was a significant increase in the share of light industry, as noted in figures 7-3 and 7-4—an observation that differentiates these two economies from the rest of the sample. Korea and Taiwan also differ from Colombia, Mexico, and Turkey in that export expansion made an increasingly significant contribution to structural change in heavy industry. In this respect, they resemble Yugoslavia and Japan.

The role of import substitution varied in the sample. In the more advanced countries—Yugoslavia, Japan, Israel, and Norway—import substitution made a low or negative contribution to structural change in both manufacturing subsectors. In the rest of the sample, import substitution was important in both subsectors in the early episodes but then declined in importance (with the exception of heavy industry in Colombia). By the end of the entire period, these countries appear to have exploited the available opportunities for "easy" import substitution. Less contribution to structural change from this source is likely in the future.

The role of changes in input-output coefficients varied widely across economies and episodes. For nearly every economy and subsector, there were episodes during which changes in input-output coefficients had a significant effect on structural change. At this level of aggregation, however, there does not appear to be any systematic relation between this source of deviation and other sources. As we discussed earlier (chapters 3 and 6), regularities in changes in the technology of intermediate inputs go along with development, but these changes are rooted in the increasing interdependence of the economy and are systemic. In the next section, we do a systemwide exploration of these changes in intermediate input technology.

---

15. In this case, note the negative contribution of import substitution in heavy manufacturing during Turkey's export expansion phase, when at least some of the foreign exchange was spent on imports of intermediate and capital goods.

Interindustry Linkages and the Complexity of Production

This section explores the implications of the observation that the share of total output devoted to intermediate use increases markedly as part of the structural changes that accompany growth. First, we study the relation between output growth and the rate of change of the intermediate use ratio at the sectoral level and separate the influence of differences in output composition on the intermediate input use ratio. Second, we examine how the observed increases in the use of intermediate inputs are related to changes in input-output coefficients. Such increases in interindustry linkages were first studied by Hirschman (1958), who focused on forward and backward linkages to identify key sectors that, in his view of "unbalanced growth," would spread an initial growth impulse in specific sectors throughout the economy. We develop linkage measures that are used to compare interindustry linkages in the sample of nine economies.

Intermediate Input Use, Growth, and Output Composition

In the discussion of the cross-country simulation model in chapter 3, it was noted that the average share of intermediate use in total domestic demand increases from about 33 to 45 percent during the period of the transformation (some fifty years). The typical change in the intermediate use ratio is about 12 percentage points over a fifty-year period; this implies a change in the ratio of 2.4 percentage points per decade. From table 7-1 (third column), it can be seen that all of the sample except Norway and Turkey have achieved faster rates than this.

In figure 3-3, the sample appears to divide into several groups according to two criteria: level of development and role of trade. Colombia, Mexico, and Turkey—large countries with relatively low trade shares—start out with lower initial intermediate use ratios and do not succeed in catching up with the other economies by the end of the period. Colombia is the most open of these three, and it exhibits the largest change in this ratio. Korea and Taiwan both experience dramatic changes in the intermediate use ratio and, by the end of the period, they are similar in structure to one another and to Japan. Israel and Norway—both small, open economies— are more developed initially and end up very close to each other. Norway, which started out with a higher ratio than Israel, changes the least of any country in the sample.

There is also a positive relation at the sectoral level between output growth and the rate of change of the intermediate use ratio. Pooling data for three sectors (consumer goods, producer goods, and machinery) and ten economies (treating prewar Japan as a separate entry) for a total of thirty observations gives the following regression for the relation:

$$G_w = -0.024 + 0.485\,G_x, \qquad R^2 = 0.765$$
$$(-3.5) \qquad (9.5)$$

where G_w is the annual growth rate of the sectoral intermediate use ratio, G_x is the growth rate of sectoral output, and the numbers in parentheses are t ratios.[16]

In general, the growth rate of producer goods and machinery exceeded that of consumer goods, and their use as intermediate inputs also expanded more rapidly. Taiwan is an exception—in it, consumer goods grew faster—but the relation still holds. Moreover, intermediate demand for consumer goods grew faster in Taiwan than it did for producer goods—a result that arises from Taiwan's export structure and the inclusion of textiles (an intermediate good) with clothing in the consumer goods sector. These results reaffirm the importance of intermediate demand as a source of growth and structural change.

The intermediate use ratio depends both on the density of the matrix of input-output coefficients and on the structure of production. To separate these effects, we constructed two standard output vectors designed to reflect the main differences in output composition by type of economy: an outward-oriented vector (an average of Taiwan in 1971 and Korea in 1970) and an inward-oriented vector (an average of Mexico in 1960 and Turkey in 1963). In terms of the typology in chapter 3, the first fits the small-industry-oriented (SM) pattern and the second the large (L) pattern. The principal difference in their composition of production is that the first has a larger share of manufacturing and the second a larger share of primary production and services. These two standard vectors were multiplied by the input-output coefficient matrices of each economy for every subperiod to generate variations in intermediate demand that depend only on variations in intermediate input technology. A similar decomposition is discussed in chapter 3 for the cross-country model.

The results of this exercise are revealing. First, in every case, the SM output structure generates greater demand for intermediate inputs than the L structure, since manufacturing is much more demanding of intermediate inputs. Second, in every case, the actual intermediate use ratio in the initial year was closer to that generated by the output vector for the L pattern, and in the terminal year it was closer to that generated by the SM pattern. Over time, all the economies became industrialized, moving from primary production to industry. Third, in most cases, well over half the change in intermediate use ratios can be explained by changes in input-output coefficients; the rest resulted from changes in output composition. Fourth, there is significant variation in input-output relations across the sample. Application of the standard output vectors yields consistently higher intermediate use ratios for Korea, Taiwan, Japan, and Israel—ranging from 43 to 50 percent—than for Turkey, Colombia, and Mexico—ranging from 31 to 38 percent (shown in table 3-9).

---

16. Similar results have been found in other studies. See, for example, Chenery, Shishido, and Watanabe (1962) and Vaccara and Simon (1968).

Linkage Measures

Various measures of linkages have been developed in the literature.[17] If principal sectors are focused on, as suggested by Hirschman (1958), attention is drawn away from the systemic phenomenon of increased interdependence or from the deepening of interindustry links commonly observed over time and across countries.[18] To focus on systemic properties and make comparisons among countries, we develop measures of interindustry linkages for the entire system. The approach we use is based on the Leontief inverse matrix.[19] The aggregate linkage measure, L, is defined as $L = \Sigma\Sigma r_{ij}f_j - 1$, where r_{ij} are the elements of the Leontief inverse $(I - A)^{-1}$ and f_j are the elements of a standardized final demand vector (consisting of shares that sum to one).

Each column of the Leontief inverse matrix describes the amount of goods directly and indirectly required to deliver one unit of sectoral output to final demand. The first term of L is a weighted sum of these column sums, with the composition of final demand as weights. Hence it shows the total value of products directly and indirectly needed for the economy to deliver a unit of aggregate final demand. The L measure is defined as this term minus one, which is the value of intermediate goods required to produce an aggregate unit of final demand with given composition. In general, the denser the input-output matrix, the higher is L.[20]

This measure is sensitive to the composition of final demand. For purposes of comparison across the sample, we use a standard or average final demand vector for a semi-industrial country that is drawn from the cross-country model described in chapter 3.[21] In this way, the comparisons will focus on the input-output structures of the different economies and hold constant their final demand structures.

There are two ways to calculate the aggregate linkage measure. One is to use the input-output matrix inclusive of imported intermediates so that all intermediate inputs are included in measurements of overall linkages. A second is to use the input-output matrix exclusive of imports—that is, the domestic matrix—so that only those interindustry linkages arising from domestic industries are included. The difference between the two measures reflects the role of imported intermediates in production.

17. See Rasmussen (1965), Chenery and Watanabe (1958), Yotopoulos and Nugent (1973), Shultz (1982), and Martin and Rodriguez (1979).
18. Chenery and Watanabe (1958); Deutsch, Syrquin, and Urata (1986); and Robinson and Markandya (1973) provide intercountry comparisons of systemwide linkage measures based on comparative input-output data.
19. It is common in this literature to start from the Leontief inverse. Our approach is similar to that of Rasmussen (1965), although there are significant differences.
20. Kubo (1982) discusses this and related measures in detail. He considers their relation to the Frobenius root of an input-output matrix. See also Kubo (1985).
21. It is the final demand vector for a typical country with per capita income of $560. See chapter 4 for the data.

Table 7-3. *Interindustry Linkages of Sample Economies per Unit of Final Demand with Standard Composition*

Economy	Year	Overall linkages (percent)	Domestic linkages (percent)
Colombia	1953	50.0	37.2
	1966	65.4	52.3
	1970	69.0	53.9
Mexico	1950	54.3	40.5
	1960	68.9	51.3
	1970	63.9	52.0
	1975	69.5	54.2
Turkey	1963	52.1	46.4
	1968	56.7	51.5
	1973	59.6	52.8
Yugoslavia	1962	82.2	67.9
	1966	79.5	61.9
	1972	87.3	59.4
Japan	1955	89.9	81.3
	1960	94.5	82.7
	1965	74.6	82.4
	1970	106.3	88.7
Korea	1963	89.9	60.9
	1970	89.8	58.7
	1973	92.8	54.6
Taiwan	1956	76.5	42.6
	1961	85.9	55.0
	1966	92.9	55.7
	1971	93.7	55.2
Israel	1958	83.7	53.8
	1965	78.6	50.5
	1972	101.5	48.1
Norway	1953	66.7	40.8
	1961	77.9	47.8
	1969	87.2	47.6

Note: See text for explanation of the linkage measure.
Source: World Bank data; described in Kubo (1983).

A Comparison of Interindustry Linkages across Countries

The results of computing the two linkage measures—overall and domestic—for the nine economies are given in table 7-3. The sample forms two distinct groups. On the one hand, Yugoslavia, Japan, Korea, Taiwan, Israel, and Norway consistently have an overall linkage value of more than 75 (that is, $75 worth of intermediate inputs are needed to support the gross production necessary to deliver $100 worth of final demand of a standard composition). On the other hand, Colombia, Mexico, and Turkey have values less than 75 in all years. The values for Norway increase during the period and overlap the two groups. The average of the overall linkage measure is about 90 for the first group and 60 for the second. Thus for the same final demand, the first group requires about 50 percent more intermediate inputs than does the second group—a remarkable difference.

For all the economies, overall linkages increase systematically over time—which is consistent with the results presented earlier and with conventional views about the process of development. A growing use of intermediate inputs is associated with an increasingly complex economic system, which is characterized by the prevalence of more roundabout means of production typical of developed economies. The first group shows rapid increases in overall linkages, and it approaches the level of Japan by the end of the period.[22]

The second column of table 7-3 gives the domestic linkage measure and provides a clue to why Korea, Taiwan, and Israel differ from Colombia, Mexico, and Turkey. If we restrict our attention to domestic linkages, the two groups look similar. The indicator of domestic linkages is about 50 for both groups, with much less pronounced change over time than the overall linkages. Furthermore, the two groups differ much less in domestic linkages than in overall linkages: the average is 53.5 for the first group and 49.2 for the second. We must look to differences in trade strategies for an explanation.

Table 7-4 presents data on the volume and structure of trade. In Korea and Taiwan, the rapid increase in export earnings led to an equally rapid increase in imports, which consisted largely of intermediate and capital goods.[23] Rapid export expansion enabled these economies to introduce at an early stage—and to maintain—systemic linkage structures and, implicitly, the underlying technologies typical of economies at a much higher level of development. Through imported inputs, they could achieve technological structures that would have been difficult or impossible to achieve through domestic production.[24] Even in the early years before exports expanded, Korea and Taiwan achieved high levels of imported inputs, which they were able to finance through high levels of foreign capital inflow and foreign aid. Israel also benefited from substantial foreign capital inflow during this period, but with lower shares of intermediate and capital goods imports.

22. Robinson and Markandya (1973) rank Japan as being as "complex" an economy (according to their measures) as was the United States by about 1960. A direct comparison with the United States and with European countries would be helpful but is beyond the scope of this book.

23. Capital goods are defined as machinery and transport equipment. Intermediate goods include rubber and chemical products, coal and oil products, nonmetallic minerals, and basic metals.

24. In later chapters, we explore further the implications of trade strategies for output and productivity growth in an explicitly dynamic framework.

Table 7-4. *The Volume and Structure of Trade in the Sample Economies*

Economy	Year	Exports as percentage of GDP[a]	Imports as percentage of GDP[a]	Share in total imports (percent)[b]	
				Capital goods	Intermediate goods
Colombia	1955	12.4	14.3	(43.8)	(33.9)
	1966	12.1	15.1	28.9	32.8
	1970	14.2	15.8	35.7	33.4
Mexico	1950	14.1	13.9	44.6	27.2
	1960	11.3	12.8	50.9	26.5
	1970	8.1	10.1	54.9	21.5
	1975	7.7	10.9	55.7	21.9
Turkey	1963	5.5	10.3	38.8	27.2
	1968	5.3	7.5	39.1	36.2
	1973	7.6	10.0	35.6	43.2
Yugoslavia	1962	16.0	17.1	48.3	20.0
	1966	19.5	20.5	39.4	25.5
	1972	22.0	24.1	36.7	30.1
Japan	1955	10.7	10.1	8.6	12.7
	1960	11.1	10.6	8.9	24.5
	1965	10.8	9.3	8.5	18.2
	1970	11.2	9.8	9.5	17.0
Korea	1963	4.8	16.4	21.4	34.3
	1970	14.8	24.9	29.4	26.2
	1973	31.7	35.0	32.6	29.9
Taiwan	1955	8.3	12.6	(21.6)	(38.2)
	1961	12.8	19.9	32.7	23.3
	1966	20.6	21.5	31.4	29.1
	1971	36.8	34.2	32.5	26.2
Israel	1955	11.5	32.8	(28.2)	(17.6)
	1965	18.9	31.9	26.6	20.5
	1972	27.3	40.1	27.9	39.4
Norway	1955	40.7	43.6	(26.5)	(19.9)
	1961	39.7	42.6	29.5	20.1
	1969	41.2	38.5	28.0	22.7

a. Taken from World Bank (1976).

b. Based on World Bank data; described in Kubo (1983). Figures in parentheses correspond to input-output year nearest to 1955 (1956 for Taiwan, 1953 for Colombia and Norway, and 1958 for Israel).

In Colombia, Mexico, and Turkey, the overall and domestic linkage measures are not very different. These countries emphasized import substitution and through conscious policy choices discriminated against exports; therefore, their export growth was not able to generate enough foreign exchange to meet their growing import needs. These countries have higher shares of intermediate and capital goods in total imports because, through a variety of controls, they allowed only essential imports. As their levels of foreign capital inflow were also relatively low, quantity restrictions and other import control measures were commonly used to cope with foreign exchange imbalances. Their lack of imports forced these countries to rely on domestic production and domestic technology. Their reliance on domestic technology in turn is reflected in the structures of their interindustry linkages. Given the difficulties of import substitution in intermediate goods, the result was a much lower level of overall linkages.

Japan stands out as having exceptionally strong domestic linkages. Considering its low dependence on imports for most manufactured products, the small difference between its domestic and overall linkages is not surprising. This high level of domestic linkages was already in place by the mid-1950s. Japan's interindustry structure was by then established, and no significant increases occurred until the end of the period. Yugoslavia is similar to Japan in overall linkages and is less dependent on imported intermediates than are Korea, Taiwan, and Israel. As noted earlier, this probably reflects a development strategy that strongly emphasized industrialization, which is typical of many socialist countries that sought to establish a broad industrial base at an early stage. In the late 1960s and early 1970s, the domestic linkages declined somewhat in Yugoslavia while overall linkages increased; this reflects the effects of the import liberalization that took place during that period (see chapter 6).

Finally, Norway exhibits one of the lowest levels of domestic linkages, although its overall linkages are comparable with those of other developed countries. A small country (with a population of 4 million in 1973), it did not try to develop a broadly based industrial structure; it specialized and relied heavily on imports. Also, in the postwar period, Norway adopted increasingly liberal trade policies and reduced its controls on imports.[25] Thus the large discrepancy between its domestic and overall linkage measures reflects both country size and policy choices. A similar explanation applies to Israel, where the discrepancy between domestic and overall linkages increased significantly in the 1965–72 episode.

There appears to be a strong relation between a country's interindustry structure (and its evolution over time) and the choice of a development strategy. When an inward-oriented, import substitution strategy is adopted, domestic linkages increase but overall linkages remain relatively low. When an open development strategy with high levels of both exports and imports is chosen, overall linkages grow rapidly even though domestic linkages do not change much. High exports permit an economy to import the intermediate input structure of an advanced economy and perhaps facilitates rapid growth.

25. See Balassa (1979a) for further discussion of Norway.

Openness and Comparative Advantage in Manufacturing

International trade plays a variety of roles in industrialization. On the output side, it permits a country to separate or "delink" the structure of production from the structure of demand. In trade theory, this separation is usually analyzed in terms of welfare gains to consumers. But trade also affects the input side. The analysis of the structure of intermediate inputs in the previous section indicates that an important gain from trade is that it allows a country to achieve through imports a more advanced intermediate input technology than would be possible through domestic production alone. This gain arises from the import side only and is consistent with the two-gap view of foreign exchange constraints on growth. The imported intermediate inputs are difficult or impossible to replace with domestic production, especially in the early phases of industrialization. In this section we study further the pattern of trade by comparing the degree of openness across countries and the patterns of comparative advantage within manufacturing.

Measuring Openness and Trade Structure

To analyze the implications of delinking, we need a measure of the degree of openness of the economy. A natural choice is the ratio of the sum of exports and imports to total supply on the domestic market: $T = \Sigma_i (E_i + M_i) / (X_i + M_i)$, where i is summed over the fourteen-sector aggregation. If all domestic production is traded, T approaches 100 percent; if it is all sold on the domestic market, T approaches zero. Thus, open economies have high values of T and closed economies have low values.

To reap the gains from pursuing comparative advantage, a country must alter its structure of production in response to changes in trade opportunities. Two different types of specialization can be observed. The first type is sectoral specialization with an increasing volume of interindustry trade, that is, high exports in some sectors and high imports in others. This is the pattern predicted by classical (and neoclassical) trade theory. The second type, which is consistent with "neotechnological" or "product cycle" views of trade, and especially with the new theory of international trade under imperfect competition, is specialization through diversification within sectors.[26] We would thus expect to see increasing intraindustry trade with both higher exports and higher imports in the manufacturing sectors.

Even though our data base is not sufficiently disaggregated to support a

26. The theory of comparative advantage in imperfectly competitive markets is expounded in Helpman and Krugman (1985).

detailed analysis of intraindustry trade, it is possible to generate a measure of the extent of such trade. Within a sector, the extent of such trade is measured by the absolute difference between the value of exports and imports. The lower the difference, the more nearly balanced are sectoral exports and imports and the more important is intraindustry trade. Summing over the manufacturing sectors, a summary measure is provided by: $B = 1.0 - \Sigma_i |E_i - M_i| / (E_i + M_i)$, where the index i is summed over the manufacturing sectors. In the absence of intraindustry trade, either exports, E, or imports, M, is zero in each sector, the second term will equal one, and B will equal zero. If there is exactly balanced intraindustry trade, E will equal M in every sector and B will equal one (or 100 percent).[27]

Table 7-5 gives the indicators of openness, T, and of the extent of intrasectoral trade, B, for the sample of economies and benchmark years. The extent of openness is, as might be expected, related in the initial year to domestic market size: a ranking by initial aggregate GDP is negatively correlated to a ranking by degree of openness (see table 6-1). During the period, however, the economies followed quite different patterns.

As discussed in chapter 4, the importance of trade increased dramatically in the postwar period, with most semi-industrial economies becoming more open. In the sample, however, Colombia, Mexico, and Turkey had low and decreasing (or roughly constant) measures of openness during the period under study. Japan, with an initial value for T about equal to that of Turkey, also registered only a slight increase. All the other economies showed significant increases in openness, with Israel, Korea, and Taiwan the leaders.

With the exception of Turkey, every economy in the sample shows an increase, sometimes dramatic, in intraindustry trade. Thus within the manufacturing sector, increasing volumes of foreign trade were reflected for each sector in a rise in both imports and exports. And with the exception of Japan, Yugoslavia, and Norway, every economy started with a very low value for the index of intraindustry trade (in part because of a large trade imbalance within manufacturing). The more developed countries in the group (Norway, Japan, and Yugoslavia) started with more intraindustry trade, which is typical of developed countries. Remarkably, Korea, Taiwan, and (to a lesser extent) Israel caught up with this pattern during the period. In contrast, Colombia, Mexico, and Turkey stand out as having maintained closed economies; they did not achieve much change in terms either of openness or of diversification in their patterns of manufacturing trade.[28]

27. The measure is sensitive to aggregation, so we compute it at the same level of aggregation for all economies. It is also sensitive to the overall balance of trade. See Grubel and Lloyd (1975) for a discussion of the measure and possible alternatives.

28. Part of the explanation for the small change in the degree of intraindustry trade for these countries is that they maintained negative trade balances in the manufacturing sector during the entire period.

Table 7-5. *Openness and Intraindustry Trade of the Manufacturing Sector of the Sample Economies*

| Economy | Year | Measure (percent)[a] | |
		T (degree of openness of economy)	B (summary of intrasectoral trade)
Colombia	1953	17.0	2.4
	1966	15.5	21.7
	1970	16.9	15.5
Mexico	1950	14.8	18.3
	1960	11.7	13.8
	1970	10.1	26.7
	1975	11.8	28.3
Turkey	1963	7.7	17.2
	1968	7.0	8.3
	1973	9.3	13.4
Yugoslavia	1962	12.7	64.2
	1966	16.4	68.2
	1972	22.3	67.9
Japan	1955	7.6	46.0
	1960	7.7	52.3
	1965	9.1	54.3
	1970	10.9	60.1
Korea	1955	15.5	6.2
	1963	15.2	31.2
	1970	21.7	42.6
	1973	30.2	59.3
Taiwan	1956	17.1	21.1
	1961	18.4	33.3
	1966	25.9	45.4
	1971	33.1	63.9
Israel	1958	22.3	26.3
	1965	26.9	38.2
	1968	33.1	46.7
	1972	39.4	39.2
Norway	1953	34.7	44.1
	1961	35.6	44.4
	1969	41.0	53.7

a. The *T* and *B* measures are defined in the text.
Source: World Bank data; described in Kubo (1983).

Comparative Advantage within Manufacturing

In the discussion so far, changes in trade diversification have been considered by using aggregate measures to summarize variations calculated at the fourteen-sector level. We now consider the impact of changes in subsectoral shares in total exports and total imports for the eight manufacturing subsectors. The idea is that such changes reflect a country's "revealed comparative advantage." The cause of such changes may lie in differing factor proportions, as assumed by classical trade theory, or in other neotechnology or imperfect competition explanations.[29] Our interest is less in explaining the changes than in establishing the stylized facts.

Table 7-6 presents the results for the eight manufacturing subsectors of each economy during the entire period. With imports and exports treated symmetrically, each entry in the table gives the rank within manufacturing for each subsector in the initial and terminal years, followed by the percentage change in share between the two benchmark years. For example, the entry for food exports for Israel (the first two columns) indicates that food ranked fourth for both benchmark years among the manufacturing subsectors in exports even though the share of food in total manufacturing exports rose by 4.1 percentage points. The last two rows of the table summarize the change in comparative advantage for each sector for the entire sample by presenting the average of the figures in the corresponding column. Similarly, the last column provides a summary measure of compositional changes in trade within the manufacturing sector for each economy by summing the absolute values of changes in shares across the subsectors.

An examination of table 7-6 reveals some striking similarities in the pattern of comparative advantage. On the one hand, subsectors that lose in revealed comparative advantage for exports in all nine economies also lose on the import side; that is, subsectors that supply a declining share of manufacturing exports also tend to receive a smaller share of manufacturing imports. These subsectors are food, textiles, paper, and other light manufacturing. Nonmetallic mineral products are an exception. On the other hand, subsectors that provide an increasing share of exports also tend to receive an increasing share of imports. These subsectors are rubber, metal products, and machinery. The tendency for diversification reflected by increased intrasectoral trade, which was discussed above, is clearly evident across the subsectors.

As the bottom row indicates, processed food (the largest exporting subsector in the initial year for several economies) averages the greatest decline in share of manufacturing exports (11.1 percentage points). Subsectors that gain in export share include rubber and especially machinery (which rises an average of 13.9 percentage points). On the import side, machinery, rubber, and metal products maintain the highest import shares throughout the period.

The last column in table 7-6 indicates that in general there was a much greater change in the structure of manufacturing exports than of imports.

---

29. The idea behind the notion of revealed comparative advantage is somewhat controversial. See Balassa (1965, 1977b).

These results are in accord with the economywide results discussed earlier (see table 7-1). Turkey and Yugoslavia are exceptions; the imports and exports of each had about the same magnitude of structural change.

Trade and Input Use

We finish our discussion of trade by analyzing the relation between trade and sectoral input use. First, we turn to the relation between export expansion and the requirements for imported intermediate inputs. Second, we explore the relative contribution to changes in the balance of payments at the sectoral level of changes in intrasectoral trade (sectoral exports and imports) and in sectoral demand for imported intermediate inputs. In this analysis, we focus on the manufacturing sector both as a source of foreign exchange through exports and as a demander through direct and induced imports.

Import Content of Exports

At the economywide level, we have discussed the importance of increased imports. We noted that increased intermediate imports permitted the deepening of input-output linkages, a form of technological change characteristic of industrialization. One of the advantages of pursuing an export-led development strategy is that foreign exchange earnings can be used to increase intermediate imports and so hasten the deepening process, which would otherwise require domestically produced intermediates. Indeed, it is often argued that the expansion of manufactured exports requires more "advanced" production technologies and high-quality intermediate inputs, both of which must be imported since—at least in the initial stages of export expansion—domestic producers cannot manufacture them. In this view, intermediate imports embody advanced technology, and their use is part of the process of technology transfer.

To analyze the relation between exports and imported intermediate inputs, we first develop a measure of the direct and indirect import content of exports, or ICE. The measure, discussed in chapter 5, is defined thus:

$$\text{ICE} = eA^m R^d S^e = e Q S^e$$

where

e = unit row vector $(1, \ldots, 1)$
A^m = matrix of intermediate import coefficients
R^d = $(I - A^d)^{-1}$, the inverse of the matrix of domestic input-output coefficients
S^e = column vector of export shares
Q = $A^m R^d$.

The ICE measure indicates the value of imported intermediates (in base year prices) needed to produce a unit value of exports of a given sectoral composition. In other words, it is the share of the cost of imported

Table 7-6. Changing Pattern of Trade in Manufacturing Subsectors

	Food						Textiles						Paper					
	Exports (rank)			Imports (rank)			Exports (rank)			Imports (rank)			Exports (rank)			Imports (rank)		
Economy	I[a]	T[b]	Change[c]	I	T	Change	I	T	Change	I	T	Change	I	T	Change	I	T	Change
Colombia	8	2	33.1	7	5	0.6	1	3	-5.9	5	7	-3.4	1	7	5.5	6	4	4.0
Mexico	1	2	-47.6	7	6	-1.0	2	5	-10.2	6	7	-3.5	8	8	1.0	5	5	-2.2
Turkey	1	1	12.8	4	5	-3.4	2	2	-1.1	6	4	-1.2	7	5	0.1	5	7	-1.1
Yugoslavia	3	6	-5.1	5	5	1.5	4	2	-6.2	4	4	2.0	8	7	1.0	8	8	0.8
Japan	5	6	-4.4	1	5	-16.5	1	5	-27.5	6	6	3.9	8	8	0.1	7	7	0.7
Korea	3	6	-17.7	5	6	-5.4	2	2	11.0	3	4	-5.7	7	7	1.4	6	7	-1.6
Taiwan	1	4	-67.4	4	6	-2.6	2	1	22.3	5	4	7.4	7	3	0.6	7	7	-0.2
Israel	4	4	4.1	2	4	-11.3	3	2	13.5	5	5	0.7	7	7	-0.1	7	8	-1.6
Norway	4	5	-7.8	5	6	0.4	7	7	2.2	3	3	-2.8	1	4	-13.1	8	7	2.1
Average change, all economies			-11.1			-4.2			1.2			-0.3			-0.4			0.1
Average rank, all economies	3.3	4.0		4.4	5.3		2.7	3.4		4.8	4.9		6.0	6.9		6.5	6.7	

214

| | Light industry | | | | | | Rubber | | | | | | Nonmetallic minerals | | | | | |
| | Exports (rank) | | | Imports (rank) | | | Exports (rank) | | | Imports (rank) | | | Exports (rank) | | | Imports (rank) | | |
Economy	I	T	Change	I	T	Change	I	T	Change	I	T	Change	I	T	Change	I	T	Change
Colombia	6	5	5.4	4	6	−3.3	3	1	26.3	3	2	7.8	4	8	−36.3	8	8	−0.2
Mexico	3	6	−1.3	4	4	−0.4	4	3	11.0	3	2	−1.8	6	1	2.1	8	8	−0.6
Turkey	6	7	0.2	8	8	−0.4	4	4	−6.4	2	2	12.5	5	3	2.6	7	6	−0.3
Yugoslavia	2	5	−5.6	6	7	0.1	6	4	4.6	2	2	3.1	7	8	−1.5	7	6	1.7
Japan	2	4	−5.7	5	4	4.2	6	3	5.3	3	1	5.1	2	7	−2.2	8	8	−0.1
Korea	1	3	−24.1	4	5	−3.8	8	5	5.7	1	2	−17.3	6	7	1.4	8	8	−0.4
Taiwan	5	3	11.4	6	5	2.5	4	5	5.7	4	3	−14.4	8	7	1.3	8	8	−1.6
Israel	1	1	−22.7	6	6	−0.3	2	3	0.7	4	3	3.1	6	6	−3.0	8	7	1.4
Norway	6	6	1.0	6	5	4.7	2	2	−4.3	2	2	2.1	8	8	0.9	7	8	−0.3
Average change, all economies			−4.3			0.4			5.4			−0.1			−3.9			−0.4
Average rank, all economies	3.6	4.4		5.4	5.6		4.3	3.3		2.3	2.1		6.3	6.6		7.7	7.4	

(Table continues on the following page.)

Table 7-6 (continued)

Economy	Metals						Machinery						Absolute change (percent)	
	Exports (rank)			Imports (rank)			Exports (rank)			Imports (rank)				
	I	T	Change	I	T	Change	I	T	Change	I	T	Change	Imports	Exports
Colombia	2	4	-28.6	2	3	-2.9	5	6	0.5	1	1	-2.7	141.6	24.90
Mexico	7	4	0.7	2	3	-3.4	1	5	34.1	1	1	12.9	118.0	25.80
Turkey	3	3	-9.5	3	3	3.4	8	6	1.4	1	1	-9.5	34.1	31.80
Yugoslavia	5	3	3.4	3	3	7.0	1	1	-3.0	1	1	-16.2	30.4	32.40
Japan	3	2	3.1	4	3	2.7	4	1	31.3	2	2	0.4	79.6	34.00
Korea	4	4	1.8	7	3	12.1	5	2	20.5	2	1	21.5	83.6	67.54
Taiwan	3	6	-0.9	3	2	-3.3	3	2	24.4	2	1	12.3	136.7	44.30
Israel	8	6	3.3	3	1	17.3	5	5	4.1	1	2	-8.5	51.5	43.10
Norway	3	1	10.1	4	4	-2.2	5	3	11.4	1	1	-3.7	50.8	18.00
Average change, all economies (percent)			-0.7			3.4			13.9			0.7		
Average rank, all economies	4.2	3.7		3.4	2.8		4.6	3.0		1.3	1.2			

Note: All rankings are for manufacturing subsectors within each economy. See text for explanation.
a. Initial year.
b. Terminal year.
c. Percentage point change in shares.
Source: World Bank data; described in Kubo (1983).

intermediate inputs in the value of exports. The ICE shares are given in table 7-7 for various benchmark years for the economies in the sample. The table also gives the import content of domestic final demand, which is calculated by replacing S^e with a vector of final demand shares. For those economies for which we did not have data on imported intermediate input coefficients, we approximated the import matrix by assuming the same average import coefficient across each row. Comparing the approxima-

Table 7-7. *Import Content of Domestic Final Demand and Exports*
(percent)

Economy	Year	Import content	
		Domestic final demand	Exports (ICE)
Colombia	1953	7.0	4.1
	1966	6.5	4.4
	1970	7.3	3.7
Mexico	1950	6.6	5.2
	1960	7.4	5.5
	1970	6.1	6.5
	1975	8.3	10.5
Turkey	1963	3.7	2.7
	1968	3.2	2.3
	1973	4.7	3.9
Yugoslavia	1962	6.0	9.6
	1966	8.6	11.9
	1972	14.1	18.7
Japan	1955	4.2	6.6
	1960	5.8	9.3
	1965	6.5	9.6
	1970	8.5	10.0
Korea	1963	11.2	15.8
	1970	14.8	18.7
	1973	17.9	25.5
Taiwan	1956	9.7	13.6
	1961	9.8	12.9
	1966	14.3	19.7
	1971	17.9	25.0
Israel	1958	12.8	12.1
	1965	13.0	11.1
	1972	27.0	21.2
Norway	1953	18.7	16.3
	1961	22.5	18.8
	1969	23.4	21.9

Source: World Bank data; described in Kubo (1983).

tion with the measure, given the full matrix, indicates that results differ somewhat with these two methods but that the basic trends stand.[30]

An examination of the table reveals three patterns. Israel and Norway are small, open economies with high and stable ICE shares. Colombia, Mexico (up to 1970), Turkey, and Japan are large, relatively closed economies with low and stable ICE shares. Korea and Taiwan are characterized by rapidly growing manufactured exports, accompanied by a sharp increase in ICE shares. Yugoslavia is a special case; its ICE share starts low but rises significantly, a pattern between that of the large economies and that of Korea and Taiwan. In the last period in both Turkey and Mexico, when the share of manufactured exports in total exports rose significantly, the ICE share rose also (see table 7-4).

These results are consistent with the view that a rapid expansion of manufactured exports requires increased intermediate imports. They are also consistent with the two-gap model, which treats foreign exchange availability as a separate constraint on growth. When import substitution is difficult, imported intermediates are needed to support manufacturing output, especially exports.

It is also interesting to note that, in both Korea and Taiwan, the import content of exports is much greater than the import content of final demand. In the closed economies (Colombia, Turkey, and Mexico), the pattern is reversed although the differences are not as great. The structure of production needed for an export-led growth strategy uses more imports. Also, as discussed above, those economies that pursued an export-led strategy tended to increase intraindustry trade, with increased imports and exports falling into the same sector classification.

Manufacturing and the Balance of Trade

In table 7-8, we decompose the contribution of the manufacturing sector to the overall balance of trade. The decomposition measure, discussed in chapter 5, is based on the following equation applied to the manufacturing sector:

$$\Delta BP = \Delta E - \Delta M^f - \Delta M^w$$

where

ΔBP = change in the balance of payments
ΔE = change in manufacturing exports
ΔM^f = change in manufacturing imports for final demand
ΔM^w = change in intermediate imports needed by the manufacturing
            sector.

The difference between the first two columns represents the change in net

30. See Kubo (1981) for a discussion of the measures and of the accuracy of the approximation. See also Kubo (1985).

Table 7-8. *Contribution of the Manufacturing Sector to the Overall Balance of Trade, Selected Sample Economies in Comparison with Cross-Country Model*
(percentage of total manufacturing exports)

	Change			
Economy and subsector	In total exports[a]	In final imports[b]	In inter-mediate imports[c]	In balance of payments[d]
Mexico				
1950–60				
Food processing	75	−3	−20	98
Consumer goods	−14	3	78	−95
Producer goods	39	30	217	−208
Machinery	0	326	199	−525
Total manufacturing	100	356	474	−730
1960–70				
Food processing	−29	95	28	−152
Consumer goods	14	47	79	−112
Producer goods	43	−9	125	−73
Machinery	72	322	162	−412
Total manufacturing	100	455	394	−749
1970–75				
Food processing	2	−7	44	−35
Consumer goods	19	16	16	−13
Producer goods	32	37	94	−99
Machinery	47	186	150	−289
Total manufacturing	100	232	304	−436
Japan				
1955–60				
Food processing	1	−6	16	−9
Consumer goods	37	−19	25	31
Producer goods	21	−19	77	−37
Machinery	41	5	10	26
Total manufacturing	100	−39	128	11
1960–65				
Food processing	2	−1	12	−9
Consumer goods	8	−2	13	−3
Producer goods	46	−31	42	35
Machinery	44	5	3	36
Total manufacturing	100	−29	70	59
1965–70				
Food processing	1	−3	6	−2
Consumer goods	16	1	16	−1
Producer goods	29	−25	46	8
Machinery	54	6	8	40
Total manufacturing	100	−21	76	45

(Table continues on the following page.)

Table 7-8 *(continued)*

Economy and subsector	In total exports[a]	In final imports[b]	In intermediate imports[c]	In balance of payments[d]
				Change
Korea				
1955–63				
Food processing	16	4	71	−59
Consumer goods	51	−26	6	71
Producer goods	28	−18	61	−15
Machinery	5	83	22	−100
Total manufacturing	100	43	160	−103
1963–70				
Food processing	5	2	15	−12
Consumer goods	76	4	58	14
Producer goods	10	2	32	−24
Machinery	9	43	16	−50
Total manufacturing	100	51	121	−72
1970–73				
Food processing	2	−1	10	−7
Consumer goods	51	3	17	31
Producer goods	18	0	20	−2
Machinery	29	14	22	−7
Total manufacturing	100	16	69	15
Taiwan				
1956–61				
Food processing	38	−11	10	39
Consumer goods	45	10	40	−5
Producer goods	13	−53	27	39
Machinery	4	57	15	−68
Total manufacturing	100	3	95	5
1961–66				
Food processing	46	6	10	30
Consumer goods	15	3	23	−11
Producer goods	24	4	33	−13
Machinery	15	35	15	−35
Total manufacturing	100	48	81	−29
1966–71				
Food processing	5	1	8	−4
Consumer goods	49	4	20	25
Producer goods	15	3	14	−2
Machinery	31	14	20	−3
Total manufacturing	100	22	62	16
Israel				
1958–65				
Food processing	7	4	19	−16
Consumer goods	70	9	26	35
Producer goods	22	9	33	−20
Machinery	1	37	26	−62
Total manufacturing	100	59	104	−63

	Change			
Economy and subsector	In total exports[a]	In final imports[b]	In inter-mediate imports[c]	In balance of payments[d]
1965–72				
Food processing	17	5	20	−8
Consumer goods	51	13	25	13
Producer goods	21	85	36	−100
Machinery	11	61	36	−86
Total manufacturing	100	164	117	−181
Cross-country model[e]				
Period 2				
($280–560)				
Food processing	17	12	20	−15
Consumer goods	37	9	20	8
Producer goods	42	19	24	−1
Machinery	4	54	7	−57
Total manufacturing	100	94	71	−65
Period 4				
($1,120–2,100)				
Food processing	20	4	11	5
Consumer goods	28	5	14	9
Producer goods	28	7	24	−3
Machinery	24	24	5	−5
Total manufacturing	100	40	54	6

Note: Economies included are those for which detailed import data are available.

a. For four manufacturing subsectors.

b. For final demand for four manufacturing subsectors.

c. Imports from all subsectors including nonmanufacturing. This column measures change in imported intermediates needed to sustain total sectoral production—not just production for sectoral final demand.

d. Difference between first column and sum of second and third columns.

e. See chapter 3 for the model.

Source: World Bank data; described in Kubo (1983).

trade in the subsector excluding intermediate import demand from other subsectors.[31]

Table 7-8 shows that, in general, even with growth in manufacturing exports, the manufacturing sector exerts a net drain on the balance of trade when both direct and indirect effects are taken into account. The pattern in Korea and Taiwan is revealing. At the time of rapid acceleration of manufacturing exports (the second episode in both cases), there was

31. Because it includes only the imports for final demand, the difference does not measure intrasectoral trade.

also a dramatic increase in induced intermediate imports to support manufacturing production, coupled with an increase in intrasectoral trade. As a result, in 1963–70 in Korea, a $100 increase in manufacturing exports is associated with a $72 worsening in the balance of trade. In 1961–66 in Taiwan, the effect is a $29 worsening in the balance of trade. Only in the final episode in both Korea and Taiwan does the manufacturing sector make a positive contribution to the change in the balance of trade because of a decline in the change in both intermediate and final imports. This is consistent with the view that these economies achieved successful import substitution in basic intermediates and in capital goods during the last phases of their export-led growth strategies.

The causes of this net negative contribution of manufacturing to changes in the balance of payments under an export-led development strategy are difficult to disentangle. An economy pursuing an export-led strategy generally has a high foreign capital inflow, which permits increased imports. There is a correlation between large imports of intermediate goods and rapid growth, which is consistent with the two-gap model of foreign exchange constraints. Whether the causal chain runs from higher exports to higher imports to higher growth, or vice versa, or both, is impossible to determine from this analysis. These links are a central concern of later chapters.

Postwar Japan is a large country which decreased its manufacturing imports for final demand in absolute terms throughout the period. The result is that, even though induced changes in intermediate imports were large, the net contribution of changes in exports to the balance of trade was positive.

Mexico, in contrast, is representative of countries that have pursued inward-oriented development strategies. Increases in manufacturing exports were associated with large increases in intermediate imports to support the expansion of manufacturing. All three episodes also saw large increases in final demand imports of machinery, which were undoubtedly mostly for investment. Thus, unlike Korea and Taiwan, Mexico was unable to reduce its need to import intermediate and investment goods. This inward-oriented development strategy led to an industrial structure highly dependent on crucial imports. As a result, economies such as Mexico and Turkey are more susceptible to a shock emanating from the foreign sector than are more open economies because they have little room for adjustment.[32] This result is also consistent with the analysis of linkages above.

Israel is an example of a small, open economy. With its expansion of manufacturing, including increases in exports, intermediate imports grew even faster than in Korea and Taiwan. Changes in final demand for

---

32. For an analysis of the reaction of Turkey and Yugoslavia to foreign shocks, see Dervis and Robinson (1982), Celasun (1983), and Robinson and Tyson (1984).

imports were also large and increased over time, so the net effect on the change in its balance of trade was very negative. In this case, which is not typical of semi-industrial countries, the main driving force was the very high level of foreign capital inflow, including aid.

The cross-country model provides a convenient comparison. The two periods tabulated are those that begin and end the industrialization phase. In the earlier period, manufacturing growth and increases in manufactured exports are associated with large increases in machinery imports for investment, which leads to a negative effect on the change in the net trade balance. In the later period, increases in machinery imports for final demand are much less; and the effect of changes in manufactured exports on the trade balance are positive even though changes in intermediate imports from manufacturing growth are the same in both periods. The standard pattern of the cross-country model thus behaves more like a moderated version of Korea and Taiwan than like an inward-oriented economy such as Mexico or Turkey.

Conclusions

The postwar experience of semi-industrial countries with growth and structural change reveals a variety of development paths. All these countries industrialized and in general did so at faster rates than would have been expected from historical comparisons with the developed countries. The nine sample economies exhibit a wide range of initial conditions and development experiences during the period. Their experiences are typical but span the range of semi-industrial countries. They thus provide enough diversity to permit some tentative conclusions to be drawn.

The process of industrialization is associated with structural changes beyond a simple increase in the share of manufacturing in output. Changes in the structure of final demand, in international trade, and in the use of intermediate inputs all contribute to the evolution of an economy. Although some basic long-run forces are common to all countries, differences in initial conditions and in the choice of a development strategy affect how these three components interact and the rate at which the process unfolds.

The main common forces include changes in the structure of demand as per capita income increases and changes in technology affecting both the primary factors (land, labor, and capital) and intermediate inputs. Engel's law—that with a rise in income the structure of demand moves strongly in favor of manufactures—is clearly valid for these economies; such changes in demand are a strong force for industrialization. Equally important are the increases in demand for intermediate inputs that accompany growth. Such increases arise both from a shift in the structure of production toward manufacturing subsectors that are heavy users of intermediate inputs and from changes in technology that lead to a more specialized and complex economy.

International trade has been very important for the semi-industrial countries in the postwar period. The countries that chose and were able to pursue open development strategies based on manufactured exports grew faster and achieved more rapid rates of structural change than did those that followed inward-oriented strategies.[33] Their improved performances are related to two different effects of international trade on an economy. On the export side, trade permits a country to specialize and thereby expand production in specific sectors beyond the constraints imposed by limited domestic demand. Expansion of manufactured exports, in turn, may promote economies of scale and hence more rapid industrialization. Thus exports permit faster change in the structure of production in countries that pursue open strategies than in those that pursue inward-oriented ones.

On the import side, equally important forces are at work. An increased availability of foreign exchange—from whatever source—enables an economy to import intermediate and capital goods that are difficult if not impossible to produce domestically at a relatively early stage of development. Industrialization entails the increasing use of "modern" intermediate inputs, but the needed technology can be acquired much faster by increasing imports than by expanding domestic production alone. Accordingly, the economies committed to open development strategies changed their input-output structures faster than did those that followed inward-oriented ones.

To achieve an open development strategy with strong reliance on manufactured exports calls for more than an appropriate choice of policies. Initial conditions are important, and more than just trade policy is involved. Economies that enjoyed high rates of growth of manufactured exports typically began with relatively high shares of manufacturing in total output (except for Korea, which started its spurt with a relatively low share). There is also some evidence of sequencing in that the economies successfully pursuing open development strategies did so after a period of significant import substitution. If it is to succeed, export expansion in manufactures evidently requires a substantial industrial base that includes increased intermediate linkages (which Korea achieved, even though the initial share was low). The development of such a base usually entails a period of significant import substitution, although it is possible to import some of the technology as the process unfolds. These conclusions are consistent with arguments for supporting infant industries, especially if they generate technology transfers and interindustry linkages.[34]

---

33. We have not considered the primary exporter pattern since, with the possible exception of Colombia, none of the sample fits this pattern. See chapter 4 for a broader discussion of alternative strategies.

34. Westphal (1982) provides a related argument for the protection of infant industries. See also the analysis of the relation between total factor productivity growth and choice of development strategy in chapter 11 as well as Teitel and Thoumi (1986).

An open development strategy promises benefits by delinking the structure of production from the structure of domestic demand. Countries can pursue two types of specialization: intersectoral, with increased exports in some sectors and increased imports in others; and intrasectoral, with increased imports and exports in the same sectors. Both trends are evident in the sample, but increases in intrasectoral trade are especially marked. Also evident are both specialization in export sectors and increased reliance on imported intermediates and capital goods within the manufacturing subsectors.

The net effect of manufacturing growth on the balance of trade is mixed. Rapid industrialization tends to increase the demand for imported intermediates, and manufactured exports are often concentrated in the sectors most dependent on imports. The net effect of manufacturing on the balance of payments is negative for much of the industrialization process. Only in the later stages, as an economy achieves import substitution in the "harder" heavy manufacturing sectors, does the net contribution to the balance of trade of changes in manufacturing turn positive.

In an export-led or open development strategy, export performance, foreign capital inflows, imports, and aggregate growth interact. Although the nature of the causal links among these forces is difficult to disentangle, it is apparent that an open development strategy, if successful, demands a difficult balancing of forces and careful timing. The gains from success are great, but the difficulties of managing the required structural changes and concomitant pressures on the balance of trade are also great.

PART III

Productivity and
Structural Change

PART II USED a common input-output framework to compare the experience of industrialization in eight semi-industrial economies. In part III, the analysis is expanded to cover the growth of factor productivity and changes in the structure of production and factor use. As in other parts of the book, a variety of approaches is presented and then applied to diverse samples determined by the availability of comparable information.

The growth of factor productivity for the whole economy often includes a structural component that arises when resources are reallocated from activities of lower productivity to activities of higher productivity. Two types of reallocation are explored: the shift of labor and other inputs from primary production to manufacturing (chapters 8 and 9) and the increase in the ratio of production for export to production for the domestic market (chapters 9 and 10). An increase in the weight of the export sector, especially of manufactured exports, can accelerate aggregate productivity if marginal factor products are higher in that sector than elsewhere in the economy. In chapters 9 and 10, it is argued that an outward orientation—which is associated with increasing the share of production for export—leads directly to higher rates of total factor productivity growth at the sectoral level in addition to contributing to higher aggregate productivity through the narrowing of productivity differentials.

Of the sources of industrialization on the supply side, differential productivity growth is probably the best established. During industrialization, productivity growth is expected to be higher in manufacturing than in other sectors; within manufacturing, a higher rate is commonly expected in heavy industry than in light industry. Such expectations are largely confirmed in chapters 8 and 10. Surprisingly, however, both chapters identify an even stronger country and period effect. The rates of labor and total factor productivity growth tend to be uniformly higher across sectors in countries with good average performance as well as within countries in periods of rapid growth of aggregate productivity. This finding suggests that the overall economic environment, which includes general macroeconomic and trade policies, is an important factor in explaining differences in productivity growth.

Chapter 8 extends the cross-country model that was described in chapter 3 and considers explicitly the long-term patterns of factor accumulation and productivity growth. Expanding the analysis to the supply side in a disaggregated framework, it offers an estimate of the contribution of resource reallocation and other effects of structural change to the growth of productivity and output.

Chapter 9 presents a statistical analysis of the sources of growth. It focuses on a much shorter period (1964–73) but broadens the coverage to all the semi-industrial countries identified in chapter 4. The results show that during this period the semi-industrial countries differed significantly in performance and in the determinants of growth from both the lower-income countries and the industrial countries.

Chapter 10 estimates the growth of total factor productivity within manufacturing at the sectoral level in four of the countries in our sample. The variation in productivity growth among sectors is shown to be related to output growth. This is not, however, the result of the simple Verdoorn effect, which implies that any expansion of the market, regardless of source, improves a sector's productivity performance. Rather, it appears to be a rise in exports that leads to higher rates of total factor productivity growth, while greater import substitution may even hamper an improvement in productivity.

8 Productivity Growth and Factor Reallocation

MOSHE SYRQUIN

CHAPTERS 2 AND 3 provided a framework for analyzing the relation between the structural transformation of an economy and the growth of its per capita income. In chapter 3, a simple multisectoral model designed to trace the effects of changes in demand and trade on the structure of production and factor use was presented. The estimation of the model from cross-country data revealed some typical patterns of transformation, which were then used as benchmarks in comparing the experiences of various economies.

This chapter, building on that analysis, considers the typical patterns of productivity growth within sectors and the reallocation of resources among sectors during successive stages of transformation. This dynamic extension of the industrialization model, also based on cross-country data, becomes a frame of reference for evaluating country experience in this chapter. The relations on the supply side in the countries studied between sectoral accumulation and productivity growth on the one hand and the level of development on the other hand are more erratic and less well documented than are the relations on the demand side underlying the simulations in chapter 3. Also, the country information available for analyzing these relations is scarcer and less reliable. The results, therefore, are more speculative than those in chapter 3; only broad trends and orders of magnitude are emphasized.

As in an earlier study (Chenery and Syrquin 1975), the stylized facts and the simulated links are regarded as reduced forms consistent with a variety of econometric structures. The range of possible structures is then narrowed by considering not only production but also demand and productivity in a general equilibrium framework. The reduced forms also reveal the implications of partial assumptions about parameters and trends and provide useful starting points for structural modeling (as is done in chapter 11).

The cross-country model of transformation is designed to cover the complete range of the transition. Although it is based on information referring mainly to the postwar period, it illustrates the interaction among the sets of processes that define economic development from the onset of self-sustained growth to the advanced stage characteristic of Western European countries in recent decades. It also helps to identify a transition stage of growth acceleration in output and productivity growth during which the structure of the economy is radically transformed. Such structural transformation is not well captured in price endogenous models, which are usually calibrated to replicate observed change during a limited portion of the transition only.

This chapter begins by deriving the rate of growth in the model and goes on to estimate factor productivity growth and the contribution of resource reallocation to aggregate growth. The final section returns to a consideration of the interactions between demand and supply that was begun in chapter 2.

The Growth of Output and Factor Use

The growth of aggregate output depends on the growth of inputs and on the efficiency of their allocation and use. A convenient summary of the outcome of the growth process is the Harrod-Domar accounting equation relating the accumulation of capital to the productivity of capital. Let I/V stand for the share of gross investment in GDP, δ for the ratio of depreciation to output, and h^* for the incremental capital-output ratio (ICOR). At every point in time, aggregate value added growth, G_V, satisfies the equation

$$(8\text{-}1) \qquad\qquad G_V = \frac{I/V - \delta}{h^*}.$$

The two elements in equation 8-1, net investment and the capital coefficient, both vary systematically with per capita income. A rise in investment was shown in chapter 3 to be a main component of the shift in the structure of demand. The share of depreciation also appears to increase with per capita income (Kuznets 1966), but without significantly affecting the rise in the share of net investment in GDP.

The evidence for the aggregate ICOR is derived indirectly from the variation in capital-output ratios at the sectoral level. The reduced-form specification of sectoral capital requirements in equation 3-16, which relates capital-output ratios to income, is the most natural one for the input-output system in chapter 3. The approach to factor requirements usually used by planners, it is easy to implement with commonly available data.

There are virtually no guidelines from economic theory about what to expect for the secular variation in capital-output ratios. From the empirical work of Kuznets (1961b) and others and from recent cross-country data, several systematic trends—or stylized facts—for broad sectors can be suggested. In agriculture, the capital-output ratio, excluding land, is relatively low in the initial stages and increases with income. The opposite pattern is typical for social overhead, the capital coefficient of which declines with rising income from a very high initial level dictated by indivisibilities in basic infrastructure. In manufacturing, although there

Table 8-1. *Labor and Capital Requirements per Unit of Gross Output for the Cross-Country Model*

Sector	Per capita income (dollars)						
	140	280	560	1,120	2,100	3,360	5,040
Capital coefficients (capital per unit of output)							
Agriculture	1.00	1.20	1.44	1.72	2.03	2.18	2.32
Mining	0.70	0.86	1.06	1.31	1.58	1.70	1.81
Manufacturing	0.63	0.66	0.69	0.71	0.74	0.75	0.76
Food processing	0.45	0.45	0.45	0.45	0.45	—	—
Consumer goods	0.70	0.70	0.70	0.70	0.70	—	—
Producer goods	1.00	1.00	1.00	1.00	1.00	—	—
Machinery	0.65	0.65	0.65	0.65	0.65	—	—
Social overhead	4.30	3.88	3.50	3.15	3.00	2.93	2.87
Services	1.30	1.27	1.24	1.21	1.19	1.19	1.19
Capital-output ratio (K/X)	1.44	1.45	1.43	1.37	1.32	1.31	1.32
Capital-value added ratio (K/V)	2.17	2.34	2.43	2.43	2.40	2.38	2.36
Labor coefficients (workers per million dollars of output)							
Agriculture	3,610	2,150	1,280	685	300	163	95
Mining	2,100	917	400	175	84	50	32
Manufacturing	678	343	167	85	45	29	20
Food processing	280	168	98	63	42	—	—
Consumer goods	1,155	540	252	126	70	—	—
Producer goods	770	315	133	57	28	—	—
Machinery	980	413	175	76	35	—	—
Social overhead	840	470	260	140	84	53	36
Services	890	590	385	252	160	108	76
Participation rate (L/N)	0.352	0.388	0.419	0.426	0.400	0.400	0.417

— Not available.
Source: Syrquin (1986b).

are few clear trends, the capital-output ratio tends to be higher for producer goods than for light industrial products or machinery. For the relation of sectoral capital-output ratios to income, see table 8-1.

For the economy as a whole, the capital-output ratio, h, is a weighted average of the sectoral h_i's, with the output weights, ρ_i, derived in chapter 3:

$$(8\text{-}2) \qquad\qquad h = \Sigma_i \rho_i h_i.$$

The marginal capital-output ratio, h^*, can then be derived from the average h and substituted into equation 8-1 to determine the implied growth rate for any income level.[1]

Use of the Harrod-Domar growth equation 8-1 does not imply the adoption of a specific growth theory or the assumption of a technologi-

1. The growth rate for an income interval in table 8-2 below is set at the mean value of the instantaneous initial and terminal rates.

Table 8-2. *Growth Rates of Aggregate Output and Inputs of the Cross-Country Model*

Period	Initial year's values			Annual growth rate (percent)						Length of time interval (years)	Stage
	Per capita income (dollars)	Net investment share	ICOR[a]	Population	Per capita income	Value added	Capital	Labor	Labor productivity		
0	100–140	8	2.20	2.55	1.26	3.81	3.90	2.56	1.25	27	I
1	140–280	10	2.30	2.78	2.02	4.80	5.03	3.06	1.74	35	
2	280–560	13	2.42	2.50	3.17	5.67	5.84	2.85	2.82	22	II
3	560–1,120	15	2.45	2.20	4.10	6.30	6.29	2.30	4.00	17	
4	1,120–2,100	16	2.40	2.00	4.58	6.58	6.52	1.81	4.77	14	
5	2,100–3,360	16	2.39	1.50	4.71	6.21	6.11	1.40	4.81	10	III
6	3,360–5,040	14	2.39	1.00	4.60	5.60	5.50	1.47	4.13	9	

Note: Chapter 3 describes the cross-country model; table 3-3 describes periods. Growth rates are continuously compounded. They are computed by $1/t \ln X_T/X_O$, where O and T are initial and terminal years for any variable X.

The growth of per capita income for a period is set equal to the mean of the instantaneous growth rates for the initial and terminal benchmarks, calculated by the ratio of the net investment share to the ICOR[a]. The corresponding figures for the last income benchmark ($5,040) are 13 percent for investment and 2.39 for the ICOR. I, II, and III correspond to the three stages in figure 3-7.

a. ICOR is the incremental capital-output ratio.

Source: World Bank data.

cally fixed capital coefficient. The growth equation is an ex post identity implicit in the set of reduced-form relations presented above and in chapter 3. It is one of a set of relations consistent with the observed average patterns of structural change. Other patterns may relate differently to growth, but such differences are difficult to infer from the present model. A structural model making explicit the behavioral and technological relations is needed for such extrapolations.

The main predetermined variable in this model is per capita income. To derive its growth rate from the growth of total output, the pattern of population growth at various income levels must be estimated.

Demographers and economists have described the fall in birth and death rates with an increasing level of development as the "demographic transition." Historically and in cross sections, the fall in mortality rates has preceded the decline in fertility; the result is an initial acceleration of population growth followed by a slowdown. Here I assume a smooth transition incorporating these observations.[2]

The specification of a growth rate of income for each interval converts the sectoral and total variations in output and inputs from chapter 3 into growth rates. The aggregate results appear in table 8-2. According to the illustrative calculations in the last column of this table, presented as rough orders of magnitude only, it takes about sixty years for a typical country to go through the first two periods and about fifty more for it to complete the industrializing stage represented by periods 2 through 4.[3] The use of purchasing power parities instead of exchange rates as the conversion factor reduces the income gap over the full range of the transition by about 30 percent. At the real growth rates in table 8-2, the time it takes for a typical country to go through the periods in the table is also reduced by about 30 percent (see appendix to chapter 3).

Growth Acceleration

The growth rates of per capita income and total value added in table 8-2 show an initial acceleration followed by a slowdown at higher income

2. Recent research has advanced our understanding of the determinants and timing of the demographic transition. The *World Development Report 1984* (World Bank 1984) presents the state of the art. Although the population growth rates in table 8-2 seem to be representative of the long-run demographic transition, the timing in specific cases has shown great variation around the trend. For specific examples, see World Bank (1984, figs. 4-1, 4-2).

3. The income range in the simulations of chapter 3 starts at $140 in 1970 dollars, equivalent to $100 in 1964 prices (see chapter 3). At this income level, the share of agriculture in value added has already come down substantially, and net investment accounts for about 10 percent of GDP. In this chapter, which deals with factor use and productivity growth, it proved convenient to illustrate an even earlier period where agriculture takes up about half total value added, net investment is below 8 percent, and growth is significantly lower. The basic information on investment and on the sectoral distribution of value added and employment was taken from Chenery and Syrquin (1975, pp. 20–21). There, we presented average figures for countries with levels of income below $100 per capita. The mean income for this group was close to $70 in 1964 prices, which amounts to about $100 at 1970 prices. The period $100–$140 is labeled period 0. The other six periods are as in chapter 3.

levels. The acceleration is the result of the increase in the rate of capital accumulation and of productivity growth (or technological change), which prevents the capital-output ratio from rising. In this long-term model the investment rate and the productivity of capital vary with the level of income but not with its growth rate. Various authors have argued, however, that saving and investment rates increase with the growth rate, while capital-output ratios decrease with it.[4] Incorporating these virtuous feedbacks would result in faster acceleration than that shown in table 8-2.

Growth acceleration is an important aspect of theories of economic development. Evidence of long-term acceleration of growth comes from the early experience of today's developed countries and from comparisons among countries grouped by income level. First, as Kuznets (1971) points out, when today's developed countries entered the stage known as modern economic growth, they must have experienced a significant acceleration of growth. Backward extrapolations of the growth rates during the epoch of modern economic growth suggest implausibly low levels of income in the not too distant past. In addition, for the more recent case of Japan, growth acceleration has been thoroughly documented and studied (Ohkawa and Rosovsky 1973, among others).

The 1950–75 period, for which the model is calibrated, was one of very fast growth in almost all regions and groups of countries. This acceleration, however, was in part a response to the disruption of world trade and production in the preceding period and to the destruction of the war. It cannot be explained only by acceleration during the transition to industrialization, since it encompassed countries at all income levels.

Indirect corroboration of growth acceleration at medium income levels comes from cross-country comparisons of growth over shorter periods of time. Table 8-3 presents the experience of groups of countries, ranked by income, since 1950. The middle-income group as defined in the *World Development Report 1983* and the transitional and newly developed groups as defined by Chenery (1977) correspond roughly to the semi-industrial group described in chapter 4. (Italy and Japan are included in the newly developed group.) In Morawetz's classification, the third and fourth groups—developing countries with a per capita income of more than $520—correspond to the semi-industrial group.

In every column in the table, growth is faster in the middle-income groups and slows down some at higher income levels. This pattern holds for both total and per capita income, and it holds for every subperiod. The pattern of growth in the model presented in table 8-2 agrees closely with this postwar configuration.

---

4. The effect on saving can be derived from the permanent income theory and the life cycle theory. Simple acceleration models imply a similar relation for investment. For the inverse relation between capital-output ratios and the growth rate, see Vanek and Studenmund (1968) and Chenery and Eckstein (1970).

Table 8-3. *Growth of Total and Per Capita Income of All but Centrally Planned Countries by Income Group*

Per capita income of country group	Annual growth rate of per capita income (percent)		Annual growth rate of GDP (percent)	
Morawetz (1977) classification (1975 dollars)				
	1950–60	1960–75		
Less than $265	1.4	1.0		
$266–$520	2.2	2.3		
$521–$1,075	2.4	3.7		
More than $1,075 (developing)	3.2	5.8		
OECD	3.0	3.5		
Chenery (1977) classification				
	1950–60	1960–73	1950–60	1960–73
Less developed	2.0	1.8	4.2	4.3
Transitional	2.7	3.9	5.6	6.8
Newly developed	5.7	7.0	6.9	8.1
Old developed	2.6	3.4	3.9	4.4
World Development Report 1983 classification				
	1960–81		1960–81	
India	1.4		3.5	
China	3.4[a]		5.4	
Other low-income	0.8		4.1	
Lower middle-income	3.4		5.3	
Upper middle-income	4.2		6.0	
Industrial market economies	3.4		4.0	

a. Computed from the growth rates of GDP and population.

Sectoral Growth Rates

Aggregate growth is a summary of sectoral growth. The main purpose of this chapter is to show how variations in aggregate growth result from what happens at the sectoral level and from the shift in sectoral weights in the generation of output and in factor use.

The comparative static runs of the cross-country model in chapter 3 derived the sectoral structure of production for each income benchmark. Sectoral factor requirements were determined by income-related factor-output coefficients in equations 3-16 and 3-17. As with the capital-output ratios, the pattern of labor-output ratios is based on the observed association of these ratios with per capita income across countries and over time. Certain stylized facts about the changes in labor productivity (the inverse of the labor-output ratio) appear to be reasonably robust. First, labor productivity increases in virtually all productive sectors but not at a uniform rate. Second, the level of labor productivity in agriculture is uniformly lower than in manufacturing or services. The gap in productivity commonly widens in the initial stage and then begins to narrow as the increase of labor productivity in agriculture accelerates, exceeding the average growth. The increase in productivity at this stage is the result of faster output growth and an eventual absolute decline in labor in agriculture. Third, average labor productivity is higher, and increases at a faster rate, in heavy industry than in light industry. The relation of labor-output ratios and income, based on cross-country data, is given in table 8-1.

Tables 8-4 and 8-5 present the growth rates of value added, labor productivity, and factor proportions for three sectors for the cross-country model and for the sample of economies used throughout this book. The uneven expansion of sectors translates into the changes in the structure of production analyzed in chapters 3, 6, and 7.

The relation between aggregate and sectoral growth can be derived from the definitions of total output, V, and labor productivity, y:

$$V = \Sigma_i V_i$$

and

$$y = \Sigma_i \frac{V_i}{L_i} \frac{L_i}{L} = \Sigma_i y_i \gamma_i$$

where γ_i is the employment share in sector i. Differentiating with respect to time gives the relations between aggregate and sectoral growth rates:

Table 8-4. *Growth Rates of Output and Inputs for the Cross-Country Model by Sector*
(average annual growth rates in percent)

Measure	Period[a]						
	0	1	2	3	4	5	6
Value added							
Primary	3.03	3.98	4.13	4.11	3.66	3.16	3.24
Manufacturing	5.36	5.65	6.79	7.57	7.84	6.18	4.95
Services	4.15	5.07	5.90	6.37	6.45	6.67	6.23
Total	3.81	4.80	5.67	6.30	6.58	6.21	5.60
Labor productivity							
Primary	0.74	1.32	2.03	3.54	5.71	6.22	5.83
Manufacturing	1.26	2.05	3.36	4.15	4.33	4.47	4.25
Services	1.31	1.33	2.13	2.77	3.20	4.12	3.85
Total	1.25	1.74	2.82	4.00	4.77	4.81	4.13
Capital-labor ratio							
Primary	0.73	2.11	3.32	5.03	7.18	7.26	7.02
Manufacturing	1.21	2.14	3.34	4.27	4.43	4.50	4.20
Services	1.18	1.24	1.94	2.46	3.04	3.84	3.52
Total	1.33	1.96	2.99	3.99	4.71	4.71	4.03

Note: Services includes social overhead.
a. Periods are explained in table 3-3.

(8-3) $$G_V = \Sigma_i \rho_i G_{V_i}$$

and

(8-4) $$G_y = \Sigma_i \rho_i G_{y_i} + \Sigma_i \rho_i G_{\gamma_i}$$

where $\rho_i = V_i/V$ is the share of sector i in total output (GDP).

The growth rate of total output, G_V, equals the sum of sectoral growth rates weighted by the sectoral output shares. The growth rate of aggregate labor productivity, G_y, has two components. The first term averages the sectoral growth rates of output per worker. The second term measures the contribution to aggregate labor productivity growth of employment shifts among sectors with different labor productivities. I denote this second term by $A(y)$ and label it the "gross allocation effect."

When aggregate growth accelerates, manufacturing typically leads the way, growing faster than any other sector. Because of its initial low output share, however, its contribution to growth, $\rho_m G_m$, is at first modest and below that of primary production (see figure 3-7). At low income levels, agriculture is the dominant activity; aggregate growth is therefore closely related to performance in that sector. As manufacturing increases its output share, its faster growth rate pulls up the aggregate growth rate of output and labor productivity.

If all sectors had the same production function and faced the same factor prices, and if resources were perfectly mobile, then labor productivity would follow the same pattern in all sectors. In actuality, both in the model simulations and in the observations in figure 8-1, labor productivity is significantly lower in agriculture than in the rest of the economy. In the early stages of development the growth of productivity in agriculture lags behind that of other sectors, which widens further the productivity gap. These sectoral differences in the *average* product of labor are partly a reflection of differences in the nature of the production function (which lead to different factor proportions) and in the rate of technological change. But they also stem from the low mobility of resources, a condition that lies behind the persistence of disequilibrium phenomena such as surplus labor in agriculture and other low productivity activities, including handicrafts and services.

When the industrial sector accelerates its growth in response to domestic demand and to changes in comparative advantage (usually with some help from commercial policies), the productivity gap tends to increase.[5] Labor starts to shift out of agriculture, at first in relative terms and eventually in absolute terms, but with a lag. Since productivity in agriculture rises even at this stage, a surplus of labor results.

---

5. In some cases where manufacturing was heavily protected, the policy-induced rise in the relative price of manufactured goods accounts for part of the acceleration of growth in that sector and for part of the increase in the productivity gap between agriculture and industry.

Table 8-5. *Growth Rates of Output and Inputs of Sample Economies by Sector*
(average annual growth rates in percent)

Measure	Colombia (1953–70)	Mexico (1950–75)	Turkey (1963–73)	Yugoslavia (1962–72)	Japan 1915–35	Japan 1955–70	Korea (1963–73)	Taiwan (1961–71)	Israel (1958–72)	Average for advanced countries[a] (1963–73)
Value added										
Primary	4.18	4.16	1.77	2.33	1.69	2.03	6.39	3.23	6.23	1.9
Manufacturing	7.41	7.34	8.72	11.55	5.00	14.47	20.15	15.81	12.06	5.9
Services	5.11	6.56	7.67	9.51	4.18	10.83	15.72	9.62	9.00	4.6
Total	5.17	6.24	6.18	8.16	3.49	10.87	13.70	10.49	9.42	4.8
Labor productivity										
Primary	3.62	3.43	2.30	3.55	2.04	5.47	6.44	2.69	7.73	6.1
Manufacturing	4.11	2.96	3.94	6.16	3.07	9.40	9.79	7.40	6.81	5.3
Services	1.28	2.34	0.97	10.67	1.58	6.27	6.47	4.59	4.43	2.2
Total	2.99	3.76	4.86	8.57	2.66	8.71	8.81	6.71	5.48	3.7
Capital-labor ratio										
Primary	—	4.01	—	—	—	10.08	10.20	4.22	8.39	8.1
Manufacturing	—	2.00	—	—	—	8.15	8.76	6.29	3.18	3.8
Services	—	1.70	—	—	—	4.83	-0.35	0.20	6.96	1.7
Total	—	3.31	—	—	—	7.81	5.02	2.82	5.94	3.0

— Not available.

Note: Services includes social overhead. Employment in Colombia is for 1951–70; labor productivity in Yugoslavia is for 1966–72.

a. The advanced countries are Belgium, Canada, Denmark, France, Italy, Netherlands, United Kingdom, and United States.

Sources: Employment in Colombia is from World Bank data. The average for advanced countries was computed from the data in Stein and Lee (1977). All other data are from World Bank and are described in Kubo (1983).

Figure 8-1. *Relative Labor Productivity of Sample Economies and Cross-Country Model*

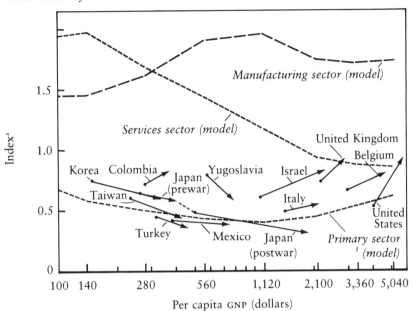

a. Index signifies labor productivity in a sector relative to labor productivity for the whole economy.

The pattern of relative productivity in figure 8-1 is related to and resembles the Kuznets curve of income inequality. The productivity gap between primary production on the one hand and industry and services on the other is greatest in the middle-income range ($500–$1,000), which is typically the period of greatest inequality of income (Chenery and others 1974).[6] It is also the period when, because of the productivity gap itself, resource shifts can make their largest contribution to aggregate growth, as discussed below.

In a second phase, once migration and capital accumulation have significantly reduced the surplus of labor, relative wages increase and a catch-up process takes place in agriculture. Capital intensity in this sector then increases faster than in other sectors. This is coupled with the continuing growth in factor productivity. As a result, agriculture begins to reduce the

6. The widening gap in the case of Korea and Taiwan reflects their exceptionally fast growth in manufacturing. It does not necessarily imply a more unequal distribution of income. In Taiwan, for example, inequality during this period was reduced according to all measures except the productivity gap. The explanation lies in part in the rapid increase in the share of off-farm income in the total income of farm families. See Kuo (1984).

productivity gap. Israel and the OECD countries represent this phase of transformation (see figure 8-1).

The acceleration of aggregate growth is only partly caused by the shift of weights implicit in differential growth rates by sector; output growth accelerates in the model in all sectors other than agriculture. The acceleration of labor productivity encompasses agriculture as well, especially at medium income levels, at which the agricultural labor force begins to decline in absolute terms. This similarity in productivity growth across sectors suggests that there are underlying factors determining the overall process of transformation. This qualifies the notion of one sector leading the process without regard to conditions elsewhere in the economy.[7]

Limits on Unbalanced Growth

During the transformation, growth proceeds at an uneven rate from sector to sector. But sectoral interdependence imposes certain constraints which if violated may retard growth. A sector is said to be a leading sector when its rate of growth exceeds the average rate for a period long enough to raise overall growth toward its rate and when it spreads its dynamism through substantial links to other sectors. A large sector, such as agriculture at very low income levels, is almost by definition excluded from this role. By its very size, however, agriculture will initially have a larger weight in determining overall performance than any emerging but still small sector.[8] Historically, agriculture has often been instrumental in igniting growth,[9] but eventually the leading role has shifted to other sectors, predominantly manufacturing.

The potential expansion of the primary sector has been limited on the demand side by low income and price elasticities for food and by the substitution of fabricated for natural raw materials and on the supply side by the availability of natural resources and technology and by low productivity growth when underemployed labor is available. When these constraints have been overcome, it has usually been through the discovery of natural resources (or price booms) and heavy reliance on the export of primary goods with little or no processing. The literature on the "staple" theory of growth gives various examples of episodes of fast growth based on the exploitation of natural resources and their export. Such episodes

---

7. A similar country effect or period effect is also observed in the following section for total factor productivity growth: differences across countries and over time for all sectors are more significant than differences across sectors for a given country and period.

8. Differences in the availability of arable land and natural resources, as well as in climate, labor supply, and the ownership structure, make it difficult to generalize about the agricultural sector, particularly at low income levels. Although the overall trend described is fairly representative, exceptions can probably be found for each specific component.

9. This has been true of newly settled areas specializing in primary exports. Argentina, Australia, Brazil, and Canada are examples of countries that went through episodes of this type of growth.

often did not lead to continuous development even when they extended over a long period of time. A measure of their success in producing self-sustained growth is the strength of the linkages to the manufacturing sector and the impetus given to the transformation of the economy.[10]

If agriculture's capacity to sustain high rates of growth is limited, too slow an expansion of this sector can nevertheless retard the growth of the economy.[11] The interdependence of agriculture and manufacturing has received much attention in the development literature.[12] Agriculture has several contributions to make during transformation: it must provide food for the urban population, raw materials for industry, markets for some of the industrial products, revenue for the state, and foreign exchange to cover the import requirements of industrialization while the capacity to export manufactured goods is being developed.[13]

Finally, as the economy industrializes there is a net flow of resources from agriculture to the expanding sectors. An elastic supply of labor facilitates the rapid expansion of manufacturing and of supporting infrastructure and services at both the early stages and higher income levels.[14] Agriculture can also finance the initial investment in manufacturing and infrastructure. The problem of maintaining the right intersectoral balance given the scarcity of capital has been aptly summarized by Kuznets: "One of the crucial problems of modern economic growth is how to extract from the product of agriculture a surplus for the financing of capital formation necessary for industrial growth without at the same time blighting the growth of agriculture, under conditions where no easy *quid pro quo* for surplus is available in the country."[15]

The importance of maintaining a proper balance among sectors is clear. Economies that have fostered the development of agriculture through government investment, extension services, and nondiscriminatory price policies have better growth performances than those that have stimulated industry and neglected agriculture. Israel, Malaysia, and Taiwan are examples of the first group and Argentina, Chile, and Uruguay of the second. In the more successful economies, sectoral transformation was marked by a rapid growth of agriculture, surpassed by an even faster growth of manufacturing. In the less successful cases, agriculture often stagnated. In

10. On the staple approach see, for example, Baldwin (1956), Watkins (1963), and Caves (1965). In the more recent literature, resource discoveries and price booms are discussed in relation to the Dutch disease (Corden and Neary 1982; Roemer 1985).

11. Nontraded goods are similar to agriculture in that they are not best suited for leading growth but can retard growth if their expansion is inadequate.

12. See, for example, Johnston (1970), Johnston and Kilby (1975), and Meier (1984, pp. 427–31).

13. International trade makes these requirements less rigid, particularly if alternative sources of foreign exchange are available, such as mineral exports or foreign capital.

14. For the role of an elastic labor supply in the postwar growth performance of Western Europe, see Kindleberger (1967) and Cornwall (1977).

15. Kuznets (1961a, p. 115), quoted in Johnston (1970).

a recent comparative study of a large number of countries for the period 1960–79, Hwa (1983) shows that the growth rate of agriculture is significantly associated with industrial growth and with the rate of increase in factor productivity.[16]

The transformation of the production structure from primary activities to manufacturing has taken place in virtually all the developed countries and is very much in evidence now in the transitional economies. As indicated in chapter 4, the timing of this transformation varies greatly and depends chiefly on the degree of participation in international trade—the main source of increased specialization.

Factor Productivity Growth

In part II, the growth of total output and of sectoral outputs was analyzed in terms of changes in the level and structure of the expenditure (demand) components of GDP. The rate of growth of total output and of labor productivity can also be accounted for by changes in three sets of interacting supply-side factors:

- Changes in primary inputs, or capital accumulation and the expansion of employment[17]
- Increases in the efficiency of factor use within sectors, or total factor productivity growth
- Resource reallocation across sectors.

This section presents a detailed supply-side growth accounting that decomposes output growth into factor contributions and productivity growth, first by sector and then for the whole economy. The aggregate growth of productivity will be seen to depend in part on the production structure of the economy, even in cases where the sectoral rates of productivity growth are exogenously given.

Aggregate Results

The data on the growth of output and inputs by sector presented in tables 8-4 and 8-5 can be used to derive the implied rates of total factor productivity growth if they are supplemented by minimal assumptions about a neoclassical production function. The production function approach complements the fixed coefficients formulation of chapter 3. At the cost of additional assumptions, it yields additional results as to the pattern of TFP growth by sector and the contribution of intersectoral resource reallocation to aggregate productivity and output growth.

In each sector, let output (value added) be produced by a differentiable

---

16. This resembles the country effect mentioned above.

17. In accounting for the growth of gross output, intermediate inputs also have to be considered. For the relation between growth accounting for gross output and for value added, see Syrquin (1985a).

production function, with constant returns to scale in capital and labor, of the form used in chapter 2:

(8-5) $$V_i = f^i(K_i, L_i, t)$$

or in intensive units (with $k = K/L$):

(8-6) $$y_i = F^i(k_i, t).$$

The rate of TFP growth, or technical change, is assumed to be Hicks neutral[18] and proceeds at a constant rate within periods. For each sector and period, the rates of change in output, inputs, and TFP growth are related by the growth accounting equation:

(8-7) $$G_{V_i} = \alpha_i G_{K_i} + (1 - \alpha_i)G_{L_i} + \lambda_i$$

where λ is the rate of TFP growth and α and $(1 - \alpha)$ are the elasticities of output with respect to capital and labor. To calculate TFP growth given the growth of output and inputs for a period, all that is needed is an estimate of the elasticity of capital, α. The exact functional form of the production function need not be specified. A point estimate for α is compatible with almost any constant-returns production function. The elasticities are not necessarily assumed to equal the factor shares in value added. Instead, I recognize the possibility of imperfect mobility, segmented labor markets, surplus labor, and other sources of friction and disequilibrium preventing the equalization of factor returns across sectors or of factor shares and elasticities within sectors. The values assumed for the elasticities in the computations below were derived from cross-country information and in most sectors vary over time according to available information on sectoral elasticities of substitution. These values appear in table 8-6.[19]

Substituting in equation 8-7 the value for the elasticity, α_i, gives the rate of TFP growth, λ_i.[20] The usual procedure in short-run models is to regard

18. Technical change is Hicks neutral if it affects the level of output but not the marginal rates of substitution between pairs of inputs.

19. Since land expansion is an important factor in the growth of output in agriculture at low income levels, I assume that any residual productivity in period 1 was attributable to land. In period 2 three-quarters of the residual is credited to land; in period 3, half. Beyond period 3, land expansion is not considered, in accordance with the common practice in growth accounting studies. See, for example, Denison and Chung (1976).

20. This is the common procedure in growth accounting. The relation of this approach to the presentation of factor-output ratios above can be clarified by restating the growth decomposition in intensive units:

$$G_{y_i} = \alpha_i G_{k_i} + \lambda_i$$

where G_{y_i} is the growth of labor productivity. Substituting $G_k = G_h + G_y$ (h being the capital-output ratio) yields

$$G_{y_i} = \frac{\alpha_i}{1 - \alpha_i} G_{h_i} + \frac{\lambda_i}{1 - \alpha_i}.$$

Given the sectoral h_i's, this is an equation in three unknowns: y_i, λ_i, and α_i. Assuming a value

(Note continues on the following page.)

TFP growth as exogenous and to derive output and labor productivity growth. Here the procedure is reversed; labor productivity growth is predetermined by estimating from cross-country data the variation in labor output ratios ($l = 1/y$), and TFP growth is then determined residually. This procedure does not imply anything about the causality or the exogeneity of technical change. Like other growth accounting exercises, it is useful in singling out potentially important effects and in providing orders of magnitude.[21]

The derived pattern of sectoral growth of TFP shown in table 8-6 is the one consistent with all the other blocks of the model. The complete model is best seen as a consistent simultaneous system that complements the more structural but data-intensive approach in chapter 11. Compared with the general equilibrium model in that chapter, this one calls for less information on specific parameters and fewer behavioral and institutional assumptions, but it stops at the reduced-form stage and is less useful for policy simulations. Its main virtue is that it incorporates into one system the various elements of growth and structure, from Engel effects to differential productivity growth. It illustrates in a simple and direct way the general equilibrium nature of the interrelations: changes in any one component imply variations throughout the system.

To apply this approach, equation 8-7 was calculated at the eight-sector level for all periods.[22] The results are tabulated in table 8-6. For manufacturing, only the total is shown since the results for its subsectors were not very different. The aggregate sources of growth are computed directly from the aggregate rates of growth of output and inputs, with the output-weighted average elasticities used as weights. When the sectoral elasticities equal the distributive shares, their output-weighted averages correspond to the factor shares in total output. To distinguish the two concepts, I denote the directly computed aggregate rate of TFP growth by $\bar{\lambda}$ and the average of the sectoral rates by $\Sigma \rho_i \lambda_i$.

The results in table 8-6 illustrate the general pattern of change in the sectoral sources of growth at various income levels. Although any individual figure may have a large margin of error, the overall pattern appears

---

for α_i yields a relation between the growth of labor productivity, G_{y_i}, and total factor productivity, λ_i. To an estimated or assumed value of one there corresponds a unique value of the other.

21. The important advances in the last twenty-five years in productivity research and in related concepts such as human capital, embodiment, and learning effect were in no small measure due to the large "residuals" reported by Abramovitz (1956) and Solow (1957).

22. The elasticities in equation 8-7 for any period are assumed to be mean weights of initial and terminal values; growth rates are computed by log differences. The index for productivity growth is thus a Tornqvist-Theil quantity index, which has been used as a discrete approximation of the Divisia index. Diewert (1976) has shown that it is exact for a homogeneous translog function, and since this can provide a second-order approximation to an arbitrary function, it is also superlative (see Diewert for definitions and references).

to be consistent with the experience of many countries. I turn now to the main results, some of which have previously been summarized in figure 3-8.

In the early periods of the transformation (represented in table 8-6 by the income levels $100–140 and $140–$280), the rate of productivity growth is quite modest and accounts for no more than 10 to 15 percent of total output growth. The initial acceleration of growth comes largely as a result of faster input growth, primarily capital accumulation. It is at this stage that most of the increase in the net investment share takes place, but since the elasticity of capital normally declines, the contribution of capital accumulation to growth stabilizes or declines. Since output growth continues to accelerate for a considerable period, the growth rate of factor productivity must increase and must also account for an increasing proportion of growth.

This is basically the argument that leads Kuznets to expect the rate of factor productivity growth in most countries to be higher in the twentieth century than it was in the nineteenth (Kuznets 1971, p. 75). In most of the countries for which long-term records are available, productivity growth did accelerate over time. A long-term acceleration has been documented for Canada and Norway (Kuznets 1971), the United Kingdom (Matthews, Feinstein, and Odling-Smee 1982), the United States (Abramovitz and David 1973), and Japan (Ohkawa and Rosovsky 1973). In the early periods in these studies, the growth of total factor productivity accounted for about 30 to 40 percent of the growth of output, and factor inputs, primarily capital, accounted for more than half. The postwar finding of very large contributions of TFP growth and correspondingly low contributions of capital and labor is therefore a recent phenomenon in the industrial countries. It does not characterize the earlier experiences of these countries or the early periods of the transformation in developing countries. At higher income levels, the contribution of capital declines and that of factor productivity increases (discussed in figure 3-8).

In chapter 2, estimates of the sources of growth for a large number of economies were summarized in figure 2-2, which plots lines of constant output growth as the sum of the combined (weighted) growth of factor inputs, G_F, and of total factor productivity, λ. These estimates cover fairly short time intervals during the postwar period. The same kind of figure can be used for comparing the long-run relation of productivity and output growth for the cross-country model and for countries for which the required information is available. Figure 8-2 adapts figure 2-2, retaining its three country clusters. The very high growth rates of the cluster C economies in figure 8-2 were achieved both by fast input expansion and by high productivity growth. Such growth rates are certainly exceptional when compared with the experiences of the developed countries and are even so when compared with the universal fast growth in the postwar period.

Table 8-6. Sources of Growth: Inputs and Productivity

Period	Per capita income (dollars)	Sector	Annual growth rate (percent)		Contributions to output growth (percent)				Elasticity of capital
			Output	TFP	TFP	Capital	Labor	Land	
0	100–140	Agriculture	2.98	0	0	39	47	14	0.40
		Mining	4.31	0.75	17	54	29	—	0.50
		Manufacturing	5.36	0.53	10	59	31	—	0.60
		Social overhead } Services	4.15	0.72	17	48	35	—	0.50
		Total	3.81	0.44	11	48	36	5	0.47
1	140–280	Agriculture	3.90	0.11	3	48	41	8	0.40
		Mining	5.51	0.90	16	56	28	—	0.50
		Manufacturing	5.65	0.91	16	54	29	—	0.54
		Social overhead	5.36	0.88	16	57	27	—	0.60
		Services	4.97	0.69	14	44	42	—	0.45
		Total	4.80	0.72	15	49	34	2	0.47
2	280–560	Agriculture	3.92	0.23	6	58	30	6	0.43
		Mining	6.50	1.43	22	57	21	—	0.50
		Manufacturing	6.79	1.61	24	51	25	—	0.51
		Social overhead	6.19	1.41	23	54	23	—	0.58
		Services	5.80	1.20	21	39	40	—	0.40
		Total	5.67	1.40	25	47	27	1	0.46

3	560–1,120	Agriculture	3.53	0.86	24	68	8	—	0.46
		Mining	7.26	1.81	25	59	16	—	0.50
		Manufacturing	7.57	2.11	28	47	25	—	0.46
		Social overhead	6.59	1.96	30	50	20	—	0.55
		Services	6.28	1.66	26	34	40	—	0.35
		Total	6.30	2.28	36	43	21	—	0.43
4	1,120–2,100	Agriculture	2.68	1.46	54	87	−41	—	0.50
		Mining	6.74	2.53	38	55	7	—	0.50
		Manufacturing	7.84	2.52	32	43	25	—	0.42
		Social overhead	6.57	1.89	29	48	23	—	0.50
		Services	6.40	2.19	34	30	36	—	0.30
		Total	6.58	2.92	44	39	15	—	0.39
5	2,100–3,360	Agriculture	1.57	1.55	99	109	−108	—	0.52
		Mining	6.07	1.78	29	58	13	—	0.48
		Manufacturing	6.18	2.67	43	40	17	—	0.40
		Social overhead	6.37	2.68	42	45	13	—	0.47
		Services	6.78	2.99	44	25	31	—	0.25
		Total	6.21	3.11	50	35	15	—	0.36
6	3,360–5,040	Agriculture	2.06	1.49	72	96	−70	—	0.52
		Mining	4.79	1.92	40	59	1	—	0.48
		Manufacturing	4.95	2.79	56	35	9	—	0.35
		Social overhead	5.60	2.43	43	42	15	—	0.44
		Services	6.48	2.91	45	25	30	—	0.25
		Total	5.60	2.80	50	32	18	—	0.33

— Negligible or zero.

Figure 8-2. *Growth of Inputs and Total Factor Productivity for Cross-Country Model and Countries that Have Long-Term Records*

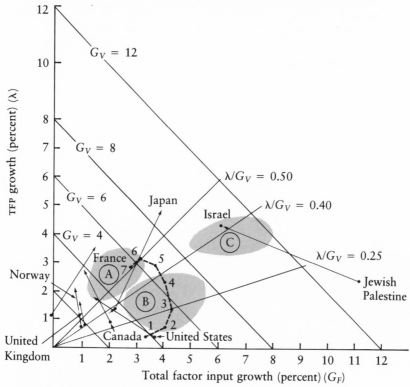

Note: G_V is growth of value added in percent.

The information for the seven periods of the model comes from table 8-6. The country data refer to the following periods:

Country	Period	Source
Canada	1891–1926	Kuznets (1971)
	1926–56	
France	1913–49	Carre, Dubois, and Malinvaud (1975)
	1949–63	
Israel (Jewish Palestine)	1922–47	Syrquin (1986)
	1950–72	
Japan	1887–1922	Ohkawa and Takamatsu (1983)
	1917–38	
	1953–71	
Norway	1879–99	Kuznets (1971)
	1899–1956	
United Kingdom	1856–1913	Matthews, Feinstein, and Odling-Smee (1982)
	1924–73, excluding 1937–51	
United States	1800–1905	Abramovitz and David (1973)
	1905–67	

The rays from the origin show the proportion of total output growth caused by TFP growth.

The three country clusters are reproduced from table 2-2 without the actual observations. Group A includes industrial countries. Group B is representative of most developing and centrally planned economies. Group C consists of semi-industrial economies with very high growth rates.

The data for the seven countries in figure 8-2 indicate a long-run acceleration of productivity growth and, except for France, an increase in productivity's contribution to output growth. The pattern derived from the cross-country model is plotted for periods 0–6. The initial acceleration of aggregate growth is the result of faster input expansion. At medium income levels, productivity growth accelerates, pulling with it the growth of aggregate output. The typical country resembles the countries in cluster B in periods 2 and 3 ($280–$1,120), which cover the bulk of the industrializing stage II. In the later periods—identified as the developed stage III—output growth diminishes but productivity continues to increase its share of growth, attaining levels similar to those in cluster A. (See figure 3-7 for explanation of the three stages.)

Sectoral Results

In agriculture, factor productivity growth is negligible at low income levels. Once the modern sectors are able to absorb a substantial portion of the excess labor in agriculture, however, capital intensity and productivity rise rapidly. The percentage of the labor force employed in agriculture shows a continuous decline, and from an income level of about $1,000 it falls in absolute terms as well. This decline, observed in virtually all countries, reflects not only the low elasticity of the demand for food but also significant increases in productivity and mechanization in the agricultural sector.

This increase in the growth of factor productivity in agriculture was observed in the three countries for which long-term records are available—the United States, the United Kingdom, and Japan (table 8-7). In Israel, the agricultural sector started in 1950 with relatively high productivity and a high priority in the allocation of investment. It also had a very high rate of TFP growth, an important element in the successful performance of the Israeli economy during the period.

Unbalanced productivity growth is one of the reasons on the supply side behind the shift in comparative advantage and the transformation of the structure of production. In the model, TFP growth in manufacturing exceeds TFP growth in agriculture by more than 1 percentage point for most periods (see table 8-6).[23]

The last column of table 8-7 indicates the gap between productivity growth in manufacturing and in agriculture for some countries. The gap is

---

23. Total factor productivity growth at the value added level is higher than at the gross output level by a factor equal to the value added ratio; see Syrquin (1985a). Since this ratio is usually higher in agriculture than in manufacturing, the productivity differential between the two sectors is correspondingly lower for gross output. In the model, the differential is reduced at the gross output level to about one-third of a percentage point. If the value added ratio in agriculture declines over time (see chapter 3), the overestimate of the productivity growth gap for value added also declines. A constant or falling gap at the value added level could then hide an increase in the gap at the gross output level, contrary to the argument in Williamson and Lindert (1980, p. 173).

Table 8-7. *Total Factor Productivity Growth in Agriculture and Manufacturing for Countries that Have Long-Term Records* (percent)

Country and years	Annual rate of TFP growth		Productivity growth gap $(\lambda m - \lambda a)$
	Agriculture (a)	Manufacturing (m)	
United States			
1839–59 ⎫			
1869–1929 ⎭	0.3	1.9	1.6
1929–66	1.8	1.9	0.1
1966–73	1.0	2.3	1.3
United Kingdom			
1856–1913	0.6	0.7	0.1
1924–73	2.6	1.8	− 0.8
Japan			
1887–1904	1.0	1.1	0.1
1904–19	1.4	2.1	0.7
1919–38	0.7	2.9	2.2
1954–76	2.4	6.1	3.7
Israel			
1950–60	6.4	0.5	− 5.9
1960–72	5.4	5.9	0.5

Sources: United States, Williamson and Lindert (1980); United Kingdom, Matthews, Feinstein, and Odling-Smee (1982); Japan, Ohkawa and Takamatsu (1983); Israel, Gaathon (1971) for 1950–60, and Metzer (1986) for 1969–72.

large in the case of the United States and Japan for most of the periods reported. In Japan, this gap rises sharply over time. In the United Kingdom, the gap is negative for most of the twentieth century; a combination of substantial productivity growth in agriculture and unimpressive productivity growth in industry is responsible. The small or negative gap in Israel has more to do with the performance of agriculture than with a lag in industry, particularly after 1960.

In the industrializing stage in the model, productivity growth in manufacturing exceeds that in services; in the developed stage, however, the situation is reversed. Because of the well-known problems of measuring output in services, I do not elaborate on these results but only note that a positive gap, such as the one at low and medium income levels, is an important element in explaining systematic departures of exchange rates from purchasing power parities in terms of a "differential productivity model" (see appendix to chapter 3). The negative gap at high income levels has much to do with the rise in the relative price of services, which Kravis, Heston, and Summers (1983), have argued wholly accounts for the rise in the output share of services.

Figure 8-3 presents the elements in the variation of productivity growth

Figure 8-3. *Components of TFP Growth for Cross-Country Model*

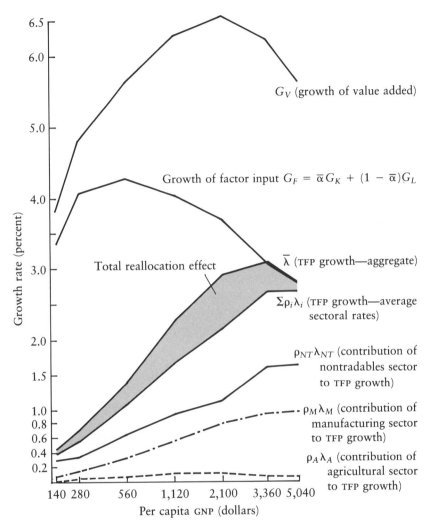

during transformation. In all sectors in table 8-6, productivity growth accelerates throughout the transition, reaching a peak during period 4. The acceleration of the aggregate rate of productivity growth, $\bar{\lambda}$, discussed above, reflects this phenomenon, but it also involves two additional elements. The first is the shift in weights from sectors with slower productivity growth (such as agriculture) to sectors with faster productivity growth (such as manufacturing). The second appears when the aggregate rate, $\bar{\lambda}$, exceeds the weighted average of the sectoral rates, $\Sigma \rho_i \lambda_i$. This difference measures the contribution to growth of resource reallocation among sectors with different marginal productivities, which is called total real-location effect (TRE; see figure). This element is discussed extensively in the following section, where it is shown to contribute significantly to the acceleration of output and productivity growth during the transformation.

Resource Reallocation as a Source of Growth

In the presence of significant differences in factor returns across sectors, structural change becomes an essential element in accounting for the rate and pattern of growth. On the one hand, that change can retard growth if its pace is too slow or its direction inefficient. On the other hand, it can contribute to growth if it improves the allocation of resources. Market forces tend to move the economic system toward equilibrium, but they are blunted by inflexibility in the system and high adjustment costs, by shocks from external events and unbalanced productivity growth, and even by government policies.

Various types of resource reallocation appear to have a significant effect on aggregate productivity growth. One of them, the shift from production for the domestic market to production for export, played a prominent role in the analysis in part II. The effect of this type of reallocation on growth in semi-industrial countries is estimated in chapter 9. A different type of reallocation, from market to nonmarket activities, or from the business to the government sector, appears in discussions of deindustrialization in industrial countries. In that case, the reallocation is seen as a source of the *slowdown* in productivity growth. In this section, I concentrate on intersectoral factor reallocation when factor returns differ across sectors.[24]

The literature includes several formulations for measuring the effect of resource shifts on productivity growth. A simple approximation of this effect is the gross allocation effect, $A(y)$, which appears in equation 8-4 as a component of the growth of aggregate labor productivity.[25] It measures the growth in aggregate labor productivity that would have taken place with the observed labor shifts, G_{γ_i}, had the relative labor productivities remained constant. The data required to compute this approximation are readily available, which is why it is often used. The gross allocation effect is a partial measure since it ignores factors other than labor and computes the gains and losses from employment shifts in terms of average and not marginal products.[26]

A positive $A(y)$ can arise in a dynamic context even when resources are optimally allocated before and after the shift. This can be illustrated with a

24. This discussion borrows liberally from Syrquin (1984).

25. Equivalent formulations are used by Kuznets (1957), OECD (1965), and Ohkawa and Rosovsky (1963), among others.

26. Denison (1967) tries to correct for these two shortcomings with a differential weighting of the gains and losses from reallocation. See Syrquin (1984) for a description and evaluation of Denison's approach.

simple example of a small country producing only two goods (at fixed international prices). By Rybczynski's theorem, an increase in the aggregate capital input under equilibrium (equal marginal products across sectors) will lead to a reallocation of labor toward the more capital-intensive good, which is also the one with a larger average product (in value terms). In each sector, marginal and average labor products remain constant, while total labor productivity rises by an amount equal to the gross allocation effect, $A(y)$. Since, by assumption, no resources are misallocated either before or after the increase in capital, the gains in labor productivity cannot be the result of the reallocation itself. A complete accounting, such as that presented below, would attribute the increase in labor productivity to the accumulation of capital. Tables 8-8 and 8-9 compare some estimates of $A(y)$ with the more complete estimates of the reallocation effect.

An intuitive way of deriving a comprehensive measure of the impact of resource shifts on growth is to start from an expression of the gross allocation effect equivalent (in the continuous case) to that in equation 8-4:

$$(8\text{-}8) \qquad A(y) = \sum_i \rho_i G_{y_i} = \frac{1}{V} \sum_i \dot{L}_i (y_i - y)$$

where a dot over a variable signifies a time derivative. This expression makes clear the dependence of $A(y)$ on intersectoral differences in average product per worker. Substituting marginal products, f_L, for average products, y, and adding an equivalent term for the input of capital, or for any other input in the production function in equation 8-5, give the measure sought—namely, the total reallocation effect or TRE:

$$(8\text{-}9) \qquad \text{TRE} = \frac{1}{V} \sum_i \dot{L}_i (f_{L_i} - f_L) + \frac{1}{V} \sum_i \dot{K}_i (f_{K_i} - f_K)$$

where $f_{L_i} (f_{K_i})$ equals the marginal product of $L(K)$ in sector i and $f_L (f_K)$ is the economywide average of these figures.

TRE is precisely the amount by which the aggregate rate of TFP growth, $\bar{\lambda}$, exceeds the weighted average of the sectoral rates, $\Sigma \rho_i \lambda_i$, when the reallocation of resources leads to a reduction in the extent of disequilibrium (see Syrquin 1984).[27] This will be the case if, on the average, sectors with above-average marginal products of labor or capital increase their share in total employment or capital. It was seen above that a positive $A(y)$ does not necessarily indicate the existence of disequilibria. But the differences in equation 8-9, and with them the total reallocation effect,

---

27. Massell (1961), who apparently was the first to publish a similar derivation, calls the weighted average of TFP growth ($\Sigma \rho_i \lambda_i$) "intraindustry technical change" and the shift terms "interindustry technical change."

Table 8-8. *Contribution of Resource Allocation to Productivity Growth for the Cross-Country Model*

Period	Per capita income (dollars)	Annual growth rate (percent) Aggregate TFP ($\bar{\lambda}$)	= Average of sectoral rates ($\Sigma \rho_i \lambda_i$)	+ TRE	TRE in relation to growth of Output (TRE/G_V)	TFP (TRE/$\bar{\lambda}$)	Share of TRE due to net allocation effect (percent)	Reallocation measures as percentage of labor productivity Gross allocation effect A(y)	Net allocation effect
0	100–140	0.44	0.40	0.04	1	9	100+	15.0	5.7
1	140–280	0.72	0.57	0.15	3	20	69	17.0	5.5
2	280–560	1.40	1.11	0.29	5	21	85	16.5	9.0
3	560–1,120	2.28	1.72	0.56	9	25	89	20.0	12.5
4	1,120–2,100	2.92	2.17	0.75	11	26	90	20.0	14.0
5	2,100–3,360	3.11	2.71	0.40	6	13	83	9.0	7.5
6	3,360–5,040	2.80	2.72	0.08	2	3	75	0.0	1.5

Table 8-9. *Contribution of Reallocation to Labor Productivity Growth for Selected Sample and Other Economies*

Economy	Years	Percentage of labor productivity growth		Net allocation effect in relation to TFP growth (NA/$\bar{\lambda}$)	Aggregate capital elasticity ($\bar{\alpha}$)
		Gross allocation effect (A[y])	Net allocation effect (NA)		
Sample					
Mexico	1950–75	30	13	22	0.48
Turkey	1963–73	61	—	—	—
Yugoslavia	1966–72	30	—	—	—
Japan (prewar)	1915–35	24	—	—	—
Japan (postwar)	1955–70	16	10	16	0.43
Korea	1963–73	16	5	6	0.40
Taiwan	1961–71	15	7	8	0.43
Israel	1958–72	5	6	11	0.40
Developed					
Italy	1963–73	14	9	14	0.40
France	1963–73	14	6	14	0.42
Belgium	1963–73	3	3	4	0.42
Canada	1963–73	8	7.5	7	0.45
Netherlands	1963–73	1	−4	−7	0.42
United Kingdom	1963–73	−1	1	1.5	0.40

— Not available.

Note: For the sample economies, the level of aggregation is three sectors for prewar Japan, six sectors for Korea, and eight sectors for the others. Social overhead is omitted in Korea because of problems with the data on capital. Capital data were not available for Turkey, Yugoslavia, and prewar Japan.

For the developed economies, the level of aggregation is four or five sectors.

Sources: For sample economies: World Bank data; described in Kubo (1983). For developed economies, Stein and Lee (1977). The values for $\bar{\alpha}$ are based on Christensen, Cummings, and Jorgenson (1980).

vanish when marginal productivities of labor and capital are equal throughout the economy.

A more convenient formulation for estimation than equation 8-9 can be derived directly by focusing on the growth of labor productivity. If the sectoral growth accounting equation (the first equation in footnote 20 above) is substituted into the expression for the growth of aggregate labor productivity 8-4 and the results are compared with those of a growth accounting exercise performed directly at the aggregate level, another formula for TRE is given:

$$(8\text{-}10) \quad \text{TRE} = \bar{\lambda} - \sum_i \rho_i \lambda_i = \frac{1}{y} \sum_i \dot{k}_i \gamma_i (f_{K_i} - f_K) + \sum_i \dot{\gamma}_i \left(\frac{y_i}{y} - \bar{\alpha} \frac{k_i}{k} \right)$$

$$= A(k) \qquad\qquad + \text{net allocation.}$$

Under full equilibrium (equal marginal products across sectors) both terms equal zero and the difference vanishes.

The first term on the right-hand side, $A(k)$, measures the difference between the contribution of sectoral capital accumulation to labor productivity growth and the contribution that would have resulted had all sectoral marginal productivities of capital equaled f_K. If k_i (not just K_i) increases faster in sectors with a higher than average marginal product, the term will be positive. This reflects the contribution of narrowing the existing disequilibrium through capital deepening in high-productivity sectors.

The second term, labeled the net allocation effect, has two components. The first component is just the gross allocation effect, $A(y)$.[28] The second component corrects for the deficiencies of the gross effect. It recognizes that for average products not to change, some net investment will usually be required. If after a reallocation of labor each worker is equipped with the same amount of capital as those who worked in the sector before, the aggregate capital-labor ratio will show a net change given by $\Sigma \, \dot{\gamma}_i k_i/k$, even if the capital intensity in each sector remains unchanged ($\dot{k}_i = 0$). This change in the aggregate capital-labor ratio, when multiplied by the average share of capital, $\bar{\alpha}$, gives the expected change in output per worker. In full equilibrium, this expected effect exactly cancels out the actual gross allocation effect, and the net allocation effect vanishes.[29] Out of equilibrium, a shift improving the allocation of labor will contribute to aggregate labor productivity over and above the expected gain through the capital requirements it generates.

The Gains from Reallocation: Empirical Results

Estimates of the contribution of resource reallocation to growth are presented in table 8-8 for the dynamic model and in table 8-9 for the sample and for some advanced countries.

The total reallocation effect is positive in every period. In its contribution to growth, it reaches a maximum during period 4 (representing high-income semi-industrial economies), when it amounts to 11 percent of output growth and more than 15 percent of labor productivity growth.

The results suggest that TRE is a significant component of aggregate TFP growth, particularly in the industrializing stage.[30] Its pattern across

---

28. $\Sigma_i \dot{\gamma}_i y_i/y = \Sigma_i \dot{\gamma}_i/\gamma_i \rho_i = A(y)$.

29. The net allocation term is equal to $1/y \; \Sigma_i \dot{\gamma}_i (y_i - f_K k_i)$. In equilibrium $f_{K_i} = f_K$, and therefore the term in parentheses reduces to f_{L_i}. Since by assumption $f_{L_i} = f_L$ and by definition $\Sigma_i \dot{\gamma}_i = 0$, the result in the text follows.

30. The figures in the fifth column of table 8-8, which show the relation of TRE to $\bar{\lambda}$, are probably too conservative. Syrquin (1984) and Kelley and Williamson (1984) review a variety of available estimates, many of which exceed the highest figure in that column. For their simulations, Kelley and Williamson chose a figure of 0.31 as representative of the experience of developing countries.

periods resembles the initial acceleration and subsequent slowdown in the growth of output and labor productivity. In the final period—which corresponds roughly to Western Europe since the late 1960s—the effect of resource reallocation almost disappears. Part of the accompanying productivity slowdown reflects the exhaustion of the shift out of agriculture as a potential source of growth. If productivity gains continue to decline at income levels beyond those in the simulation, however, it will no longer be attributable, even partially, to the reduced shift out of agriculture. A different—and negative—allocation effect may become important as labor continues to shift into services, a low-productivity sector.

The total reallocation effect can be decomposed into two terms, as in equation 8-10. The second term in the formula, the net allocation effect, accounts for 70 to 90 percent of TRE after the first period. This net effect can be computed without any information on sectoral production functions. Besides data on outputs and inputs, its computation requires only one parameter—an estimate of the aggregate elasticity of capital, $\bar{\alpha}$. It is therefore possible to calculate the net allocation effect for many economies, as is done in table 8-9. When evaluating these results, however, it must be recalled that they refer to only a part of the total reallocation effect, though it may well be the predominant part, as the numbers in table 8-8 suggest.

The last two columns of table 8-8 compare the gross and the net allocation effects in relation to the growth of output per worker. The gross effect generally exceeds the net effect, but in the last period the gross effect vanishes while the net effect remains positive.[31] The comparison of the two measures shows that the gross allocation effect is only a crude approximation of the gains from reducing disequilibrium through resource shifts.

I turn now to some country comparisons of resource reallocation and productivity growth. Table 8-9 presents the contribution to labor growth of intersectoral shifts in the simple form of the gross allocation effect, $A(y)$, as well as of the net allocation effect of equation 8-10. The net effect is also shown as a share of the aggregate rate of growth of TFP, $\bar{\lambda}$, implied by the aggregate figures for labor productivity and capital intensity together with the assumed value for $\bar{\alpha}$.

The gross allocation effect accounts for a significant part of the growth in labor productivity. The relative contribution is much lower in the industrial countries, and it shows a sizable decline in Japan over time. When capital accumulation is taken into account in the net effect, the contribution to growth is reduced to about 10 percent in the sample[32] and

---

31. By the last period, the large shift from industry to services actually reduces capital requirements, thus allowing for a positive effect of labor reallocation by saving capital, even when average products of labor do not differ across sectors.

32. The figure for Korea may indicate that the initial disequilibrium was low. The estimate, however, is much affected by the data on capital in the service sector. When only the

to less than 10 percent in the industrial countries. This latter group exhibits an interesting contrast between France and Italy on the one hand and the Netherlands and the United Kingdom on the other. At the beginning of the period, the first pair's employment in agriculture is still high and productivity of labor in agriculture low. So these countries can yet benefit from the shift out of agriculture. But the second pair's employment in agriculture is quite low and productivity high; the shift is into services, which yields no gain in growth and may even retard it.

Compared with the aggregate rate of TFP growth, $\bar{\lambda}$, the contribution of resource reallocation is more significant. In the rough calculations for the sample, the figures are generally close to or above the highest figure in the cross-country model (table 8-8). In the group of industrial countries, resource reallocation accounts for a smaller fraction of $\bar{\lambda}$, reaching a high of 14 percent in France and Italy.

Assessing the Results

The effect of resource reallocation can be identified only at the aggregate level. When total output growth is aggregated from the sectoral results, there is no place for resource reallocation as an independent source of growth. Any such effect has already been accounted for in the contribution of inputs. It may nonetheless be of interest to present the effect separately, but in interpreting the results the resource shifts must be recognized as not being exogenous. Potential gains from reallocation may be present, as in the case of embodied technological change. But to realize the gains, some triggering mechanisms, with costs of their own—migration, investment, and so on—may be needed.

The estimated contributions of structural change to growth probably understate the effect of resource shifts. The broad definition of sectors, even in fairly disaggregated studies, hides all factor reallocations within those sectors. This is important for industrial economies and for rapidly growing ones. About Taiwan, for example, Kuznets (1979, p. 73) argues that the high rate of growth of product per worker called for "a much greater rate of shift [than the] one now suggested in the three-sector classification and that the shifts from old to new subbranches within these sectors are particularly neglected."

Another potential source of underestimation of the importance of resource shifts lies in the static and partial nature of the measures. According to Cornwall (1977, p. 124), who regards the manufacturing sector as the engine of growth, "these estimates . . . assume that the level and rate of

---

primary and manufacturing sectors are considered, the net allocation effect is twice as high as the figure in table 8-9. In a recent application of Denison's method to Korea, Kim and Park (1984) give an estimate of the contribution of "contraction of agricultural inputs" equal to 12 percent of the growth of national income per person employed during 1963–72.

growth of productivity in the sector expanding inputs and output are independent of the expansion process itself. This rules out the possibility of various economies of scale in manufacturing." A more general and dynamic approach would explicitly recognize that resource shifts may facilitate or directly trigger higher productivity growth.

A possible source of overestimation of the importance of resource reallocation is the assumption of input homogeneity. Differences in returns to labor and capital across sectors may reflect quality differences as well as disequilibrium. A reallocation of resources from sectors with low returns to those with high returns would then reflect a reduction in the misallocation of resources and an improvement in the average quality of inputs. The total reallocation effect includes both the reduction of disequilibrium and the upgrading of the quality of inputs. The contribution of resource reallocation to growth could also be overstated if the higher productivity observed in manufacturing when it is compared with agriculture reflects, in part, a distorted domestic price structure.

A complete evaluation of the role of compositional changes in development would have to include a systematic treatment of the relevant mechanisms. Rapid shifts may help accelerate growth, but at the same time they may not be feasible without high rates of growth and investment. Similarly, just as the effect of resource shifts on growth may be underestimated, so the contribution of investment to growth may also be underestimated if the increase in flexibility caused by the higher investment rates is not considered.

Productivity and Growth: Demand-Supply Interactions

In the extreme supply approach, exogenous productivity growth drives the economy. Combined with the growth of inputs, this leads to output growth. It has already been shown that for two reasons the *aggregate* rate of TFP growth, $\bar{\lambda}$, cannot be regarded as exogenous even when the *sectoral* rates, λ_i, are. First, the output weights needed to aggregate the sectoral rates are clearly not independent of demand. Second, the aggregate rate of productivity growth includes as a component the gains from resource shifts in a disequilibrium situation. In addition to these two reasons, if the sectoral rates of TFP growth are themselves endogenously determined, the extreme supply-determined approach to growth analysis becomes untenable.

Some additional links between the demand side and productivity growth at the aggregate as well as sectoral levels can be derived by a priori reasoning and well-established empirical regularities. In most cases, however, serious identification problems make it difficult to determine causality. The empirical associations are indicative only of demand-supply interactions, which probably reinforce each other regardless of the initiating mechanism.

Economic Environment

In disaggregated cross-country comparisons or in a single country over time, one finds a high degree of uniformity of productivity change across sectors for a given country or period. Although the diversity among industries is far from negligible, it is difficult to point to particular industries as being consistently the best or worst performers irrespective of time and place. In his study of long-term growth in the United Kingdom, Matthews (1974) found no support for the view that certain industries have persistently high rates of technical progress. Similarly, in his study of the United States, Kendrick (1961, p. 178) concluded that ". . . there are certain forces that promote productive efficiency throughout the economy." In the detailed comparison of four countries reported in chapter 10, productivity growth is found to be uniformly higher in some countries than others. This country effect emerges much more clearly than does any sector effect. This suggests that, in addition to any intrinsic productivity potential of an industry, the overall economic environment is important in explaining the general level of productivity growth.

This country effect (or period effect within a country) is strongly associated with general macroeconomic policies. It has been observed that productivity growth in developed countries has a large cyclical component related to capacity utilization. In developing countries, productivity growth is affected by stop-go episodes caused by balance of payments problems. Such cyclical phenomena will not only affect the measured rate of TFP growth, but will probably also influence the pace of advance of technological innovation (Nelson 1981).[33] A large part of the better performance of outward-oriented economies can probably be traced to their successfully having avoided stop-go cycles by preventing foreign exchange shortages. Denison (1967) and Maddison (1980) also stress the importance of general macroeconomic policies for technological progress.

Endogenous Technical Change

The rate of technological progress in a sector or activity is in part a response to changes in economic variables within the sector. A high rate of investment is essential for realizing the potential gains from capital-embodied technological change. The rates of investment and output growth are key elements in theories of endogenous technical change such as Arrow's "learning by doing" (1962)—in which labor productivity increases with the level of cumulative gross investment or output—and Schmookler's argument (1966) that inventive activity gravitates toward industries experiencing rapid growth of demand.

Learning effects play an important role in rationalizations of the high

---

33. Kornai (1980) has also emphasized the beneficial aspects of "taut" utilization of capacity.

correlation commonly found between the rates of growth of productivity and output, either across industries (primarily manufacturing) or for a given industry over time.[34] The association is often presented as capturing the effect on measured productivity of endogenous technical change and economies of scale through the expansion of output. A faster rate of output growth facilitates the adoption of new technology, leads to a reduction in the average age of the capital stock, enhances efficiency by learning, and increases productivity through economies of scale, both static and dynamic.[35] In this view, the impact of the growth of output on the growth of productivity incorporates most of the demand-supply links discussed above. In numerous empirical studies, this approach has proved successful in accounting for interindustry and intercountry differences in the growth of labor productivity. The causal chain could run from faster productivity growth to faster output growth through changes in relative prices with elastic demands.[36] Given the complexity of the relation, however, it is not likely that the direction of causality at the aggregate level—the level at which the relation is usually examined—can be determined. Some authors recognize the reciprocal nature of the relation but conclude after comparing the strength of various correlations (productivity and prices, prices and quantities, and so on) that the dominant influence goes from output to productivity (Kendrick 1961; Kennedy 1971).[37]

A similar debate over causality is found in the literature on trade. Is a good export performance the result of productivity growth, or does the growth of exports contribute to a rise in productivity? Here again the relation is probably reciprocal. For the typical semi-industrial country that has gone through a period of inward-oriented industrialization, an internal change that raises productivity might be needed before exports can expand significantly. Sustained growth of exports, on the other hand, may contribute to further productivity growth in a variety of ways: through economies of scale, through relaxation of the foreign exchange constraint, or through a host of positive side effects that are sometimes said to accompany an outward orientation (see, for example, chapter 9 and Krueger 1983).[38]

---

34. In the literature, this relation often appears as Verdoorn's law (1949), which is examined in chapter 2. It is also one of Kaldor's "laws" (1967). See Kennedy (1971) for a critical evaluation, as well as the recent symposium in the *Journal of Post-Keynesian Economics* (1983).

35. Ohkawa and Rosovsky (1973, p. 77) discuss the organizational changes that must take place for "a faster expansion of the market to lead to more rapid productivity." They also make clear that it is increasing the scale relative to the size of the market that is relevant, rather than increasing returns to scale on the production side.

36. If technical progress is directed to the more price-elastic goods, then the link through prices from productivity to output growth is in part an endogenous response to demand characteristics (see Kennedy 1971, chap. 6).

37. See Caves (1968) for the opposite view for the United Kingdom.

38. Kelley and Williamson (1974) review the historical literature and the Japanese experience. Also relevant for Japan is Kanamori's study (1968): by examining fifty-five manufactur-

(Note continues on the following page.)

One important factor usually ignored in the simple correlations between productivity growth and either output or export expansion is the *type* of output or trade involved. For example, a rise in domestic demand stimulated by a budget deficit would have a different effect than would a rise in world demand for machinery (Cornwall 1977). Similarly, a greater exposure to trade might lead to faster productivity growth in the case of producer goods but not in the case of consumer goods or of manufacturing overall (Wragg and Robertson 1977; quoted in Caves 1980). This point is explicitly considered in chapter 10, which will distinguish between export expansion and import substitution as sources of output growth.

---

ing industries for 1955–64, he shows that, at the sectoral level, higher rates of export increase were associated with high rates of investment growth and of domestic demand expansion.

9 Growth in Semi-Industrial Countries: A Statistical Analysis

GERSHON FEDER

THIS CHAPTER seeks to identify the factors that account for the growth experience of the group of semi-industrial countries described in chapter 4. The analysis is based on cross-section regression analysis. The simplest approach—the one presented in chapter 2—assumes an underlying aggregate production function, and it attributes changes in output to changes in the capital stock and in the labor force. But most researchers recognize that other elements also contribute to the variation in growth experience among countries. Thus Wheeler (1980) emphasizes human capital and the quality of labor; Hagen and Havrylyshyn (1969) introduce a set of variables accounting for school enrollment, social mobility, communications, and so on; and Balassa (1978), Michalopoulos and Jay (1973), and Tyler (1981) stress the importance of exports.

This chapter extends the analysis begun in chapter 8. It focuses on the role of disequilibrium—that is, of differences in productivity among sectors. Growth comes not only from increasing aggregate inputs but also from reallocating resources to more productive sectors. This is the central hypothesis of a study by Robinson (1971), who constructs a model that explicitly incorporates the shift of resources from the traditional (less efficient) to the modern (more efficient) sectors.

The possibility of two types of disequilibrium is considered: that between industrial and nonindustrial sectors and that between export and nonexport sectors. First, a general two-sector disequilibrium model is described, and the results based on the regression specifications suggested by the model are presented for each type of disequilibrium. Second, a four-sector framework is developed to allow an estimation that incorporates the two types of disequilibrium simultaneously. Third, the possibility that the results reflect some other underlying explanation is considered.

The Disequilibrium Model

The first task is to construct an analytical framework that will both facilitate the design of the empirical work on sources of economic growth

A partial version of this chapter appeared in the *Journal of Development Economics* 12 (1983): 59–73. It is reprinted here with permission of the North-Holland Publishing Company.

and suggest possible interpretations of the estimated parameters. In developing this framework, one has to bear in mind the likely limitations in the data available for a cross section of developing countries. Variables have to be specified at a high level of aggregation. Nevertheless, the formulation offered here should make possible an assessment of the effect of resource reallocation on growth so that the disequilibrium hypothesis can be tested.

Suppose the economy consists of two sectors with outputs Y_1 and Y_2. Each sector's output is determined by a production function that depends on sectoral inputs:

$$(9\text{-}1) \qquad\qquad Y_i = F^i(K_i, L_i)$$

where $i = 1$ or 2, K_i and L_i denote sectoral capital and labor inputs, respectively. The change in output over time is thus:

$$(9\text{-}2) \qquad \Delta Y_i = F_K^i \Delta K_i + F_L^i \Delta L_i = F_K^i I_i + F_L^i \Delta L_i$$

where F_K^i and F_L^i denote marginal factor productivities and I_i denotes sectoral investment. Were the economy in equilibrium with optimal resource allocation, marginal factor productivities would be equal across sectors.[1] But this formulation does not impose equilibrium. Rather, marginal factor productivities are assumed to differ by a given proportion such that

$$(9\text{-}3) \qquad\qquad \frac{F_K^2}{F_K^1} = 1 + \delta$$

and

$$(9\text{-}4) \qquad\qquad \frac{F_L^2}{F_L^1} = 1 + \mu$$

where δ and μ can take any sign.

Let Y, which is the sum of Y_1 and Y_2, denote GDP. Then equation 9-2 implies that

$$(9\text{-}5) \qquad \Delta Y = \sum_{i=1}^{2} \Delta Y_i = \sum_{i=1}^{2} F_K^i I_i + \sum_{i=1}^{2} F_L^i \Delta L_i.$$

Substituting equations 9-3 and 9-4 in equation 9-5 gives

$$(9\text{-}6) \qquad \Delta Y = F_K^1 I_1 + (1 + \delta) F_K^1 I_2 + F_L^1 \Delta L_1 + (1 + \mu) F_L^1 \Delta L_2$$
$$= F_K^1 (I_1 + I_2) + F_L^1 (\Delta L_1 + \Delta L_2) + \delta F_K^1 I_2 + \mu F_L^1 \Delta L_2.$$

Next, if $I = I_1 + I_2$ and $\Delta L = \Delta L_1 + \Delta L_2$, equation 9-6 can be rewritten:

1. Since constant prices are assumed, no distinction is made between quantities and values.

$$(9\text{-}7) \qquad \Delta Y = F_K^1 I + F_L^1 \Delta L + \frac{\delta}{1+\delta} + F_K^2 I_2 + \frac{\mu}{1+\mu} F_L^2 \Delta L_2$$

$$= F_K^1 I + F_L^1 \Delta L + \frac{\delta}{1+\delta} (F_K^2 I_2 + F_L^2 \Delta L_2)$$

$$+ (\frac{\mu}{1+\mu} - \frac{\delta}{1+\delta}) F_L^2 \Delta L_2.$$

Following arguments similar to those presented by Bruno (1968), I suppose that a linear relation exists between the marginal productivity of labor in a given sector and the average output per worker in the economy:

$$(9\text{-}8) \qquad\qquad F_L^i = \beta_i \cdot \frac{Y}{L}.$$

If equation 9-7 is divided by Y and the results in equations 9-2 and 9-8 are used (and G_z stands for the growth rate of a variable z), the result is:

$$G_Y = F_K^1 \cdot \frac{I}{Y} + \beta_1 \cdot G_L + \frac{\delta}{1+\delta} \cdot (G_{Y_2} \cdot \frac{Y_2}{Y}) + (\frac{\mu}{1+\mu} - \frac{\delta}{1+\delta}) \cdot \beta_2$$
$$(9\text{-}9) \qquad \cdot (G_{L_2} \cdot \frac{L_2}{L}).$$

Equation 9-9 reduces to the familiar neoclassical growth equation when $\delta = \mu = 0$, that is, when marginal factor productivities are equal across sectors. In the more general case, however, it offers the possibility of estimating the contribution to growth of resource shifts from sectors of low productivity to sectors of high productivity. The data requirements are modest: the growth ratios of aggregate investment and labor are commonly used in the neoclassical formulation, and the growth rate of sectoral output is usually available. The sectoral growth rate of labor (the last term on the right-hand side of equation 9-9) may be available for at least some sectors for a large group of countries. Note that, if a case can be made for a particular sectoral decomposition of the economy, and if the ratios of marginal productivities are equal across sectors (that is, if $\delta = \mu$), then only sectoral growth rates are required to assess the effect of factor shifts.

Even though equation 9-9 is fairly straightforward and is valid subject to the assumptions made earlier in this section, its estimation by regression analysis raises a host of econometric problems. Some of these problems are common in cross-country studies of sources of growth (see the detailed discussions in Hagen and Havrylyshyn 1969 and in Chenery, Elkington, and Sims 1970); they include errors in variables, simultaneity, variation of parameters across countries, and so on.[2] The use of data averaged over time ameliorates but does not eliminate some of these problems. Moreover, results of regressions using the variables indicated by the present analysis could in fact reflect different underlying frameworks, with different interpretations for the estimated parameters. Although the present formulation introduces disequilibrium, which in general provides a more realistic description of an economy than would otherwise be possible, the analysis assumes that all the economies studied are in the same type of disequilibrium. Yet more than one type of disequilibrium may be present, and some economies may be affected more by one type than another. These qualifications and limitations should be borne in mind when the results in the following sections are considered.

Disequilibrium between Industrial and Nonindustrial Sectors

The dual-economy model of growth suggests a relevant two-sector decomposition of the economy into traditional and modern sectors. The common argument (supported in several empirical studies) is that marginal labor productivity is higher in the modern sector; therefore, expanding the labor force in the modern sector through shifts out of the traditional sector makes a contribution to growth.

In many dual-economy models, the traditional sector is assumed to produce with labor but without capital, so the issue of the differential marginal productivity of capital is not discussed. But in fact capital is used in all sectors of the economy, and persistent differences in the marginal productivity of capital across sectors are possible. Empirical evidence is not as abundant as in the case of labor. De Melo (1977) provides figures for Colombia which suggest that its industrial sector enjoys rates of return on capital higher than those observed for agriculture and services.[3] Robinson (1971) has constructed a model of the sources of growth that allows for higher marginal productivities of both capital and labor in the industrial sector than in the nonindustrial sector. His empirical results suggest substantial differences between these two sectors, although the statistical significance for capital parameters is on the borderline. (See also chapter 8.)

This chapter uses two definitions of the industrial sector. The narrower definition includes the manufacturing sector only; the broader one combines manufacturing and construction.[4] The two sets of results obtained do not seem to differ substantially.

---

2. An application of equation 9-9 that uses a cross-country sample implicitly assumes that the marginal productivities of capital are identical throughout the sample; thus they can be treated as parameters. In addition, the parameters β_1, β_2, δ, and μ are assumed to be identical for all countries.

3. De Melo (1977, p. 400) comments, however, that reliance on shaky estimates of capital stocks may seriously bias the calculated rates of return.

4. These two sectors comprise "industry" in the analysis of patterns of development in Chenery and Syrquin (1975).

The equation estimated in this section is therefore

$$(9\text{-}10) \qquad G_Y = a_0 + a_1\frac{I}{Y} + a_2G_L + a_3\left(G_M\frac{M}{Y}\right) + a_4G_{L_m}\frac{L_m}{L}$$

where M denotes industrial output and L_m denotes industrial labor force. Interpretation of the parameters a_i follows from equation 9-9.

As is common in cross-section studies, averages over a long time are used for both GDP growth and explanatory variables. The reasoning is that nonsystematic changes are thereby averaged out and the problem of lags between investment and production is reduced. But the post-1973 era has been subjected to effects not properly covered by the simple disequilibrium model developed above. This, and data problems for the years before 1964, dictated that the analysis be confined largely to the period 1964–73, although some results for an earlier period will also be discussed.

The analytical framework is designed for cross-country data. Yet it may be argued that grouping all developing countries in one sample would excessively stretch the assumption about the constancy of parameters across the sample. The group of semi-industrial economies identified in chapter 4 seems to offer a relatively homogeneous sample. Some results for another group of developing countries substantiate the decision to focus on the semi-industrial economies.

Table 9-1 reports regression results comparing the common neoclassical formulation (which assumes equal marginal factor productivities across sectors) with the formulation of equation 9-10. Several observations follow from these results:

- The two variants of the disequilibrium model—referred to in the table as models I and II—produce very similar parameter estimates.
- The disequilibrium formulation explains the variability of average growth rates much better than the simple neoclassical model does. (The adjusted R^2 is about 50 percent higher.) This is consistent with the indication of a significant disparity between marginal factor productivities in favor of the industrial sector. (The coefficient of $G_M \cdot [M/Y]$ is significantly larger than zero at the 99 percent confidence level.)
- The lack of statistical significance for the parameter associated with industrial labor growth, $G_{L_m} \cdot (L_m/L)$, seems to suggest that the ratio of marginal labor productivities in the two sectors is not much different from the ratio of marginal capital productivities (that is, $\mu = \delta$ in the notation of equation 9-9).[5]
- The coefficient associated with the investment variable, I/Y, is interpreted in the simple neoclassical formulation as the average of the marginal productivities of capital for all sectors of the economy. In the

5. However, this indication does not amount to a rigorous test of the hypothesis $\mu = \delta$.

Table 9-1. *Regression Results for Semi-Industrial Countries, 1964–73; Neoclassical and Industry/Nonindustry Disequilibrium Models*

Variable or result	Neoclassical model	Disequilibrium model I (equation 9-10; industry defined as manufacturing only)	Disequilibrium model II (equation 9-10; industry defined as manufacturing and construction)
I/Y	0.247	0.139	0.112
	(4.059)	(2.558)	(2.125)
G_L	0.779	0.429	0.383
	(3.457)	(2.023)	(1.922)
$G_M \cdot (M/Y)$		0.801	0.871
		(3.406)	(4.105)
$G_{L_m} \cdot (L_m/L)$		0.791	0.729
		(1.116)	(1.109)
Constant	−0.002	0.007	0.010
	(0.128)	(0.652)	(0.935)
Adjusted R^2	0.460	0.665	0.707
Standard error of regression (percent)	1.616	1.272	1.190
Number of observations	30	30	30

Note: Numbers in parentheses are t values.
Source: World Bank data.

disequilibrium formulation, this coefficient is interpreted as the marginal productivity of capital in the less productive of the two sectors of the economy. This apparently affords a partial explanation for the sizable decline in the magnitude of the investment coefficient when the disequilibrium specification is used.

The decomposition of the sources of growth is reported in table 9-2. The contribution of industrial expansion is substantial—about 2 percentage points, or almost a third of total growth. But this needs to be interpreted carefully. The 2 percent contribution measures the gain from the greater productivity of factors of production in the industrial sector. It is equal to the difference between the actual growth rate and the hypothetical growth rate if marginal productivities in all sectors were the same as those estimated for the nonindustrial sector.

A better assessment of the effect of the reallocation of resources can be derived from this hypothetical calculation: holding sectoral labor inputs and the capital stock constant, suppose that capital amounting to 1 percent of GDP is transferred from the nonindustrial sector to the indus-

Table 9-2. *Sources of Growth in Semi-Industrial Countries, 1964–73; Neoclassical and Industry/Nonindustry Disequilibrium Models*

Variable or result	Sample mean	Contribution to growth	
		Neoclassical model	Disequilibrium model (equation 9-10; industry defined as manufacturing)
I/Y	20.09	4.971	2.797
G_L	2.07	1.616	0.888
$G_M \cdot (M/Y)$	1.84		1.475 ⎫
$G_{L_m} \cdot (L_m/L)$	0.67		0.530 ⎬ 2.005
Constant		−0.176	0.720
GDP growth[a]		6.410	6.410

Note: All numbers are multiplied by 100.
a. Numbers may not add to totals because of rounding.
Source: World Bank data.

trial sector. This would yield an increase of about 0.5 percent in GDP, which is a substantial gain from reallocation alone.[6]

In view of the magnitude of marginal factor differentials, the question arises why market forces have not brought about a much greater shift of resources, which would shrink the gaps. The answer may lie partly in constraints on factor mobility caused by segmented markets, government intervention in investment allocation, continuing technological change, and so on. But it is also conceivable that some part of the marginal productivity of factors in manufacturing is not taken into account by the individual economic agents because of intrasectoral externalities. Specifically, the tendency of industrial activities to be concentrated in urban centers gives rise to positive agglomeration effects—both vertical and horizontal—that are not fully considered by individual firms. Nonmanufacturing activities seem to enjoy many fewer benefits of this type. Other beneficial effects may be generated through training and on-the-job learning. If skilled workers and managers are highly mobile within a sector, there will be additional externalities not fully reflected in a firm's calculations.

6. The real extent of these gains, however, may be biased upward because of distorted prices. If the industrial sector is protected from foreign competition, then domestic prices in that sector are higher than world prices. The real difference between marginal factor productivities (if measured in world prices) would be lower than the difference implied by the present estimates (where GDP growth was calculated from a time series in constant domestic prices).

Table 9-3. *Regression Results for Less Developed Countries, 1964–73; Neoclassical and Industry/Nonindustry Disequilibrium Models*

Variable or result	Neoclassical model	Disequilibrium model I (equation 9-10; industry defined as manufacturing only)	Disequilibrium model II (equation 9-10; industry defined as manufacturing and construction)
I/Y	0.055	−0.016	−0.012
	(0.841)	(0.245)	(0.186)
G_L	0.541	0.379	0.409
	(1.354)	(0.964)	(1.065)
$G_M \cdot (M/Y)$		1.603	1.382
		(2.032)	(2.384)
$G_{L_m} \cdot (L_m/L)$		2.384	1.742
		(1.406)	(1.023)
Constant	0.024	0.019	0.018
	(1.910)	(1.580)	(1.585)
Adjusted R^2	0.032	0.166	0.205
Standard error of regression (percent)	1.835	1.703	1.663
Number of observations	33	33	33

Note: Numbers in parentheses are *t* values.
Source: World Bank data.

Experimentation with another group of less developed countries that are not semi-industrialized tended to support the hypothesis that the semi-industrial countries are more homogeneous and are therefore a more appropriate group for this type of analysis. As is apparent from table 9-3, the neoclassical formulation and the two disequilibrium models explain very little of the variability in GDP growth rates among these less developed countries. Although the coefficient associated with the growth of industrial output differs significantly from zero, the point estimate is clearly not compatible with the underlying model, for it cannot theoretically exceed the value of one.[7] The lack of statistical significance for any of the other explanatory variables and the overall weakness of the results may suggest the need for a different growth model that emphasizes other factors more

7. The hypothesis that this coefficient is in fact 0.8 or 0.9 (the values obtained for semi-industrial countries) cannot, however, be rejected. Furthermore, a Chow test implies that the hypothesis that the two groups of developing countries have the same parameters for equation 9-10 can also not be rejected. But this is not strong enough evidence to suggest that the two samples should be combined. The estimates for the less developed countries have such a high variance that many alternative hypotheses cannot be rejected.

Table 9-4. *Regression Results for Semi-Industrial Countries, 1955–63;*
Neoclassical and Industry/Nonindustry Disequilibrium Models

Variable or result	Neoclassical model	Disequilibrium model I (equation 9-10; industry defined as manufacturing only)	Disequilibrium model II (equation 9-10; industry defined as manufacturing and construction)
I/Y	0.135	0.067	0.053
	(2.261)	(0.816)	(0.656)
G_L	0.740	0.848	0.878
	(2.549)	(2.264)	(2.417)
$G_M \cdot (M/Y)$		0.977	0.822
		(1.603)	(2.046)
Constant	0.007	0.007	0.007
	(0.538)	(0.332)	(0.366)
Adjusted R^2	0.258	0.134	0.186
Standard error of regression (percent)	1.770	2.013	1.952
Number of observations	31	27	27

Note: Numbers in parentheses are t values.
Source: World Bank data.

relevant for such economies. A discussion of these issues, however, is
beyond the scope of this chapter.

   Consideration of an earlier time period for the group of semi-industrial
economies was complicated by data problems. Since labor force data
(whether aggregate or by industrial sector) were not readily available, the
growth of the total labor force was approximated by population growth (a
practice quite common in cross-country studies of the sources of growth).
Estimating sectoral labor growth demanded the assumption that $\delta = \mu$
(see equation 9-9)—that is, that the ratios of respective marginal factor
productivities are equal across sectors. As indicated earlier, for the period
1964–73 there was no strong indication of a substantial difference between δ and μ. The results for the period 1955–63, presented in table 9-4,
indicate that none of the models explains much of the variation in growth.
The coefficient of investment (which according to the analytical
framework measures marginal capital productivity in the nonindustrial
sector) is small in absolute value, but it has a high standard deviation. In
general, the hypothesis that parameters have remained constant over time
cannot be rejected. But the low R^2 may imply that important variables
were left out, which could bias the estimates. Also, differences in the

parameters among countries may have been larger. No convincing argument exists, therefore, for pooling observations over time.[8]

In summary, the results reported in this section suggest that a substantial difference existed in the period 1964–73 between marginal factor productivities in the industrial and in the nonindustrial sectors of the sample group of semi-industrial countries. Consequently, those countries that pursued accelerated industrial growth tended—all else being equal—to grow faster than other countries in the group since resource allocation was closer to being optimal.

Disequilibrium between Export and Nonexport Sectors

The relation between export performance and economic growth has been a subject of considerable interest to development economists in recent years. (The presentation in this section draws on my earlier paper [Feder 1983].) A substantial body of literature suggests that distinguishing between outward-oriented and inward-oriented sectors might be useful in comparing countries' growth experiences. Empirical comparisons of countries tend to demonstrate that developing countries with favorable export growth records have generally enjoyed higher rates of growth of national income than other developing countries. Since exports are a component of aggregate output, a positive correlation coefficient is to be expected (Kravis 1970). But several empirical studies argue that rising exports contribute more to GDP growth than the change in the volume of exports alone would suggest (Balassa 1978; Heller and Porter 1978; Michaely 1977; Michalopoulos and Jay 1973).

Explanations for these observations have been discussed by many economists. They point to various benefits of export activity—such as greater capacity utilization, economies of scale, incentives for technological improvements, and more efficient management—that arise from competitive pressures abroad (see Balassa 1978; Bhagwati and Srinivasan 1978; Keesing 1967, 1979; and Krueger 1980). These discussions imply substantial differences between marginal factor productivities in outward-oriented and inward-oriented industries, with the former having the higher factor productivity. It follows that countries which have adopted policies less biased against exports have benefited from resource allocation that is closer to being optimal—and from faster growth.

In accordance with the disequilibrium framework developed earlier in this chapter, an economy is viewed as being composed of two distinct sectors, one producing for the domestic market and the other for the foreign market.[9] Two modifications to the model summarized by equation

8. Results for the less developed countries in the period 1955–63 were very poor. The adjusted R^2 was close to zero. There was no point in comparing these results with those for the later period or for the semi-industrial countries.

9. Clearly this is an abstraction, as many firms produce for both domestic and foreign markets. It may be argued that, even so, the domestically marketed output of such firms has

9-9 are needed. The first is dictated by the lack of information on the growth of labor in the export sector. This means that equation 9-9 can be used only under the assumption that $\delta = \mu$, that is, that the ratio of marginal capital productivities in the two sectors is the same as the ratio of marginal labor productivities. If the main sources of disequilibrium are the distortions in product markets (rather than in factor markets), then the imposition of $\delta = \mu$ is not a source of serious bias.

The second modification to the original framework relates to the specification of externalities. In the case of the disequilibrium between the industrial and nonindustrial sectors, an argument was made for the possibility of substantial *intra*sectoral externalities in manufacturing. In the case of the disequilibrium between the export and nonexport sectors, an argument can be made for significant *inter*sectoral externalities. These follow from the beneficial effects of export activities on other sectors in the economy through the development of efficient and internationally competitive management, the introduction of improved production techniques, the training of skilled workers, and the spillover consequences of scale expansion (Keesing 1967, p. 311; 1979, pp. 4, 5). For modeling purposes, such effects are best represented by introducing in equation 9-1 the volume of output of the export sector as a factor affecting output of the nonexport sector. Equation 9-2 can then be rewritten:

(9-11) $$Y_1 = F_K^1 \, \Delta K_1 + F_L^1 \, \Delta L_1 + F_X^1 \, \Delta Y_2$$

and

(9-12) $$Y_2 = F_K^2 \, \Delta K_2 + F_L^2 \, \Delta L_2$$

where 1 denotes the nonexport sector, 2 the export sector, and F_X^1 the marginal effect of exports on the output of the nonexport sector (that is, $\partial Y_1 / \partial Y_2$).

Combining equations 9-11 and 9-12 with equations 9-3, 9-4, and 9-8, and assuming $\delta = \mu$, yields a slightly modified version of equation 9-9:

(9-13) $$G_Y = F_K^1 \frac{I}{Y} + \beta_1 \cdot G_L + \left(\frac{\delta}{1 + \delta} + F_X^1 \right) \left(G_{Y_2} \frac{Y_2}{Y} \right).$$

If F_X^1 is treated as a constant parameter, equation 9-13 is not different from equation 9-9 for econometric purposes, except for the assumption $\delta = \mu$. But if a specific form is adopted for F_X^1—one which hypothesizes that the extent of intersectoral externalities depends on the size of the export and nonexport sectors—then the specification of the econometric model is affected. Suppose that the relation between nonexports and exports is governed by a fixed elasticity, θ, such that

---

the same qualities (and factor productivities) as the exported output. To the extent that the growth of exports represents a good approximation of changes in the volume of production of such firms, the results are still valid.

Table 9-5. *Regression Results for Semi-Industrial Countries, 1964–73;*
Neoclassical and Export/Nonexport Disequilibrium Models

Variable or result	Neoclassical model	Disequilibrium model III (equation 9-13)	Disequilibrium model IV (equation 9-15)
I/Y	0.242	0.148	0.104
	(3.670)	(3.008)	(2.674)
G_L	0.612	0.606	0.593
	(1.827)	(2.563)	(3.283)
$G_X \cdot (X/Y)$		0.446	0.302
		(5.676)	(4.496)
G_X			0.145
			(4.732)
Constant	0.000	0.010	0.010
	(0.005)	(0.768)	(1.092)
Adjusted R^2	0.273	0.638	0.789
Standard error of regression (percent)	1.827	1.289	0.985
Number of observations	34	34	34

Note: Numbers in parentheses are *t* values.
Source: World Bank data.

$$(9\text{-}14) \qquad\qquad Y_1 = Y_2^\theta \cdot H(K_1, L_1)$$

where H is some function of sectoral inputs. Then $F_X^1 = \theta Y_1/Y_2$, and since
by definition $Y_1 = Y - Y_2$, equation 9-13 can be written:

$$(9\text{-}15) \qquad G_Y = F_K^1 \frac{I}{Y} + \beta_1 G_L + \left(\frac{\delta}{1+\delta} - \theta\right)\left(G_X \frac{X}{Y}\right) + \theta G_X$$

where $X = Y_2$, the output of the export sector.

This formulation allows the externality effect to be separated from other
effects that may cause deviation between marginal factor productivities,
albeit at the cost of adopting a specific form for F_X^1. Results will be
presented for both equations 9-13 and 9-15, which will be labeled disequilibrium models III and IV respectively.[10]

The same considerations that led me in the preceding section to focus on
semi-industrial economies in the period 1964–73 apply to this analysis, as
will be shown.[11] The results in table 9-5 suggest that the export sector has

10. The work of Chenery, Elkington, and Sims (1970) includes some estimates that are
identical to equation 9-13. The papers by Balassa (1978), Michalopoulos and Jay (1973), and
Tyler (1981) include the rate of growth of exports and are thus equivalent to equation 9-15
under the assumption that $\delta/(1 + \delta) = \theta$.

11. All results in this section use population growth to approximate labor force growth.
Population data are available for the full period 1964–73, labor force data only for the period
1960–70.

higher factor productivity at the margin. Comparing models III and IV tends to support the formulation that allows variability among countries in the extent of intersectoral externalities.

As in the preceding section, the coefficient associated with investment decreases when a disequilibrium formulation replaces the neoclassical formulation. The explanation is, as before, that in the neoclassical model this parameter represents some "average" marginal productivity of capital, whereas in the disequilibrium model it represents the marginal productivity in the less productive sector.

The difference in productivity between the export and nonexport sectors is substantial, especially in economies where the export sector is small. It is true that the "average" productivity differential factor (as implied by the parameter of $G_X \cdot [X/Y]$ in model III) is only about half the estimated coefficient associated with industrial expansion. But the differential, when measured in world prices, is understated in the export/nonexport model because of the protection granted to the nonexport sector in most countries and the distorted prices that result.

Table 9-6 presents the sources of growth for the semi-industrial economies as implied by model IV. The higher productivity of resources in the export sector contributes 1.85 percentage points to GDP growth, or about 30 percent of overall growth. Put differently, average growth would be lower by 1.85 percentage points if all sectors of the economy had the same marginal factor productivities as those observed in the nonexport sector. Thus, the success of export-led growth—as experienced by Korea and Taiwan—comes largely from the shift of resources into high-productivity sectors and from the establishment of new export-oriented and efficient industries.

Table 9-6. *Sources of Growth in Semi-Industrial Countries, 1964–73; Neoclassical and Export/Nonexport Disequilibrium Models*

		Contribution to growth	
		Neo-	Disequilibrium
Variable[a]	*Sample*	*classical*	*model IV*
or result	*mean*	*model*	*(equation 9-15)*
I/Y	20.61	4.986	2.141
G_L	2.35	1.439	1.394
$G_X \cdot (X/Y)$	2.21		0.668 ⎫ 1.851
G_X	8.16		1.183 ⎭
Constant		0.008	1.044
GDP growth[a]		6.43	6.43

Note: All numbers are multiplied by 100. The small differences in the figures for sample means and for the neoclassical model from those in table 9-2 are due to differences in samples.

a. Numbers may not sum to totals because of rounding.

Source: World Bank data.

Table 9-7. *Regression Results for Less Developed Countries, 1964–73; Neoclassical and Export/Nonexport Disequilibrium Models*

Variable or result	Neoclassical model	Disequilibrium model III (equation 9-13)	Disequilibrium model IV (equation 9-15)
I/Y	0.106	0.059	0.053
	(2.037)	(1.163)	(0.983)
G_L	0.518	0.727	0.710
	(0.840)	(1.269)	(1.222)
$G_X \cdot (X/Y)$		0.652	0.793
		(2.811)	(1.830)
G_X			−0.042
			(0.388)
Constant	0.013	0.007	0.009
	(0.769)	(0.430)	(0.517)
Adjusted R^2	0.074	0.214	0.196
Standard error of regression (percent)	1.879	1.732	1.752
Number of observations	42	42	42

Note: Numbers in parentheses are *t* values.
Source: World Bank data.

The export/nonexport disequilibrium model seems to provide a reasonable explanation for much of the variation in growth among semi-industrial countries. Experiments with the sample of non-semi-industrial developing countries yielded results similar to those obtained for this group using the industry/nonindustry disequilibrium model: the underlying production function framework does not explain much of the variation in growth (see table 9-7). Also, although the coefficient of $G_X \cdot (X/Y)$ is significantly different from zero, the coefficients of investment and labor growth are not significant. Assessment of the superior marginal productivity of factors employed in the export sector is therefore not meaningful.[12]

The results for the period 1955–63 for semi-industrial countries are not very different from the results for 1964–73 with respect to parameter estimates, but the significance of the estimates is generally low and the unexplained variation is large (see table 9-8). Regressions for the same period for less developed countries provide a very poor explanation of the growth experience. Thus for both the export/nonexport and industry/nonindustry models it seems that data problems as well as the influence of

12. The hypothesis that the parameters of the corresponding regressions for semi-industrial and less developed countries are identical is rejected by a Chow test for models III and IV. This substantiates the decision to treat these two groups separately.

Table 9-8. *Regression Results for Semi-Industrial Countries, 1955–63; Neoclassical and Export/Nonexport Disequilibrium Models*

Variable or result	Neoclassical model	Disequilibrium model III (equation 9-13)	Disequilibrium model IV (equation 9-15)
I/Y	0.135	0.108	0.092
	(2.261)	(1.789)	(1.447)
G_L	0.740	0.536	0.569
	(2.549)	(1.756)	(1.837)
$G_X \cdot (X/Y)$		0.429	0.370
		(1.704)	(1.408)
G_X			0.056
			(0.829)
Constant	0.007	0.011	0.010
	(0.538)	(0.856)	(0.777)
Adjusted R^2	0.258	0.305	0.297
Standard error of regression (percent)	1.770	1.713	1.723
Number of observations	31	31	31

Note: Numbers in parentheses are *t* values.
Source: World Bank data.

other factors on growth make the early period less suitable for analysis. Regressions for the years 1974–77 for both groups of countries have a low R^2, and no insight is gained since the parameters of both investment and labor growth have large standard deviations.

In summary, the export/nonexport disequilibrium model seems to provide a suitable framework for analyzing the growth of semi-industrial countries but not of other developing countries. The results suggest that, for the group of semi-industrial countries in the period 1964–73, substantial differences existed between marginal factor productivities in the export and nonexport sectors. These differences were in part caused by externalities generated by the export sector and benefiting the nonexport sector. The shift of resources toward export industries is thus one of the important sources of growth in this group.

A Synthesis: Disequilibrium among Industry, Nonindustry, Export, and Nonexport Sectors

The existence of significant differences between marginal factor productivities in industrial and nonindustrial sectors as well as in export and nonexport sectors has been demonstrated. It is natural to attempt a reformulation of the analytical framework to allow the coexistence of both sources of disequilibrium. In this section, we construct a four-sector framework. With some simplifying assumptions, this permits a reestimation that takes into account both types of disequilibrium simultaneously.

The economy is assumed to consist of four sectors:

- Nonindustrial goods for the domestic market (denoted by superscript nm and subscript nx)
- Nonindustrial goods for export (denoted by superscript nm and subscript x)
- Industrial goods for the domestic market (denoted by superscript m and subscript nx)
- Industrial goods for export (denoted by a superscript m and subscript x).

To facilitate the derivation of the model and allow for data limitations, two simplifications are introduced. First, the ratios of marginal capital productivities between any two sectors are assumed to equal the corresponding ratios of marginal labor productivities.[13] Second, marginal intersectoral externality effects of each of the two export sectors on the other two sectors are fixed. With sectoral outputs denoted by Y_i^j (where $j = m$ and nm, and $i = x$ and nx), the externality effects are given by these six equalities:

$$\frac{\partial Y_{nx}^{nm}}{\partial Y_x^{nm}} = \lambda_x^{nm} \qquad\qquad \frac{\partial Y_{nx}^{nm}}{\partial Y_x^{m}} = \lambda_x^{m}$$

$$\frac{\partial Y_{nx}^{m}}{\partial Y_x^{nm}} = \mu_x^{nm} \qquad\qquad \frac{\partial Y_{nx}^{m}}{\partial Y_x^{m}} = \mu_x^{m}$$

$$\frac{\partial Y_{x}^{m}}{\partial Y_x^{nm}} = \gamma_x^{nm} \qquad\qquad \frac{\partial Y_{x}^{nm}}{\partial Y_x^{m}} = \gamma_x^{m}$$

The assumed relations between marginal productivities are

(9-16)
$$\frac{\text{MPK}_{nx}^{m}}{\text{MPK}_{nx}^{nm}} = \frac{\text{MPL}_{nx}^{m}}{\text{MPL}_{nx}^{nm}} = 1 + \delta$$

(9-17)
$$\frac{\text{MPK}_{x}^{nm}}{\text{MPK}_{nx}^{nm}} = \frac{\text{MPL}_{x}^{nm}}{\text{MPL}_{nx}^{nm}} = 1 + \theta$$

and

(9-18)
$$\frac{\text{MPK}_{x}^{m}}{\text{MPK}_{nx}^{m}} = \frac{\text{MPL}_{x}^{m}}{\text{MPL}_{nx}^{m}} = 1 + \eta.$$

The growth of GDP can now be expressed as

---

13. This assumption was already used in the formulation of the export/nonexport disequilibrium model.

$$G_Y = MPK_{nx}^{nm} \cdot \frac{I}{Y} + \beta \cdot G_L + \left(\frac{\theta}{1+\theta} + \alpha_1\right) G_X \cdot \frac{X}{Y} + \frac{\delta}{1+\delta} G_M \cdot \frac{M}{Y}$$

(9-19)

$$+ \left[\frac{\eta}{(1+\eta)(1+\delta)} - \frac{\theta}{1+\theta} + \alpha_2 - \alpha_1\right] \cdot G_{Y_x^m} \cdot \frac{Y_x^m}{Y}$$

where

$$\alpha_1 = \lambda_x^{nm} + \frac{1}{1+\delta} \mu_x^{nm} + \frac{1}{(1+\eta)(1+\delta)} \cdot \gamma_x^{nm}$$

$$\alpha_2 = \lambda_x^m + \frac{1}{1+\delta} \mu_x^m + \frac{1}{(1+\theta)} \cdot \gamma_x^m$$

$$X = Y_x^m + Y_x^{nm}$$

$$M = Y_x^m + Y_{nx}^m$$

and β is a fixed ratio between marginal labor productivity in the nonindustrial domestic sector and average output per worker in the economy (analogous to the formulation in equation 9-8). Equation 9-19, which will be estimated in this section, includes one additional variable: the share-weighted growth of manufactured exports. Whereas the parameters of all other variables are expected to be greater than zero (if the marginal productivity of factors in industrial and export sectors is higher than it is in nonindustrial and nonexport sectors), the parameter associated with exports of manufactured goods could be positive or negative, depending on the relative magnitudes of the other parameters in the equation.

Table 9-9 presents the estimates of equation 9-19 for the group of semi-industrial countries using each of the definitions of the industrial sector discussed earlier: manufacturing only, which will be labeled disequilibrium model V, and manufacturing and construction, which will be labeled disequilibrium model VI. As in earlier regressions, the results are not much affected by how the industrial sector is defined. Furthermore, comparisons with tables 9-1 and 9-5 show that parameter estimates are not much different. As predicted, the parameters associated with export growth and industrial growth are significantly positive. The parameter of manufactured export growth is negative but not significantly different from zero. A direct estimate of η (the parameter incorporating the hypothesized higher productivity of manufacturing industries that produce exports over other manufacturing industries) cannot be obtained, but some indication that manufactured exports have higher marginal productivity than other manufactured goods can be inferred. Adding $\theta/(1 + \theta) + \alpha_1$ to the parameter of manufactured export growth yields an estimate of $\eta/(1 + \eta) \cdot (1 + \delta) + \alpha_2$ (see equation 9-19), which according to table 9-9 is approximately 0.18. Since δ is positive, the figure 0.18 is lower than $\eta/(1 + \eta) + \alpha_2$. But since the parameter of manufactured export growth

Table 9-9. *Regression Results for Semi-Industrial Countries, 1964–73; Four-Sector Disequilibrium Models*

Variable or result	Disequilibrium model			
	(Equation 9-19)	*(Equation 9-19)*	V'	VI'
I/Y	0.105	0.082	0.135	0.109
	(2.048)	(1.833)	(2.959)	(2.656)
G_L	0.598	0.580	0.766	0.741
	(2.442)	(2.745)	(3.730)	(4.150)
$G_X \cdot (X/Y)$	0.338	0.312	0.246	0.228
	(3.240)	(3.437)	(2.959)	(3.231)
$G_M \cdot (M/Y)$	0.832	0.898	0.809	0.898
	(3.421)	(4.804)	(3.681)	(5.072)
$G_{Y_x^m} \cdot (Y_x^m/Y)$	-0.153	-0.132		
	(1.227)	(1.258)		
Constant	0.009	0.010	-0.002	0.000
	(0.641)	(0.813)	(0.132)	(0.006)
Adjusted R^2	0.723	0.791	0.752	0.809
Standard error of regression (percent)	1.071	0.929	1.072	0.940
Number of observations	29	29	32	32

Note: Numbers in parentheses are t values.
Source: World Bank data.

has a large standard deviation, many numerical values can theoretically apply.

Next, this parameter was assumed to be approximately zero,[14] thereby excluding manufactured export growth, and models V and VI were reestimated. The results, labeled models V' and VI' in table 9-9, indicate the same order of magnitude for estimated parameters. The conclusions drawn from these results, therefore, confirm what was said above about the sources of growth: the shift of resources into industrial and export sectors—that is, into sectors with higher productivity—characterizes countries that grow faster. The sources-of-growth accounting detailed in table 9-10 indicates that growth would have been lower by more than 2 percent if all sectors had had the same productivity as the domestic-oriented nonindustrial sector.

Alternative Interpretations of the Results

The interpretation given to the results so far is both plausible and consistent with the underlying framework. But it is not necessarily the only

14. This would still be consistent with positive values for η and the externality effects generated by manufacturing exports.

Table 9-10. *Sources of Growth in Semi-Industrial Countries, 1964–73: Models V' and VI'*

Variable or result	Sample mean	Disequilibrium model V'	Disequilibrium model VI'
I/Y	20.18	2.727	2.195
G_L	2.32	1.778	1.720
$G_X \cdot (X/Y)$	2.21	0.542 ⎱	0.503 ⎱
G_M (M/Y)		1.489 ⎰ 2.031	0.503
Manufacturing	1.84		⎱ 2.461
Manufacturing and construction	2.18		1.958 ⎰
Constant		−0.150	0.010
GDP growth		6.386	6.386

Note: All numbers are multiplied by 100.
Source: World Bank data.

possible interpretation. Alternative frameworks can be constructed that would yield specifications similar to the ones used. This is demonstrated below for the export/nonexport disequilibrium model, for which there is an alternative a priori reasoning that is plausible.

Foreign exchange may be considered an important determinant of GDP growth. In fact, the simple trade-gap model implies that when the foreign exchange constraint is binding, growth depends only on foreign exchange inflows (from aid, borrowing, and exports). Even in a less rigid model, larger amounts of foreign exchange allow more flexibility and efficiency in production: bottlenecks are minimized, the need for using lower-quality domestic components is reduced, and the pressure for inefficient import substitution may be lower. It is, therefore, possible that the significant positive association between export growth and GDP growth indicated by the earlier analysis stems from the fact that exports are the main source of foreign exchange.

Let us construct a model that considers the foreign exchange aspect of exports. Suppose that GDP is generated subject to the production function

$$(9\text{-}20) \qquad Y = F\left[\min\left(\frac{K_d}{\alpha}, \frac{K_m}{\beta}\right), W_m, L\right]$$

where K_d and K_m denote domestic and foreign-made capital, W_m denotes imports of intermediate goods, and L denotes labor. Assume that the supply of domestic investment is linearly related to GDP:

$$(9\text{-}21) \qquad \dot{K}_d = \gamma_0 + \gamma_1 Y.$$

Assume also that consumption imports, M_c, are a fixed proportion of GDP:

$$(9\text{-}22) \qquad M_c = \delta Y.$$

Efficiency considerations dictate that

(9-23) $$M_K \equiv \dot{K}_m = \alpha \frac{\dot{K}_d}{\beta}$$

where M_K denotes imports of capital goods and the dots over the variables denote time derivatives: $\dot{K} = dK/dt$, and so forth. The change in GDP is

(9-24) $$\dot{Y} = F_1 \cdot \dot{K}_d + F_2 \cdot \dot{W}_m + F_3 \cdot \dot{L}.$$

With total supply of foreign exchange denoted by S, it must hold that

(9-25) $$\dot{W}_m = \dot{S} - \dot{M}_c - \dot{M}_K = \dot{S} - \delta\dot{Y} - \frac{\alpha\dot{K}_d}{\beta} = \dot{S} - \delta\dot{Y} - \frac{\alpha}{\beta}\cdot\gamma_1\cdot\dot{Y}.$$

Given equations 9-21 and 9-25, and denoting $(\alpha\gamma_1/\beta) \equiv \gamma$, equation 9-24 can be written as

(9-26) $$\dot{Y} = F_1\cdot\dot{K}_d + F_2\cdot[\dot{S} - (\delta + \gamma)\dot{Y}] + F_3\dot{L}.$$

Note that $I \equiv \dot{K}_d + \dot{K}_m = (1 + \alpha/\beta)\dot{K}_d$ (by equation 9.22). Rearranging the terms of equation 9-26 yields

(9-27) $$\dot{Y} = \frac{F_1}{(1 + \frac{\alpha}{\beta})[1 + (\delta + \gamma)\cdot F_2]}\cdot I + \frac{F_2}{[1 + F_2\cdot(\delta + \gamma)]}\dot{S}$$
$$+ \frac{F_3}{[1 + F_2\cdot(\delta + \gamma)]}\dot{L}.$$

Manipulating equation 9-27 and adopting an assumption analogous to equation 9-8 regarding the relation between marginal labor productivity and average output per worker, one eventually obtains

(9-28) $$G_Y = a_1\cdot\frac{I}{Y} + a_2\cdot G_S\cdot\frac{S}{Y} + a_3\cdot G_L.$$

Note that $G_S \cdot (S/Y) = G_X \cdot (X/Y) + G_F \cdot F/Y$, where F denotes foreign exchange inflows other than export revenues. If $G_X \cdot (X/Y)$ is highly correlated with $G_S \cdot (S/Y)$, then estimation of equation 9-28 will yield results not much different from equation 9-15. Indeed, an estimate of equation 9-28 for the semi-industrial countries in the period 1964–73 yields

$$G_Y = 0.009 + 0.139 \cdot\frac{I}{Y} + 0.404\cdot G_S\cdot\frac{S}{Y} + 0.704\,G_L; \; (\bar{R}^2 = 0.626).$$
$$\quad\;\;(0.682)\quad(2.738)\qquad(5.50)\qquad\quad(2.924)$$

Comparison with table 9-5 verifies that no substantial difference exists between the two formulations.

The conclusion is that both the earlier explanation based on marginal productivity differences and the trade-gap explanation may be valid simultaneously. For some countries, one explanation may be more appropriate than the other, but this cannot be discerned from the results reported in this chapter.

10 Productivity Growth in Manufacturing

MIEKO NISHIMIZU

SHERMAN ROBINSON

THE LAST two chapters explored a number of issues related to sectoral differences in factor productivity and the contribution of structural change to aggregate growth. In developing countries, there are many constraints on how fast employable resources can grow and on how easily they can be transferred across sectors. Aggregate growth depends not only on factor accumulation and its sectoral allocation, but also on total factor productivity growth. In a constrained economy, achieving rapid rates of TFP growth is therefore a real issue in alleviating economic bottlenecks. Furthermore, as discussed in chapters 6 and 7, an important part of the "catching up" process involves exploiting changing comparative advantage, which provides a significant driving force for structural change. Differential sectoral rates of TFP growth are crucial determinants of evolving comparative advantage and have a great effect on both growth and structural change in the medium to long run.

Two issues concerning TFP growth are especially relevant for development policy. First, what range of TFP growth rates can one reasonably expect? Confidence intervals for TFP growth rates can in principle be obtained from historical records of firms, industries, or economies operating under varying production environments. They provide information useful for answering various questions about development. For example: First, what is the appropriate duration of infant industry protection or promotion policies? Is five years too short? Is twenty years too long? Should the duration be uniform among industries, or should it differ from industry to industry? Second, what are the causes or sources of TFP growth? For example, does protection from competing imports destroy incentives to improve efficiency in production? Can some policies improve productivity—for example, subsidies tailored to specific factors such as fiscal incentives for accelerated depreciation or support for employee training?

Over the years, the empirical literature on TFP change has accumulated a

This chapter originally appeared in a slightly different form in the *Journal of Development Economics* 16 (1984): 177–206. It is reprinted here with permission.

substantial body of stylized facts about the contribution of productivity change and factor input growth to economic performance in various economies.[1] Perhaps the most significant stylized fact to emerge is the importance of TFP change in contributing to growth: as much as one-third to one-half of growth in output can be attributed to TFP change. Until quite recently, much of what we knew was in terms of macro aggregates.[2] There is now, however, a small but growing empirical literature on TFP change at a disaggregated level.[3] The first objective of this chapter is to add to this body of stylized facts by analyzing time-series data developed at the World Bank on TFP growth at the sectoral level within manufacturing for three countries: Korea, Turkey, and Yugoslavia. We include Japan in the sample as a comparator; data for it were developed by Jorgenson and Nishimizu (1981).

In contrast to the growing stock of empirical estimates on TFP growth, sufficient evidence has not yet been accumulated to establish the causes of productivity change. As surveyed and discussed extensively by Nelson (1981), the literature on productivity change offers a wide variety of possible causes but no consensus as to which deserve most attention. In the development literature, the role of trade policy in increasing growth and efficiency has long been a main theme. Therefore, the second and more important objective of this chapter is to examine the effects of various development strategies, especially trade policies, on sectoral TFP growth. Our analysis is exploratory and considers several of the suggested hypotheses—of which there is certainly no shortage. Indeed, it is difficult to sort out the differences among them and to define the appropriate measures and tests required to assess each one. Our analysis does indicate important links between trade policies and productivity performance, and it raises some issues for further research.

One hypothesis put forward in the literature is that a positive relation exists between productivity change and the rate of growth of output. Expressed in terms of labor productivity, this relation has been called

---

1. For a review of the literature, see Nadiri (1970, 1972). For an excellent critical survey of the productivity literature, see Nelson (1981).

2. See, for example, Christensen and Jorgenson (1973); Christensen, Cummings, and Jorgenson (1980); Denison (1967, 1974); Denison and Chung (1976); Ezaki and Jorgenson (1973); and Griliches and Jorgenson (1967) for studies on developed countries. For developing countries, see Christensen, Cummings, and Jorgenson (1980), who included Korea in their international comparison, and Bruton (1967) and Elias (1978), who studied Latin American countries. See also Robinson (1971), Feder (chapter 9), and studies cited by them as well as by Nadiri (1972).

3. See, for example, Kendrick (1961, 1973) and Gollop and Jorgenson (1980) for the United States; Nishimizu and Hulten (1978) and Kuroda and Imamura (1981) for Japan; and a comparative study of the United States and Japan by Jorgenson and Nishimizu (1981). In addition, there are productivity studies of regulated industries or firms in the United States and Canada; see, for example, Cowing and Stevenson, eds. (1981). A comprehensive study of Indian manufacturing industries was made by Ahluwalia (1985). See also Ezaki (1975) on the Philippines, Kuo (1983) on Taiwan, and Kim and Son (1979) on Korea.

Verdoorn's law after P. J. Verdoorn, who suggested it in 1949. Among those who have investigated this relation, Kaldor (1967) has argued that the fundamental explanation for it lies in economies of scale.[4] He has also noted that it is observed most prominently in manufacturing and other industrial activities. In developing countries, economies of scale and size of market have long been considered important in determining growth and structural change.[5] The existence of scale economies, or any other justification for Verdoorn's law, implies that widening the market through trade should lead to reductions in production costs. The argument is usually made in terms of the benefits of an expansion in demand through increased exports. Although the argument depends on the size of domestic markets, it should in principle apply to import substitution as well.

A quite different trade policy hypothesis is that opening up to international competition will spur increases in domestic efficiency. There is an implicit challenge-response mechanism induced by competition; domestic industries are forced to adopt new technologies, to reduce "X-inefficiency," and generally to reduce costs wherever possible. According to this argument, export expansion is good and so is import liberalization. While a policy of increasing imports may restrict the market for domestic goods, it also increases competition and hence induces greater efficiency. The converse is also widely asserted: protectionist policies designed to promote import substitution reduce competitiveness and lead to inefficiency in production. One must be careful not to overstate the argument. Infant industry protection, by definition, is afforded to high-cost industries that cannot compete with imports until they "grow up" and become internationally competitive. Yet export promotion policies such as excessive export subsidies may distort incentives and lead to increasing inefficiency. It is important to focus on the causal mechanism assumed to be working: export expansion and import substitution policies may increase or decrease TFP (levels or growth rates) depending on their impact on competitive, cost-reducing incentives to producers in the medium to long run.

The literature on foreign exchange constraints provides yet another hypothesis for a link between trade and productivity. A stylized fact characterizing developing countries is that intermediate and capital goods are not very substitutable with domestically produced goods. In a sense, these imported inputs embody technologies that are unavailable to domestic producers and can only be attained through imports. Policies that limit the availability of such imports, or make them more expensive, will lead to poor productivity performance. In contrast, policies that increase the availability of imported inputs or lower their costs—such as increased foreign aid or an export-led development strategy—will reduce costs for

4. See also Salter (1960) and Kaldor (1961).
5. See Balassa (1967) and Chenery and Westphal (1979).

domestic industries and lead to better productivity performance. In this view, exports are important only as a source of foreign exchange; they permit industries to buy inputs that can be produced domestically only at a much greater cost, if at all.

These hypotheses about possible links between alternative development strategies distinguished by trade policies and TFP growth are not mutually exclusive. They may all be true, and the postulated effects need not be independent of one another. Given the current state of knowledge, it is not possible to discriminate finely among these hypotheses. Indeed, it is not even possible to state with any real confidence what is the direction of causation. It is just as likely, for example, that exogenous TFP growth in a sector generates a shift in the supply curve and, if domestic demand is limited, provides a strong incentive to open up export markets. The possible relationships are myriad and probably have to be sorted out case by case.

In this chapter, we begin by looking at the experiences of four countries and try to identify similarities and differences among them at the sectoral level. We then explore some of the hypotheses discussed above by analyzing additional data on the nature of the development process in these countries, which at different times have pursued a variety of development strategies and supporting trade policy regimes. This variety yields experiments in which different effects dominate the results and enables us to explore the relative importance of factors such as import substitution and export expansion. Before considering the empirical results, however, we first discuss the nature of the TFP measures we use. The measures embody some strong assumptions that affect how they should be interpreted and what they capture as productivity change.

The Analytical Framework for Measuring Total Factor Productivity

The analytical framework for TFP measurement is founded on the economic theory of cost and production. In recent decades, developments in the field of productivity research have been accompanied by advances in closely related areas of economic theory and measurement. They include duality theory, the theory of index numbers, and the development of flexible functional forms that are less restrictive in representing economic relationships such as production functions and cost functions.[6] Advances in these areas have strengthened the theoretical foundations of TFP measurement.[7]

Indexes of TFP change are usually given in terms of output per unit of

___

6. Caves, Christensen, and Diewert (1981, 1982a,b) provide a good and concise summary of the literature and references. See also Gollop and Jorgenson (1980).

7. In this section, we shall provide a brief exposition of the analytical framework. For a more detailed and technical discussion, see the references cited above.

total factor inputs and are functions of scale elasticities, output and input elasticities, and quantities (or prices) of outputs and inputs. It is usually assumed that output and input markets are competitive and that firms maximize profit subject to a constant-returns-to-scale production function and to market prices that are taken as parameters. Under these assumptions, output and input elasticities are equivalent to the observed cost shares of factor inputs and revenue shares of each output produced.[8] The index of TFP change can then be computed using only the prices and quantities of outputs and inputs; it equals the difference between revenue-share-weighted output growth rates and cost-share-weighted input growth rates. There is an extensive literature on the choice of an appropriate index of TFP change.[9] Essentially, one must specify something about the form of the production function (or, alternatively, of the cost function) in order to justify a particular form of an index. We have chosen the translog production function and the resulting translog index number in our methodology.[10]

This framework for TFP measurement has some shortcomings since the simple stylization of production and markets ignores a number of factors and constraints that may be important. In his review of the productivity literature, Nelson (1981) provides detailed criticism and evaluation of the approach. Several issues he raises are worth emphasizing since they affect the interpretation of our empirical results.

A production process can be seen as the application of technology to the production of goods and services. Technology, however, is more than machines, tools, and equipment. It may be embodied in workers and managers, in the physical characteristics of material inputs, or in procedures and organizational principles that determine how various inputs are combined. It may also be embodied in produced outputs themselves. As Nelson discusses at length, TFP changes may therefore result from all sorts of changes in this broadly interpreted technology as applied to the production process.

Nelson also points out that production takes place within "production environments" that are defined by the nature of the markets for inputs and

8. When these assumptions are not tenable—as in Yugoslavia—direct estimates of output and input elasticities and scale elasticities must be generated. See Nishimizu and Page (1982).

9. For a survey on the theory of index numbers, see Diewert (1979).

10. For a detailed exposition of this approach, see Diewert (1976) for a theoretical discussion and Gollop and Jorgenson (1980) for applications. There is an issue of whether one should work with a value added production function (excluding intermediate input) or with a gross production function (including intermediate input). We have chosen the gross production function approach because we believe that intermediate inputs matter in sectoral TFP change and that it is misleading to assume that intermediate inputs are separable from capital and labor. There is an extensive literature on this issue, but the most comprehensive treatment can be found in Gollop and Jorgenson (1979). Gollop and Jorgenson (1979) also provide a comprehensive treatment and survey of the literature on aggregation over sectoral TFP estimates and on the impact of intersectoral resource shifts on TFP change at the macro level.

outputs and by a set of market and nonmarket constraints such as government policies. Changes in production environments ultimately affect productivity performance by altering production constraints through changes in prices, quantities, or qualities of inputs and outputs. They may also have an important shorter-run impact on TFP changes during the process of adjustment to new conditions in production environments.

Our empirical results on TFP change thus should not be interpreted as measuring technical change only in the sense of a shift in the frontier of production possibilities because of the implementation of a new generation of technical knowledge. Instead, the measures must be interpreted quite broadly to include such factors as industrial and plant organization, engineering know-how, or changes in response to disruptions in the production process that affect capacity utilization in the short run. The measures really treat production units as a black box. We measure the inputs and the outputs but make no real attempt to describe exactly what is going on inside the plant gate. Figuring out how the black box works is important, but it is beyond the scope of this book.[11] We seek to delineate the stylized facts at a fairly aggregate level and will necessarily be modest in our attempts to generalize and to discern causal links.

Growth and Productivity Change in the Manufacturing Industries

In this section, we attempt to distinguish systematic patterns of output, input, and TFP growth in the manufacturing industries of Japan, Korea, Turkey, and Yugoslavia. The period we consider is from the late 1950s to the late 1970s. One characteristic that unites the development experiences of these four countries during this period is that they are all semi-industrialized countries (Japan graduated to industrial status during the 1960s). Among the four countries, however, a variety of development strategies and supporting trade policy regimes has been followed. If factors related to stage of development or trade policy have a significant effect on productivity performance, we should be able to see systematic similarities and differences among the four countries caused by these factors.

Our empirical analysis is based on data for Japan developed by Jorgenson and Nishimizu (1981) and on data on TFP growth in manufacturing industries in Korea, Turkey, and Yugoslavia developed at the World Bank.[12] To summarize, data on gross output, labor, capital, and material

11. See Nelson (1981) for a survey of the relevant literature. Research toward this objective is under way at the World Bank in two research projects: "Acquisition of Technological Capability" (RPO 672-48) by Carl Dahlman and Larry Westphal, and "Productivity Change in Infant Industries" (RPO 672-86) by Mieko Nishimizu and John M. Page, Jr.

12. The data come from two World Bank research projects: "Sources of Growth and Productivity Change: A Comparative Analysis" and "Productivity Change in Yugoslavia." More detailed discussions of the results are available in separate papers. See Krueger and Tuncer (1980b) on Turkey, Rhee (1980) on Korea, and Nishimizu and Page (1982) on Yugoslavia for a more comprehensive comparison of the countries.

input in current and constant prices were assembled for the manufacturing industries in these four countries.[13] Conceptually similar methodologies were used in defining the variables and in aggregating to achieve comparability.[14] Gross output and material input by industry are in constant 1970 prices in each country. Capital is defined as net capital stock at replacement cost in 1970 prices and includes all nonresidential structures and producers' durables. Land and inventories unfortunately could not be included because of the unavailability of data for the three developing countries. Labor is defined as persons employed since, again, data on hours worked were not readily available for the developing countries. A summary of the industry estimates is presented in tables 10-1, 10-2, and 10-3.

In an essay on economic growth, Kaldor (1967, p. 7) stated—with empirical support—that "fast rates of growth are almost invariably associated with the fast rate of growth of the secondary sector, mainly manufacturing, and . . . this is an attribute of an intermediate stage of development." Table 10-4 presents the average annual growth rates of TFP and gross output and of capital, labor, and material input, as well as the standard sources-of-growth decomposition, for aggregate manufacturing in Japan, Korea, Turkey, and Yugoslavia. These countries all demonstrate rapid growth in manufacturing and seem to fit Kaldor's stylization of being at an intermediate stage of development. Figure 10-1 plots output growth rates of different industries for each country (from table 10-1), along with the sample mean and sample standard deviation. The figure shows that the rapid manufacturing growth in these countries is the result of many industries growing uniformly fast. More than two-thirds of all industries have growth rates that range from 9 to 15 percent in Japan, 17 to 27 percent in Korea, 9 to 18 percent in Turkey, and 6 to 13 percent in Yugoslavia.[15] In Japan, Korea, and Turkey, there are no industries characterized by slow growth; and in Yugoslavia, only two industries have growth rates of less than 6 percent a year.

Earlier, we noted that size of market may be an important factor in determining growth and productivity change. One way in which this scale effect comes about is through interindustry linkages. Balassa (1967, p. 97) has argued that "cost reductions tend to have a cumulative effect: improvements in particular industries are transmitted to other sectors through input-output relationships and through the effects of higher incomes on the demand for consumer goods." These intersectoral links,

13. Data for Korea include 52 manufacturing industries; for Turkey, 33; for Yugoslavia, 19; and for Japan, 21. We have aggregated the data for each country to 16 comparable sectors (roughly the ISIC two-digit classification).

14. The methodology for Yugoslavia differs from that for the others because it could not be assumed that cost-share data reflected the workings of a competitive market (see Nishimizu and Page 1982).

15. Note that the sample means of figure 10-1 differ from aggregate manufacturing output growth given in table 10-1 (first row) since the latter is computed as a weighted average.

Table 10-1. *Output, Input, and Total Factor Productivity Growth in Four Countries by Industry*
(percent)

Industry	Japan (1955–73)					Korea (1960–77)				
	1	2	3	4	5	1	2	3	4	5
Food processing	9.36	9.96	3.22	7.11	2.21	16.09	8.50	4.49	13.24	5.26
Textile	7.49	5.98	1.42	7.06	1.70	18.88	13.09	6.68	16.40	4.51
Apparel	12.52	16.23	6.48	11.28	1.94	23.34	22.11	12.75	22.98	1.62
Leather	11.15	8.45	5.09	11.63	0.95	25.20	14.78	18.91	25.46	2.80
Lumber and wood	7.94	7.45	1.98	7.88	1.12	16.32	5.56	4.89	13.00	5.62
Furniture	11.83	9.65	4.97	14.73	−0.09	13.49	4.93	3.74	11.90	4.88
Paper	11.25	10.75	4.96	10.38	1.62	19.41	6.73	7.61	19.37	4.52
Chemicals	12.23	10.86	2.38	10.73	2.50	21.33	14.42	5.93	19.46	4.49
Petroleum and coal	15.28	13.58	3.31	16.69	−0.43	22.81	20.40	2.24	24.06	0.68
Rubber	9.79	14.08	5.14	11.71	−1.22	20.90	16.80	11.02	15.44	5.88
Stone, clay, and glass	12.43	13.22	4.30	12.30	1.73	18.93	11.12	7.20	18.73	4.53
Basic metals	12.11	13.08	4.50	11.85	0.96	25.68	25.58	4.90	25.52	1.87
Fabricated metals	14.33	16.35	7.30	15.20	0.84	22.19	12.49	10.17	19.01	6.01
Machinery	15.90	13.87	6.12	14.56	3.14	23.01	13.31	7.88	21.91	5.73
Electrical machinery	18.26	12.20	7.68	15.72	4.42	36.00	25.87	17.48	31.88	7.25
Transportation equipment	16.69	13.27	6.25	15.89	2.53	28.68	13.64	8.66	30.76	5.10

Note: Column 1 is gross output growth; column 2 is capital input growth; column 3 is labor input growth; column 4 is material input growth; and column 5 is total factor productivity growth.

while significant in developed countries, are especially important in developing countries that are undergoing major changes in input-output structure and in the composition of final demand as part of the process of development.[16] It is characteristic of the intermediate stage of development that the share of intermediate demand in total gross production increases significantly over time. This trend would lead one to expect consistently higher output growth in the sectors turning out producer goods across all four countries. And, without prejudging causation, where one sees high output growth one also expects to see high TFP growth.

Although it is difficult to map our industry classification strictly according to producer goods sectors, we can divide the industries into the following four groups: consumer goods, light intermediates, heavy intermediates, and investment goods. For each country, industries are ranked with respect to both output and TFP growth. The use of such rankings allows us to separate the differences among countries in the

16. Rapid structural change, especially if it also leads to sustained disequilibrium in the factor markets (that is, different marginal productivities across sectors), also has a profound effect on aggregate growth. We shall not pursue this issue further; see chapters 8 and 9 and Robinson (1971).

Turkey (1963–76)					Yugoslavia (1965–78)					
1	2	3	4	5	1	2	3	4	5	Yugoslav industry
8.47	8.30	3.39	6.40	1.91	7.20	7.28	4.55	8.24	−0.65	Food processing
					5.74	7.47	−2.04	13.89	−1.71	Tobacco
9.47	10.88	3.35	8.09	1.44	9.77	7.78	3.50	12.87	−0.17	Textile and apparel
18.30	14.80	8.46	17.63	2.74						
6.41	16.39	3.25	6.41	−0.98	11.69	8.21	5.29	15.45	−0.14	Leather
7.35	11.28	4.92	8.39	−1.20	10.85	7.89	1.94	15.45	−0.60	Lumber and wood,
12.37	19.13	4.34	9.28	3.23						furniture
13.53	12.34	4.24	13.93	1.41	10.77	7.18	3.64	13.01	0.07	Paper
15.23	12.13	7.65	15.55	1.62	12.14	8.19	4.15	14.06	0.10	Chemicals
16.60	17.68	−0.81	14.99	0.45	10.09	9.32	1.02	12.72	0.18	Petroleum
					1.32	6.40	−2.91	5.05	1.10	Coal
19.19	13.29	3.59	15.85	5.80	13.19	10.74	5.36	17.55	2.35	Rubber
12.80	13.91	7.05	13.66	0.26	9.90	8.05	1.94	13.70	−0.05	Building materials
					8.90	6.99	2.08	12.64	1.72	Nonmetallic minerals
14.98	14.52	11.41	14.62	0.87	6.08	6.85	0.37	7.84	−0.63	Ferrous metals
					7.54	8.00	1.13	9.85	−0.65	Nonferrous metals
7.57	9.68	−0.88	6.55	1.51	12.58	7.35	4.18	16.31	0.60	Metal products
17.61	13.64	13.97	17.81	1.33						
19.34	19.44	10.99	17.76	1.83	15.55	10.78	4.28	19.29	−0.25	Electrical machinery
19.48	16.05	7.51	19.65	3.33	3.09	6.52	1.35	5.21	−0.25	Shipbuilding

Source: World Bank data.

average growth rates. Table 10-5 presents these industry rankings. Table 10-6 further summarizes the results by giving a frequency count of industries in each ranking across countries within the four industrial groups.

The industry ranking of output and TFP growth arranged in this manner shows a strikingly similar pattern across the four countries of faster growth in heavy industries and slower growth in light industries. Investment goods industries are the fastest growing, followed by heavy intermediate goods industries and then the two light industry groups. Kendall's (multiple) rank correlation coefficient, which measures the similarity in rankings across all four countries together, is 0.75 for output growth excluding Yugoslavia (for which the industry classification differs somewhat from the other three countries) and 0.52 including Yugoslavia. A similar but weaker correlation is observed in the industry ranking of TFP growth rates among the four countries. Similarly, a chi-square test treating table 10-6 as a contingency table yields values of 25.4 and 15.7 for the output growth and TFP growth respectively. These values indicate a significant association between the four industrial groups and their rank according to both output and TFP growth, although the latter is significant at only the 90–95 percent confidence level.

Given these broad similarities, what are the main differences among the

Table 10-2. Sources of Growth by Industry
(percent)

Industry	Japan (1955–73)				Korea (1960–77)				Turkey (1963–76)				Yugoslavia (1965–78)				Yugoslav industry
	1	2	3	4	1	2	3	4	1	2	3	4	1	2	3	4	
Food processing	23.5	19.7	3.7	52.9	32.6	17.9	2.1	47.2	22.6	24.1	3.0	50.2	-9.0	1.7	4.5	102.8	Food processing
													-29.8	69.8	-3.8	63.8	Tobacco
Textile	22.6	4.9	2.8	69.5	23.8	16.3	3.8	55.9	15.2	26.1	4.9	53.7	-1.7	20.9	6.6	74.1	Textile and apparel
Apparel	15.5	9.2	10.2	65.0	6.9	21.7	17.1	64.1	14.9	13.8	8.2	62.9					
Leather	8.5	4.7	8.0	78.6	11.1	11.8	8.0	68.9	-15.2	34.6	4.6	76.0	-1.1	3.3	14.0	83.7	Leather
Lumber and wood	14.1	6.8	4.0	74.9	34.4	6.5	1.8	57.2	-16.2	33.7	9.5	72.9	-5.5	2.1	5.5	97.8	Lumber and wood, furniture
Furniture	-0.7	4.9	11.4	84.3	36.1	8.3	5.1	50.3	26.1	35.2	-4.1	28.2					
Paper	14.4	9.2	6.7	69.5	23.3	8.8	3.4	64.3	10.4	28.2	5.3	55.9	0.6	3.4	7.2	88.7	Paper
Chemicals	20.4	19.6	2.4	57.3	21.0	21.1	2.5	55.3	10.6	22.8	6.1	60.4	0.8	0.0	6.9	92.2	Chemicals
Petroleum and coal	-2.7	12.4	1.0	89.3	2.9	22.8	0.9	73.1	2.7	58.5	-0.1	38.9	1.8	11.5	0.1	86.5	Petroleum
													82.8	63.6	-138.3	91.8	Coal
Rubber	-12.4	27.2	7.4	77.7	28.1	14.8	6.5	50.4	30.2	21.3	1.8	46.5	17.7	0.0	22.5	59.7	Rubber
Stone, clay, and glass	13.9	18.1	8.1	59.7	23.9	21.1	5.0	49.9	2.0	38.8	10.4	48.6	-0.4	41.0	1.8	57.5	Building materials
													19.3	17.4	9.4	53.6	Nonmetallic minerals
Basic metals	7.9	12.8	4.3	74.9	7.2	18.1	0.9	73.6	5.8	30.1	8.9	55.1	-10.4	7.2	0.4	102.6	Ferrous metals
													-8.6	9.2	1.9	97.4	Nonferrous metals
Fabricated metals	5.8	14.7	11.8	67.5	27.0	13.3	6.5	53.0	19.9	28.2	-2.2	54.1	4.8	3.8	10.7	80.6	Metal products
Machinery	19.7	12.4	8.7	59.0	24.9	14.1	5.3	55.5	7.5	18.2	9.6	64.5					
Electrical machinery	24.2	10.1	7.6	57.9	20.1	19.9	5.6	54.1	9.4	26.6	7.8	56.1	-1.5	2.0	5.0	94.4	Electrical machinery
Transportation equipment	15.1	10.3	6.1	68.3	17.7	11.5	3.8	66.9	17.0	17.8	7.4	57.6	-7.9	47.3	24.6	35.9	Shipbuilding

Note: Column 1 is total factor productivity growth divided by gross output growth; column 2 is the contribution of capital input growth divided by gross output growth; column 3 is the contribution of labor input growth divided by gross output growth; and column 4 is the contribution of material input growth divided by gross output growth.

Source: World Bank data.

Table 10-3. *Factor Input Shares by Industry*
(percent)

Industry	Japan (1955–73)			Korea (1960–77)			Turkey (1963–76)			Yugoslavia (1965–78)			Yugoslav industry
	1	2	3	1	2	3	1	2	3	1	2	3	
Food processing	18.6	10.9	69.8	34.0	7.6	57.4	24.6	7.4	66.5	1.6	7.3	89.8	Food processing
										53.7	10.8	26.3	Tobacco
Textile	6.2	14.8	73.4	23.6	10.8	64.4	22.7	13.7	62.9	26.3	18.5	56.3	Textile and apparel
Apparel	7.1	19.8	72.2	23.0	13.1	65.2	17.1	17.8	65.4				
Leather	6.3	17.7	75.4	20.2	10.8	68.2	13.5	9.2	76.0	4.8	31.0	63.4	Leather
Lumber and wood	7.4	16.2	75.5	19.1	6.1	71.8	22.0	14.2	63.9	3.0	30.9	67.0	Lumber and wood, furniture
Furniture	6.1	27.2	67.8	22.7	18.9	57.1	21.7	13.2	63.3				
Paper	9.9	15.3	75.4	25.6	8.9	64.5	31.0	17.0	54.3	5.2	21.4	73.5	Paper
Chemicals	22.2	12.6	65.3	31.3	9.1	60.6	28.7	12.3	59.2	0.0	20.2	79.7	Chemicals
Petroleum and coal	13.9	4.5	81.8	25.5	9.8	64.5	55.0	3.7	43.1	13.5	17.5	68.9	Petroleum
										13.1	62.9	24.2	Coal
Rubber	19.0	14.2	65.0	18.5	12.3	68.3	30.9	10.0	56.3	0.0	55.4	44.9	Rubber
Stone, clay, and glass	17.1	23.5	60.4	36.0	13.2	50.5	35.7	19.0	45.6	50.6	9.8	41.6	Building materials
										22.3	40.4	37.8	Nonmetallic minerals
Basic metals	11.9	11.6	76.6	18.2	5.3	74.1	31.1	11.7	56.5	8.7	13.3	78.1	Ferrous metals
										11.9	15.4	74.2	Nonferrous metals
Fabricated metals	12.9	23.3	63.7	23.7	14.4	61.9	21.3	14.9	64.3	6.5	32.3	62.2	Metal products
Machinery	14.3	22.7	64.5	24.5	15.5	58.4	23.5	12.2	63.8				
Electrical machinery	15.2	18.2	67.4	27.8	11.7	61.2	26.5	13.7	61.1	3.0	18.2	76.2	Electrical machinery
Transportation equipment	13.0	16.3	71.8	24.2	12.6	62.4	21.7	19.3	57.2	22.4	56.3	21.3	Shipbuilding

Note: Column 1 is capital input share; column 2 is labor input share; and column 3 is material input share.
Source: World Bank data.

Table 10-4. *Sources of Growth for the Manufacturing Sector*
(percent per year)

Measure	Japan (1955–73)		Korea (1960–77)		Turkey (1963–76)		Yugoslavia (1965–78)	
Gross output	11.59		17.94		10.71		9.78	
Capital input	10.84		12.98		11.24		7.72	
Labor input	4.50		5.32		5.05		2.99	
Material input	10.41		16.29		9.29		11.55	
Weighted capital input[a]	1.51	(0.130)	3.50	(0.195)	3.23	(0.302)	0.78	(0.080)
Weighted labor input[a]	0.70	(0.060)	0.46	(0.026)	0.55	(0.051)	0.67	(0.069)
Weighted material input[a]	7.34	(0.633)	10.28	(0.573)	5.60	(0.523)	7.85	(0.802)
Total factor productivity change[a]	2.04	(0.176)	3.71	(0.207)	1.33	(0.124)	0.48	(0.049)

a. Ratios of weighted capital, labor, and material input growth as well as total factor productivity change to gross output growth are given in parentheses.

Source: Tables 10-1 and 10-2.

four countries? In particular, are there systematic differences in productivity performance by industries among the four countries? The country differences in TFP growth can be summarized statistically. For this purpose, we estimate a log-linear time-trend equation for TFP change over the individual industry's annual time series pooled across countries. The ordinary least squares regression (with standard errors given in parentheses) is

$$\ln \text{TFP} = \underset{(0.0054)}{0.0085} + \underset{(0.0014)}{0.0194t} + \underset{(0.0020)}{0.0177Kt} - \underset{(0.0023)}{0.0105Tt} - \underset{(0.0020)}{0.0195Yt}$$

where R^2 is 0.475; the sample size is 1,054; the variable t is time; and the variables K, T, and Y are country dummies set to one for Korea, Turkey, and Yugoslavia respectively and to zero otherwise. All estimated coefficients are significant at the 99 percent level, other than the intercept term (as should be expected since the level index of TFP is one in the base year). These results indicate that the sectoral TFP growth rates in Korea, Turkey, and Yugoslavia differ significantly from the rate in Japan. In Korea, TFP growth is 1.77 percent above Japan, in Turkey it is 1.05 percent below Japan, and in Yugoslavia it is 1.95 percent below Japan. The difference in TFP growth rates is also statistically significant between Korea and Turkey, Korea and Yugoslavia, and Turkey and Yugoslavia. Furthermore, Yugoslavia's TFP growth rate is the only one not significantly different from zero.

Returning briefly to the aggregate manufacturing estimates in table 10-4, we note that differences in TFP growth reflect another marked difference in the manufacturing growth process of these four countries—that between the relative importance of TFP growth and of factor input growth in output growth (see the last four rows in table 10-4). Japan and Korea are similar in that TFP change is as important as capital and labor

Figure 10-1. *Distribution of Sectoral Growth Rates*

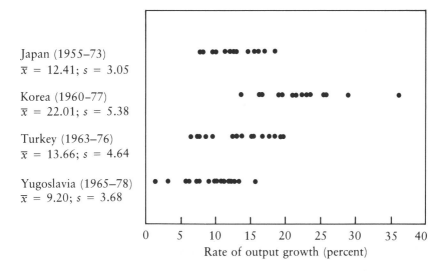

Japan (1955–73)
$\bar{x}$ = 12.41; s = 3.05

Korea (1960–77)
$\bar{x}$ = 22.01; s = 5.38

Turkey (1963–76)
$\bar{x}$ = 13.66; s = 4.64

Yugoslavia (1965–78)
$\bar{x}$ = 9.20; s = 3.68

Rate of output growth (percent)

Note: Each dot represents a sector. Sector definitions are given in table 10-1. The variable $\bar{x}$ is a sample mean; s is standard deviation.

input growth combined.[17] For Turkey, although the rate of TFP growth is respectable, its contribution to output growth is significantly less than that of capital and labor combined. In sharp contrast, Yugoslavia's manufacturing growth involves very little TFP growth—virtually all growth is derived from increases in the quantity of inputs.

The relative importance of TFP growth on the one hand and of capital and labor growth on the other at the disaggregated industry level can be examined in figure 10-2. From the data in table 10-2, the share of TFP growth in output growth is plotted against the share of capital plus labor growth in output growth in each industry by country, with the 45-degree line indicating equal contributions. These industry results also show that Japan and Korea differ from Turkey and Yugoslavia as noted above. In Turkey and Yugoslavia, the individual industry results mirror the aggregate pattern; with only one exception, the contribution of sectoral TFP growth is less important than that of capital and labor input combined. In Yugoslavia, almost all industries derive their growth in output from increases in factor inputs, with zero or negative contribution from TFP growth.

17. Since the contribution of material input growth to gross output growth is always the dominating factor in manufacturing, we shall focus on the relative importance of TFP, capital, and labor growth in our discussion.

Table 10-5. Ranking of Gross Output Growth and Total Factor Productivity Growth

Gross output growth

Industry	Rank 1–4 J	K	T	Y	Rank 5–8 J	K	T	Y	Rank 9–12 J	K	T	Y	Rank 13–16 J	K	T	Y
Consumer goods																
Food processing[a]													(14)	(15)	(13)	(14)
Textile[b]					(6)	(5)			(12)	(11)	11		(16)	(13)		
Apparel[b]		4									11					
Leather	4					6		12							16	
Light intermediates																
Lumber and wood[c]					7								(15)	(14)	(15)	
Furniture[c]					7				(10)	(11)					16	
Paper									(11)	(11)	(9)	(9)				

Total factor productivity growth

Industry	Rank 1–4 J	K	T	Y	Rank 5–8 J	K	T	Y	Rank 9–12 J	K	T	Y	Rank 13–16 J	K	T	Y
Consumer goods																
Food processing[a]					(5)	(6)	(5)									16
Textile[b]						8			(11)	(9)	(9)	9				
Apparel[b]			4			6									15	
Leather						8		12					(13)	(15)		
Light intermediates																
Lumber and wood[c]			3			5			10							
Furniture[c]						8							(16)	(13)		
Paper							7		(9)	(10)	(10)		(14)	(13)		

Heavy intermediates

Industry								
Chemicals	4	8 ⑦ ⑤	9	⑦ ⑥	12		⑮ ⑯ 13	
Petroleum and coal[d]	③ ②	⑦ ⑥	10	5		16		
Rubber	7	10	13	9	14			
Stone, clay, and glass[e]	⑫ ⑩	8	9	⑪ ⑫	⑭ 15		13	
Basic metals[f]	3	9	13	15	⑭ 15			

Investment goods

Industry								
Fabricated metals[g]	3 ⑤ ⑧	③	14	②	8	13		
Machinery[g]	③ ⑥ ⑤	② ④ ③	11	11				
Electrical machinery	① ② ①	① ①	6	11				
Transport equipment[h]	② ② ①	③ ②	7	16	11			

Note: In columns, J stands for Japan, K for Korea, T for Turkey, and Y for Yugoslavia. Rankings are grouped in quartiles; circled rankings indicate that there is a similar industry ranking in more than one country within each quartile.

Kendall's rank correlation coefficient (excluding Yugoslavia) is 0.75 for output growth and 0.47 for TFP growth; significant at the 99.5 percent and 75 percent levels, respectively. Kendall's rank correlation coefficient (including Yugoslavia) is 0.52 for output growth and 0.30 for input growth; significant at the 99 percent and 75 percent levels, respectively.

a. Excluding tobacco in Yugoslavia.
b. Textile and apparel are considered a tie ranking for Yugoslavia.
c. Lumber and wood and furniture are considered a tie ranking for Yugoslavia.
d. Excluding coal for Yugoslavia.
e. Average of building materials and nonmetallic minerals for Yugoslavia.
f. Average of ferrous and nonferrous metals for Yugoslavia.
g. Fabricated metals and machinery are considered a tie ranking for Yugoslavia.
h. Shipbuilding only for Yugoslavia.

Source: World Bank data.

Table 10-6. *Sectoral Frequencies across Countries of Ranks of Output and* TFP *Growth*

Aggregate sector	Rank				Row sum
	1–4	5–8	9–12	13–16	
	Gross output growth				
Consumer goods	2	3	4	7	16
Light intermediates	0	2	6	4	12
Heavy intermediates	4	7	6	3	20
Investment goods	10	4	0	2	16
Column sum	16	16	16	16	64
	TFP *growth*				
Consumer goods	1	6	5	4	16
Light intermediates	1	3	4	4	12
Heavy intermediates	5	4	4	7	20
Investment goods	9	3	3	1	16
Column sum	16	16	16	16	64

Note: For industries included in each aggregate sector, see table 10-5.
Source: Table 10-5.

The differences in productivity performance among countries might be at least partly caused by the nature of the economic policies pursued by each country. One important element distinguishing Japan, Korea, Turkey, and Yugoslavia from each other is the choice of trade policies in their development strategies. Korea and Yugoslavia (in that order) have manufacturing sectors that are relatively more open to trade, whereas Turkey and Japan are relatively more closed—the former by design and the latter mainly because of the size of the domestic market. As we shall discuss in the next section, Korea's development strategy has been distinguished by strong export promotion policies, often applied to selected industries. Turkey has long pursued import substitution policies for much of its manufacturing sector, many industries in which are dominated by state enterprises. Yugoslavia has pursued strong import liberalization accompanied by export expansion. In addition, it has long sought regional and sectoral equalization of productive performance by designing wage, employment, and investment policies to affect all industries similarly. Japan has made use of mixed export promotion and import substitution policies at different times. In the next section, we shall examine the relation between the growth and productivity performance of manufacturing industries and the effect of choosing either an open, export-led development strategy or a closed, import substitution strategy.

Trade Strategies and TFP Growth

In the introduction to this chapter, we discussed three hypotheses linking TFP growth and trade policies. First, there is a positive link between

Figure 10-2. *Relative Contributions of TFP and Primary Inputs to Growth of Output for Disaggregated Industries*

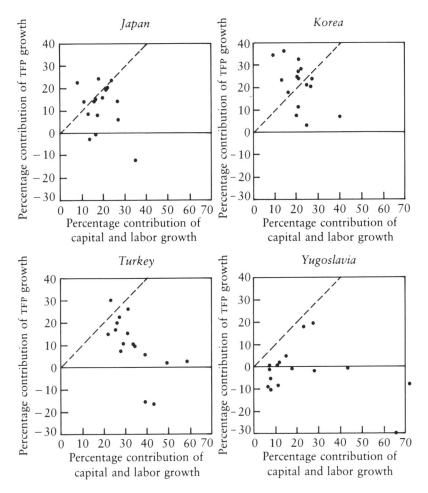

higher exports or (depending on the size of the domestic market) increased import substitution and TFP growth, arising from Verdoorn's law and from the role of export expansion and import substitution policies in increasing the size of the market. Second, there is a positive link between higher exports and TFP growth and a negative link with import substitution (or a positive link with import liberalization), arising from competitive cost-reducing incentives or lack thereof. Third, there is a positive link between export expansion, import liberalization, and TFP growth, arising from the importance of foreign exchange constraints and nonsubstitutable imports of intermediate inputs and capital goods.

It is likely that what is observed is the net effect of all these hypothesized forces. As noted earlier, the hypotheses are not mutually exclusive, and distinguishing among them can be quite difficult. They can all be seen as involving a supply response in terms of TFP change to changes in two components of demand: export expansion and import substitution. Taking these components as exogenous, or as determined by exogenous policy regimes, we can then relate TFP growth to changes in the sources of demand growth. One must be very cautious, however, in implying the direction of causality in the relation. For example, it may be that higher rates of exogenous TFP change lead to rapid growth in demand through lower costs and prices. Regardless of causality, however, the existence of any statistically significant relation will provide an interesting starting point for further investigation.

The single equation model to be estimated is TFPG $= \beta_0 + \beta_{EE}x_{EE} + \beta_{IS}x_{IS} + \varepsilon$, where TFPG, x_{EE}, and x_{IS} are, respectively, annual rates of TFP growth, output growth allocated to export expansion, and output growth allocated to import substitution, and ε is the random disturbance term.[18]

For each industry in Japan, Korea, Turkey, and Yugoslavia, we use as the dependent variable our estimate of annual rate of TFP change.[19] For the explanatory variables, we combine our estimates of annual output growth rates with demand-side sources of growth decomposition measures.[20] For each industry, total demand can be decomposed into four terms: $\Delta X = \hat{u}_t\Delta D + \hat{u}_t\Delta W + \Delta E + \Delta\hat{u}(D_{t+1} + W_{t+1})$ where $\hat{u}$ is the diagonal matrix of domestic demand ratios (that is, ratios of domestic demand to domestic plus import demand); D, W, and E are final demand, intermediate demand, and export demand respectively; and the subscript refers to the time period.[21] The third and fourth terms in the decomposition give the export expansion and import substitution components of demand changes. Dividing each of these two terms by ΔX, we obtain share measures of export

18. Strictly speaking, the model should also include output growth allocated to domestic demand growth. We found, however, high colinearity between export and domestic demand growth (whereas no such colinearity problem arose between import substitution and domestic demand) for most industries in all countries except Japan. It therefore becomes difficult to make a clear statistical distinction between the effect of export expansion and of domestic demand in these cases. Although we can sum the two growth rates, this imposes equality of coefficients between them. We choose instead to omit the domestic demand growth in the analysis below, although it may result in biased estimates particularly of export coefficients, and ask that care be taken in interpreting our results.

19. Note that in tables 10-8 and 10-9 we aggregate to thirteen industries (from those appearing in table 10-5) to achieve consistent data on demand components for all countries.

20. See chapter 5 for a description of the methodology and the data.

21. There is also a total decomposition equation which uses the input-output matrix and therefore incorporates indirect linkages into the decomposition. Since we are concerned with the supply response of individual sectors to changes in demand, the direct decomposition equation is more appropriate for our purpose than the total decomposition equation. There is also an index number problem arising from the choice of initial or terminal weights. We use an average of the analogous Paasche and Laspeyres indexes. See chapter 5 for further discussion of the measures.

Table 10-7. *Decomposition of Growth of Manufacturing Demand*
(percent)

Economy and years	Manufacturing		Growth decomposition[c]		
	Output share[a]	Growth rate[b]	Domestic demand expansion	Export expansion	Import substitution
Japan					
1955–60	47.2	12.6	95.4	5.8	−1.2
1960–65	50.4	10.8	90.2	9.9	−0.1
1965–70	54.6	16.5	92.1	8.1	−0.2
Korea					
1955–63	32.1	10.4	64.3	7.2	28.5
1963–70	41.9	18.9	81.8	18.0	0.2
1970–73	49.6	23.8	62.9	38.1	−1.0
Turkey					
1953–63	27.9	6.4	90.6	1.3	8.1
1963–68	31.8	9.9	89.6	3.2	7.2
1968–73	36.5	9.4	94.2	6.7	−0.9
Yugoslavia					
1962–66	39.0	16.6	90.0	12.7	−2.7
1966–72	45.0	9.1	91.5	21.2	−12.7

a. Average share of manufacturing in aggregate gross output during the period.

b. Average annual rate of growth of gross output.

c. The decomposition methodology is described in the text and in chapter 5. The three components sum to 100 percent. The first, domestic demand expansion, includes both intermediate and final demand.

Source: World Bank data; described in Kubo (1983).

expansion and import substitution in gross output changes for each industry in each country. We then multiply these share measures by the annual growth rates of gross output of each industry.[22]

Table 10-7 provides a summary of the decomposition results at the aggregate level for the four countries. Note, first, the considerable variation in the relative roles of domestic demand expansion, export expansion, and import substitution, both over time and across countries. In every country the role of export expansion increases over time—dramatically so in Korea and Yugoslavia—and in every country but Japan the role of import substitution decreases. Yugoslavia actually shows significant import liberalization (that is, negative import substitution). Korea and Tur-

22. Since the share measures are based on data for a few episodes, we apply the nearest benchmark shares to output growth rates for intervening years in the benchmark periods. The effect is to assume that the share measures reflect a regime that is uniform for each period. Although not ideal, this procedure does provide measures of the two explanatory variables. The episodes for each country are: Japan (1955–60, 1960–65, 1965–70), Korea (1963–70, 1970–73), Turkey (1963–68, 1968–73), and Yugoslavia (1966–72, 1972–78). See chapter 6 for further analysis of the relation between policy regimes and episodes.

key appear to have distinct phases, with a period characterized by significant import substitution followed by a period of export expansion—
although Turkey's short export expansion phase is hardly dramatic, especially compared with Korea's. In Japan, although export expansion is
significant in all three periods, the country is very large and the domestic
market is the dominant component of demand. All in all, these four
countries represent a variety of development experiences. With the exception of Japan, each one underwent a significant shift in development
strategy during the period under study, so they should constitute a good
sample for statistical analysis.

Whether or not trade policies are tailored to particular industries, there
is no a priori reason to expect that the manner in which they affect
productivity performance is similar for different manufacturing industries. Applying covariance analyses to our panel data reveals significant
differences in the estimated regressions among industries in each country
and across countries in each industry. Therefore, we report a separate
regression for each industry in each country in table 10-8.

The regressions reported in table 10-8 indicate that, in general, substantial portions of the variation in TFP growth rates are explained by output
growth allocated to export expansion and import substitution in Korea,
Turkey, and Yugoslavia—but (interestingly) not in Japan. There are also
significant differences among manufacturing industries. In Korea, 13 to 83
percent of the variance in TFP change is explained by export expansion and
import substitution. Only three industries show less than 30 percent of the
variance explained. In Turkey, the range is 13 to 95 percent, with only
three industries less than 30 percent. In Yugoslavia, industries range from
a low of 3 percent to a high of 93 percent, with four industries less than 30
percent. In Japan, in contrast, the range is from 2 to 41 percent, with all
industries other than textiles and apparel showing less than 30 percent of
variance in TFP change explained. Note also in table 10-8 that all the
statistically significant constant terms ($\hat{\beta}_0$) for Korea, Turkey, and Yugoslavia are negative, whereas they are all positive for Japan. Negative
constant terms in the three developing countries imply reductions in TFP
levels (that is, increases in the unit cost of production) unless they are offset
by sufficiently large positive contributions from a growth in output
through export expansion or import substitution. These striking contrasts
between Korea, Turkey, and Yugoslavia on the one hand and Japan on the
other point to the relative importance of trade and trade policies in the
three developing countries. The results are also consistent with the view
that domestic demand has been the prime source of growth in Japan.

We also observe in table 10-8 that the estimated elasticities of TFP
change with respect to growth through export expansion and import
substitution are distinctly larger (in absolute values) in Turkey than in the
other countries. Also in Turkey, in all industries except paper products,
the elasticities with respect to export expansion are greater than those with

respect to import substitution. Turkey is probably the most closed economy of the four, and these results emphasize the importance of trade at the margin for such an economy.[23]

Table 10-9 presents a summary of the regression results and gives only the signs of the statistically significant estimated coefficients. The table also provides an indication of export-oriented and import-competing industries in each country. Export-oriented industries are defined as those with exports greater than 10 percent of total production and import-competing industries as those with imports greater than 10 percent of total domestic supply. Aggregate export and import shares are also given; they indicate the relative openness of the manufacturing sector in these countries.

Table 10-9 reveals some interesting results that are hard to observe in table 10-8. Of the twenty-eight cases for which statistically significant elasticities with respect to export expansion are estimated, only two are negative. In contrast, thirteen out of twenty-one significant elasticities with respect to import substitution are negative. Import substitution regimes seem to be negatively correlated with TFP change, whereas export expansion regimes seem to be positively correlated with TFP change. In Korea, no industry suffers from export expansion, and those industries that benefit from it are concentrated in the light manufacturing and heavy intermediate categories. In Turkey, the concentration shifts down toward heavy industries. Yugoslavia shows no clear pattern of concentration. Paper products in Turkey and petroleum and coal products in Yugoslavia are the only two industries that show an adverse impact on productivity from export expansion. In Japan, only two industries benefit significantly from export expansion. Industries that experience a significant effect from import substitution are concentrated in Korea and Turkey. More of these are heavy industries in Turkey than in Korea. Only four industries in Yugoslavia and one in Japan show a significant effect from import substitution.

These results support some of the hypotheses outlined above and suggest four new hypotheses worth examining in future work. First, the results do not confirm the simple version of Verdoorn's law, which implies that any expansion of the market, regardless of source, improves productivity performance. There are significant and strong differences in the effect of export expansion versus import substitution. Second, the results are consistent with the hypothesis that export expansion leads to higher TFP growth through economies of scale or through competitive incentives. Third, the results are also consistent with the converse hypothesis that increased import substitution leads to lower TFP growth, perhaps by reducing competitive cost-reduction incentives; or that import liberaliza-

---

23. See Celasun (1983) for an analysis of the structure of Turkish growth during the period under study.

Table 10-8. *Effect of Export Expansion and Import Substitution on Total Factor Productivity Changes, Multiple Regression Results*

	Japan (1955–73)					Korea (1960–77)				
Industry	$\hat{\beta}_0$	$\hat{\beta}_{EE}$	$\hat{\beta}_{IS}$	R^2	Durbin-Watson statistic	$\hat{\beta}_0$	$\hat{\beta}_{EE}$	$\hat{\beta}_{IS}$	R^2	Durbin-Watson statistic
Food processing	−0.013 (0.023)	13.740 (12.796)	−4.534 (3.318)	0.189	1.441 (0.030)	−0.030 (0.034)	11.164* (4.088)	−1.212 (7.234)	0.352	2.042 (0.064)
Textile and apparel	0.036* (0.017)	6.399* (2.491)	−3.291 (3.680)	0.408	1.685 (0.061)	−0.005 (0.015)	0.224* (0.129)	−1.437* (0.766)	0.236	2.020 (0.054)
Leather	0.000 (0.023)	.543 (3.349)	−1.252 (3.550)	0.023	1.631 (0.046)	−0.088 (0.053)	1.305* (0.541)	9.233 (7.042)	0.340	1.567 (0.132)
Lumber and wood, furniture	−0.008 (0.016)	7.026 (5.649)	−1.848 (3.085)	0.045	2.219 (0.046)	0.003 (0.019)	0.518** (0.130)	−0.729 (20.301)	0.402	2.579 (0.090)
Paper	−0.001 (0.026)	4.341 (6.262)	−8.659 (14.770)	0.034	1.982 (0.040)	−0.042* (0.015)	3.051** (0.876)	−1.790** (0.300)	0.835	1.997 (0.047)
Chemicals	−0.018 (0.024)	4.127* (2.245)	−2.351 (1.626)	0.187	1.920 (0.036)	−0.068** (0.018)	1.729 (2.795)	5.096** (1.334)	0.822	2.200 (0.044)
Petroleum and coal	−0.002 (0.011)	1.411 (2.173)	−2.039 (1.959)	0.094	1.643 (0.029)	−0.161* (0.056)	99.614** (27.424)	−24.019** (7.023)	0.568	1.419 (0.142)
Rubber	−0.018 (0.017)	−0.070 (0.678)	−18.812 (24.831)	0.037	2.016 (0.043)	−0.017 (0.034)	0.682* (0.303)	3.582 (18.995)	0.421	2.033 (0.078)
Stone, clay, and glass	0.010 (0.008)	1.673 (1.492)	−5.265 (18.631)	0.106	1.779 (0.027)	−0.055 (0.041)	2.133* (1.232)	6.651* (2.344)	0.372	1.582 (0.077)
Basic metals	0.021 (0.022)	−1.316 (1.970)	4.593 (3.537)	0.102	1.489 (0.061)	0.016 (0.021)	0.241 (0.333)	−0.298 (0.516)	0.129	2.484 (0.049)
Fabricated metals and machinery	0.003 (0.012)	1.352 (0.875)	−0.671 (2.517)	0.076	1.799 (0.046)	0.029 (0.020)	0.483* (0.265)	0.019 (0.335)	0.136	1.999 (0.088)
Electrical machinery	0.048** (0.011)	0.205 (0.554)	−7.185* (3.765)	0.213	2.146 (0.021)	−0.024 (0.044)	0.375 (0.253)	−0.614* (0.324)	0.320	1.870 (0.089)
Transportation equipment	0.027* (0.010)	−0.214 (0.377)	3.501 (2.145)	0.158	1.974 (0.017)	−0.012 (0.025)	0.314 (0.243)	3.475* (1.175)	0.439	1.705 (0.068)

Industry	Turkey (1963–76)					Yugoslavia (1965–78)				
	$\hat{\beta}_0$	β_{EE}	β_{IS}	R^2	Durbin-Watson statistic	$\hat{\beta}_0$	$\hat{\beta}_{EE}$	$\hat{\beta}_{IS}$	R^2	Durbin-Watson statistic
Food processing	-0.064* (0.020)	6.416* (1.100)	-9.917* (4.138)	0.774	2.871 (0.048)	-0.024** (0.007)	0.703** (0.233)	0.056 (1.128)	0.605	2.201 (0.036)
Textile and apparel	-0.008 (0.020)	0.665 (0.430)	-2.248 (1.436)	0.202	2.221 (0.082)	-0.011* (0.004)	0.478* (0.190)	0.170 (0.265)	0.387	1.738 (0.008)
Leather	-0.059* (0.023)	26.639* (10.643)	-40.567* (13.711)	0.821	(1.734) (0.066)	-0.005 (0.007)	0.081 (0.161)	-0.625 (0.575)	0.449	2.004 (0.016)
Lumber and wood, furniture	0.009 (0.019)	8.539 (6.011)	-4.503 (6.189)	0.125	2.007 (0.082)	-0.012 (0.007)	0.493 (0.475)	0.139 (0.713)	0.108	2.040 (0.016)
Paper	-0.070 (0.043)	-3800.580* (1291.160)	163.570* (54.911)	0.496	1.757 (0.110)	-0.009 (0.009)	-1.186 (1.271)	-1.988 (1.600)	0.169	1.900 (0.021)
Chemicals	-0.069** (0.018)	0.798 (55.418)	-10.198 (9.707)	0.741	2.929 (0.032)	-0.001 (0.013)	-0.124 (0.864)	-0.264 (0.664)	0.032	1.396 (0.027)
Petroleum and coal	-0.144** (0.037)	373.362* (60.403)	-852.478* (138.861)	0.794	1.917 (0.102)	0.002 (0.009)	-0.748* (0.288)	-0.199* (0.080)	0.226	1.777 (0.044)
Rubber	-0.084** (0.018)	134.499* (21.511)	2.029* (0.144)	0.952	2.018 (0.040)	-0.013 (0.008)	2.522** (0.465)	0.138 (0.154)	0.772	2.775 (0.017)
Stone, clay, and glass	-0.067* (0.021)	32.684** (7.702)	-38.329** (9.463)	0.643	1.601 (0.044)	-0.005 (0.004)	2.005** (0.364)	-0.805* (0.289)	0.576	1.806 (0.018)
Basic metals	-0.068 (0.038)	36.644** (5.522)	4.715** (0.868)	0.843	(1.724) (0.064)	-0.008 (0.006)	0.004 (0.109)	-0.100 (0.131)	0.222	(1.707) (0.021)
Fabricated metals and machinery	-0.005 (0.018)	13.165* (5.197)	0.109 (0.674)	0.224	2.308 (0.072)	-0.013* (0.004)	1.119** (0.233)	0.052 (0.079)	0.700	1.855 (0.007)
Electrical machinery	-0.000 (0.027)	30.900** (7.856)	-2.002 (1.366)	0.621	2.952 (0.054)	-0.011 (0.010)	2.222** (0.682)	-9.051* (3.106)	0.515	1.783 (0.018)
Transportation equipment	-0.017 (0.022)	221.755** (67.220)	0.471* (0.221)	0.560	1.629 (0.060)	-0.030* (0.012)	-0.048 (0.044)	14.654** (1.604)	0.929	1.883 (0.029)

** and * imply coefficient significantly different from zero at 99 and 90 percent levels, respectively.

Note: Regression equation: $\text{TFPG} = \beta_0 + \beta_{EE} x_{EE} + \beta_{IS} x_{IS} + \epsilon$. Standard errors of coefficients are reported in parentheses below each coefficient. Standard errors of estimate are reported in parentheses below Durbin-Watson statistics. Durbin-Watson statistics in parentheses imply that the Cochrane-Orcutt correction was applied. See also notes a–h in table 10-5.

Source: World Bank data.

Table 10-9. *Summary of Regression Results*

Industry	Export expansion				Import substitution			
	Japan	*Korea*	*Turkey*	*Yugoslavia*	*Japan*	*Korea*	*Turkey*	*Yugoslavia*
Food processing	+EO	+	+	+	MC		−	−
Textiles and apparel	+EO	+EO	+	+EO		−MC		MC
Leather		+EO	+	EO			−	
Lumber and wood, furniture		+EO	−	EO				
Paper		+				−MC	+	MC
Chemicals	+			EO		+MC	MC	MC
Petroleum and coal			+	−		−	−	−MC
Rubber	EO	+EO	+	+			+	MC
Stone, clay, and glass		+EO	+	+EO		+	−	−MC
Basic metals		EO	+	EO		MC	+MC	MC
Fabricated metals and machinery		+EO	+	+EO		MC	MC	MC
Electrical machinery			+	+EO		−MC	MC	−MC
Transport equipment	EO			EO	−	+MC	+MC	+MC
Total manufacturing share of export/production	0.081	0.254	0.037	0.164				
Total manufacturing share of import/domestic supply					0.044	0.278	0.112	0.237

Note: EO, export-oriented industry (exports greater than 10 percent of total production); MC, import-competing industry (imports greater than 10 percent of total domestic supply, that is, imports plus total production less exports). These export and import shares were computed for 1973 in Korea and Turkey, for 1972 in Yugoslavia, and for 1970 in Japan.

Source: World Bank data.

tion leads to higher TFP growth, by increasing competitive cost-reduction incentives. Fourth, the results are also consistent with the hypothesis that export expansion and import liberalization increase TFP growth by relaxing the foreign exchange constraint and facilitating imports of nonsubstitutable intermediate and capital goods.

Such results provide some interesting material for the debate on infant industry protection policies. In every case but one in Korea and in Yugoslavia, and in every case in Turkey, sectors with a statistically significant negative effect of import substitution on TFP growth are also sectors with a significant positive effect of export expansion. Westphal (1982) has recently revived the infant industry argument for selective protection by noting a strong link at the micro level between protection and export performance. He concludes (p. 274) that he has identified "one possible reason why the industrial sector in a country like Korea, following an outward-looking strategy, performs so well; namely, the possibility that its selectively promoted infant industries exhibit superior performance as a result of their export activity." Our results for Korea are consistent with this argument.[24]

Krueger and Tuncer (1982) consider the standard infant industry argument in Turkey and conclude (p. 1149) that "input per unit of output must fall more rapidly in more protected industries if there is to be any rationale for infant industry protection. In the Turkish case, there was no such tendency over the period covered." In Turkey, in contrast to Korea, the export expansion phase was very short and not that strong. It can be stated, therefore, that the positive effect of export expansion on TFP growth that we found did not offset the negative effect of import substitution. Our results are consistent with those of Krueger and Tuncer, but we would be more diffident in concluding that protection was not justified. The positive relation between TFP growth and export performance in Turkey indicates the possibility that it could have followed the Korean example of selective protection, with export performance providing a test of success. Indeed, it still might do so.

One final point is worth noting. In both Korea and Turkey, an import substitution phase was followed by a phase with significant export contribution to growth. Although the Turkish export phase from 1970–73 turned out to be abortive, largely because the government allowed incentives to move against exports, the country is currently entering a new period of rapid and successful export promotion. The observed phasing suggests the hypothesis that a period of protected import substitution is

---

24. Our results may be somewhat distorted, however, by aggregation problems. Within any one of our "sectors," exports and import substitutes may be very different products. The colinearity issue discussed in footnote 18 needs to be recalled, and care should be taken in interpreting our comments on export expansion, since the estimates may be biased to reflect the domestic demand effect. See also Westphal and others (1985).

useful—perhaps even necessary—to build a base from which a successful export drive, with associated positive TFP growth, can be launched.[25] Westphal's argument holds out the hope that the benefits of export expansion for TFP growth can be realized simultaneously with the protection phase, but only if the incentives are tied to export performance. Such was not the case in Turkey, nor was there such an intention on the part of the policymakers. But the question of whether a period of protected import substitution, with associated negative effect on TFP growth, is worth the costs is not so easily answered. The crucial policy issue is one of timing. How long must one wait for an infant to mature? And is it possible to devise a policy mix that hastens the maturation process by tying policy incentives to performance (especially when it comes to exports)?

The results we have presented have raised as many questions as they have answered. At this stage in productivity research, such a state of affairs is probably desirable. There is a real need to coordinate research at the micro and aggregate levels. The sort of stylized facts we have been considering must be tested against work at the micro level to see if they make sense. Similarly, the micro work must be tested against comparative data at more aggregate levels to see what kind of generalizations are reasonable.

Also unresolved are questions about the interdependence of different policies. A development strategy implies a coordinated effort to devise a consistent set of policies covering many areas. By definition, such a strategy affects a large part of the total economic activity in a country. The existence of linkages and externalities implies that it will be difficult if not impossible to consider the effect of such strategies in a partial equilibrium framework. The work that has been done indicates that studying how different development strategies and TFP growth are related is important, if not crucial, to gaining an understanding of what constitutes a successful development strategy.

25. See also chapter 6 and Kubo and Robinson (1984), who present data on such phasing in other countries, and Balassa (1979b).

PART IV

Development Strategy

THROUGHOUT THIS BOOK, we have used a variety of analytical techniques to investigate the forms that structural transformation has taken in different countries. In part I, we studied a large group of semi-industrial countries by applying the techniques of growth accounting, augmented by a simple model of stuctural change. In part II, we probed the experience of industrialization in nine economies in more detail, using an input-output framework to make comparisons among different policy episodes. These efforts have led to a better understanding of the causes of industrialization and the identification of characteristic sequences of structural change.

Up to now, the causal relation between policy and performance has been inferred from each economy's trade regimes and capital inflows, which help to determine the exogenous elements in input-output models. While this procedure serves to establish quantitative links between various aspects of structural change, it leaves many questions about the effects of policy on performance unanswered. For this purpose, we need to know not only the historical results of a particular set of policies but also the probable consequences of varying these policies. In other words, we need to establish the essential links between specific policy instruments and the other variables in the model.

Chapter 11 is an exploratory attempt to use general equilibrium modeling for this purpose. We shall draw on experimental applications of computable general equilibrium models for two countries in our sample—Korea and Turkey—to develop some quantifiable relations between development policy and economic performance. Although the general equilibrium approach requires some specification of all commodity and factor markets, we shall concentrate on the external aspects that have received primary emphasis in earlier chapters, namely trade policy and capital inflow.

General equilibrium modeling of long-run growth is still in an experimental stage. Our results are best interpreted as quantitative illustrations of phenomena that can otherwise be described only in general terms.

Chapter 11 thus serves two purposes: to determine how the conclusions from the fixed coefficient models of earlier chapters are modified by the introduction of price effects and to characterize development strategies in terms of changing relative prices as well as quantities. Chapter 12 explores the implications of our findings for the choice of a development strategy and highlights some unanswered questions for further research.

11 Alternative Routes to Development

HOLLIS CHENERY

JEFFREY LEWIS

JAIME DE MELO

SHERMAN ROBINSON

UP TO NOW, our analysis has focused on real activity in the economy and its implications for aggregate growth, factor accumulation, resource allocation, productivity growth, and changes in the structure of production and of demand. The role of market mechanisms and of relative prices in determining resource allocation and structural change has been left in the background. Yet in mixed economies, the policy instruments that are designed to promote development work through markets and prices. In this chapter, therefore, we explicitly consider how market mechanisms and relative prices affect industrialization under different development strategies.

Similarly, the models we have used up to now to provide the framework for the analysis have focused on real variables and neglected the role of prices. In this chapter, we turn to the Walrasian model, in which market-clearing prices achieve equilibrium in a set of interdependent commodity and factor markets. Specifically, we use a computable general equilibrium (CGE) model that simulates the operation of a market economy and into which price incentive policies such as taxes, subsidies, and tariffs are explicitly incorporated. With this framework, we can sort out some of the main causal mechanisms that operate through changes in relative prices and that determine the effects of different policy choices.

Our approach is to use a CGE model of a single country as a simulation laboratory for doing controlled experiments designed to explore different development strategies. Chapter 3 used a model of several representative or archetypal economies that was based entirely on comparative data. In this chapter, we start instead with data for a particular country, Korea, in 1963. At that time, Korea had just completed a period of growth based primarily on import substitution and was poised for a major shift in development strategy. In many ways, its economic structure at that time was typical of those of other semi-industrial countries setting out on a path of rapid industrialization. Where Korea differs from the average, we have adjusted the data to obtain a more typical economy. We are interested in creating a stylized version of Korea for the purpose of comparative analysis, not in analyzing the strategic choices available to Korea in 1963.[1]

The first section defines three development strategies that differ mainly in their trade policies and that span the range of strategies actually followed in semi-industrial countries. We also consider how differences in the external environment—such as the nature of export markets and access to foreign capital—can affect the success of a given strategy choice. The second section describes the theoretical structure of the dynamic CGE model, and the third section analyzes the macroeconomic features of some model experiments designed to isolate the chief mechanisms at work. In the fourth section, we provide a more detailed analysis of the experimental results at the sectoral level, focusing on the role of changes in commodity and factor prices and in the exchange rate.

Three Development Strategies

We have seen in earlier chapters that even in those economies in which manufactured exports burgeoned following the shift to an outward-oriented development strategy, rapid industrialization led to increasing demands for imports of intermediate and capital goods. Only late in the process did the industrial sector become a net contributor of foreign exchange. In an industrializing economy, the balance of payments pressure arising from increases in import demand can be met in three ways: by import substitution, by export expansion, or by increased foreign borrowing. Either the demand for imports must be limited or the supply of foreign exchange must be increased. As shown in chapter 6, different trade strategies can be classified according to the relative importance they give to each of these components.

We define three options that cover a spectrum wide enough to encompass the experience of most semi-industrial countries. These three options provide the starting point for the experiments with the CGE model. In all cases, we assume an economy that has achieved a significant industrial base and that is not rich in natural resources—and so cannot generate ample supplies of foreign exchange through primary exports.

The first option is the strategy of export expansion, which is illustrated in an extreme form by the experience of Korea after 1963. Starting from a situation in which production for the domestic market had been strongly favored, Korea implemented a strategy that called for, first, reduced protection to imports; second, real devaluation to provide incentives to shift resources toward the tradable sectors; and third, elimination of incentives with a bias against exporting. Among the economies that have pursued such a strategy for a shorter or longer time, the most successful—in addition to Korea—include Malaysia, Singapore, and Taiwan.

1. For an analysis of the Korean case, see Kim and Roemer (1979). Chapters 4, 6, and 7 provide comparative data that include Korea.

Common features of their experience are export expansion well in excess of GNP growth, substantial reduction of the bias in incentives against exports, and sufficient foreign capital inflow to permit a sustained period of trade liberalization.

The second option is the strategy of import substitution, the elements of which are also taken from the experience of countries that have followed it with some success—Mexico and Turkey in our sample. Its three essential characteristics are a limitation on imports through both tariff protection and foreign exchange rationing; maintenance of an overvalued real exchange rate, which exacerbates the bias in incentives against exporting; and a relatively low foreign capital inflow, the result primarily of creditworthiness constraints arising from the low level of exports.

These two options represent extreme cases. In terms of policy choice, they are mutually exclusive. The protectionist policies supporting the import substitution strategy necessarily generate a bias against sales abroad and in favor of the domestic market; this applies to nontradables as well as tradables. Slower export growth also leads to less foreign borrowing, and this leads to still more limitations on imports.

Between the two extremes of export expansion and import substitution, a third option, a balanced strategy, combines elements of both. This alternative calls for more equal adjustments in the three components and a phasing of capital inflows. Import demand is limited through exchange rate policy rather than through tariff protection and foreign exchange rationing. The net effect is less bias against exporting and hence more exports than in the import substitution strategy. Since removing the bias against exports generally takes time, the strategy leads to more foreign borrowing in the early periods to finance more imports and so requires less devaluation of the real exchange rate. The components of the strategy include a reduction in import growth as a result of devaluation, but less than in the second option; an increase in exports, but less than in the first option; and higher foreign capital inflows in the early period. For countries with access to foreign capital, this strategy is less demanding than either the first option, which calls for a rapid shift of resources toward exports, or the second option, which calls for severe constraints on imports. In the sample, Israel is the best example of a country pursuing such a strategy.[2]

A Dynamic Computable General Equilibrium Model

The computable general equilibrium model presented in this section provides a framework for making systematic comparisons among the

2. Although the choice among these three options is primarily a domestic policy matter, external factors may impinge on a country's ability to pursue a given strategy successfully. For example, export performance is responsive to economic conditions and policies in the developed countries, and access to foreign borrowing is also affected by world economic conditions.

three strategies. Given our emphasis on alternative trade strategies, the model focuses on the markets for tradable commodities and on the incentives facing domestic producers and demanders of imports. Moreover, since our concern is with the effect of alternative development strategies on growth and structural change in the long run, the model is simulated for a twenty-year period (in five four-year intervals).[3] The long-run CGE model incorporates the market mechanisms through which domestic policy choices affect incentives, and it endogenizes the supply and demand reactions of domestic economic actors to such policies. Because the model is for a single economy, external conditions are reflected in exogenous variables.

In the development literature, CGE models trace their lineage back to the multisector input-output models widely applied to problems of planning in developing countries in the 1960s.[4] While firmly based on the foundation of Walrasian general equilibrium theory, CGE models can also be seen as a logical culmination of a trend in the literature on planning models to add more and more substitutability and nonlinearity to the basic input-output model.[5] The models tend to be highly nonlinear—to have neoclassical production and expenditure functions—and to incorporate a variety of substitution possibilities in production, demand, and trade.

CGE models applied to developed countries have generally stayed relatively close to the Walrasian paradigm.[6] In applications to developing countries, however, most researchers have introduced certain structuralist features into CGE models to capture the stylized facts characterizing these countries. Our model is very much in this tradition; it starts from a family of models developed by Dervis, de Melo, and Robinson to explore questions of foreign trade policy in semi-industrial countries characterized by many structural rigidities.[7] The model is presented in three stages. First, we outline the model structure, distinguishing between the static part, during which an equilibrium is achieved, and the dynamic part, which updates exogenous variables and parameters. A description of markets, agents in

---

3. The model is not designed to explore the short-run problems of making a transition to a new development strategy. Such issues of "structural adjustment"—in the terminology of the World Bank—are better addressed with an annual model designed to track the adjustment process in more detail.

4. The model of the Norwegian economy developed by Johansen (1960) was the first empirical implementation of a general equilibrium model in a developed country.

5. There are also theoretical similarities between CGE models that simulate a multisector market equilibrium and planning models, either linear or nonlinear, that specify an explicit objective function within the framework of a programming model. See Ginsburgh and Robinson (1984) for a discussion of the relationship.

6. For a survey of CGE models focusing on issues of tax policy and international trade in developed countries, see Shoven and Whalley (1984).

7. See Dervis, de Melo, and Robinson (1982) for a detailed discussion of the structure and theoretical properties of CGE models in general and of models applied to problems of foreign trade in particular. See also Robinson (1986).

the markets, and functional forms governing agents' behavior follows. Second, we outline the adjustment mechanisms that operate under each of the three development strategies defined above. Third, we describe the dynamic processes that drive the model forward in time.

Structure of the Model

The dynamic model consists of two parts. First, there is a static CGE model which solves for a one-year equilibrium. In this model, a set of markets for factors, commodities, and foreign exchange is assumed to clear subject to a variety of structural rigidities and to choices of exogenous variables, including policy parameters. Given these constraints, the static equilibrium represents an optimum for producers and consumers. Second, intertemporal linkage equations update exogenous variables and parameters that are dependent on policy choices and specify cumulative dynamic processes such as factor accumulation and productivity growth. The intertemporal equations provide all exogenous variables needed for the next period (four years later) by the CGE model, which is then solved for a new equilibrium. The model is thus solved forward in a dynamically recursive fashion, with each static solution depending only on current and past variables. The model does not incorporate any behavioral role for future expectations, and in its present form it cannot be used to explore issues of dynamic optimality except through sensitivity analysis.

Table 11-1 schematically organizes the main features of the model around blocks of equations and equilibrium conditions. The first two columns describe the overall structure of the within-period CGE model, while the third column summarizes the cumulative processes incorporated into the dynamic part. The equilibrium conditions in the CGE model include a supply-demand balance in three different types of market: labor, commodities, and foreign exchange. A fourth macroeconomic equilibrium condition is a balance between investment and savings—the macro "closure" of the model. A detailed description of the mathematical equations of the CGE model, supplementing the briefer discussion here, will be found in appendix A to this chapter.

The CGE model simulates the working of a market economy. In each period, it solves for wages, prices, and an exchange rate (or import premium rate) that clear the markets for labor, commodities, and foreign exchange. The model is Walrasian in that only relative prices matter. The numeraire against which all relative prices are measured is defined as an index of domestic prices.[8] The model also satisfies Walras's law so that, by construction, there cannot be a situation of aggregate excess demand or supply. Thus the model cannot address macro issues such as the role of

---

8. This choice is especially important in interpreting the role of the exchange rate, which will be discussed in more detail below.

Table 11-1. *Schematic Outline of the Static and Dynamic* CGE *Models*

| Economic relations | Static model | | Dynamic model: cumulative processes |
	Principal relations	Structural features	
Factor markets			
Labor	Labor demand equations	Segmented rural-urban labor markets	Labor force growth
Capital	Marginal product equations	Fixed sectoral capital stocks	Capital stock growth
Product markets			
Production	Production functions	—	Productivity growth
Demand	Expenditure functions	—	Composition changes
Foreign trade			
Exports	Export supply functions	Segmented domestic and export markets	World market trends
Imports	Trade aggregation functions	Imperfect substitutability	Induced import substitution
Trade balance	Exchange rate or premium rate	Foreign exchange rationing, exogenous inflow	Sequence of capital inflows
Macroeconomic balance			
Savings-investment	Domestic savings rates	—	Trends in savings rates
External capital	Endogenous foreign capital inflows	Fixed exchange rate	—

— Not applicable.

inflation or Keynesian unemployment. Given its long-run focus, it is appropriate to ignore such cyclical effects.[9]

Except for the structuralist features listed in table 11-1, the model is very neoclassical in spirit. Sectoral production is given by mixed two-level constant elasticity of substitution (CES) and linear functions. Intermediate inputs are required according to fixed input-output coefficients, aggregate labor and capital are combined to create value added according to a CES function, aggregate labor is a CES aggregation of labor of different types,

9. There are CGE models that have been designed to explore issues of inflation and unemployment, with some strain to the Walrasian paradigm. See J. D. Lewis (1986) for such a model and for a discussion of the modeling issues raised.

and the aggregate capital used in each sector is a linear aggregation of capital goods from different sectors. Sectors are assumed to maximize profits, and labor demand functions come from the first order conditions equating the wage with the marginal revenue product of labor of each category.

The labor market is segmented, with four distinct categories of labor: agricultural, unskilled, skilled (in the industrial sector), and service-oriented. Migration from the agricultural sector is specified exogenously over time; there is no mobility within periods. There is full employment of aggregate labor in each period, with the sectoral allocation of labor by different categories determined endogenously.[10] Sectoral capital stocks are fixed within periods; they change over time given aggregate growth of the capital stock and the sectoral allocation of investment. Investment in the industrial sectors is allocated endogenously to make sectoral rental rates approximately equal by the terminal year (although the rates differ across sectors in the intervening years).

Expenditure functions for demanders arise from Cobb-Douglas utility functions, which yield constant expenditure shares and unitary income elasticities of demand within periods. To capture the impact of Engel's law, exogenous trends are imposed on the expenditure shares dynamically. Thus, income elasticities all equal one within periods but differ from one over time. The model determines the flow of funds to all economic agents, including wage earners, recipients of capital income, and government (whose income consists of tax revenue).

The supply of exports by sector is a function of the ratio of the price in domestic currency of exports (determined by the world price, the exchange rate, and any subsidies) to the price of output sold in the domestic market. This treatment partially segments the export and domestic markets. Prices in the two markets are linked but need not be identical. Imports and domestic products are assumed to be imperfect substitutes—an assumption widely used in CGE models of trade. Imports and domestic goods are combined according to a CES trade aggregation function, with consumers demanding the resulting composite good.[11] The trade substitution elasticity determines the extent to which import shares adjust in response to changes in relative prices. For both exports and imports, the world price in dollars is assumed to be constant—the small country assumption.

Adjustment Mechanisms under Alternative Strategies

There are three mechanisms by which the CGE model can achieve equilibrium in the balance of trade under different assumptions about the

10. The model thus has no surplus labor or underemployment. It would be feasible to specify a model with surplus labor (and a fixed real wage). See de Melo and Robinson (1982), who explore the effect of trade policy on income distribution in such a model.

11. See Dervis, de Melo, and Robinson (1982) and de Melo and Robinson (1985) for a discussion of the implications of this treatment. Armington (1969) used this specification in

(Note continues on the following page.)

availability of foreign borrowing. These alternative mechanisms are used in different experiments depending on the issues being addressed. Two of them assume a fixed foreign capital inflow, reflected in an exogenous value for the balance of trade, so that adjustment depends primarily on relative price effects.

For the first mechanism, endogenous variation in the real exchange rate provides the equilibrating mechanism. The real exchange rate is defined as the relative price of tradables and nontradables. Since we use an index of domestic prices as numeraire, variations in the nominal exchange rate in the model directly affect the ratio of the price—in domestic currency—of imports and exports to the price of domestic sales and so represent a change in the real exchange rate. For example, a devaluation raises the domestic price of imports and exports relative to domestic sales and so encourages exports and import substitution. The model determines the equilibrium real exchange rate by manipulating the nominal rate relative to the fixed numeraire index of domestic prices.

For the second mechanism, import rationing provides the equilibrating mechanism. We assume that the rationing is efficient in that the marginal value of a dollar is the same across sectors: this is equivalent to assuming that import licenses can be sold in an open market.[12] In effect, a uniform import premium is imposed on top of any official tariffs; the premium rate is determined endogenously to equate import demand with the available aggregate supply, given exports and the exogenous foreign capital inflow. The result is the same as a devaluation applied only to imports, and the scheme yields a bias in incentives against exporting since it operates like a tariff.

For the third mechanism, we assume that the exchange rate is fixed and the balance of trade is endogenous, so that foreign capital inflow adjusts. Given the numeraire, this specification effectively fixes the real exchange rate. With a fixed relative price, the model achieves equilibrium through a quantity adjustment mechanism—in this case, through changes in foreign capital inflow. Because of the dual role of foreign capital inflow in permitting both increased investment and imports (as in two-gap models), external capital plays an important macroeconomic role as well.

The balance between savings and investment in the model is achieved by setting total investment equal to the sum of domestic and foreign savings.[13]

---

estimating import demand functions: the trade aggregation function is sometimes called an Armington function.

12. This treatment is a proxy for the wide range of second-best quantitative and licensing restrictions that are often imposed in developing, as well as developed, economies. For a discussion of modeling alternative rationing schemes, see Dervis, de Melo, and Robinson (1982).

13. This specification is termed neoclassical closure. Much of the debate on the appropriate macro closure revolves around issues of adjustments in the short to medium run in models that allow unemployment by, for example, assuming a fixed wage. Given our long-run focus and full-employment assumption, the neoclassical closure is an obvious choice. See Rattso (1982), Lysy (1983), and Robinson (1986) for surveys of the issues involved.

Domestic savings is modeled as a rising function of real GDP, so that a higher growth rate is associated with an increase in the domestic savings effort. The specification of foreign savings reflects empirical evidence that the propensity to save out of foreign capital inflows is less than one. In the CGE model, 40 percent of the inflow goes directly into savings. The remainder is funneled to capitalists, who in turn save a fraction; the remainder is consumed or taxed. The net effect is that the overall marginal savings rate from external resources is about 0.6, a value similar to that estimated by Chenery and Syrquin (1975).

Cumulative Dynamic Processes

The dynamic equations capture cumulative processes that drive the CGE model forward in time. These processes reflect three different types of forces: exogenous trends, policy choices, and past history incorporating solutions of the model for previous periods. The variables and parameters that are updated dynamically in the model can be classified into three categories:

- Updated by exogenous trends
   Aggregate labor force growth
   Sectoral total factor productivity growth
   Input-output coefficients
   Government consumption shares
   Private consumption shares
- Updated by policy choices
   Tariff rates
   Foreign capital inflows
   Exchange rate
- Updated by economic behavior
   Sectoral investment allocation
   Sectoral capital stocks
   Labor force allocation by category
   Sectoral export shares
   Sectoral import ratios

Variables updated by exogenous trends follow the same dynamic path in all experiments. The aggregate labor force is assumed to grow 3 percent annually. Total factor productivity growth rates are drawn from the results discussed in chapter 10. The other parameters—input-output coefficients and expenditure shares—are interpolated in each period between exogenously specified initial and terminal values.

Variables updated by policy choices are the chief policy instruments of the three trade strategies. While the CGE model includes a large number of policy instruments, the variations in these three define the three trade strategies. We vary different combinations of these instruments and solve others endogenously to meet certain targets.

Variables updated by economic behavior have values that are generated as part of the history of the model. The sectoral allocation of investment is assumed to adjust over time to equate rental rates in the industrial sectors by the terminal year.[14] Sectoral capital stocks in any year depend on investment allocation and the depreciation rate. Whereas aggregate growth of the labor force is exogenous, the composition by category is determined by a combination of two factors: exogenously specified migration of agricultural labor to one of the three categories of urban labor and migration among categories in response to changing real wage differentials. Over time, real wage differentials will induce an offsetting migration response.

Within a period, export supply shares and import demand shares respond to changes in relative prices. In some experiments, we also add a trend component to these shares. For exports, the assumption is that changes in world demand or increased market penetration lead to increased exports without any change in relative prices in the domestic market. With only supply behavior included in the model, such a specification is necessary to capture actual export behavior under the export expansion trade strategy.[15]

The dynamic specification of import demand also varies according to the trade strategy pursued. Under an import substitution strategy or a balanced strategy, it is assumed that the long-run trade substitution elasticity is higher than the short-run elasticity.[16] The effect is to allow for "successful" import substitution: the efficient ratio of imports to domestic supply for a given set of relative prices will gradually fall. Demanders can replace imports with domestic production more easily between periods than within periods and so avoid experiencing diminishing returns to further import substitution.

Macroeconomics of Alternative Strategies

In this section we describe the simulations of the three strategies in general terms and discuss their policy differences. All simulations begin from a common starting point in the base year, after which policy choices and the paths of exogenous variables differ. The purpose is to measure the effect of each strategy under different conditions, to illustrate the effects of various policy packages, and to examine the strains that emerge from the interactions among groups of policies.

14. In the base year, by construction, the economy is assumed to start from an initial solution with equal rental rates across the industrial sectors.

15. We chose not to include both supply and demand functions for exports because we did not wish to endogenize the effects of international terms of trade. Models with such behavior are described in Dervis, de Melo, and Robinson (1982).

16. There is a long-run envelope curve for each level of composite good (analogous to isoquants in production functions) with the short-run curves applicable to each period tangent to the long-run curve at a point.

Table 11-2. *Representative Trade Strategies*

Components	Import substitution (IS)	Balanced (B)	Export promotion (EP)
Trade policy			
Sectoral trends	Import reduction	Import reduction	Export penetration/ import liberalization
Main policy instruments	Tariffs/import rationing	Real exchange rate	Real exchange rate
Trade bias	Inward	Neutral	Outward
Trade shares	Low/falling	Constant	Rising
Borrowing policy	Limited by low exports	Maintain neutrality	Sustain trade liberalization
Indirect effects			
Productivity growth	Low/intermediate	Intermediate	High
Capital goods	High cost	World prices	World prices
Examples (1960s)[a]	*Turkey*	*Israel*	*Korea*
	Mexico	*Thailand*	*Taiwan*
	Philippines	Tunisia	Singapore
	Colombia	Greece	Malaysia
	Argentina		
	Brazil		

a. Examples are taken from chapter 4. Economies in italics are those analyzed in chapters 6 and 7.

The main features of each strategy are compared in table 11-2, and the influence of these factors on growth is summarized in table 11-3.[17] Each strategy is characterized by typical exogenous elements, the policy rules for maintaining external balance, and other policy choices.

A successful export promotion (EP) strategy is reflected in an average export growth of 14 percent annually.[18] Given the pattern and cumulative level of capital inflow, the real exchange rate varies to achieve external balance. Over a twenty-year period, this strategy results in substantial trade liberalization, shown by the rise in the share of imports in GDP from 14 to 24 percent. The capital inflow required to finance import requirements declines steadily from an initial level of 8 percent of GDP to less than 1 percent in the terminal year. GDP growth averages 6.5 percent, of which 1.7 percent is the result of assumed growth of total factor productivity.[19]

17. The numbers cited in table 11-3 and in the description of strategies are for a moderate level of foreign capital inflow for each strategy. The implications of different cumulative inflows are discussed more fully below.

18. Of this 14 percent, about 2.5 percent is attributable to market penetration and other effects not reflected in relative prices.

19. While this GDP growth is representative of the outward-oriented economies identified in table 4-4, it is less than the growth rate of 8 to 9 percent observed in Korea and Taiwan during the 1960s.

Table 11-3. *Macroeconomic Indicators of Alternative Trade Strategies*

Indicator	Import substitution (IS-2)	Balanced (B-2)	Export promotion (EP-2)
Average ratio of capital inflow to GDP	4.5	4.4	4.1
Ratio of imports to GDP, terminal period	10.7	18.1	24.0
Incremental capital-output ratio, terminal period	3.26	3.02	2.95
Export growth rate	7.9	10.3	14.1
Import growth rate	4.5	6.4	9.3
GDP growth rate	5.7	6.2	6.5

Note: In the abbreviations IS-2, B-2, and EP-2, the number "2" refers to one of four levels of capital inflow, defined in table 11-4 as 1,900 million 1964 dollars. All figures are percentages except for the incremental capital-output ratio.

The import substitution (IS) (inward-oriented) strategy maintains external balance by rationing foreign exchange through an import premium that provides incentives for import substitution. By increasing the cost of imported inputs, this strategy also makes exports less profitable. To maintain this policy over the twenty-year period, the import premium rises rapidly. This steadily increases the incentive bias in favor of import substitution over export promotion. The implications of this bias for relative prices are discussed more fully in the next section.

The macroeconomic effect of the IS strategy is a considerable closing of the economy. Imports fall from 14 percent of GDP to under 11 percent. The incremental capital-output ratio is 10 percent higher in the terminal year than it is in the EP strategy, and average GDP growth declines by nearly a percentage point.

The balanced (B) strategy contains elements of both the EP and IS strategies. The balanced strategy eliminates the inefficiency and price distortions associated with protection in the IS strategy without calling for the rapid growth of exports of the EP strategy. This is accomplished by combining successful import substitution with devaluation of the real exchange rate, which encourages exports and avoids the anti-export bias inherent in the IS strategy. Elimination of this bias increases export growth to 10 percent, which permits substantially more rapid growth in imports.[20] GDP growth over the period is 6.2 percent, only slightly less than growth with the EP strategy.

In summary, the balanced strategy combines efficient import substitution with moderate export expansion. In some of the countries pursuing

20. The balanced strategy simulations do not include the export growth through market penetration that is part of the export promotion simulations.

this strategy, access to more external borrowing and the resulting increase in investment can offset the gains from further specialization that occur in the export-led strategy. The choice between the two strategies then depends on the preferences of a country and the feasibility of implementing the necessary trade and borrowing policies.

In considering the three alternative strategies, it is important to emphasize that the sectoral rates of total factor productivity growth used in each strategy have been held constant. This assumption conflicts with the conclusions of chapters 2, 8, and 9, in which it was argued that the import restrictions, price distortions, and loss of specialization inherent in the aggressive pursuit of an import substitution strategy result in significantly lower rates of total factor productivity growth. We have assumed similar productivity growth to facilitate comparisons across strategies; however, we explore in other experiments how economic performance is affected by assuming lower factor productivity growth rates in the IS strategy.

Elements of Policy

To clarify the effects of the main elements of external policy—the trade bias, degree of openness, and capital inflow—it is useful to vary them separately while holding other aspects constant. This procedure is illustrated in table 11-4, which gives solutions for each strategy with the cumulative capital inflow held constant at four different levels. This set of simulations is used to identify the effects of individual policy changes when all else remains unchanged.

TRADE BIAS. The effect on growth of eliminating the trade bias (holding capital inflow constant) is shown in table 11-4 by comparing the balanced strategy (B) with the inward-oriented strategy (IS) in column 1. The import premium as an endogenous equilibrating variable is replaced by a flexible exchange rate, so that external balance is achieved both by increasing exports and by reducing imports in proportion to their respective elasticities. The exchange rate devaluation needed is only 35 percent instead of the 170 percent premium needed in IS. More than half the adjustment in the B strategy takes place through expanding exports.

This shift to a neutral trade policy raises GDP growth from 5.2 to 5.9 percent. In addition to the small static allocative gains from more efficient trade, the decline in the relative cost of investment goods leads to a significant rise in the real rate of investment and contributes to GDP growth.[21]

The marginal benefits of eliminating the trade bias decline as the capital inflow rises because the more plentiful supply of foreign exchange reduces the need for import substitution. Whereas the elimination of trade bias at

---

21. This phenomenon will be analyzed in more detail in the section below on prices, incentives, and structural change.

Table 11-4. *Trade Strategies, Capital Inflows, and Growth*

Strategy	Level of cumulative capital inflow (millions of 1964 dollars)			
	900 (1)	1,900 (2)	3,000 (3)	4,500 (4)
Import substitution (IS)				
GDP growth rate (percent)	5.2	5.7	6.2	—
Elasticity of imports to GDP	0.65	0.79	0.97	—
Ratio of imports to GDP, terminal period (percent)	9.4	10.7	13.4	—
Ratio of total debt to GDP, terminal period (percent)	0.31	0.54	0.78	—
Ratio of average capital inflow to average GDP (percent)	2.9	4.5	6.3	—
Balanced (B)				
GDP growth rate (percent)	5.9	6.2	—	6.6
Elasticity of imports to GDP	1.07	1.05	—	1.17
Ratio of imports to GDP, terminal period (percent)	17.6	18.1	—	17.7
Ratio of total debt to GDP, terminal period (percent)	0.27	0.50	—	1.10
Ratio of average capital inflow to average GDP (percent)	2.7	4.4	—	8.4
Export promotion (EP)				
GDP growth rate (percent)	6.3	6.5	—	6.9
Elasticity of imports to GDP	1.49	1.43	—	1.50
Ratio of imports to GDP, terminal period (percent)	23.9	24.0	—	24.0
Ratio of total debt to GDP, terminal period (percent)	0.26	0.47	—	1.02
Ratio of average capital inflow to average GDP (percent)	2.6	4.1	—	8.4

— Figures are not available because simulations with that cumulative capital inflow were not undertaken.
Note: Levels of capital inflow are identified by column numbers.

low levels of capital inflow (IS-1 versus B-1, where "1" refers to column 1 in table 11-4) increases GDP growth by 0.7 percentage points, doing so at moderate levels of inflow (IS-2 versus B-2) increases GDP growth by only 0.5 percentage points. With capital inflows as high as in B-4, the premium falls to zero, eliminating the bias between the IS and B strategies.

OPENNESS. An increase in exports and imports beyond the level specified by the balanced strategy leads to greater specialization and lower resource costs for tradable goods as a whole. This result is the essence of trade liberalization (see chapter 6). The increase in export growth from 10 percent in B-2 to 14 percent in EP-2 leads to cumulative levels of both imports and exports that are 50 percent higher over twenty years.

The aggregate effect of this greater specialization is to increase the growth rate by 0.4 percentage points, which is about half the effect of eliminating the trade bias at low levels of capital inflow. Although the increase in openness (as measured by the ratio of imports to GDP) from B-1 to EP-1 is similar to the increase from IS-1 to B-1, the reduction in the resource cost for tradable goods is considerably less.

CAPITAL INFLOW. External resources perform two distinct functions in a development strategy: they add to the level of investment and they supply additional imports. In modeling the first function, we have assumed that 60 to 70 percent of the capital inflow represents a net addition to investment, in line with econometric estimates of this effect.[22]

On the trade side, capital inflows are not a perfect substitute for exports since they do not have the cumulative benefits of market penetration and eventually need to be repaid. In addition, slower export growth limits the amount of external borrowing that can be sustained over the long run.[23] Borrowing does alleviate the need to undertake types of import substitution or export subsidization that may prove inefficient once export performance improves. It also allows a lower real exchange rate in the early period of import substitution.

The examples in table 11-4 suggest that an increase in capital inflow may add half a percentage point to the long-run growth rate within the feasible limit of the debt-export ratio. This increased growth from higher borrowing capability adds to the direct benefits of shifting from an inward-oriented to an outward-oriented strategy.

Dynamic Growth Paths

We now turn from a consideration of the cumulative effects of alternative strategies to an examination of the dynamic aspects of growth. How do trade bias, openness, and capital inflows interact to determine the pattern of growth under each strategy? Table 11-5 and figures 11-1, 11-2, and 11-3 show the dynamic effect of changes in these policy components.

The effects of trade policy on the openness of the economy (as measured by the ratio of imports to GDP) and on the growth of GDP are shown in

22. The proportion varies somewhat depending on the level of real GDP since the domestic savings effort is a rising function of national income.
23. In the model simulations, we approximate the borrowing constraint by restricting cumulative foreign borrowing to four times the level of exports. Among major borrowers, this was approximately the ratio of Argentina, Mexico, and the Phillipines in 1983. It was exceeded by Brazil (5.3) and Turkey (4.5). In contrast, the outward-oriented countries (for example, Korea, Malaysia, Thailand, and Yugoslavia) had ratios ranging from 0.9 to 2.0.

Table 11-5. *Dynamics of Alternative Strategies*

Period or variable	Base Time 0[a]	Import substitution (IS-2)		Balanced (B-2)		Export promotion (EP-2)	
		Time 2	Time 5	Time 2	Time 5	Time 2	Time 5
Variable—internal aspects							
Percent of GDP							
Domestic savings	8.6	13.8	24.3	13.5	24.7	13.5	26.3
Foreign savings	5.1	3.5	1.9	4.2	2.3	4.4	0.6
Investment	13.7	17.3	26.2	17.7	26.9	17.9	26.9
Real investment	13.7	17.2	23.6	17.5	26.4	18.0	27.1
Growth rate[b]							
Primary output		3.5	2.9	3.3	2.9	3.5	3.2
Manufacturing output		7.4	9.1	8.9	11.6	9.1	11.5
GDP		5.6	6.4	5.7	7.3	6.0	7.9
Incremental capital-GDP ratio		2.83	3.26	2.78	3.02	2.65	2.95
Variable—external aspects							
Percent of GDP							
Import share	14.1	11.6	10.7	15.1	18.1	17.3	24.0
Export share	5.7	6.3	8.1	8.7	15.1	10.5	23.3
Trade balance	8.4	5.4	2.6	6.5	3.0	6.8	0.8
Growth rate[b]							
Imports		3.5	6.8	5.0	9.8	8.8	10.7
Exports		7.3	9.5	9.6	11.3	14.2	14.4
Exchange rate	1.00	1.00	1.00	1.19	1.22	1.00	1.00
Premium rate (percent)	0	35	118	0	0	0	0

Note: The cumulative trade balance in all runs is the same.

a. Each twenty-year simulation is composed of five four-year "times." Time 0 is the base year; time 2 is eight years later; time 5 is the last year in the twenty-year simulation.

b. Growth rates for time 2 are for the first eight years; growth rates for time 5 are for the last four years.

figure 11-1. In the import substitution strategy (IS-2), the initial import ratio of 14 percent falls to 11 percent by the fourth four-year period.[24] This decline in openness is accompanied by lower GDP growth. The balanced strategy (B-2) is characterized by a steady rise in the import ratio, which reaches 18 percent by the end of the twenty-year span; in the export promotion strategy (EP-2), the import ratio reaches 24 percent.

Figure 11-2 shows the changing import ratio, and the relative importance of exports and of capital inflows in financing imports, for the three trade strategies. The moderate capital inflow of EP-2 is sufficient to maintain a constant real exchange rate over the twenty years.[25] External capital

24. Recall that each twenty-year simulation with the model is composed of five four-year periods. Declines of this magnitude have been observed in Argentina, Brazil, Turkey, and some other countries following implementation of an inward-oriented policy. Such declines eventually end either because of the increasing cost of import substitution or because of a change in policy to offset the anti-export bias in selected sectors.

25. This result was achieved by construction to provide a base for comparisons. The model was run with a fixed exchange rate and endogenous capital inflow.

Figure 11-1. *Import Requirements under Alternative Strategies*

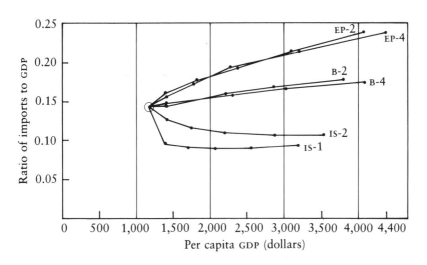

Figure 11-2. *Financing of Imports under Alternative Strategies*

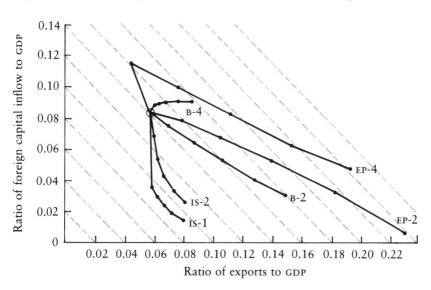

Note: See table 11-4 for key to simulations in figure. Dashed lines indicate ratios of investment to GDP.

Figure 11-3. *Financing of Investment under Alternative Strategies*

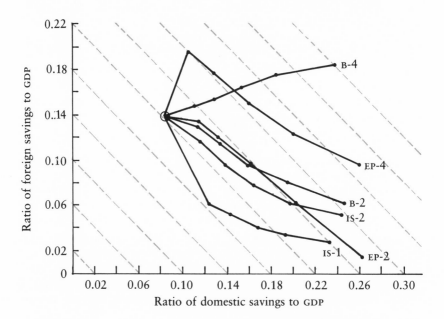

Note: See table 11-4 for key to simulations in figure. Dashed lines indicate ratios of investment to GDP.

is more concentrated in the earlier periods, during which it sustains higher imports and more rapid growth.[26] With the high capital inflow of EP-4, the importance of exports in GDP actually declines in the second period, as the large capital inflow results in a revaluation of the exchange rate and a corresponding decline in export growth.[27]

The moderate inflow of B-2 is also distributed in a manner which maintains a fairly constant real exchange rate from the second period onward.[28] It is characteristic of this strategy to reduce dependence on external capital more slowly. Although the opening up of the economy takes place more slowly than in EP-2, the corresponding loss in aggregate growth is relatively small. With the initial increase in external dependence associated with the higher inflow of EP-4, dependence is actually lower in B-4 than in EP-4 in the second period. The export growth of EP-4 rapidly

26. Analysis of the optimal distribution of capital inflows (Chenery and MacEwan 1966) shows that this pattern persists under a wide variety of assumptions.

27. This initial decline in the contribution of exports under an export promotion strategy is in keeping with the empirical conclusions of chapter 7.

28. Although the CGE model does not determine optimal aid patterns, experiments with alternative paths for capital inflow showed very little improvement over the pattern in B-2.

overtakes the balanced path, however, so that from the third period onward, the balanced path is more dependent on external inflows. After twenty years, dependence on external resources in B-4 remains unchanged.

Table 11-5 compares the economy's performance during time 2, after the major dislocations associated with policy changes have occurred, to that during time 5, which reflects the cumulative effects of twenty years of growth and structural change. From this table, which supplements figures 11-2 and 11-3, we can distinguish the common features of all strategies as well as the main differences among them:

- Acceleration of aggregate growth takes place in all strategies. GDP growth rates increase nearly 30 percent in the two neutral strategies (EP-2 and B-2). The increase is less with import substitution.
- Accelerated growth has two main sources: a rise in the domestic savings rate for a given income level and increasing openness of the economy. Whereas the first effect is similar in all strategies, the second occurs only in the two neutral strategies.
- Several factors act to offset accelerated growth. Higher domestic savings are partially offset by declining foreign savings (figure 11-3) and by rising incremental capital-output ratios. Greater openness is partly offset by rising import costs, particularly under the import substitution strategy.
- The combined effects of these factors is to widen the range of growth rates, since the slower growth that characterizes the inward-oriented strategy is more affected by the adverse factors than the other strategies. For the runs reported in table 11-4, GDP growth rates toward the end of the period range from less than 6 percent to more than 8 percent, three times the range observed at the beginning.

A summary of the effects on terminal GDP and terminal capital stocks of varying both the choice of strategy and the level of capital inflow is given in figure 11-4. The greater efficiency of the outward-oriented strategies is shown by the higher output-capital ratios of the EP and B curves compared with the IS curve. The relative slopes of these curves reveal the marginal productivity of external capital in each case. Since the inward-oriented strategy becomes increasingly inefficient at low import levels, the marginal productivity of external resources is correspondingly higher, as indicated by the steeper slope of the IS curve starting from the low inflow of IS-1.

Productivity Growth and Trade Strategies

Evidence from earlier chapters points to a strong positive association between the outward orientation of an economy and the growth rates of total factor productivity in the economy. In the characterizations of alternative strategies undertaken thus far, however, no distinction has been made in the sectoral rates of productivity growth according to the strategy pursued. If inward-oriented, import substitution strategies do

Figure 11-4. *Productivity of Capital under Alternative Strategies*

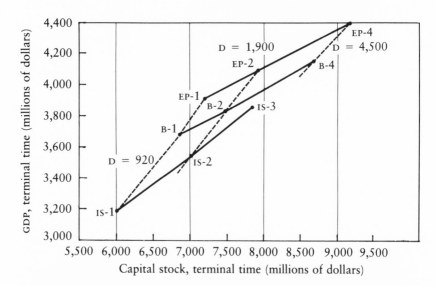

Note: See table 11-4 for key to simulations in figure. The points on the dashed lines indicate terminal-time GDP and capital stocks under different strategies for a given level of cumulative capital inflow (D). Lines further from the origin indicate higher capital inflow. The slopes of the solid lines indicate the marginal productivity of capital under each strategy.

imply lower rates of productivity growth, then the differences in growth performance by strategy will be larger than those described above.

To provide some indication of how economic performance is affected by the lower productivity growth associated with inward-oriented strategies, table 11-6 compares IS-1 with a scenario (IS-1L) in which sectoral rates of productivity growth are reduced by half. All other policies are the same, so that differences in performance are attributable to the lower productivity growth.

The reduction in TFP growth slows GDP growth by about 1 percent.[29] Nominal investment, which rises with GDP growth, remains lower as well. Incremental capital-output ratios are substantially higher in IS-1L, with even larger differentials observed in earlier periods. The slower growth does reduce import requirements, so that the premium rate required to achieve external balance is actually lower than in IS-1 (134 percent compared with 170 percent), although it remains quite high. The openness of the economy is largely unchanged, although export and import growth is slower since GDP growth has dropped. GDP growth accelerates less, in-

29. The TFP growth is assumed to apply only to value added. Changes in intermediate input coefficients are specified separately and are not altered in this experiment.

Table 11-6. *The Effect of Lower Productivity Growth*

Variable	Normal productivity (IS-1)	Low productivity (IS-1L)
Percentage of GDP, *terminal year*		
Domestic savings	23.2	19.5
Foreign savings	1.0	1.3
Investment	24.2	20.8
Real investment	20.9	18.0
Imports	9.4	9.7
Exports	7.9	7.8
Growth rate		
Primary output	3.0	2.0
Manufacturing output	8.8	7.5
GDP	5.2	4.0
Imports	7.3	6.0
Exports	3.4	2.4
Other values		
Incremental capital- GDP ratio	3.14	3.38
Premium rate (percent)	170	134

Note: For a description of these experiments, see the text. Further discussion of these results can be found in appendix B.

creasing from 3.5 percent in the first four-year period to 4.5 percent in the final four-year period. By incorporating the adverse impact of inward-oriented strategies on productivity growth, IS-1L is more representative of the experience of countries pursuing such strategies over a long time.

Although not reported here, additional experiments were conducted to analyze the sensitivity of the results to such main elasticity assumptions as trade substitution elasticities and capital-labor substitution elasticities.[30] The principal finding is that the IS strategy is more adversely affected than the others by reductions in the substitution elasticities: when both trade substitution and capital-labor elasticities are reduced by 50 percent, the GDP growth acceleration disappears completely. In the two neutral strategies (EP and B), acceleration is reduced but not eliminated. As substitution possibilities are reduced, the economy behaves more like the traditional two-gap model.

Prices, Incentives, and Structural Change

The macroeconomic policy choices discussed in the previous section work primarily through their influence on relative prices. Since sectoral

30. These sensitivity experiments are discussed in detail in appendix B to this chapter.

factor allocation responds to price incentives, we can trace the mechanisms through which policy changes affect structural change and hence the growth of the economy. After a discussion of the structural features of the economy and the sectoral sources of growth, we focus on the relative price movements underlying the alternative trade strategies. In particular, we examine the exchange rate regime and the bias it creates toward producing for export markets or for domestic import substitution, and the relative price of capital goods and its influence on real capital accumulation.

Structural Change and Development Strategy

Each strategy leads to a different economic structure in the terminal period, primarily because of the differing pattern of international trade. In particular, the degree of tradability of a sector—defined here in terms of the share of imports and exports in domestic supply—together with the responsiveness of output supply determine the distribution of adjustment across sectors. For example, more tradable sectors will benefit from a depreciation of the real exchange rate since both import substitution and export expansion will be stimulated.

The columns of table 11-7 contain measures of sectoral trade dependence and supply responsiveness. Sectors with low value added ratios are more adversely affected than others by a rise in the price of intermediate goods.[31] The ratio of imported intermediates to total intermediates measures the dependence of each producing sector on imported goods—the higher the ratio, the greater the impact of an increase in the prices of imported intermediate goods. Since capital stocks are fixed within a given period, the capital-labor ratio is a proxy for the supply elasticity of the sector. The trade substitution elasticity measures the substitutability of domestic for imported goods, which together with the composition of final demand will determine demand elasticities.[32]

To summarize the pattern of structural change implicit in the three strategies, we decompose the growth of output using the sources-of-growth methodology developed in chapter 5. Sectoral output growth is decomposed into four components: domestic demand expansion, export expansion, import substitution, and changes in input-output coefficients.[33]

Table 11-8 contains the sectoral growth decompositions for the full twenty-year period. (The three service sectors have been aggregated.) The

31. This is especially true in a model such as this one that assumes fixed input-output coefficients, since no price-responsive substitution between intermediates and value added is possible. Note, however, that there is substitution between imports and domestic goods within each cell of the input-output matrix.

32. The composition of final demand is important because different components of final demand have different elasticities of demand. Intermediate demand has a zero price elasticity, while consumption has an elasticity of one.

33. Since the changes in input-output coefficients are exogenous and identical in all strategies, the contribution of this component varies little, with aggregate differences explained by variations in the composition of output.

Table 11-7. *Sectoral Trade Dependence and Elasticities*

Sector	Gross output structure	Value added ratio	Imported inter-mediate ratio	Export supply ratio	Import supply ratio	Capital-labor ratio	Trade elastic-ity
Primary	32.6	73.7	10.8	2.4	10.9	0.22	1.10
Food processing	9.4	10.8	8.2	3.7	6.4	0.21	1.30
Consumer goods	16.0	33.6	6.3	3.0	3.4	0.63	1.10
Intermediate goods	7.9	33.6	12.7	4.7	38.7	0.68	0.60
Machinery	3.0	42.4	20.3	2.6	64.5	0.49	0.50
Construction	5.6	33.3	16.2	2.0	0.0	0.12	0.33
Social overhead	4.7	51.3	15.4	7.5	1.1	2.19	0.33
Services	20.8	69.6	5.5	3.9	1.1	1.02	0.33
Total	100.0	53.2	10.0	3.3	9.9	0.51	—

— Not applicable.

Note: Imported intermediate ratio = ratio of imported intermediates to total intermediates
Export supply ratio = ratio of exports to domestic output
Import supply ratio = ratio of imports to domestic supply
(domestic supply = domestic output – exports)
Trade elasticity = elasticity between imports and domestic goods

Source: World Bank data.

economywide results reveal the importance of trade strategy to the pattern of growth in the economy. With an export-led strategy, export expansion accounts for 27 percent of the overall expansion in output, while import substitution is negligible. In the more neutral balanced strategy, the contribution of export expansion falls to 13 percent, only half that of the export-led strategy but still substantially larger than the 6 percent contribution of import substitution. Finally, in the import substitution strategy, the import substitution contribution reaches 12 percent, surpassing the export contribution of 8 percent.

The sources of growth presented in table 11-8 are comparable with the empirical results presented in chapter 6 (see, for example, table 6-4). The typical strategies analyzed here avoid the extreme episodes observed for limited periods in certain economies; this reflects the focus on long-run structural change. The negligible contribution of import substitution to growth under the export promotion strategy differs from the experience of some outward-oriented economies and arises from the assumption of a degree of trade liberalization as part of the strategy.

Effects of the Trade Incentive Bias

One direct impact of alternative development policies is reflected in the incentives to domestic producers to sell products in domestic rather than foreign markets. The policies that influence these incentives include sectoral policy instruments such as tariffs and subsidies as well as macroeconomic variables such as the real exchange rate.

The upper graph of figure 11-5 shows the incentive to substitute for imports, represented by the ratio of import to domestic prices.[34] The lower graph portrays the bias of the trade regime, which corresponds to the ratio of import prices to export prices—in domestic currency—and summarizes the aggregate incentives for import substitution and for export. A higher bias value signals relatively greater incentives to produce import substitutes rather than exports.[35]

The differences in strategy are apparent in the figure. With the EP strategy, the rapid growth in export earnings achieved through market penetration and increased market shares is sufficient to finance import needs without substantial import substitution. Price incentives further encourage increased exports as average tariffs are lowered from 17 to 11 percent by the end of the period. The successful penetration of export markets and the availability of adequate capital inflows obviates the need for increased export incentives that would require real devaluations of the exchange rate.[36]

With the B strategy, an exclusive reliance on export expansion is replaced by more neutral policies that increase exports as well as gradually reduce import dependence through successful import substitution. With lower export growth and the same inflow as with EP-2, external balance is achieved through devaluations of the real exchange rate. Since devaluation affects export and import prices uniformly, the bias of the trade regime remains unchanged. The real devaluation necessary is about 20–25 percent, and it occurs in the early portion of the twenty-year period.[37]

The IS strategy assumes the same successful import substitution as in the B strategy. The real exchange rate is held constant, however, so that adjustment to the foreign exchange constraint occurs entirely through import reduction brought about by a rising import premium. Since this premium affects import prices but not export prices, the bias of the trade regime more than doubles as increasingly costly and inefficient import

34. Although the results shown are only for a moderate level of capital inflow, the pattern is largely unchanged for other levels of inflow as well.

35. A measure of the bias is given by B, defined as:

$$B = \frac{M_i}{E_i} \frac{\text{PWM}_i}{\text{PWE}_i} \frac{(1 + \text{TM}_i}{(1 + \text{TE}_i)} \frac{+ \text{PR})\,\text{ER}}{\text{ER}},$$

where M and E are base-year weights, PWE and PWM are world prices, TE and TM are subsidies and tariffs, PR is the import premium, and ER is the exchange rate. In the current case, however, with no export subsidies and no change in world prices, the bias is determined as $B = (1 + \text{ATM} + \text{PR})$, where ATM is the appropriate average tariff rate.

36. This pattern is in fact characteristic of the East Asian superexporters. Westphal (1978) shows, for example, that the real exchange rate in Korea remained constant throughout a period of substantial penetration of foreign markets.

37. This policy is representative of the crawling peg policies pursued by some Latin American and other countries starting in the mid-1960s; the real exchange rate was held constant, with periodic discrete devaluations to increase export competitiveness and curtail imports.

Table 11-8. *Sources of Output Growth*
for Twenty-Year Simulation Period

Strategy and sector	Output growth	Share of output change	Percentage contribution			
			Domestic demand	Exports	Import substitution	Change in input-output coefficients
EP-2						
Agriculture	3.2	9.0	103.4	31.2	−4.6	−30.2
Food processing	7.3	9.1	79.4	23.4	−0.7	−2.1
Consumer goods	9.4	24.9	64.4	38.1	0.2	−2.6
Intermediate goods	12.4	23.0	51.0	30.9	1.7	16.4
Machinery	12.6	8.9	70.1	16.4	−1.5	14.9
Services	6.6	25.1	89.5	14.9	0.1	−4.5
Total	7.5	100.0	73.0	26.7	−0.2	0.4
B-2						
Agriculture	3.2	9.4	101.3	16.6	13.2	−31.1
Food processing	6.8	8.6	89.2	10.0	3.4	−2.6
Consumer goods	8.1	20.0	85.5	13.9	3.8	−3.2
Intermediate goods	12.6	25.5	56.2	17.0	9.4	17.5
Machinery	12.9	10.1	70.4	6.4	6.4	16.8
Services	6.5	26.4	90.4	11.6	2.3	−4.3
Total	7.2	100.0	79.6	13.2	5.9	1.2
IS-2						
Agriculture	3.2	10.2	95.3	8.8	26.8	−30.8
Food processing	6.6	8.7	89.8	5.4	7.5	−2.7
Consumer goods	7.9	20.1	86.7	9.1	7.1	−3.0
Intermediate goods	12.3	25.9	52.6	11.4	17.0	19.1
Machinery	12.2	9.5	65.4	3.5	12.2	18.9
Services	6.2	25.6	92.4	7.6	4.3	−4.3
Total	6.9	100.0	78.4	8.4	11.5	1.7

Note: The first column gives sectoral output growth rates. The second column expresses sectoral growth as a share of total change in output. The remaining four columns show the percentage contribution of each demand component to sectoral output change and sum to 100.0 for each sector.

substitution opportunities are pursued. Thus, although the large foreign borrowing in the base year (8 percent of GDP) has been substantially reduced, evidence of continued external imbalance is apparent in the import premium of nearly 200 percent in the terminal period.[38]

The Cost of Capital and Growth

One important implication of the choice of a development strategy—an implication stemming from sectoral interdependence—concerns the rela-

---

38. In practice, of course, such continued disequilibrium would almost inevitably result in major policy changes as the economy was increasingly crippled by a shortage of foreign exchange. The results described here illustrate the strains inherent in such circumstances but have nothing to say about how the situation would be resolved.

Figure 11-5. *The Level of Incentives*

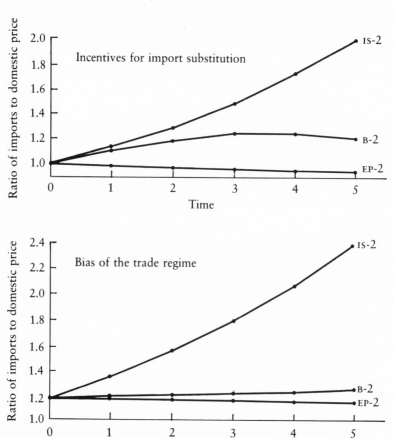

Note: See table 11-4 for key to simulations in figure. See table 11-5 for explanation of times.

tive price of capital goods and its effect on capital accumulation and growth. Capital accumulation in the economy occurs as investors in each sector purchase capital goods. As noted in chapter 8, a unit of capital goods is composed primarily of machinery and construction inputs in a proportion that remains more or less stable over the course of development.[39]

The relative price of capital goods will determine the real investment resulting from a given investment expenditure. This capital goods price is,

39. In the data used in this chapter, the average composition is: machinery, 36 percent; construction, 56 percent; other sectors, 8 percent.

in turn, strongly influenced by trade policy, since a large portion (40 percent in the base year) of the machinery purchased domestically is imported. Thus any policy that raises the domestic price of imported machinery will raise the price of capital goods, since substitution possibilities are limited.

Figure 11-6 illustrates this effect for the three trade strategies. In the upper graph, the average price of a unit of capital goods is plotted for the moderate inflow simulation of each strategy. For the export promotion strategy, the relative price of capital goods declines over most of the period. This fall in capital costs has been noted for Korea, where the relative price of capital goods declined by over 40 percent between 1962–65 and 1972–75.[40]

The average price of capital goods in the final period is 20 percent higher with the IS strategy than with the EP strategy. Furthermore, the price is rising most rapidly in the final period, reflecting the increasing scarcity of foreign exchange manifested in a rising import premium. The implication for real investment and growth is shown in the lower graph of figure 11-6. The divergence in the unit cost of capital goods translates into a ratio of real investment to GDP that is 2 percentage points higher with the EP strategy than with the IS strategy.[41] This real investment differential yields an aggregate capital stock that is 13 percent higher in the EP strategy than in the IS strategy.

In the IS strategy, the 16 percent rise in the average price of capital goods masks substantial sectoral variation. In the final period, increases in the prices of sectoral capital goods range from 1 percent in the construction and services sectors to 25–30 percent in the manufacturing sectors. These sectoral differences are caused by compositional differences in capital goods. The high premium rate of the IS strategy raises the price of machinery to domestic purchasers because of the high share of imports in total supply. Capital goods prices for the manufacturing sectors increase since machinery is the largest component of the capital stock in these sectors. In the service sector, in contrast, the share of machinery is smaller and that of construction (a nontraded good) larger, so that the impact of higher import prices is less severe.

Conclusions

The CGE model has proved useful for tracing the causal mechanisms through which trade policies affect economic performance in a market economy. In exploring the effects of the three development strategies

40. See Williamson (1979, p. 350). This effect is analyzed in Corden (1971) and de Melo and Dervis (1977).
41. The difference in investment rates also reflects the impact of savings propensities rising with GDP growth, but this effect is quite small compared with the relative price effect. Ratios of nominal investment to GDP differ by only 0.7 percentage points across the three strategies in the final period.

Figure 11-6. *The Cost of Capital Goods and Real Investment*

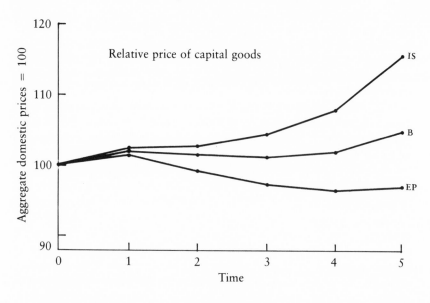

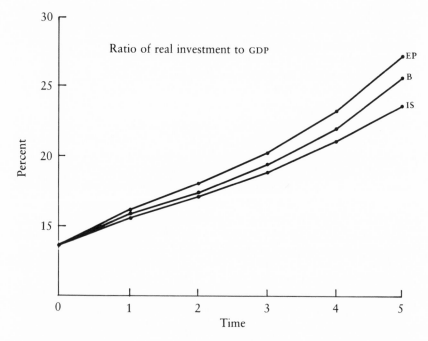

Note: See table 11-4 for key to simulations in figure. See table 11-5 for explanation of times.

(export promotion, import substitution, and balanced), we have been able to follow the links from incentive policies through changes in prices to changes in resource allocation, output, and trade. Our experiments with the CGE model also indicate some of the limitations of an exclusive focus on price incentives and market mechanisms in policy analysis. These are not the whole story, especially in developing countries where structural rigidities and more limited substitution possibilities constrain the effective operation of some markets and the responsiveness of the system as a whole.

In our experiments with the model based on the Korean experience, we found only moderate variation in aggregate growth rates under different development strategies—certainly less variation than we have observed among the semi-industrial countries whose experience was analyzed in chapter 4. The main reason for this is that our model was designed to describe an economy that starts with a significant industrial base (although it need not be a large share of GDP) and reasonably effective factor markets. For example, the model assumes that the choice of development strategy does not affect aggregate employment in the long run. This assumption is reasonable for an economy such as Korea's, which reached the end of its surplus labor phase in the late 1960s. In a dualistic economy characterized by massive underemployment, one would seek to model the employment creation effects arising from different development strategies. This would increase the contrasts between strategies.

Our results indicate the importance of interactions between foreign capital inflows and domestic investment. Holding either one fixed, we found significant diminishing returns in terms of growth from increases in the other. Note that the causal mechanisms are complex and involve changes in the structure of production arising from shifts in demand, variations in sectoral factor proportion, and the composition of sectoral investment. Thus even though the model embodies a variety of substitution possibilities in production, demand, and trade, it nonetheless exhibits the behavior characteristic of a two-gap model. Although there are no binding constraints of the type that a programming model would exhibit, there are increasing costs (and corresponding declines in growth) when an economy is forced to adjust to large imbalances in trade and in its domestic structure.

In many ways, the model economy embodies our current state of knowledge about the interactions among the various components of a development strategy. We focus on market incentives and leave out exogenous factors whose links with policy are only imperfectly understood. Especially important among these are: the relation between total factor productivity growth and policy choices; the determinants of successful import substitution, whereby domestic producers acquire the technological capability to produce close substitutes for foreign goods (exports as well as import substitutes); and the determinants of export supply behavior beyond simple price differential incentives, including issues of quality and market penetration. In each of these areas, we were forced to specify exogenous trends, the effect of which could therefore only be explored by parametric variation. These elements are empirically very important. Endogenous effects working through incentives and market channels only explain a part of the differences in performance.

Policies designed to "get the prices right" may be necessary to achieve rapid growth and structural change, but at this stage of our knowledge we cannot conclude that they suffice. Our results in this chapter support the analysis in chapter 4 and part III suggesting that a combination of factors influences performance. The success of an export promotion development strategy cannot be entirely attributed to the direct effects of the trade strategy.

Appendix A. Equations of the CGE Model

The Flexible Exchange Rate Version

This appendix gives a more formal mathematical description of the static CGE model used in chapter 11.

Capital letters without a bar denote endogenous variables. Lower-case letters, Greek letters, and letters with a bar are exogenous variables or parameters. The subscripts i and j refer to sectors and the subscript k refers to labor categories. There are n sectors and m labor categories. Nonlinear functions are not written out explicitly. Instead, the symbol for a function $f(-)$ is used, and the form of the particular function is explained with each such equation.

PRICES

$$(11\text{-}1) \qquad PM_i = \overline{PW}_i(1 + tm_i)\,ER$$

$$(11\text{-}2) \qquad PE_i = \overline{PWE}_i(1 + te_i)\,ER$$

$$(11\text{-}3) \qquad P_i = f(PD_i, PM_i)$$

$$(11\text{-}4) \qquad PS_i = S_i^e PE_i + (1 - S_i^e)\,PD_i$$

$$(11\text{-}5) \qquad PN_i = PS_i(1 - td_i) - \Sigma_j a_{ji} P_j$$

$$(11\text{-}6) \qquad \Sigma \vartheta_i PD_i = \bar{P}$$

Endogenous variables:

   ER = exchange rate
   PM_i = domestic price of imports
   PE_i = domestic price of exports
    P_i = price of a composite good
   PS_i = average price of domestic and export sales
   PN_i = net or value added price

PD_i = domestic price of domestic sales
a_{ji} = input-output coefficients
S_i^e = export share in sectoral sales

Exogenous variables and functions:

$\overline{PW}_i$ = world price of imports
$\overline{PWE}_i$ = world price of exports
tm_i = tariff rate
te_i = export subsidy rate
td_i = indirect tax rate
Ω_i = aggregate price index weights
$\bar{P}$ = exogenous level of price index
$f(x)$ = equation 11-3, cost function dual of the CES trade aggregation function (CES is the constant elasticity of substitution).

PRODUCTION AND EMPLOYMENT

(11-7) $$X_i^S = f(\bar{K}_i, L_i, VD_i)$$

(11-8) $$L_i = f(L_{li}, \ldots, L_{mi})$$

(11-9) $$VD_i = \Sigma_j\, a_{ji}\, X_i^s$$

(11-10) $$WL_k = (1 - tv_i)\, PN_i (\partial X_i / \partial L_i)\, (\partial L_i / \partial L_{ki}) / \gamma_{ki}$$

(11-11) $$WK_i = (1 - tv_i)\, PN_i (\partial X_i / \partial K_i)$$

(11-12) $$L_k^D = \Sigma_i L_{ki}$$

(11-13) $$L_k^D - \bar{L}_k^S = 0$$

Endogenous variables:

X_i^S = sectoral production
L_i = aggregate labor input
VD_i = aggregate intermediate input by sector of destination
L_{ki} = labor of category k in sector i
WL_k = average wage of labor category k
WK_i = market profitability rate
L_k^D = demand for labor of category k

Exogenous variables and functions:

$\bar{K}_i$ = exogenous sectoral capital stock
tv_i = value added tax
γ_{ki} = ratio of sectoral wage rate to average wage rate for labor category k
$\bar{L}_k^S$ = exogenous labor supply of category k
$f(x)$ = equation 11-7, two-level Cobb-Douglas or CES production function
$f(x)$ = equation 11-8, Cobb-Douglas or CES labor aggregation function

FOREIGN TRADE

$$(11\text{-}14) \qquad S_i^e = f(PE_i/PD_i)$$

$$(11\text{-}15) \qquad E_i = S_i^e \cdot X_i^S$$

$$(11\text{-}16) \qquad M_i/D_i = f(PD_i/PM_i)$$

$$(11\text{-}17) \qquad \Sigma \overline{PW_i} M_i - \Sigma \overline{PWE_i} E_i - \bar{F} = 0$$

Endogenous variables:

E_i = exports
M_i = imports
D_i = domestic demand for domestic production

Exogenous variables and functions:

$\bar{F}$ = exogenous net inflow of foreign exchange
$f(x)$ = equation 11-16 derived from first-order conditions associated
   with the trade aggregation function

INCOME AND FLOW OF FUNDS

Endogenous variables calculated:

$$(11\text{-}18) \qquad GY = \text{total government revenue}$$

$$(11\text{-}19) \qquad HY = \text{total income of households}$$

$$(11\text{-}20) \qquad TZ = \text{total investment}$$

$$(11\text{-}21) \qquad GC = \text{total government consumption}$$

$$(11\text{-}22) \qquad HC = \text{total consumption by households}$$

Total investment, TZ, is equal to the sum of domestic and foreign savings. A fixed fraction of the foreign capital inflow is assumed to enter directly into savings, while the rest is distributed to institutions, with part of it being saved and part of it ending up as household consumption. Domestic savings is made up of government and private savings, with the private savings rate assumed to be an increasing function of GDP.

PRODUCT MARKETS

$$(11\text{-}23) \qquad ZD_i = \overline{SZ_i} TZ/\Sigma_j b_{ji} P_j$$

$$(11\text{-}24) \qquad Z_i = \Sigma_j b_{ij} ZD_j$$

$$(11\text{-}25) \qquad G_i = \frac{\overline{SG_i} GC}{P_i}$$

$$(11\text{-}26) \qquad C_i = \frac{\overline{SP_i} HC}{P_i}$$

$$(11\text{-}27) \qquad V_i = \Sigma_j a_{ij} X_j^S$$

$$(11\text{-}28) \qquad D_i = S_i^d (Z_i + G_i + C_i + V_i)$$

$$(11\text{-}29) \qquad S_i^d = f(PD_i/PM_i)$$

$$(11\text{-}30) \qquad X_i^D = D_i + E_i$$

$$(11\text{-}31) \qquad X_i^D - X_i^S = 0$$

Endogenous variables:

ZD_i = investment by sector of destination
Z_i = investment by sector of origin
G_i = government demand by sector
C_i = private demand by households
V_i = intermediate demand by sector of origin
S_i^d = domestic demand ratio
X_i^D = total demand for domestic production

Exogenous variables and functions:

$\overline{SZ_i}$ = total sectoral investment allocation shares ($\Sigma_i \overline{SZ_i} = 1$)
b_{ji} = capital composition coefficients ($\Sigma_j b_{ji} = 1$)
$\overline{SG_i}$ = government expenditure shares ($\Sigma_i \overline{SG_i} = 1$)
$\overline{SP_i}$ = private expenditure shares ($\Sigma_i \overline{SP_i} = 1$)
$f(x)$ = equation 11-29, derived from first-order conditions associated with the trade aggregation function

The Import Premium Version

The equations above describe the flexible exchange rate version of the static CGE model. In certain simulations in chapter 11, the exchange rate is fixed, and an endogenous premium on imports is the equilibrating variable in the foreign exchange market. Since this premium generates an income flow, certain equations must be modified. The import and export price equations become:

$$(11\text{-}1a) \qquad PM_i = \overline{PW_i}(1 + tm_i + PR)\overline{ER}$$

$$(11\text{-}2a) \qquad PE_i = \overline{PWE_i}(1 + te_i)\overline{ER}$$

where

$\overline{PR}$ = uniform import premium rate
$\overline{ER}$ = exogenously fixed exchange rate

All other variables are defined as before. Total income of households (equation 11-19) now includes premium income, which equals $ER \cdot PR \cdot \Sigma pw_i M_i$.

Appendix B. The Critical Parameters of the CGE Model

This appendix explores systematically the macroeconomic effects of alternative assumptions about three sets of parameters: the rate of productivity growth; the substitutability of domestic production for imports; and the substitutability of labor for capital.

Productivity Growth

In chapter 11, we assumed relatively high rates of total factor productivity (TFP) growth, averaging 1.7 percent across all sectors. The rates were unaffected by the choice of a development strategy, a specification which is contrary to the evidence of chapters 9 and 10 but enables us to isolate the effects of other factors. We shall now assume that this rate of productivity growth is associated with trade liberalization and examine the effects of lower TFP growth on the other two strategies.

Lower productivity growth initially implies a smaller increase in output and in income from a given increase in capital and labor. In subsequent periods, lower income leads to less savings and investment, which augments the initial effects. The total adjustment to lower productivity growth through the general equilibrium model is shown in the terminal-year figures in table 11-9 for both the import substitution and the balanced strategies. There is a cumulative reduction of about 17 percent in the rates of saving and real investment under both strategies. The growth rate of GDP declines by about 1.2 percentage points, which is comparable with the effects of either a change in strategy or the maximum variation in capital inflow, as discussed previously.

There is much more reason to associate lower productivity growth with the excessive import substitution and distorted prices characteristic of the inward-oriented strategy than with the balanced strategy, in which the trade bias has been eliminated. Chapters 9 and 10 point to an association of lower productivity growth with the policy environment of inward-oriented countries rather than with particular types of sectors. Within our sample, the export-promoting economies (Korea and Taiwan) have clearly benefited from high productivity growth, while the import substitution economies (Mexico and Turkey) were shown in chapters 2 and 9 to be average performers. The difference between the two pairs is of the same order of magnitude as that assumed here. There are clearly other factors than trade policy, however, that explain productivity growth (see chapter 8).

Substitution in Production and Trade

The basic difference between the CGE model and the input-output model of earlier chapters is the omission from the latter of almost all forms of substitution: between capital and aggregate labor in each sector, between domestic production and imports in satisfying domestic demand, and

Table 11-9. *Lower Productivity Growth and Trade Strategy*

	Trade strategy			
	Import substitution		balanced	
Variable	IS-1	IS-1L	B-1	B-1L
Percentage of GDP, terminal year				
Domestic savings	23.2	19.5	24.3	20.1
Foreign savings	1.0	1.3	1.2	1.4
Investment	24.2	20.8	25.5	21.5
Real investment	20.9	18.0	25.2	21.1
Imports	9.4	9.7	17.6	16.8
Exports	7.9	7.8	16.0	14.8
Growth rate				
Primary output	3.0	2.0	3.0	2.0
Manufacturing output	8.8	7.5	9.4	8.0
GDP	5.2	4.0	5.9	4.6
Imports	7.3	6.0	6.3	4.9
Exports	3.4	2.4	11.9	9.1
Other values				
Incremental capital-GDP ratio	3.14	3.38	2.83	3.38
Premium rate (percent)	170	134	0	0
Exchange rate	1.00	1.00	1.15	1.12

Note: IS-1L and B-1L have TFP growth rates reduced by 50 percent in all sectors compared with the growth rates used in IS-1 and B-1. The trade strategies are identified in table 11-4.

between exports and supplying domestic markets.[42] Since we have assumed relatively high elasticities for each of these relations, the performance of the economy is quite neoclassical in its ability to adjust to changes in the constraints on labor, capital, and foreign exchange that have been considered.

We now investigate how assuming lower elasticities of substitution in critical areas affects the aggregate performance of the economy. For example, the effects of limited capital-labor substitution have been analyzed in general terms in the surplus labor model, in which capital becomes the principal determinant of growth as the productivity of labor falls. The limited substitutability of domestic production for certain types of imports plays a similar role in two-gap models of development. Both these phenomena are produced in the present model when the relevant elasticities of substitution are sufficiently reduced. Furthermore, since trade provides an

42. The formulation of these relations has been discussed in appendix A. Substitution among commodities in domestic demand is omitted in the present specification, in which Cobb-Douglas expenditure shares are used.

indirect way of substituting capital for labor, the effects of lowering both elasticities together tend to be cumulative.[43]

Here we are concerned with the differential effects of lower elasticities on the three external strategies. Our experiment consists of lowering the elasticities of capital-labor substitution and imports-domestic production (or trade) substitution first by 50 percent and then by 75 percent in each sector. For capital-labor substitution, reductions of this magnitude cover the range of estimates of this parameter in empirical studies. Since trade substitution—which means replacing imports of commodities such as machinery and capital-intensive intermediate goods by domestic production—involves a complex combination of factors, such as quality differentials and economies of scale, there are few statistical estimates available.

The results of selected simulations for different strategies, levels of capital inflow, and combinations of elasticities are given in table 11-10. They illustrate the following conclusions for each strategy:

- The import substitution strategy is quite sensitive to the reduction in trade elasticities but is much less affected by capital-labor substitution. Reducing trade elasticities by 50 percent forces the premium rate to more than double (from 118 to 276) and produces a moderate reduction in the growth rate of GDP (from 5.7 to 5.4 percent). If the supply of foreign exchange is further reduced by cutting the capital inflow, the effect on growth is quite marked, and the required premium (385 percent) becomes implausibly high. In effect, this is the CGE equivalent of a two-gap model in which foreign exchange becomes the main factor limiting growth. Since discrimination against exports is inherent in this strategy, the elasticity of demand for exports is irrelevant to the outcome. In these experiments, changing the capital-labor elasticity has relatively little effect.
- The balanced strategy is much less sensitive to lower trade elasticities than is the import substitution strategy. When both elasticities are lowered by 50 percent, the economy adjusts by expanding exports to offset the more limited opportunities for import substitution. This is accomplished by a moderate increase in the devaluation required (from 20 to 30 percent). It is only under the extreme assumptions of a 75 percent reduction in both elasticities combined with lower capital inflow that growth drops substantially (from 6.1 to 5.6 percent).[44]

The reason for the greater sensitivity of the import substitution strategy to lower elasticities of substitution between capital and labor is easy to

43. The interaction among elasticities of substitution in production, domestic demand, and trade is analyzed in Chenery and Raduchel (1979).

44. These conclusions derive from a more extensive process of sensitivity analysis, which is not reported in the table. The results for export promotion were less sensitive and are omitted from the discussion here.

Table 11-10. *Effects of Lower Substitution Elasticities*

Trade strategy experiment	Elasticities		Exchange rate		Premium rate (percent)		GDP growth (percent)
	Capital-labor	Trade	Time 2	Time 5	Time 2	Time 5	
Import substitution							
IS-2	1.00	1.00	1.0	1.0	35	118	5.7
IS-2A	1.00	0.50	1.0	1.0	70	276	5.4
IS-2B	0.50	0.50	1.0	1.0	68	256	5.3
IS-1	1.00	1.00	1.0	1.0	84	170	5.2
IS-1A	0.50	0.50	1.0	1.0	182	385	4.5
Balanced							
B-2	1.00	1.00	1.19	1.20	0	0	6.2
B-2A	0.50	0.50	1.30	1.17	0	0	6.0
B-2B	0.25	1.00	1.19	1.16	0	0	5.8
B-2C	0.25	0.25	1.39	1.13	0	0	5.7

Note: The elasticity numbers shown are the multiplicative factors applied to the original sectoral elasticities in each run. The trade strategy experiments are identified in table 11-4; the times in table 11-5.

understand: a lower elasticity value only matters when the economy departs from a "balanced" growth path, that is, from the set of relative prices in the base year around which the model is calibrated. Since the import substitution strategy is the strategy for which relative product and factor prices change the most, it is the strategy for which the effect of low elasticity of substitution is the greatest. This holds for both the trade substitution and capital-labor substitution elasticities.

It has been shown that more pessimistic assumptions about trade elasticities increase the differences between the import substitution strategy and the two neutral strategies. These differences could in turn be reduced by cutting the export elasticity in the neutral strategies.

12 Growth and Structure: A Synthesis

THE OBJECT of this book has been to explore the interrelations between the growth of developing countries and the changing structure of their economies. Traditional studies of the sources of growth have been based on the neoclassical framework in which structural change is essentially a by-product of growth, which in turn is produced by increases in factor supplies and productivity. Our evaluation of the results of growth accounting for developing countries (chapter 2) showed the need for a less aggregated analysis that takes account of the reallocation of resources among sectors.

This study shifts the focus of attention from factor accumulation to long-run structural change, or what we have called the structural transformation. Our general approach has been labeled "demand-side analysis" although it also incorporates the effects of income-related changes in comparative advantage. This methodology has been developed to explore three questions:

- What are the principal causes of the observed uniformities in the structural transformation?
- What are the effects of factors that may be expected to cause different sequences of industrialization, such as the availability of natural resources, market size, and external policies?
- How is productivity growth associated with the reallocation of resources among sectors?

The study of these questions has uncovered a number of uniform structural features and has also added to the list of unresolved issues. Principal among the latter is the nature of the causation underlying the statistical associations that have been identified. In the preceding chapter, we explored some of these issues in the context of a more complete general equilibrium model, which incorporates both demand and supply changes. This model helps sort out the effects of typical shifts from inward to outward policies into their principal components. In the following discussion, we use the CGE framework to help interpret the findings of earlier chapters.

The Structural Transformation

The task of this book would have been greatly simplified if all the semi-industrial economies shared the same set of demand and production functions. In that case, the observed variations in the structural transformation could have been attributed to differences in initial conditions or development policies. While clearly not universally valid, the assumption of similarities in tastes and technology does provide a useful starting point, especially for long-run comparisons.

In the present volume, the relations between growth and structural change were divided for analytical convenience into two parts: the effects of growth in per capita income on structure (the demand side); and the effects of changing structure and productivity increase on growth (the supply side).

The multisectoral, cross-country model of chapter 3 addressed the demand side, which is based on three sets of relationships that essentially drive the model:

- Income elasticities of demand for each commodity
- Input-output relations that are a function of per capita income
- Export demands and import proportions that reflect the factor endowments and policies of different groups of countries.

This static model was solved for exogenous increases in per capita income and yielded numerical relationships between the rise in manufacturing (and other changes in the structure of production) and the four factors that cause these changes: domestic demand expansion, export expansion, import substitution, and changing input-output coefficients. This model was extended in chapter 8 to analyze the changing composition of employment and differences in labor productivity growth by sector.

In the first two parts of the book, this model of the structural transformation was presented in a simple form that can be applied to both cross-country and time-series data. This procedure led first to an interpretation of the average or "standard" pattern of transformation, in which the findings from the cross-country model were checked against historical data for industrializing countries.

The main empirical findings as to the general nature of the transformation include observations regarding the standard pattern, alternative patterns, and the need to industrialize.

The Standard Pattern

In the standard pattern the share of manufacturing in total output and value added more than doubles during the transformation (table 3-7), and the decline of primary production is even more pronounced. Although this shift is usually attributed to Engel effects on domestic demands, both cross-country simulations and historical studies indicate that the changing composition of trade is of greater importance. The increase in intermediate use (change in input-output coefficients) also contributes significantly to the rising share of manufacturing in most countries (table 6-4).

Alternative Patterns

Systematic deviations from the standard pattern of industrialization can be attributed largely to differences in comparative advantage and trade policies. Our analysis traced the effects on the transformation of variations in primary resources and market size, which are combined in three typical patterns: large (L), small and primary-oriented (SP), and small and industry-oriented (SM). Most of our nine sample economies can be identified with one of these three patterns (tables 4-3, 6-4). The timing of industrialization is accelerated by import substitution in the L pattern and by increasing manufactured exports in the SM pattern; it is retarded by continued primary specialization in the SP pattern. Since each of these results could be produced by efficient adaptation of trade to factor endowments, there is no presumption that early industrialization is either a necessary or sufficient condition for accelerated growth.

The Need to Industrialize

Is industrialization necessary to continued growth? Our models of the transformation suggest that the answer is generally yes. However, there are three conditions under which this might not be true. The first is an early shift in demand in which the average income elasticity for manufactured goods falls below unity at an income level less than $1,000. The second is the persistence of the Dutch disease phenomenon, in which the share of primary exports in GNP expands fast enough to offset the combined effects of increasing final demand for manufactured goods plus rising intermediate demands. Neither condition is at all probable. While a few specialized mineral exporters—notably Ecuador and Iraq—satisfied the second condition during the period 1960–80 (table 4-6), it is unlikely to persist throughout the transformation. The third theoretical possibility is that there could be early development of service exports such as tourism or finance, but this appears equally unlikely to offset the increasing demand for manufactures in economies of any size.

In summary, we conclude that—on both empirical and theoretical grounds—a period in which the share of manufacturing rises substantially is a virtually universal feature of the structural transformation. The fact that the share of manufacturing has recently been declining in advanced countries does not argue against an earlier period of industrialization. This conclusion, however, is of little value for development policy without further analysis of the several functions performed by industrialization and the conditions necessary for their success.

The Role of Industrialization

To define the role of industrialization in more detail, we have studied it in a variety of country settings. Since the input-output model used in these comparisons ignores the effects of changes in relative prices, it can only be used to consider income effects and shifts in comparative advantage. The subsequent analysis of industrialization in a CGE framework examines the effects of changes in relative prices.

The following characteristics of manufacturing industries help to define their role in a multisectoral framework:

- The income elasticity of demand for manufactured goods is relatively high.
- Manufactures are highly tradable, but with differing degrees of substitutability between domestic and foreign products.
- The establishment of industries in accordance with comparative advantage permits the reallocation of labor and capital to more productive uses and exploits potential gains from specialization and economies of scale.
- Manufacturing growth is one of the main sources of technological change.

The first two factors were incorporated into our basic model, which yielded a solution for the growth of each sector in the form of the four components of equation 5-11, two internal and two external.

Our country studies support several generalizations about the determinants of industrial growth. Perhaps most important, the differences in country experiences are concentrated in the two external factors: export expansion and import substitution. Once allowance is made for the level of income, there is much less variation in the two domestic factors: final and intermediate demand. These observations influenced the design of both the cross-country input-output and CGE models, which assume that the main differences in development strategies are those reflected in the several types of external adjustment: import substitution, export expansion, and—by implication—capital inflows. The CGE model provides a more general framework in which shifts in external factors are generated by different policies for managing the balance of payments.

Table 12-1 summarizes our central findings as to the effects of industrialization in the three typical patterns of external adjustment. It includes the seven economies that are representative of these three patterns, as well as the simulations of both the input-output and CGE models. Since the results are given in detail in tables 6-3, 6-4, and 11-8, table 12-1 concentrates on the long-term effects of meeting the balance of payments constraint in different ways.

The addition of the CGE model results strengthens our earlier conclusion that resource endowments and trade policy are the major sources of the observed differences in the transformation. The outward-oriented—or export promotion—strategy reported here is a generalized version of Korean experience in which export growth is somewhat less rapid than that actually observed (14 versus 20 percent). The allocation of resources to maintain external balance is determined by profit maximization in each

Table 12-1. Sources of Growth for Simulations and Economies; Contributions of Demand Components to Total Increase in Output
(percent)

| Pattern (showing rise in GNP per capita) | Internal components | | | External components | | | | | | | |
| | Domestic demand | Input-output coefficients | Total | Exports | | | | | Import substitution | Total |
				Primary	Light industry	Heavy industry	Services	Total		
Inward-looking										
Turkey										
($240–$460)	87	3	91	1	2	1	3	7	2	9
Mexico										
($380–$750)	91	2	93	1	0	2	1	4	4	8
Cross-country (large)										
$260–$580	85	3	88	1	3	3	3	10	2	12
$560–$1,120	85	2	87	1	4	4	3	12	1	13
CGE (is-2)	78	2	80	1	2	3	2	8	11	20

Primary-oriented										
Colombia ($270–$370)	74	5	79	9	1	1	3	14	7	21
Cross-country ($280–$560)	74	3	77	11	3	1	3	18	4	23
Outward-oriented: industry										
Japan (prewar) ($260–$420)	74	0	74	3	11	4	9	27	0	26
Korea ($130–$320)	68	−3	65	3	15	11	6	35	0	35
Taiwan ($200–$430)	55	0	55	5	18	14	7	44	1	45
Israel ($1,070–$2,320)	72	3	75	4	12	6	14	36	−11	25
Cross-country: small, industry-oriented ($280–$560)	70	1	71	5	10	3	10	28	2	29
CGE (EP-2)	73	0	73	3	12	9	4	27	0	27

Sources: Tables 6-3, 6-4, 11-8.

sector at a fixed exchange rate. The solution illustrated (EP-2) assumes that the entire adjustment takes place through export expansion, which produces a sectoral distribution of external effects on growth in which light-industry exports predominate. This is quite similar to that observed in prewar Japan, Korea, and Taiwan but notably different from the other two strategies.

The inward-looking (IS-2) strategy shown in table 12-1 differs from the outward-oriented simulation in its use of protection to maintain external balance, with the total capital inflow being held constant. The resulting antitrade bias reduces exports as a source of output growth from 27 to 8 percent, which is similar to the experience of Turkey and the large-country pattern from the cross-country model. It also raises import substitution to 11 percent of growth because of the need to reduce the high level of capital inflow, which is characteristic of the earlier periods of our sample economies.

Since the CGE results are similar to the cross-country input-output model and, in most respects, to the country experience, they help to illuminate the underlying causes. In the CGE model, there is a drop in the growth rate of about 15 percent as a result of shifting from export promotion to import substitution. Since manufacturing contributes some 70 percent of the external adjustment in both cases, the lower growth is mainly attributable to less efficient choices within manufacturing, particularly in heavy industry.

Productivity

Identifying the source of increased productivity is the major conundrum for any attempt to explain growth. In the neoclassical framework examined in chapter 2, the residual labeled total factor productivity typically accounts for half the growth of advanced countries and 30 percent of less developed economies. Furthermore, the difference between low and high growth in less developed countries is owed more to higher productivity than to higher rates of factor accumulation.

In this volume we have concentrated on sources of increased productivity that are associated with the structural transformation. Several kinds of factors are examined:

- Pure sector effects associated with internal factors such as technological change or economies of scale
- Effects of reallocating factors from low to higher productivity sectors
- Choice of trade strategy
- Systemwide effects, such as reducing market imperfections.

The existence of sectoral differentials in productivity growth was assumed in the dynamic model of chapter 8 and tested by Nishimizu and Robinson as one of several hypotheses in chapter 10. The latter provides evidence of systematic differences in productivity growth among four groups of manufacturing industries—consumer goods, light intermediates, heavy intermediates, and investment goods—and among four countries. It also finds significantly higher productivity growth associated with export expansion than with import substitution.

Among these findings, the evidence for differences among manufacturing sectors is the weakest and that for systemwide (country) differences is the most pronounced. With Japan as a reference point, chapter 10 estimated the following percentages for the country effects on productivity growth: Korea, $+1.8$; Turkey, -1.0; Yugoslavia, -2.0. This ranking is consistent with the reallocation hypothesis, which implies that a rapidly industrializing country (such as Korea) will have higher growth from shifting labor to higher productivity uses than a mature economy (such as Japan) which has fewer remaining opportunities for such shifts.

An extensive econometric test of the reallocation hypothesis was carried out by Feder in chapter 9. In the context of the present volume, he treated the semi-industrial countries as a sample separate from the other less developed countries. Reallocation effects were shown to be strong in the former and not significant in the latter.

Feder's analysis was based on a general two-sector model in which one sector is assumed to have a higher marginal productivity of labor and capital than the other; the effect on growth is determined by the magnitude of the shifts of factors to the higher productivity sector. The model was applied first to a Lewis-type economy in which industry is the modern (high-productivity) sector and then to an economy in which exports have higher productivity. Both formulations produced statistically satisfactory results and imputed some 2 percentage points of growth (out of 6.4 percent) to either industrialization or export expansion. When the two hypotheses were combined, the explanation was improved and exports appeared to be the more powerful influence on growth.

Several of these empirical findings were incorporated into Syrquin's dynamic version of the cross-country simulation model in chapter 8. He developed a specification of the effects of factor movements among sectors under conditions of initial disequilibrium that can be embedded in our multisectoral framework. He was then able to estimate reallocation effects for our sample countries as well as a general pattern of accelerating growth for the cross-country model.

Although most findings as to the nature of productivity growth are subject to alternative interpretations, the scenario in table 8-4, in which changing demand and trade patterns lead to growth acceleration of 2.5 percentage points, seems quite plausible. Within this total, reallocation accounts for 20–30 percent in typical simulations.

Policy

Since our main purpose has been to reexamine the role of industrialization in a postwar setting, policy changes have appeared mainly as exogenous variables. Only in chapter 11 did we go further and attempt to model directly the effects of shifts in policy. For this purpose, we concentrated on the shift from an inward- to an outward-oriented strategy, probably the major policy issue of the past twenty years.

We found that the input-output framework provides a useful way of interpreting historical data on structural change but that it is necessary to incorporate market behavior and relative prices in order to explore the effects of varying policy regimes. Although we have experimented with alternatives, the specification of the Korea-based CGE model in chapter 11 is rooted in neoclassical theory. The simulations of alternative external policies of particular relevance to this volume yield two results.

First, the shift from tariff-induced import substitution to a neutral trade policy can account for an increase of as much as 1 percentage point in growth (holding capital inflow, productivity growth, and other indirect effects constant). With more structuralist assumptions, such as lower substitutability between domestic production and imports, this figure might double.

Second, capital inflows, in addition to outward-oriented policies, can add significantly to the effects of higher exports and help to explain the acceleration of growth in Korea and Taiwan.

The use of both input-output and CGE models provides different perspectives on the sources of growth. Given the diversity of the data bases to which they have been applied, these insights are largely complementary. Together they make better use of the available information than does any one of them alone.

Supply-Side Analysis

The principal result of our comparison of the results of neoclassical growth accounting is to bring out the differences between developed and developing countries. The advanced countries appear to fit the neoclassical assumptions better, while the explanations of growth of semi-industrial countries are improved by the addition of structuralist elements. In comparing the three factors in the Solow growth equation (labor, capital, and productivity growth), we found that a higher proportion of the somewhat higher growth in developing countries is explained by increases in the quantity and quality of labor and capital. This is not true of the most rapidly growing semi-industrial countries, however, in which rising productivity contributes half of total growth.

Although this accounting framework does not lead directly to policy conclusions, it helps to identify the relatively efficient countries for further analysis. It also demonstrates that the difference between the average and the best growth performances is caused largely by variations in economic efficiency rather than in capital accumulation.

Supply and Demand Interactions

In part II and chapter 11, several attempts were made to bring together the analysis of growth from the supply and demand sides. In chapter 8, the initial decomposition based on demand and trade was extended to identify the contribution of shifts of factors among sectors. This analysis implies continuing disequilibrium in that the marginal products of capital and labor are assumed to differ across sectors for long periods. Potentially there is a causal linkage running from shifts in factors from low to high productivity sectors, which results in higher growth. This theme was continued in chapter 10, which compared patterns of productivity growth by sector in four countries.

The CGE model used in chapter 11 incorporated the disequilibrium features of the earlier chapters but also added two new sorts of disequilibrium. First, it incorporated features of two-gap models in which there are problems in achieving simultaneous internal and external balance. Second, it focused on policy-induced distortions that affect market prices and hence incentives, especially in the area of trade policy. We have explored the importance of these persistent disequilibria and examined the role of foreign borrowing as well as the effects of varying choices of trade policies with respect to protection and the exchange rate.

Development economists have long acknowledged the existence of persistent disequilibria. Such phenomena make it difficult to analyze dynamic processes. For example, one cannot make much use of dynamic models which quickly settle onto a well-behaved, steady-state growth path. Instead, one must consider problems of adjustment lags and dynamic responses to continuing market disequilibrium.

While the existence of rigidities and persistent disequilibrium raises problems of analysis, that in no way invalidates the use of neoclassical tools in studying developing countries. Much of our analysis was based on multisectoral models, production functions, demand functions, and so forth, which are strongly neoclassical in form. We also found it necessary, however, to adapt the framework to take account of the structural features that characterize the economies we studied. In this effort, we follow a long tradition of development economics.

Policy Instruments

While most of our work has sought to sort out regularities in the industrial transformation and to analyze linkages among the different processes involved, we have also been concerned with the instruments of policy. How can policymakers affect the process of industrialization? What development strategies will hasten or retard growth? What are the links between particular policy instruments and the performance of the economy?

On these questions, our conclusions are more tentative. It is easier to establish correlations than causal chains. In studying the semi-industrial economies which have grown rapidly in the postwar period, it is difficult to sort out necessary conditions from the sets of sufficient conditions that underlie the successful cases. In a number of places—especially chapters 6, 7, 10, and 11—we considered the links between industrialization and the choice of an open development strategy, which involves incentives for greater exports of manufactures.

By now, the conventional wisdom is that an open development strategy is the preferred route to industrialization. Our results certainly do not conflict with this view. We found that economies which pursued export-led growth—as opposed to a strategy of import substitution—grew faster, industrialized sooner, had higher rates of total factor productivity growth, and tended to achieve the input-output structure of an advanced economy faster. In a more speculative vein, the results of chapters 6 and 7 indicate that there may be a necessary sequence from growth dominated by import substitution to a shift to manufacturing exports as the major engine. It appears that an economy must develop a certain industrial base and set of technical skills before it can pursue manufactured exports. Chapter 10 indicates that there has also been sequencing at the sectoral level, with import substitution associated with low TFP growth rates followed in the same sectors with high export-led growth and high TFP growth. Whether these observed sequences are necessary or not cannot be determined from our data, but they are suggestive.

An open development strategy that relies on manufacturing exports also involves some risks. If the component processes falter for some reason, the overall result may not be sustainable. In particular, relatively high rates of sectoral TFP growth are a necessary part of the success of outward orientation. There also appears to be a preferred sequencing in capital flow requirements.[1] If an economy borrows heavily to acquire intermediate and capital goods imports that are needed to fuel the process, the eventual failure of rapid export growth to materialize will leave the economy with a serious debt overhang.

In sum, our analysis stresses that industrialization must be examined in several dimensions. It may well be that all the associated elements follow naturally from a policy regime of sensible incentives in an environment of free markets. However, such a conclusion is certainly not obvious, and examination of the experiences of the countries which have successfully pursued export-led growth shows that their governments followed active interventionist policies, albeit with heavy reliance on market incentives.[2]

---

1. See the analysis with the CGE model in chapter 11. Also, Kubo, Robinson, and Urata (1986) find similar results using a dynamic input-output model.
2. See Westphal (1982).

Our analysis has little to add to this debate directly, but it does suggest that a certain modesty in claims made for particular policy choices is called for. Since our analysis of the shift from inward- to outward-oriented policies in the Korea-based model of chapter 11 succeeded in explaining only about half the actual acceleration achieved, it is likely that other important system effects are also involved.

References

Abramovitz, M. 1956. "Resource and Output Trends in the United States since 1870." *American Economic Review* 46 (May): 5–23.

Abramovitz, M., and P. A. David. 1973. "Reinterpreting Economic Growth: Parables and Realities." *American Economic Review* 63 (May): 428–39.

Adelman, I., and S. Robinson. 1978. *Income Distribution Policy in Developing Countries: A Case Study of Korea.* Stanford, Calif.: Stanford University Press.

Ahluwalia, I. J. 1985. *Industrial Growth in India: Stagnation since the Mid-Sixties.* New Delhi: Oxford University Press.

Armington, P. 1969. "A Theory of Demand for Products Distinguished by Place of Production." *IMF Staff Papers* 16: 159–78.

Arrow, K. J. 1954. "Import Substitution in Leontief Models." *Econometrica* 22 (October): 481–92.

———. 1962. "The Economic Implications of Learning by Doing." *Review of Economic Studies* 29 (June): 154–74.

Aukrust, O. 1965. "Factors of Economic Development: A Review of Recent Research." *Productivity Measurement Review* 40 (February): 6–22.

Balassa, B. 1964. "The Purchasing Power Parity Doctrine: A Reappraisal." *Journal of Political Economy* 72 (December): 584–96.

———. 1965. "Trade Liberalization and 'Revealed' Comparative Advantage." *Manchester School of Economic and Social Studies*, May: 99–121.

———. 1967. *Trade Liberalization among Industrialized Countries: Objectives and Alternatives.* New York: McGraw-Hill.

———. 1977a. *Policy Reform in Developing Countries,* New York: Pergamon.

———. 1977b. "Revealed Comparative Advantage Revisited: An Analysis of Relative Export Shares of the Industrial Countries, 1953–71." *Manchester School of Economic and Social Studies*, December: 327–44.

———. 1978. "Exports and Economic Growth: Further Evidence." *Journal of Development Economics* 5, no. 2 (June): 181–89.

———. 1979a. "Accounting for Economic Growth: The Case of Norway." *Oxford Economic Papers* (November): 415–36.

———. 1979b. "'A Stages Approach' to Comparative Advantage." In I. Adelman, ed., *Economic Growth and Resources,* vol. 4: *National and International Policies.* London: Macmillan.

———. 1981. *The Newly Industrializing Countries in the World Economy.* New York: Pergamon.

Balassa, B., and T. Bertrand. 1970. "Growth Performances of Eastern European Economies and Comparable Western European Countries." *American Economic Review* (May): 314–20.

Balassa, B., and Associates. 1971. *The Structure of Protection in Developing Countries.* Baltimore: Johns Hopkins University Press.

————. 1982. *Development Strategies in Semi-Industrial Countries*. Baltimore, Md.: Johns Hopkins University Press.

Baldwin, R. E. 1956. "Patterns of Development in Newly Settled Regions." *Manchester School of Economic and Social Studies* 24: 161–79.

Bergsman, J. 1979. *Growth and Equity in Semi-Industrialized Countries*. World Bank Staff Working Paper 351. Washington, D.C.

Bhagwati, J. N. 1978. *Foreign Trade Regimes and Economic Development: Anatomy and Consequences of Exchange Control Regimes*. Cambridge, Mass.: Ballinger.

————. ed. 1982. *Import Competition and Response*. Chicago: University of Chicago Press.

————. 1984. "Why Are Services Cheaper in the Poor Countries?" *Economic Journal* 94 (June): 279–86.

Bhagwati, J. N., and T. N. Srinivasan. 1978. "Trade Policy and Development." In R. Dornbusch and J. A. Frenkel, eds., *International Economic Policy: Theory and Evidence*. Baltimore, Md.: Johns Hopkins University Press.

Blitzer, C. R., P. B. Clark, and L. J. Taylor. 1975. *Economy-Wide Models and Development Planning*. London: Oxford University Press.

Boretsky, M. 1966. "Comparative Progress in Technology, Productivity and Economic Efficiency: U.S.S.R. vs. U.S.A." In U.S. Congress, Joint Economic Committee, *New Directions in the Soviet Economy*. Washington, D.C.: U.S. Government Printing Office.

Branson, W. H. 1979. *Macroeconomic Theory and Policy*. 2d ed. New York: Harper & Row.

Brown, G. T. 1973. *Korean Pricing Policies and Economic Development in the 1960s*. Baltimore, Md.: Johns Hopkins University Press.

Bruno, M. 1966. "A Programming Model for Israel." In I. Adelman and E. Thorbecke, eds., *The Theory and Design of Economic Development*. Baltimore, Md.: Johns Hopkins University Press.

————. 1968. "Estimation of Factor Contribution to Growth under Structural Disequilibrium." *International Economic Review* 9 (February): 49–62.

————. 1978. "Duality, Intermediate Inputs and Value Added." In M. Fuss and D. McFadden, eds., *Production Economics: A Dual Approach to Theory and Applications*, vol. 2. Amsterdam: North-Holland.

Bruton, H. J. 1967. "Productivity Growth in Latin America." *American Economic Review* 57 (December): 1099–116.

————. 1970. "The Import Substitution Strategy of Economic Development." *Pakistan Development Review* 10 (Summer): 123–46.

Carre, J. J., P. Dubois, and E. Malinvaud. 1975. *French Economic Growth*. Stanford, Calif.: Stanford University Press.

Caves, R. E. 1965. "'Vent for Surplus' Models of Trade and Growth." In R. E. Baldwin and others, eds., *Trade, Growth and the Balance of Payments*. Chicago: Rand McNally.

————. 1968. "Market Organization, Performance, and Public Policy." In R. E. Caves, ed., *Britain's Economic Prospects*. Washington, D.C.: Brookings Institution.

———. 1980. "Productivity in Britain: An Interindustry Approach." In R. E. Caves and L. B. Krause, eds., *Britain's Economic Performance.* Washington, D.C.: Brookings Institution.

Caves, D. W., L. R. Christensen, and W. E. Diewert. 1981. "A New Approach to Index Number Theory and the Measurement of Input, Output, and Productivity." *Journal of Political Economy* 88: 958–76.

———. 1982a. "The Economic Theory of Index Numbers and the Measurement of Input, Output, and Productivity." *Econometrica* 50: 1393–1414.

———. 1982b. "Multilateral Comparisons of Output, Input and Productivity Using Superlative Index Numbers." *Economic Journal* 92: 73–86.

Celasun, M. 1983. *Sources of Industrial Growth and Structural Change: The Case of Turkey.* World Bank Staff Working Paper 614. Washington, D.C.

Chen, E. K. Y. 1977. "Factor Inputs, TFP, and Economic Growth: The Asian Case." *Developing Economies* 15 (June): 121–43.

Chenery, H. B. 1960. "Patterns of Industrial Growth." *American Economic Review* 50 (September): 624–54.

———. 1963. "The Use of Interindustry Analysis in Development Programming." In T. Barna, ed., *Structural Interdependence and Economic Development.* New York: St. Martin's.

———. 1969. *The Process of Industrialization.* Harvard University Center for International Affairs, Economic Development Report 146 (December). Cambridge, Mass.

———. 1977. "Transitional Growth and World Industrialization." In B. Ohlin, P. O. Hesselborn, and P. M. Wijkman, eds., *The International Allocation of Economic Activity.* London: Macmillan.

———. 1979. *Structural Change and Development Policy.* New York: Oxford University Press.

———. 1980. "Interactions between Industrialization and Exports." *American Economic Review* 70 (May): 281–87.

Chenery, H. B., M. S. Ahluwalia, C. Bell, J. H. Duloy, and R. Jolly. 1974. *Redistribution with Growth.* London: Oxford University Press.

Chenery, H. B., and P. Eckstein. 1970. "Development Alternatives for Latin America." *Journal of Political Economy* 78 (July–August): 966–1006.

Chenery, H. B., H. Elkington, and C. Sims. 1970. *A Uniform Analysis of Development Patterns.* Harvard University Center for International Affairs, Economic Development Report 148 (July). Cambridge, Mass.

Chenery, H. B., and A. MacEwan. 1966. "Optimal Patterns of Growth and Aid: The Case of Pakistan." In I. Adelman and E. Thorbecke, eds., *The Theory and Design of Economic Development.* Baltimore, Md.: Johns Hopkins University Press.

Chenery, H. B., and W. J. Raduchel. 1979. "Substitution and Structural Change." In Chenery 1979: 143–72.

Chenery, H. B., S. Shishido, and T. Watanabe. 1962. "The Pattern of Japanese Growth, 1914–1954." *Econometrica* 30 (January): 98–139.

Chenery, H. B., and M. Syrquin. 1975. *Patterns of Development, 1950–1970.* London: Oxford University Press.

———. 1980. "A Comparative Analysis of Industrial Growth." In R. C. O. Matthews, ed., *Economic Growth and Resources*, vol. 2: *Trends and Factors*. New York: Macmillan.

Chenery, H. B., and L. Taylor. 1968. "Development Patterns among Countries and over Time." *Review of Economics and Statistics* 50 (November): 391–416.

Chenery, H. B., and T. Watanabe. 1958. "International Comparisons of the Structure of Production." *Econometrica* 26 (October): 487–521.

———. 1976. *Role of Industrialization in Japanese Development*. World Bank Development Research Department (January). Washington, D.C. Processed.

Chenery, H. B., and L. E. Westphal. 1979. "Economies of Scale and Investment over Time." In Chenery 1979: 217–65.

Christensen, L. R., D. Cummings, and D. W. Jorgenson. 1980. "Economic Growth 1947–73: An International Comparison." In J. W. Kendrick and B. N. Vaccara, eds., *New Developments in Productivity Measurement and Analysis*. National Bureau of Economic Research Studies in Income and Wealth 44. Chicago: University of Chicago Press.

Christensen, L. R., and D. W. Jorgenson. 1973. Measuring Economic Performance in the Private Sector. In M. Moss, ed., *Measuring Economic and Social Performance*. New York: National Bureau of Economic Research.

Clark, C. 1940. *The Conditions of Economic Progress*. London: Macmillan.

Clague, C. K. 1985. "A Model of Real National Price Levels." *Southern Economic Journal* 51 (April): 998–1017.

Cole, D., and P. Lyman. 1971. *Korean Development: The Interplay of Politics and Economics*. Cambridge, Mass.: Harvard University Press.

Corden, W. M. 1971. "The Effects of Trade on the Rate of Growth." In J. Bhagwati, and others, eds., *Trade, Balance of Payments and Growth: Papers in Honor of C. P. Kindleberger*. Amsterdam: North-Holland.

Corden, W. M., and J. P. Neary. 1982. "Booming Sector and De-Industrialization in a Small Open Economy." *Economic Journal* 92: 825–48.

Cornwall, J. 1977. *Modern Capitalism: Its Growth and Transformation*. New York: St. Martin's.

Correa, H. 1970. "Sources of Economic Growth in Latin America." *Southern Economic Journal* 37 (July): 17–31.

Cowing, T. G., and R. E. Stevenson, eds. 1981. *Productivity Measurement in Regulated Industries*. London: Academic.

Datta-Choudhuri, M. E. 1981. "Industrialization and Foreign Trade: The Development Experiences of South Korea and the Philippines." In E. Lee, ed., *Export-Led Industrialization and Development*. Geneva: International Labour Office.

David, P. A. 1962. "The Deflation of Value Added." *Review of Economics and Statistics* 44 (May): 148–55.

Denison, E. F. 1962. "Sources of Economic Growth in the United States and the Alternatives before Us." Supplementary Paper 13. New York: Committee for Economic Development.

———. 1967. *"Why Economic Growth Rates Differ: Postwar Experience in Nine Western Countries."* Washington, D.C.: Brookings Institution.

————. 1974. *Accounting for United States Economic Growth 1929–1969*. Washington, D.C.: Brookings Institution.

Denison, E., and W. Chung. 1976a. "Economic Growth and Its Sources." In H. Patrick and H. Rosovsky, eds., *Asia's New Giant, How the Japanese Economy Works*. Washington, D.C.: Brookings Institution.

————. 1976b. *How Japan's Economy Grew So Fast: The Sources of Postwar Expansion*. Washington, D.C.: Brookings Institution.

Dervis, K., J. de Melo, and S. Robinson. 1982. *General Equilibrium Models for Development Policy*. Cambridge, England: Cambridge University Press.

Dervis, K., and S. Robinson. 1978. *The Foreign Exchange Gap, Growth, and Industrial Strategy in Turkey 1973–1983*. World Bank Staff Working Paper 306. Washington, D.C.

————. 1982. "A General Equilibrium Analysis of the Causes of a Foreign Exchange Crisis: The Case of Turkey." *Weltwirtschaftliches Archiv*, Band 118, Heft 2, 259–80.

Desai, P. 1969. "Alternative Measures of Import Substitution." *Oxford Economic Papers* 21 (November): 311–24.

Deutsch, J., M. Syrquin, and S. Urata. 1986. "Economic Development and the Structure of Production." Processed.

Diaz-Alejandro, C. F. 1975. "Trade Policies and Economic Development." In P. B. Kenen, ed., *International Trade and Finance*. Cambridge, England: Cambridge University Press.

————. 1976. *Foreign Trade Regimes and Economic Development: Colombia*. New York: National Bureau of Economic Research.

Diewert, W. E. 1976. "Exact and Superlative Index Numbers." *Journal of Econometrics* 4 (May): 115–45.

————. 1979. "The Economic Theory of Index Numbers." Survey Discussion Paper 79–09. Department of Economics, University of British Columbia, Vancouver.

Donges, J. 1976. "A Comparative Survey of Industrialization Policies in Fifteen Semi-Industrial Countries." *Weltwirtschaftliches Archiv* 112 (4): 626–59.

ECE (Economic Commission for Europe). 1964. *Some Factors in Economic Growth in Europe during the 1950s*. Geneva: United Nations.

Elias, V. J. 1978. "Sources of Economic Growth in Latin American Countries." *Review of Economics and Statistics* 60 (August): 363–70.

Ezaki, M. 1975. "Growth Accounting of the Philippines: A Comparative Study of the 1965 and 1969 Input-Output Tables." *Philippine Economic Journal* 14: 399–435.

Ezaki, M., and D. W. Jorgenson. 1973. "Measurement of Macroeconomic Performance in Japan, 1951–1968." In K. Ohkawa and Y. Hayami, eds., *Economic Growth: The Japanese Experience since the Mejii Era*. Tokyo: Japan Economic Research Center.

Fane, G. 1971. "Import Substitution and Export Expansion: Their Measurement and an Example of their Application." *Pakistan Development Review* 11 (Spring): 1–17.

————. 1973. "Consistent Measures of Import Substitution." *Oxford Economic Papers* 25 (July): 251–61.

Feder, G. 1983. "On Exports and Economic Growth." *Journal of Development Economics* 12, no. 1 (March/April): 59–73.

Fei, J. C. H., G. Ranis, and S. W. Y. Kuo. 1980. *Growth with Equity: The Taiwan Case*. New York: Oxford University Press.

Fleming, M. 1955. "External Economies and the Doctrine of Balanced Growth." *Economic Journal* 65 (June): 241–56.

Frank, C. R., K. S. Kim, and L. E. Westphal. 1975. *Foreign Trade Regimes and Economic Development: South Korea*. New York: National Bureau of Economic Research.

Frankel, M. 1983. "Sources of Growth Data for Israel." In Kubo 1983.

Gaathon, A. L. 1971. *Economic Productivity in Israel*. New York: Praeger.

Ginsburgh, V., and S. Robinson. 1984. "Equilibrium and Prices in Multisector Models." In M. Syrquin, L. Taylor, and L. E. Westphal, eds., *Economic Structure and Performance: Essays in Honor of Hollis B. Chenery*. New York: Academic, 429–50.

Giovanni, A. 1983. "The Interest Elasticity of Savings in Developing Countries: The Existing Evidence." *World Development* 601–07.

Gollop, F. M., and D. W. Jorgenson. 1979. "U.S. Economic Growth: 1948–1973." Unpublished.

———. 1980. "U.S. Productivity Growth by Industry, 1947–73." In J. W. Kendrick and B. N. Vaccara, eds., *New Developments in Productivity Measurement and Analysis*. Chicago: University of Chicago Press.

Griliches, Z., and D. W. Jorgenson. 1967. "The Explanation of Productivity Change." *Review of Economic Studies* 34 (99): 249–83.

———. 1966. "Sources of Measured Productivity Change: Capital Input." *American Economic Review* 55 (May): 50–61.

Grubel, H., and P. J. Lloyd. 1975. *Intra-Industry Trade: The Theory and Measurement of International Trade in Differentiated Products*. London: Macmillan and Halsted.

Hadne, F. 1983. *The Norwegian Economy, 1920–1980*. New York: St. Martin's.

Hagen, E. E., and O. Havrylyshyn. 1969. "Analysis of World Income and Growth, 1955–1965." *Economic Development and Cultural Change* 18 (October): 1–96.

Heller, P. S., and R. C. Porter. 1978. "Exports and Growth: An Empirical Re-Investigation." *Journal of Development Economics* 5, no. 2 (June): 191–93.

Helpman, E., and P. R. Krugman. 1985. *Market Structure and Foreign Trade*. Cambridge, Mass.: MIT Press.

Hirschman, A. 1958. *The Strategy of Economic Development*, New Haven, Conn.: Yale University Press.

Humphries, J. 1976. "Causes of Growth." *Economic Development and Cultural Change* 24, no. 2 (January): 339–53.

Hwa, E. C. 1983. *The Contribution of Agriculture to Economic Growth*. World Bank Staff Working Paper 619. Washington, D.C.

Johansen, L. 1960. *A Multisectoral Study of Economic Growth*. Amsterdam: North-Holland.

Johnston, B. F. 1970. "Agriculture and Structural Transformation in Developing Countries: A Survey of Research." *Journal of Economic Literature* 8 (June): 369–404.

Johnston, B. F., and P. Kilby. 1975. *Agriculture and Structural Transformation: Strategies for Late Developing Countries.* New York: Oxford University Press.

Jorgenson, D. W., and M. Nishimizu. 1978. "U.S. and Japanese Economic Growth. 1952–1974: An International Comparison." *Economic Journal* 88: 707–26.

———. 1981. "International Differences in Levels of Technology: A Comparison between U.S. and Japanese Industries." In *International Roundtable Congress Proceedings.* Tokyo: Institute of Statistical Mathematics.

Journal of Post-Keynesian Economics. 1983. "Symposium: Kaldor's Growth Laws." Spring.

Kaldor, N. 1961. "Capital Accumulation and Economic Growth." In F. A. Lutz and D. C. Hague, eds., *The Theory of Capital.* London: Macmillan.

———. 1967. *Strategic Factors in Economic Development.* Ithaca, New York: Cornell University Press.

Kanamori, H. 1968. "Economic Growth and Exports." In L. Klein and K. Ohkawa, eds., *Economic Growth: The Japanese Experience since the Meiji Era.* Homewood, Ill.: Irwin.

Keesing, D. B. 1967. "Outward-Looking Policies and Economic Development." *Economic Journal* 77, no. 306 (June): 303–20.

———. 1979. *Trade Policy for Developing Countries.* World Bank Staff Working Paper 353. Washington, D.C.

Kelley, A. C., and J. G. Williamson. 1974. *Lessons from Japanese Development.* Chicago: University of Chicago Press.

———. 1984. *What Drives Third World City Growth? A Dynamic General Equilibrium Approach.* Princeton, N.J.: Princeton University Press.

Kendrick, J. W. 1961. *Productivity Trends in the United States.* Princeton, N.J.: Princeton University Press.

———. 1973. *Postwar Productivity Trends in the United States, 1948–1969.* New York: National Bureau of Economic Research.

———. 1982. "International Comparisons of Recent Productivity Trends." In W. Fellner, ed., *Essays in Contemporary Economic Problems.* Washington, D.C.: American Enterprise Institute.

Kennedy, K. A. 1971. *Productivity and Industrial Growth: The Irish Experience.* London: Oxford University Press.

Kim, K. S. 1977. *Sources of Industrial Growth and Structural Change in Korea.* Korea Development Institute Working Paper 77-03. Seoul.

———. 1978. *Industrialization and Structural Change in Korea.* Seoul: Korea Development Institute.

Kim, K. S., C. Frank, and L. Westphal. 1975. *Foreign Trade Regimes and Economic Development.* New Haven, Conn.: Yale University Press.

Kim, K. S., and J. K. Park. 1984. *Accounting for Korea's Rapid Economic Growth: 1963–1982.* Korea Development Institute Working Paper 84-01. Seoul.

Kim, K. S., and M. Roemer. 1979. *Growth and Structural Transformation.* Harvard East Asian Monograph. Cambridge, Mass.: Harvard University Press.

Kim, C. K., and C. H. Son. 1979. "Productivity Analysis of Korean Manufacturing 1966–75" (in Korean). Korea Development Institute Research Paper 79-01. Seoul.

Kindleberger, C. 1967. *Europe's Postwar Growth: The Role of Labor Supply.* Cambridge, Mass.: Harvard University Press.

Kornai, J. 1980. *Economics of Shortage.* Amsterdam: North-Holland.

Kravis, I. B. 1970. "Trade as a Handmaiden of Growth: Similarities between the Nineteenth and Twentieth Centuries." *Economic Journal* 80, no. 320 (December): 850–72.

———. 1984. "Comparative Studies of National Incomes and Prices." *Journal of Economic Literature* 22 (March): 1–39.

Kravis, I. B., A. W. Heston, and R. Summers. 1978. "Real GDP Per Capita for More than One Hundred Countries." *Economic Journal* 88 (June): 215–42.

———. 1982. *World Product and Income: International Comparisons of Real Gross Product.* Baltimore, Md.: Johns Hopkins University Press.

———. 1983. "The Share of Services in Economic Growth." In F. G. Adams and B. Hickman, eds., *Global Econometrics.* Cambridge, Mass.: MIT Press.

Kravis, I. B., and R. E. Lipsey. 1983. *Towards an Explanation of National Price Levels.* Special Studies in International Finance 52. Princeton, N.J.: Princeton University Press.

Krueger, A. O. 1974. *Foreign Trade Regimes and Economic Development: Turkey.* New York: Columbia University Press.

———. 1978. *Foreign Trade Regimes and Economic Development: Liberalization Attempts and Consequences.* New York: National Bureau of Economic Research.

———. 1980a. *The Development Role of the Foreign Sector and Aid: Studies in the Modernization of the Republic of Korea, 1945–75.* Cambridge, Mass.: Harvard University, Council on East Asian Studies.

———. 1980b. "Trade Policy as an Input to Development." *American Economic Review* 70, no. 2 (May): 288–92.

———. 1983. *Trade and Employment in Developing Countries,* vol. 3: *Synthesis and Conclusions.* Chicago: University of Chicago Press.

———. 1984. "Comparative Advantage and Development Policy Twenty Years Later." In M. Syrquin, L. Taylor, and L. E. Westphal, eds., *Economic Structure and Performance: Essays in Honor of Hollis B. Chenery.* New York: Academic.

Krueger, A., and B. Tuncer. 1980a. "Estimates of Total Factor Productivity Growth for the Turkish Economy." World Bank Development Research Department (April). Washington, D.C.

———. 1980b. *Estimating Total Factor Productivity Growth in a Developing Country.* World Bank Staff Working Paper 422. Washington, D.C.

———. 1982. "An Empirical Test of the Infant Industry Argument." *American Economic Review* 72 (December): 1142–52.

Kubo, Y. 1980. *Methodology for Measuring Sources of Industrial Growth and*

Structural Change. World Bank Development Economics Department (April). Washington, D.C. Processed.

———. 1981. "Interindustry Linkages and Industrial Development." Institute of Socio-Economic Planning Discussion Paper Series 133 (81-34). Tsukuba, Japan: University of Tsukuba.

———. 1983. "Detailed Input-Output Data Bank of the Sources of Industrial Growth Project." Sources Project Data Base. World Bank Development Economics Department Memorandum (September). Washington, D.C.

———. 1985. "A Cross-Country Comparison of Interindustry Linkages and the Role of Imported Intermediate Inputs." *World Development* 13, no. 12: 1278–98.

Kubo, Y., and S. Robinson. 1984. "Sources of Industrial Growth and Structural Change: A Comparative Analysis of Eight Economies." In UNIDO, *Proceedings of the Seventh International Conference on Input-Output Techniques.* New York: United Nations.

Kubo, Y., J. D. Lewis, J. de Melo, and S. Robinson. 1983. *Multisector Models and the Analysis of Alternative Development Strategies: An Application to Korea.* World Bank Staff Working Paper 563. Washington, D.C. (Also published in Spanish in *Cuadernos de Economia* 20, no. 61 (December): 313–43.)

Kubo, Y., S. Robinson, and S. Urata. 1986. "The Impact of Alternative Development Strategies: Simulations with a Dynamic Input-Output Model." Department of Agricultural and Resource Economics, University of California, Berkeley. Processed.

Kuo, S. W. 1979. *Economic Growth and Structural Change in the Republic of China.* World Bank Development Research Department. Washington, D.C. Processed.

———. 1983. *The Taiwan Economy in Transition.* Boulder, Colo.: Westview Press.

———. 1984. "Urbanization and Income Distribution: The Case of Taiwan, 1966–1980." In M. Syrquin, L. Taylor, and L. E. Westphal, eds., *Economic Structure and Performance: Essays in Honor of Hollis B. Chenery.* New York: Academic.

Kuroda, M., and H. Imamura. 1981. "Productivity and Market Performance, Time-Series Analysis (1960–1977) in the Japanese Economy." In *International Roundtable Congress Proceedings.* Tokyo: Institute of Statistical Mathematics.

Kuznets, S. 1957. "Quantitative Aspects of the Economic Growth of Nations: II. Industrial Distribution of National Product and Labor Force." *Economic Development and Cultural Change* 5 (July): supplement.

———. 1961a. "Economic Growth and the Contribution of Agriculture: Notes on Measurements." *International Journal of Agrarian Affairs* (April).

———. 1961b. "Quantitative Aspects of the Economic Growth of Nations: IV. Long Term Trends in Capital Formation Proportions." *Economic Development and Cultural Change* 9 (July, part II): 1–124.

———. 1966. *Modern Economic Growth.* New Haven, Conn.: Yale University Press.

——. 1971. *Economic Growth of Nations: Total Output and Production Structure.* Cambridge, Mass.: Harvard University Press.

——. 1979. "Growth and Structural Shifts." In W. Galenson, ed., *Economic Growth and Structural Change in Taiwan: The Postwar Experience of the Republic of China.* Ithaca, N.Y.: Cornell University Press.

Lampman, R. J. 1967. "The Sources of Post-War Economic Growth in the Philippines." *Philippine Economic Journal* 6, no. 2: 170–88.

Leontief, W. W. 1951. *The Structure of the American Economy.* New York: Oxford University Press.

Leontief, W. W., and others. 1953. *Studies in the Structure of the American Economy.* New York: Oxford University Press.

Lewis, J. D. 1986. "Stabilization and Structural Adjustment Policies in Semi-Industrial Countries: Experiments with a General Equilibrium Model." Ph.D. dissertation, Stanford University.

Lewis, J. D., and S. Urata. 1984. "Anatomy of a Balance-of-Payments Crisis: Application of a Computable General Equilibrium Model to Turkey, 1978–1980." *Economic Modelling* 1, no. 3: 281–303.

Lewis, W. A. 1954. "Economic Development with Unlimited Supplies of Labor." *Manchester School of Economic and Social Studies* 22 (May): 139–91.

——. 1980. "The Slowing Down of the Engine of Growth." *American Economic Review* 70, no. 4: 535–64.

Little, I. M. D. 1982. *Economic Development: Theory, Policy, and International Relations.* New York: Basic Books.

Little, I. M. D., T. Scitovsky, and M. Scott. 1970. *Industry and Trade in Some Developing Countries: A Comparative Study.* London: Oxford University Press.

Lluch, C., A. A. Powell, and R. A. Williams. 1977. *Patterns in Household Demand and Savings.* New York: Oxford University Press.

Lysy, F. J. 1983. "The Character of General Equilibrium Models under Alternative Closures." World Bank Development Research Department. Washington, D.C. Processed.

Macario, S. 1964. "Protectionism and Industrialization in Latin America." *Economic Bulletin for Latin America* 9: 61–101.

Machlup, F. 1963. *Essays in Economic Semantics.* Englewood Cliffs, N.J.: Prentice-Hall.

McKinnon, R. 1973. *Money and Capital in Economic Development.* Washington, D.C.: Brookings Institution.

——. 1979. "Foreign Trade Regimes and Economic Development: A Review Article." *Journal of International Economics* 9, no. 3: 429–52.

Maddison, A. 1980. "Western Economic Performance in the 1970s: A Perspective." *Banca Nazionale di Lavoro Quarterly Review* (September): 247–88.

——. 1983. "A Comparison of Levels of GDP Per Capita in Developed and Developing Countries, 1700–1980." *Journal of Economic History* 43 (March): 27–41.

Mahalanobis, P. C. 1955. "The Approach of Operational Research to Planning in India." *Sankhya* 16 (December): 3–131.

Mandelbaum, K. 1945. *The Industrialization of Backward Areas*. Oxford: Black-well.

Marris, R. 1981. "International Comparisons of Real Product." World Bank Economic Analysis and Projections Department. Washington, D.C.

Martin Rodriguez, M. 1979. "International Comparisons of Industrial Structure: Common Market vs. Spain, 1970." Paper read at Seventh International Conference on Input-Output Techniques, April. Innsbruck, Austria.

Mason, E. S., and others. 1980. *The Economic and Social Modernization of the Republic of Korea*. Cambridge, Mass.: Harvard Council on East Asian Studies.

Massell, B. F. 1961. "A Disaggregated View of Technical Change." *Journal of Political Economy* 59 (December): 547–57.

Matthews, R. C. O. 1974. "Some Aspects of Postwar Growth in the British Economy in Relation to Historical Experience." In R. Floud, ed., *Essays in Quantitative Economic History*. Oxford: Clarendon Press. (First published in 1964–65.)

Matthews, R. C. O., C. Feinstein, and C. Odling-Smee. 1982. *British Economic Growth*. Oxford: Oxford University Press.

Meier, G. M. 1984. *Leading Issues in Economic Development*. 4th ed. New York: Oxford University Press.

Melo, J. de. 1977. "Distortions in the Factor Market: Some General Equilibrium Estimates." *Review of Economics and Statistics* 54 (November): 398–405.

———. 1983. "Sources of Growth Data for Colombia." In Kubo 1983.

———. 1985. "Sources of Growth and Structural Change in the Republic of Korea and Taiwan: Some Comparisons." In V. Corbo and others, eds., *Export-Oriented Development Strategies: The Success of Five Newly Industrialized Countries*. Boulder, Colo.: Westview Press.

Melo, J. de, and K. Dervis. 1977. "Modelling the Effects of Protection in a Dynamic Framework." *Journal of Development Economics* 4: 149–72.

Melo, J. de, and S. Robinson. 1982. "Trade, Policy, Employment, and Income Distribution in a Small, Open, Developing Economy." In S. B. Dahiya, ed., *Development Planning Models*, vol. 2. New Delhi: Inter-India Publications.

———. 1985. "Product Differentiation and Trade Dependence of the Domestic Price System in Computable General Equilibrium Trade Models." In T. Peeters, P. Praet, and P. Reding, eds., *International Trade and Exchange Rates in the Late Eighties*. Amsterdam: North-Holland.

Metzer, J. 1986. "The Slowdown of Economic Growth in Israel: A Passing Phase or the End of the Big Spurt?" (Maurice Falk Institute for Economic Research in Israel Discussion Paper 83-03. Jerusalem. In Y. Ben Porath, ed., *The Israeli Economy: Maturing through Crises*. Cambridge, Mass.: Harvard University Press.

Michaely, M. 1975. *Foreign Trade Regimes and Economic Development: Israel*. New York: National Bureau of Economic Research.

———. 1977. "Exports and Growth: An Empirical Investigation." *Journal of Development Economics* 4, no. 1 (March): 49–53.

Michalopoulos, C., and K. Jay. 1973. "Growth of Exports and Income in the

Developing World: A Neoclassical View." AID Discussion Paper 28. Washington, D.C. (November): U.S. Agency for International Development.

Morawetz, D. 1977. *Twenty-Five Years of Economic Development, 1950 to 1975.* Washington, D.C.: World Bank.

————. 1981. *Why the Emperor's New Clothes Are Not Made in Colombia: A Case Study in Latin American and East Asian Exports.* New York: Oxford University Press.

Morley, S. H., and G. W. Smith. 1970. "On the Measurement of Import Substitution." *American Economic Review* 60 (September): 728–35.

Nadiri, M. I. 1970. "Some Approaches to the Theory of Measurement of Total Factor Productivity: A Survey." *Journal of Economic Literature* 8 (December): 1137–77.

————. 1972. "International Studies of Factor Inputs and Total Factor Productivity: A Brief Survey." *Review of Income and Wealth* 18 (June): 194–254.

Nelson, R. R. 1981. "Research on Productivity Growth and Productivity Differences: Dead Ends and New Departures." *Journal of Economic Literature* 19 (September): 1029–64.

Nelson, R. R., T. P. Schultz, and R. Slighton. 1971. *Structural Change in a Developing Economy: Colombia's Problems and Prospects.* Princeton, N.J.: Princeton University Press.

Nishimizu, M., and C. R. Hulten. 1978. "The Sources of Japanese Economic Growth: 1955–1971." *Review of Economics and Statistics* 40: 351–61.

Nishimizu, M., and J. M. Page, Jr. 1982. "Total Factor Productivity Growth, Technological Progress, and Technical Efficiency Change: Dimensions of Productivity Change in Yugoslavia, 1965–1978." *Economic Journal* 92: 920–36.

Nishimizu, M., and S. Robinson. 1984. "Trade Policies and Productivity Change in Semi-Industrialized Countries." *Journal of Development Economics* 16, nos. 1–2 (September–October): 177–206.

Nurkse, R. 1961. "Balanced and Unbalanced Growth." In G. Haberler and R. M. Stern, eds., *Equilibrium and Growth in the World Economy.* Cambridge, Mass.: Harvard University Press.

OECD (Organisation for Economic Co-operation and Development). 1965. *Agriculture and Economic Growth: A Report by a Group of Experts,* Paris.

————. 1979. *The Impact of the Newly Industrializing Countries on Production and Trade in Manufactures.* Paris.

Ohkawa, K., and H. Rosovsky. 1963. "Recent Japanese Growth in Historical Perspective." *American Economic Review* 53 (May): 578–88.

————. 1973. *Japanese Economic Growth: Trend Acceleration in the Twentieth Century.* Stanford, Calif.: Stanford University Press.

Ohkawa, K., and N. Takamatsu. 1983. "Capital Formation, Productivity, and Employment: Japan's Historical Experience and Its Possible Relevance to LDCs." International Development Center of Japan Working Paper 26. Tokyo.

Pesmazoglu, J. 1972. "Growth, Investment, and Saving Ratios: Some Long- and Medium-Term Associations by Groups of Countries." *Bulletin of Oxford University Institute of Economics and Statistics* 34, no. 4 (November): 309–28.

Poduval, N. 1978. "Data Bank and Data Management Programs for Analyzing Patterns of Industrial Development." World Bank Development Economics Department. Washington, D.C.

Prebisch, R. 1950. *The Economic Development of Latin America and Its Principal Problems.* New York: United Nations Economic Commission for Latin America.

Ranis, G. 1981. "Challenges and Opportunities Posed by Asia's Superexporters: Implications for Manufactured Exports from Latin America." In W. Baer and M. Gillis, eds., *Export Diversification and the New Protectionism.* Urbana: University of Illinois Bureau of Economic and Business Research.

———. 1984. "Typology in Development Theory: Retrospective and Prospects." In M. Syrquin, L. Taylor, and L. E. Westphal, eds., *Economic Structure and Performance: Essays in Honor of Hollis B. Chenery.* New York: Academic Press.

Rasmussen, P. N. 1965. *Studies in Intersectoral Relations.* Amsterdam: North-Holland.

Rattso, J. 1982. "Different Macroclosures of the Original Johansen Model and Their Impact on Policy Evaluation." *Journal of Policy Modelling* 4, no. 1 (March): 85–97.

Rhee, S. Y. 1980. "Total Factor Productivity Growth in Korean Mining and Manufacturing Industries." Processed. World Bank Development Research Department. Washington, D.C.

Robinson, S. 1969. "Aggregate Production Functions and Growth Models in Economic Development: A Cross-Section Study." Ph.D. dissertation, Harvard University.

———. 1971. "Sources of Growth in Less Developed Countries." *Quarterly Journal of Economics* 85, no. 3 (August): 391–408.

———. 1986. *Multisectoral Models of Developing Countries: A Survey.* Working Paper 401, Department of Agricultural and Resource Economics, University of California, Berkeley.

Robinson, S., and A. Markandya. 1973. "Complexity and Adjustment in Input-Output Systems." *Oxford Bulletin of Economics and Statistics* 35, no. 2 (May): 119–34.

Robinson, S., and L. D. Tyson. 1984. "Modelling Structural Adjustment: Micro and Macro Elements in a General Equilibrium Framework." In H. Scarf and J. Shoven, eds., *Applied General Equilibrium Analysis.* Cambridge, England: Cambridge University Press.

———. 1985. "Foreign Trade, Resource Allocation, and Structural Adjustment in Yugoslavia: 1976–1980." *Journal of Comparative Economics* 9: 46–70.

Roemer, M. 1985. "Dutch Disease in Developing Countries: Taking Bitter Medicine." In M. Lundahl, ed., *The Primary Sector in Economic Development.* New York: St. Martin's.

Rosenstein-Rodan, P. 1943. "Problems of Industrialization in Eastern and Southeastern Europe." *Economic Journal* 53 (June–September): 202–11.

———. 1961. "Notes on the Theory of the 'Big Push'." In H. S. Ellis and H. C. Wallich, eds., *Economic Development for Latin America.* London: Macmillan.

Salter, W. E. G. 1960. *Productivity and Technical Change.* Cambridge, England: Cambridge University Press.

Samuelson, P. A. 1964. "Theoretical Notes on Trade Problems." *Review of Economics and Statistics* 46 (May): 145–54.

Schmookler, J. 1966. *Invention and Economic Growth.* Cambridge, Mass.: Harvard University Press.

Schrenk, M., C. Ardalan, and N. A. El-Tatawy. 1979. *Yugoslavia: Self-Management Socialism and the Challenges of Development.* Baltimore: Johns Hopkins University Press.

Scitovsky, T. 1954. "Two Concepts of External Economics." *Journal of Political Economy* 62 (April): 143–51.

———. 1959. "Growth—Balanced or Unbalanced." In M. Abramovitz and others. *The Allocation of Economic Resources.* Stanford, Calif.: Stanford University Press.

Sen, A. K. 1963. "Neo-Classical and Neo-Keynesian Theories of Distribution." *Economic Record* 39: 53–66.

Shaw, E. 1973. *Financial Deepening in Economic Development.* London: Oxford University Press.

Shoven, J. B., and J. Whalley. 1984. "Applied General-Equilibrium Models of Taxation and International Trade: An Introduction and Survey." *Journal of Economic Literature* 22 (September): 1007–51.

Shultz, T. P. 1982. "Effective Protection and the Distribution of Personal Income in Colombia." In A. O. Krueger, ed., *Trade and Employment in Developing Countries: Factor Supply and Substitution.* Chicago: University of Chicago Press.

Singer, H. W. 1950. "The Distribution of Gains between Investing and Borrowing Countries." *American Economic Review* 40 (May): 473–85.

Solow, R. M. 1957. "Technical Change and the Aggregate Production Function." *Review of Economics and Statistics* 39 (August): 312–20.

Stein, J. P., and A. Lee. 1977. *Productivity Growth in Industrial Countries at the Sectoral Level, 1963–1974.* Santa Monica, Calif.: Rand Corporation for Council on International Economic Policy.

Stern, J., and J. D. Lewis. 1980. *Employment Patterns and Income Growth.* World Bank Staff Working Paper 419. Washington, D.C.

Streeten, P. 1959. "Unbalanced Growth." *Oxford Economic Papers* 11 (June): 167–90.

———. 1982. "A Cool Look at Outward-Looking Strategies for Development." *World Economy* 5 (September): 159–69.

Summers, R., I. B. Kravis, and A. W. Heston. 1980. "International Comparison of Real Product and Its Composition." *Review of Income and Wealth* 26 (March): 19–66.

Syrquin, M. 1976. "Sources of Industrial Growth and Change: An Alternative Measure." Paper read at European Meeting of Econometric Society, August. Helsinki, Finland.

———. 1983. "Sources of Growth Data for Mexico." In Kubo 1983.

————. 1984. "Resource Reallocation and Productivity Growth." In M. Syrquin, L. Taylor, and L. E. Westphal, eds., *Economic Structure and Performance: Essays in Honor of Hollis B. Chenery*. New York: Academic Press.

————. 1985a. "Growth Accounting with Intermediate Inputs and the Transmission of Productivity Growth." Processed.

————. 1985b. "Measuring the Contributions to Growth and Structural Change from the Demand Side." Processed.

————. 1985c. "Patterns of Development since 1960: A Comparison for China." Processed.

————. 1986. "Economic Growth and Structural Change in Israel: An International Perspective." In Y. Ben Porath, ed., *The Israeli Economy: Maturing Through Crises*. Cambridge, Mass.: Harvard University Press.

Syrquin, M., and H. Elkington. 1978. "The Data Base for the Simulation Model." World Bank Development Economics Department Memorandum (November). Washington, D.C.

Syrquin, M., and S. Teitel, eds. 1982. *Trade, Stability, Technology, and Equity in Latin America*. New York: Academic.

Syrquin, M., and S. Urata. Forthcoming. "Sources of Changes in Factor Intensity of Trade." *Journal of Development Economics*.

Taylor, L. J. 1979. *Macro Models for Developing Countries*. New York: McGraw-Hill.

————. 1981. "IS-LM in the Tropics: Diagrammatics of the New Structuralist Macro Critique." In W. R. Cline and S. Weintraub, eds., *Economic Stabilization in Developing Countries*. Washington, D.C.: Brookings Institution.

————. 1983. *Structuralist Macroeconomics: Applicable Models for the Third World*. New York: Basic Books.

Taylor, L., and F. J. Lysy. 1979. "Vanishing Income Redistributions: Keynesian Clues about Model Surprises in the Short Run." *Journal of Development Economics* 6, no. 1: 11–30.

Teitel, S., and F. E. Thoumi. 1986. "From Import Substitution to Exports: The Manufacturing Exports Experience of Argentina and Brazil." *Economic Development and Cultural Change* 34 (April) : 455–90.

Temin, P. 1967. "A Time-Series Test of Patterns of Industrial Growth." *Economic Development and Cultural Change* 15 (January): 174–82.

Tharakan, P. K. M. 1983. *Intra-Industry Trade: Empirical and Methodological Aspects*. Amsterdam: North-Holland.

Tobin, J. 1969. "A General Equilibrium Approach to Monetary Theory." *Journal of Money, Credit, and Banking* 1: 1–29.

Tsao, Y. 1980. "Growth and Productivity in Singapore: A Supply Side Analysis." Ph.D. dissertation, Harvard University.

Tyler, W. 1981. "Growth and Export Expansion in Developing Countries: Some Empirical Evidence." *Journal of Developing Economics* 9, no. 3 (August): 121–30.

Tyson, L. D. 1980. *The Yugoslav Economic System and Its Performance in the 1970s*. Berkeley, Calif.: Institute of International Studies.

United Nations. 1958. *International Standard Industrial Classification of All Economic Activity* (ISIC). New York.

Vaccara, B. N., and N. Simon. 1968. "Factors Affecting the Postwar Industrial Composition of Product." In *Studies in Income and Wealth* 32. New York: Columbia University Press.

Vanek, J., and A. H. Studenmund. 1968. "Toward a Better Understanding of the Incremental Capital-Output Ratio." *Quarterly Journal of Economics* 82 (August): 435–51.

Verdoorn, P. J. 1949. "Fattori che Regolano lo Sviluppo della Produttivita del Lavoro," *L'Industria*, 3–11.

Villarreal, R. 1976. *El Desequilibrio Externo en la Industrializacion de Mexico, 1929–1975: Un Enfoque Estructuralista*. Mexico: Fondo de Cultura Economica.

Viner, J. 1952. *International Trade and Economic Development*. Glencoe, Ill.: Free Press.

Watkins, M. H. 1963. "A Staple Theory of Economy Growth." *Canadian Journal of Economics and Political Science* 29: 141–158.

Weisskopf, T. E. 1971. "Alternative Patterns of Import Substitution in India." In H. B. Chenery, ed., *Studies in Development Planning*. Cambridge, Mass.: Harvard University Press.

Westphal, L. E. 1978. "The Republic of Korea's Experience with Export-Led Industrial Development." *World Development* 6, no. 3: 347–82.

———. 1982. "Fostering Technological Mystery by Means of Selective Industry Promotion." In M. Syrquin and S. Teitel, eds., *Trade, Stability, Technology and Equity in Latin America*. New York: Academic.

Westphal, L. E., L. Kim, and C. Dahlman. 1985. "Reflections on Korea's Acquisition of Technological Capability." In N. Rosenberg and C. Frischtak, eds., *International Technology Transfer*. New York: Praeger.

Wheeler, D. 1980. "Basic Needs Fulfillment and Economic Growth: A Simultaneous Model." *Journal of Development Economics* 7 (December): 435–51.

Williamson, J. G. 1979. "Why Do Koreans Save So Little?" *Journal of Development Economics* 6, no. 3: 343–62.

Williamson, J. G., and P. H. Lindert. 1980. *American Inequality: A Macroeconomic History*. New York: Academic.

World Bank. 1976. *World Tables*. Baltimore: Johns Hopkins University Press.

———. 1977. *The World Bank Atlas 1977*. Washington, D.C.

———. 1978. *World Development Report 1978*. New York: Oxford University Press.

———. 1980a. *Turkey: Policies and Prospects for Growth*. Washington, D.C.

———. 1980b. *World Development Report 1980*. New York: Oxford University Press.

———. 1980c. *World Tables*. Baltimore: Johns Hopkins University Press.

———. 1981. *World Development Report 1981*. New York: Oxford University Press.

―――. 1982. *World Development Report 1982*. New York: Oxford University Press.

―――. 1983. *World Development Report 1983*. New York: Oxford University Press.

―――. 1984. *World Development Report 1984*. New York: Oxford University Press.

Wragg, R., and J. Robertson. 1977. *Post-War Trends in Employment, Productivity Output, Labor Costs, and Prices by Industry in the United Kingdom*, Department of Employment, Research Paper 3. London: Her Majesty's Stationery Office.

Yotopoulos, P., and J. Nugent. 1973. "A Balanced-Growth Version of the Linkage Hypothesis: A Test." *Quarterly Journal of Economics* 87, no. 2 (May): 157–71.

Index

213–23; specialization and, 74–75, 76; structural change and, 77; structural transformation and changes in, 32, 33, 37; structural transformation model and external, 44–45; TFP growth and, 284, 285, 298–308; trade incentive bias (in CGE model) and, 333–35. *See also names of study sample economies*; Trade, balance of; Trade strategies

Trade, balance of: input-output model and, 142; manufacturing and, 218–23, 225

Tradables, 35, 71

Trade orientation index, 114–18

Trade strategies: aggregate performance of sample economies and, 149–52; analysis of CGE model and, 337–40; categorization of, 148–49; demand and output change and, 153–65; development, CGE model, and, 313–20, 351; factor markets and, 166; industry and, 172–87; industrialization typology and, 87; macroeconomics of, 320–31; regimes of, 165–72; structural change, relative prices, and, 332–37; study analysis and, 357–59. *See also* Inward-oriented trade strategies; Outward-oriented trade strategies

Transformation. *See* Structural transformation

Tuncer, B., 307

Tunisia, 94, 106

Turkey, 95, 96, 103, 108, 213, 309; balance of trade of, 222, 223; data sources for, 7; demand in and output of, 158, 162, 164; employment in, 66; exchange rates of, 171; growth pattern of, 76, 198, 201; ICE of, 218; income of, 54, 56; industrialization of, 191; interindustry linkages in, 205–06, 207, 211; intermediate use in, 61, 202; productivity of, 284, 288, 289, 294, 295, 298, 300, 301–07, 308, 355; trade strategy of, 168, 170, 172, 176, 178, 180, 181, 187, 313

United Kingdom, 245, 249, 250, 258, 260

United States, 24, 189, 245, 249, 250, 260

Value added, 66, 68, 108, 152; growth, specialization, and, 74–75; intermediate use analysis and, 62–63; primary inputs and, 142; in primary production, 102; sectoral growth rates and, 236; static input-output model and, 124, 127; structural transformation and, 349

Verdoorn's law, 285, 299, 303

Watanabe, T., 39

Yugoslavia, 94, 96, 98, 103, 114, 213; data sources for, 7; demand in and output of, 157–58, 162; employment in, 66; growth pattern of, 76, 149, 195; ICE of, 218; income of, 54; industrialization of, 190; interindusry linkages in, 205, 208, 211; intermediate use in, 61; productivity of, 284, 288, 289, 291, 294, 295, 298, 300, 301, 302, 303, 355; trade strategy of, 168–69, 170, 172, 176, 177, 178

T TO
Y RE...

DATE DUE

MAY 1 2 1990 VOID			
AUG 0 9 2011			
GAYLORD			PRINTED IN U.S.A.